INDUSTRIAL TRIBUNAL PRACTICE IN SCOTLAND

BY

WILLIAM LESLIE

B.A. (Cantab.), LL.B. (Aberd.), W.S.

A Chairman of the Industrial Tribunals (Scotland)

EDINBURGH

W. GREEN & SON LTD.

2 St. Giles Street

1981

First published . . . 1981

ISBN 0 41400680 1

Printed in Great Britain
by
McQUEEN PRINTERS LTD.
GALASHIELS, SCOTLAND

INDUSTRIAL TRIBUNAL PRACTICE IN SCOTLAND

IN MEMORIAM
J. M. S.
"Fidus Achates"

FOREWORD

By the Hon. Lord McDonald, M.C., Scottish judicial member of the Employment Appeal Tribunal.

It is a privilege to have been given a preview of Mr Leslie's book on the law and practice relating to industrial tribunals in Scotland. As he points out, the thinking which gave rise to the establishment of these tribunals was that they should work flexibly, informally and expeditiously.

It is easy to state such a basic principle. To achieve it in practice is a different matter, as this careful and comprehensive account of the work of industrial tribunals illustrates. Too much flexibility, informality and expedition may lead to injustice. Excessive rigidity, unnecessary formality and unpardonable delay may create more than injustice. They can cause resentment and disenchantment with the legal process. These latter were factors which brought the ordinary courts of the land into disfavour in the first half of the twentieth century when the Workmens' Compensation Acts were administered and interpreted by them.

The author of this book is alive to the dangers inherent in these two extremes. He has dealt with them in an admirable fashion. There is a lesson for the over-zealous lawyer. Do not approach a case before an industrial tribunal in the same way as in the ordinary courts. There is a lesson for the management or trade union official or other interested person who, although not legally qualified, finds himself involved in tribunal work. Many aspects of industrial legislation are complex—perhaps unnecessarily so. Where such issues arise, the astute official will quickly recognise them and will not disdain to seek legal advice and help.

This work will be of value to all Scottish lawyers who practise before industrial tribunals, and also to academics and students interested in this branch of the law. It will be of equal, if not greater value to management and trade union officials at all levels, and to others who find themselves before industrial tribunals without legal assistance.

Although it is primarily directed at tribunal law and practice in Scotland, it should be a useful book of reference south of the border as well.

May, 1981

PREFACE

Industrial tribunals have jurisdiction over a wide variety of matters in the employment field, which they operate with procedures which are relatively speedy, simple and inexpensive. A substantial number of cases are conducted by parties themselves, or by representatives who have no legal qualification. But the extent and, in some respects, the complexities of the law which they administer, and the volume of cases which it attracts—both at first instance and on appeal—have had the result, one might say inevitably, that even with a comparatively uncomplicated framework of procedural regulations a considerable body of rules and methods of practice has evolved, with significant differences in operation between Scotland and England and Wales. This work arose from the need for the practice of industrial tribunals in Scotland to be collated for those in all walks of life who sit in and administer them, and who appear before them.

One of the problems in writing for the unqualified as well as the legally qualified reader has been to avoid the use of jargon, in the interest of intelligibility, without sacrificing the accuracy which technical language may impart to a technical subject. I have tried to steer a course between the Scylla of the one and the Charybdis of the other by explaining legal concepts and expressions where that has been practicable. I hope that in the result I do not suffer the common fate of those who try to be all things to all men. (Here with the spirit, if not the letter, of the Sex Discrimination Act 1975 in mind, may I enlist s.6 of the Interpretation Act 1978 to excuse the use of the masculine gender in any context where the inelegant suffix "person" might be more strictly appropriate.)

The other problem has been where to draw the boundary between practice and substantive law, which in some areas can be indeterminate. The decisions of appellate courts contain dicta and guidelines on how tribunals should approach the merits of their cases, but such matters seem to me outwith the scope of the present work, except in so far as they illustrate a broad principle or a point of actual procedure. Other writers have expounded, more ably than I could, and at greater length than has been available to me, the general law on such topics as unfair dismissal and redundancy. But I have thought it proper to include a summary of the law affecting the jurisdiction of tribunals, since that is a matter for consideration at the outset, before the merits of a case can be investigated. I would have liked also to have included a full discussion of the remedies available under the various grounds of jurisdiction, but this has not proved possible within the space available. So I have had to confine myself to considering the quantification of monetary remedies in the hope of affording some guidance on this subject for the preparation and conduct of cases. Much of these two passages has had to be a catalogue of many complex statutory provisions, the dreariness of which I hope the reader will ascribe in some measure at least to our legislators, and not only to me.

The inspirer of this work has been the President of the Industrial Tribunals in Scotland, Mr Ian MacDonald, Q.C.* I cannot sufficiently express my gratitude for the support and encouragement I have received from him and my colleagues, and especially Mr Ian M. Thomson, W.S., but for which it could not have been written. They have made many valuable suggestions, but I take sole responsibility for the contents. I must also thank the Hon. Lord McDonald, for kindly writing the foreword.

The chapter on appeals was considered in draft by Mr James Watson, Deputy Principal Clerk of the Court of Session, and Mr G. A. Paterson, Deputy Registrar of the Employment Appeal Tribunal in Scotland, to whom I am grateful for various helpful suggestions, as also to Mr A. E. Anton of the Scottish Law Commission and Mr C. McLay, Assistant Sheriff Clerk at Edinburgh, for advice on various aspects of the law of enforcement and sheriff court practice. I am also greatly obliged to Miss Elaine Sutherland, who prepared the table of cases, and my special thanks are due to Miss Elizabeth Carr, who typed most of the manuscript, and to Miss I. Stewart and Mr D. Purdom of W. Green & Son for advice and assistance during production, and for coping with my prentice efforts in this field. Finally, may I acknowledge the debt I owe to the various writers upon whose works I have drawn.

The law has been generally stated as at 31 December 1980, but reference has been made to certain orders and rules which have come into force since then, and to certain decisions taken prior to but not published until after that date. I do not pretend that the citation of cases is exhaustive, particularly in the passages relating to jurisdiction and remedies, but I have tried to include those decisions which state principles or significant points of statutory construction. But in this developing field the flow of legislation and decision continues unabated, and it has not been practicable to note all of the substantial number of relevant decisions published or taken during production.

WILLIAM LESLIE

May, 1981

*Now the Hon. Lord Mayfield

TABLE OF CONTENTS

CHAPTER 10—EXPENSES

CHAPTER 11—REVIEW

CHAPTER 12—APPEAL

APPENDICES

TABLE OF CASES

(For guide to citation of cases see table of abbreviations, p. xxxxi)

TABLE OF STATUTES

TABLE OF STATUTORY INSTRUMENTS

TABLE OF ABBREVIATIONS

Note on industrial tribunal cases

There are three series of reports of decisions in industrial tribunal cases:

(1) Industrial Cases Reports. Commenced 1972. Cited as [19] I.C.R.

(2) Industrial Relations Law Reports. Commenced 1972. Cited as [19] I.R.L.R.

(3) Industrial Tribunal Reports. Commenced 1966, and discontinued after vol. 13 (1978). Cited as (1966) 1 I.T.R., etc.

Unreported cases are cited by reference to the case number or the date of the decision.

Other abbreviations:

A.C.=Appeal Cases (Law Reports—House of Lords and Privy Council).

All E.R.=All England Law Reports

E.C.R.=European Court Reports

F.=Court of Session Reports 1898-1906 (edited by Fraser)

H.L.=House of Lords (Reports in Session Cases)

J.C.=Justiciary Cases (Criminal Reports in Session Cases)

Q.B.=Queen's Bench (Law Reports—Queen's Bench Division and Court of Appeal)

R.=Court of Session Reports 1873-1898 (edited by Rettie)

S.C.=Session Cases (Court of Session Reports)

S.L.T.=Scots Law Times

T.L.R.=Times Law Reports

CHAPTER 1

HISTORY AND GROUNDS OF JURISDICTION

HISTORICAL INTRODUCTION

Industrial tribunals had an inconspicuous origin in s. 12 of the Industrial Training Act 1964, which conferred on the Minister of Labour the power to establish tribunals to determine appeals by persons assessed to levy under the Act. The title "industrial tribunal" first occurs in regulations made in exercise of that power, the Industrial Tribunals (Scotland) Regulations 1965 (S.I. 1965/1157). (In the various levy orders made under the principal Act, in which provision is made for persons aggrieved by assessments to levy to appeal to a tribunal established under s. 12, the tribunals are commonly referred to as "appeal tribunals").

Since then the jurisdiction of industrial tribunals has been greatly expanded in subsequent employment legislation, and principally in the Redundancy Payments Act 1965, the Equal Pay Act 1970, the Industrial Relations Act 1971 (repealed by the Trade Union and Labour Relations Act 1974, but the unfair dismissal provisions were re-enacted (with amendments) in Sched. 1), the Employment Protection Act 1975, the Sex Discrimination Act 1975, and the Race Relations Act 1976. Certain other Acts, referred to below, also conferred jurisdiction on industrial tribunals.

The grounds of jurisdiction and related provisions concerning industrial tribunals in the Redundancy Payments Act 1965, the Contracts of Employment Act 1972, the Trade Union and Labour Relations Act 1974, and the Employment Protection Act 1975, with the exception of those in Pt. IV (ss. 99 to 107) of the latter Act, were consolidated and re-enacted in the Employment Protection (Consolidation) Act 1978. Further grounds of jurisdiction have since been conferred by the Employment Act 1980.

Industrial tribunals were designed as a forum where procedural rules would be relatively simple so far as consistent with order and dignity, with a view to avoiding the expense, delay and formality which are endemic in litigation in the traditional courts, so that parties should not feel inhibited from using them, and presenting their cases in person, without professional representation, if they so wished. A tribunal normally consists of three members—a legally qualified Chairman, a member representative of the employers' side of industry, and a member representative of employees, although in certain circumstances a tribunal may consist of a Chairman and one other member or a

Chairman alone. For the constitution of a tribunal, see Chapter 3. Successive Governments have entrusted industrial tribunals with the responsibility of adjudicating upon disputes between individual employees and employers in a wide variety of situations. A number of disputes between individuals (both employees and employers) and the State in the employment field have also been put under their jurisdiction, and most recently, in the Employment Act 1980, they have been given the task of hearing complaints against trade unions about refusal of membership or expulsion from membership in a "closed shop" situation. While these grounds of jurisdiction may produce proceedings of a multiple nature, industrial tribunals have not generally been given the task of adjudicating upon disputes in the collective field.[1] In effect they now constitute a system of industrial courts operating, in their own distinctive manner, what is recognised to be a judicial process,[2] and not a process of arbitration.[3] In some cases the jurisdiction is expressly stated to be exclusive,[4] while in others it is alternative to that of the sheriff court,[5] or it may arise by virtue of a reference to the tribunal by a sheriff court.[6]

Although the jurisdictions conferred on industrial tribunals have so far been identical in Scotland and in England and Wales, the tribunals in Scotland have from their inception been separate in constitution, operation and (in various respects) practice from those in England and Wales, and governed by separate, though very similar, regulations and rules of procedure. Comparisons between the practice of the tribunals in the two countries are therefore apt, although distinctions have to be made. Industrial tribunals in Northern Ireland have had a somewhat different history, and no attempt has been made to draw comparisons with the practice of tribunals there.

GROUNDS OF JURISDICTION

(1) The Employment Protection (Consolidation) Act 1978

As observed above, many of the important jurisdictions conferred on

---

1 The exceptions are the rights conferred on trade unions to complain under s. 101 of the Employment Protection Act 1975, (failure to consult in impending redundancy situations) and s. 2 of the Employment Act 1980 (failure to provide facilities for a ballot).

2 See *Green and Anr.* v. *Hampshire County Council* [1979] I.C.R. 861, where it was held that a fully reasoned decision by an industrial tribunal was a judicial decision by a judicial tribunal for the purposes of the doctrine of *res judicata*. As to *res judicata*, see Chap. 4, p. 37.

3 Paragraph 4 of Sched. 9 to the Employment Protection (Consolidation) Act 1978 provides that the Arbitration Act 1950 (which only has limited application in Scotland) shall not apply to any proceedings before an industrial tribunal.

4 In s. 129 of the Employment Protection (Consolidation) Act 1978; s. 108(1) of the Employment Protection Act 1975; and s. 2(8) of the Employment Act 1980.

5 Under s. 131 of the Employment Protection (Consolidation) Act 1978.

6 Under s. 51 of the Docks and Harbours Act 1966.

industrial tribunals under previous legislation have been consolidated in the 1978 Act. They are as follows:

Part I (Particulars of terms of employment)

Section 11 (written particulars of terms of employment). An employee may require a reference to be made to an industrial tribunal to determine what particulars ought to have been included or referred to in a written statement so as to comply with the requirements of the relevant sections (s. 1 (written particulars of terms of employment), s. 4(1) (written particulars of change in terms of employment), or s. 8 (itemised pay statements)).

Part II (Rights arising in course of employment)

Section 17 (Guarantee payments). An employee may complain that his employer has failed to pay the whole or any part of a guarantee payment to which he is entitled.

Section 22 (Suspension from work on medical grounds). An employee may complain that his employer has failed to pay the whole or any part of the remuneration to which the employee is entitled under s. 19.

Section 24 (Trade union membership and activities). An employee may complain that action has been taken against him by his employer in contravention of his rights under s. 23 not to have action (short of dismissal) taken against him for the purpose of preventing or deterring him from membership of an independent trade union or taking part in trade union activities, or penalising him for doing so, or compelling him to become a member of a trade union which is not independent.

Section 27(7) (Time off work for carrying out trade union duties). An official of an independent trade union recognised by his employer may complain that his employer has failed to permit him to take time off during working hours for the purpose of enabling him to carry out duties concerned with industrial relations, or to undergo training in relevant aspects of industrial relations approved by his union or the Trades Union Congress. He may also complain that his employer has failed to pay for such time off.

Section 28(4) (Time off for trade union activities). A member of an independent trade union recognised by his employer may complain that his employer has failed to permit him to take time off for the purpose of taking part in specified trade union activities.

Section 29(6) (Time off for public duties). An employee may complain that his employer has failed to permit him to take time off to enable him to perform certain specified public duties.

Section 31(6) (Time off to look for work or make arrangements for training). An employee under notice by reason of redundancy, who is entitled under s. 31 to reasonable time off in order to look for new employment or make arrangements for training for future employment, may complain that his employer has unreasonably refused to allow him such time off or has failed to pay the whole or any part of any remuneration to which he is entitled under the section.

Section 31A(6) (Time off for ante-natal care).[7] An employee may complain that her employer has unreasonably refused her time off as required by s. 31A for the purpose of receiving ante-natal care, or that he has failed to pay her the whole or part of any remuneration to which she is entitled under s. 31A (4) for time off for that purpose.

Part III (Maternity)

Section 36 (Maternity pay). An employee may complain that her employer has failed to pay her the whole or any part of any maternity pay to which she is entitled.

Section 43 (Payments out of the Maternity Pay Fund). An employer or an employee may complain under s. 43(1) or 43(3) (as the case may be) that the Secretary of State has failed or refused to make a payment of maternity pay or maternity pay rebate (as is appropriate), or on the ground that the amount paid by him was less than the amount which should have been paid. An employer may also appeal under s. 43(4) against a determination by the Secretary of State as to an amount to be recovered from him under s. 41.

Section 46 (Right to return to work). The remedies of an employee who has been absent from work because of pregnancy or confinement but is not permitted to return to work are those conferred by ss. 56 and 86 and Sched. 2. The effect of these provisions, broadly speaking, is to extend (as may be appropriate) the right not to be unfairly dismissed and the right to a redundancy payment to such employees and, by the same token, to extend to such cases the jurisdiction of industrial tribunals in Pts. V and VI of the Act, subject to the modifications provided in Pts. I and II of Sched. 2. Part III of that Schedule also confers unfair dismissal rights on employees dismissed during a period of absence on account of pregnancy or confinement. Schedule 2 modifies the provisions of Pts. V and VI of the Act in such cases.

Part IV (Termination of employment)

Section 53(4) (Written statement of reasons for dismissal). An employee whose contract of employment has been terminated by his employer, or an employee on a fixed term contract which has expired without being renewed, may complain that his employer has unreason-

[7] Added by the Employment Act 1980, s. 13. Effective from October 1, 1980 (The Employment Act 1980 (Commencement No. 1) Order 1980 (S.I. 1980/1170)).

ably refused to provide a written statement under s. 53(1) or that the particulars or reasons given in purported compliance with that subsection are inadequate or untrue. The right does not extend to an employee who resigns whether or not the circumstances constitute a constructive dismissal.

Part V (Unfair dismissal)

Section 67 (Unfair dismissal). A complaint may be presented against an employer by any *person*[8] that he was unfairly dismissed. This is by far the commonest ground of complaint to industrial tribunals. The complainant's position in relation to the employer must, however, have been that of employee as defined in s. 153(1),[9] since it is that relationship which confers the right not to be unfairly dismissed by virtue of s. 54. Any other form of relationship (e.g. under a contract to perform services, as opposed to a contract of service) does not confer such a right (see Chapter 4, pp. 54 to 58).

Sections 77 and 79 (Interim relief). An employee who complains that he has been unfairly dismissed and claims that the reason for the dismissal (or, if more than one, the principal reason) was that he was or proposed to become a member of a particular independent trade union, or had taken or proposed to take part in the activities of such a union, may apply under s. 77 for an order for interim relief pending the determination of his complaint. If such relief is ordered the employer or employee may apply under s. 79 for the order to be revoked or varied on the ground of change of circumstances at any time before the complaint is determined.

Part VI (Redundancy payments)

Section 91 (Right to redundancy payment). Any question arising under Pt. VI of the Act as to the right of an employee to a redundancy payment or as to the amount of a redundancy payment is to be referred to and determined by an industrial tribunal. Section 91(3) brings certain questions arising in relation to lay-off or short-time within the ambit of a question as to the right of an employee to a redundancy payment.

Section 108 (Payments out of the Redundancy Fund). Section 108(2) provides for referring to an industrial tribunal various questions which may arise where (under s. 108(1)(*a*)) a claim is made for redundancy rebate based on an employer's payment, or where notice is given that such a claim may arise, or where (under s. 108(1)(*b*)) an application is

---

[8] (Author's italics).

[9] Where "employee" is defined as an individual who has entered into or works under (or, where the employment has ceased, worked under) a contract of employment, and contract of employment is defined as a contract of service or apprenticeship, whether express or implied.

made to the Secretary of State by an employee for such a payment under s. 106 because he has been unable to recover it from his employer. The questions to be referred are:

(a) any question as to the liability of the employer to pay the employer's payment;
(b) in a case falling within s. 108(1)(*a*), any question as to the amount of the rebate payable; and
(c) in a case falling within s. 108(1)(*b*), any question as to the amount of the sum payable.

Section 108(4) provides that an employer may appeal against the refusal of rebate by the Secretary of State in the exercise of his discretion under s. 104(3)—*i.e.* in cases where the employer has paid a redundancy payment in circumstances in which, by virtue of s. 101, the employee had no right to it. Section 108(5) provides that an employer may appeal against a withholding of or reduction in the amount of a redundancy rebate by the Secretary of State in pursuance of s. 104(7) (failure to give timeous notice of intention to claim) or s. 106(4) (where the employer's failure to pay is without reasonable excuse).

Section 112 (Payments equivalent to redundancy payments). This section provides for referring to an industrial tribunal questions which arise in the case of persons in certain employments in the public service and in the service of the Queen or the Duchies of Lancaster or Cornwall who are barred from entitlement to a redundancy payment under s. 99, but may be entitled to an equivalent payment under s. 111. The questions which may be so referred are similar to those in s. 91.

Part VII (Insolvency of employer)

Section 124 (Payments by Secretary of State). By s. 124(1) a person who has applied to the Secretary of State under s. 122 for payment of a debt due to him by an insolvent employer may complain that the Secretary of State has failed to make any such payment or that any such payment which has been made is less than the amount which should have been paid. Section 124(2) confers a similar right on persons who are competent to act in respect of an occupational pension scheme and who have applied to the Secretary of State under s. 123 for a payment to be made into the resources of the scheme.

Part VIII (Resolution of disputes relating to employment)

Section 130 (Jurisdiction of referees). By s. 130(1) any question which by any statutory provision is to be determined by a referee or board of referees constituted under any of the statutory provisions specified in Sched. 10, or which is so directed to be determined in the absence of agreement to the contrary, is to be referred to and determined by an industrial tribunal. The statutory provisions in question are too numerous for repetition here.

Section 131 (Damages etc., for breach of contract of employment). By s. 131(1), if so provided by statutory order made (in Scotland) by the Secretary of State,[10] proceedings in any claim to which s. 131 applies, for the recovery of damages or any other sum (except damages or a sum due in respect of personal injuries), may be brought before an industrial tribunal. Section 131 applies to:—

> a claim for damages for breach of a contract of employment or any other contract connected with employment;
> a claim for a sum due under such a contract; and
> a claim for the recovery of a sum in pursuance of any enactment relating to the terms or performance of such a contract.

In each case the claim must be such that a court would have jurisdiction to hear and determine an action in respect of it, and can only be one which either arises or is outstanding on the termination of the employee's employment, or arises in circumstances which also give rise to proceedings already or simultaneously brought before an industrial tribunal (otherwise than by virtue of s. 131). If the statutory order so provides, the claim must satisfy both the last mentioned conditions (s. 131(2) and (3)). Any jurisdiction conferred on an industrial tribunal by virtue of s. 131 cannot exclude that of any court in England and Wales or in Scotland, as the case may be, which has jurisdiction to hear and to determine an action in respect of the claim. By contrast, s. 129 confers exclusive jurisdiction on industrial tribunals where provision is made for a complaint or reference of a question to a tribunal as the remedy for infringement of any of the rights conferred on employees by ss. 8 and 53 and Pts. II, III, V and VII of the Act. No order has as yet been made under s. 131.

Part IX (Miscellaneous and supplementary)

Section 139 (Provisions as to House of Commons staff). Subsection (6) provides that where any proceedings are brought against the House of Commons Commission or Mr Speaker or any person designated as the employer in their place, the person against whom the proceedings are brought may apply to the court or the industrial tribunal, as the case may be, to have some other person against whom the proceedings could at the time of the application be brought substituted for him as a party to those proceedings. In practice, this jurisdiction would not apply in Scotland, by virtue of the Industrial Tribunals (Rules of Procedure) Scotland Regulations 1980, reg. 3.

---

[10] See s. 131(7).

(2) The Industrial Training Act 1964

The origin of this ground of jurisdiction in s. 12 of the Act has already been referred to.[11] The various levy orders made under the Act provide for an appeal to an industrial tribunal (generally referred to in such orders as an "appeal tribunal") by a person assessed to levy under the order.

(3) The Docks and Harbours Act 1966

By s. 51(1), a dispute between a person and the National Dock Labour Board or a licensing authority about a question whether any work is dock work or whether a place is within the ambit of a dock labour scheme,[12] may be referred to an industrial tribunal either by an interested person or a trade union official on his behalf, or (where the question arises in any proceedings before a sheriff) by the sheriff.

(4) The Selective Employment Payments Act 1966 and the Industrial Relations Act 1971

The grounds of jurisdiction under these Acts no longer exist, except to the extent that the unfair dismissal provisions in the 1971 Act were re-enacted (with changes) in the Trade Union and Labour Relations Act 1974.

(5) The Equal Pay Act 1970 (as amended by the Sex Discrimination Act 1975)

By s. 2(1) any claim in respect of the contravention of a term in a contract of employment modified or included by virtue of an equality clause, including a claim for arrears of remuneration or damages in respect of the contravention, may be presented by way of complaint to an industrial tribunal.[13]

By s. 2(1A), where a dispute arises in relation to the effect of an equality clause the employer may apply for an order declaring the rights of the employer and the employee in relation to the matter in question.[14]

By s. 2(2) the Secretary of State may refer to an industrial tribunal a question whether an employer is or has been contravening a term

---

[11] See p. 1 above.

[12] But not a question relating to work in an area in which there is in force the scheme under the Dock Work Regulation Act 1976 (see s. 12(3) of that Act).

[13] In cases involving a contravention of the equal access requirements (ss. 53 to 56) of the Social Security Pensions Act 1975 the jurisdiction of industrial tribunals has been modified in certain respects by regs. 11 and 12 of the Occupational Pension Schemes (Equal Access to Membership) Regulations 1976 (S.I. 1976/142), made under that Act.

[14] But see previous footnote as to cases relating to the equal access requirements of the Social Security Pensions Act 1975.

modified or included by virtue of an equality clause, if it appears to him that it is not reasonable to expect the employees concerned to take steps to have the question determined.

Section 2(3) provides that where it appears to the court in which any proceedings are pending that a claim or a counter claim in respect of the operation of an equality clause could be more conveniently disposed of by an industrial tribunal, the court may direct that the claim or counter claim shall be struck out; and where in proceedings before any court a question arises as to the operation of an equality clause, the court may on the application of any party to the proceedings or otherwise refer that question, or direct it to be referred by a party to the proceedings, to an industrial tribunal for determination by the tribunal, and may stay or sist the proceedings in the meantime.

(6) **Acts relating to local government, etc.**

Provisions in various Acts relating to the local administration of government and justice in Scotland enable the Secretary of State by regulations to provide for the payment of compensation to persons who suffer loss of employment and consequential loss or diminution of emoluments attributable to any provisions of the Acts, and that the regulations may *inter alia* include provision for the determination of all questions arising thereunder.

The Acts in question are:

The Water Officers' Compensation Act 1960, s. 1, as amended by the Water (Scotland) Acts 1967 and 1980.

The Registration of Births, Deaths and Marriages (Scotland) Act 1965, s. 7(11).

The Social Work (Scotland) Act 1968, s. 85.

The Sheriff Courts (Scotland) Act 1971, s. 27.

The Superannuation Act 1972, s. 24.

The Local Government (Scotland) Act 1973, s. 219.

The District Courts (Scotland) Act 1975, s. 19.

In *Gordon District Council* v. *Hay*, 1978 S.L.T. 2 (O.H.) the jurisdiction of an industrial tribunal to determine a compensation question arising under the Local Government (Compensation) (Scotland) Regulations 1975, made under s. 219(3) of the Local Government (Scotland) Act 1973 was unsuccessfully challenged. The decision in the Outer House was upheld on appeal by the Second Division in the Inner House, although on slightly different grounds. (The Inner House decision is not reported).

(7) **The Health and Safety at Work, etc. Act 1974**

By s. 24(2) a person on whom an improvement notice or a prohibition notice is served may appeal to an industrial tribunal.

Regulation 11(1) of the Safety Representatives and Safety Committees Regulations 1977 (S.I. 1977/500) (which, under the powers in s. 2 of the Act, provide *inter alia* for the appointment of safety representatives and prescribe their functions) provides that a safety representative may complain to an industrial tribunal that the employer has failed to permit him to take time off or to pay him for such time off in accordance with the regulations. This jurisdiction was constituted under powers conferred by s. 80 of the Act to repeal or modify by statutory regulation various other statutory provisions and regulations, including (in subsection (3)) modifications relating to the enforcement of provisions to which s. 80 applies. Regulation 11(5) made an appropriate modification to para. 16 of Sched. 1 to the Trade Union and Labour Relations Act 1974, which prescribed the areas of jurisdiction of industrial tribunals, so as to bring this particular ground of jurisdiction within the ambit of para. 16. Paragraph 16 was repealed by the Employment Protection (Consolidation) Act 1978,[15] and was not expressly re-enacted as modified, but in *White* v. *Pressed Steel Fisher* [1980] I.R.L.R. 176 the jurisdiction was held to be preserved by virtue of para. 4 of Sched. 15 to the Employment Protection (Consolidation) Act 1978.

(8) **The Sex Discrimination Act 1975**

Section 63(1) provides that a complaint of unlawful discrimination by virtue of Pt. II of the Act (which deals with discrimination in the employment field), or by virtue of an act which is to be treated as such discrimination under ss. 41 or 42 (which create vicarious liabilities of different kinds), may be presented to an industrial tribunal. But, by s. 66(1) and (2), proceedings for discrimination in other fields, as specified in Pt. III, or by virtue of an act which is to be treated as such discrimination by virtue of s. 41 or s. 42, may in Scotland only be taken in the sheriff court.

By s. 68(1) a person may appeal against any requirement of a non-discrimination notice, so far as the requirement relates to acts which are within the jurisdiction of the tribunal, or to a sheriff court so far as the requirement relates to acts which are within the jurisdiction of the court and are not within the jurisdiction of an industrial tribunal. The "acts" referred to in s. 68(1) are those specified in the notice appealed against, so far as within the jurisdiction of the tribunal, *i.e.* by virtue of s. 63(1).

Section 72, subss. (2) and (3) make provision for an application to an industrial tribunal by the Equal Opportunities Commission *inter alia* for

[15] Sched. 17.

a decision on a contravention of ss. 38, 39 or 40 (relating to discriminatory advertisements, instructions to discriminate and pressure to discriminate) in a case based on any provision of Pt. II of the Act; in any other case the application must be made to the sheriff court.

Section 73(1) provides that with a view to making an application to the sheriff court under ss. 71(1) or 72(4) (which enable the Commission to apply for an order to restrain a person from repeated contraventions of the Act) the Commission may complain to an industrial tribunal that the person concerned has done an unlawful act within the jurisdiction of an industrial tribunal. Section 73(4) defines "an act within the jurisdiction of an industrial tribunal", for the purposes of ss. 71 to 73, as those in respect of which jurisdiction is conferred by ss. 63 and 72 of the Act and by s. 2 of the Equal Pay Act 1970, *i.e.* of unlawful discrimination in the employment field or contravening a term of a contract of employment modified by an equality clause.

(9) **The Social Security Pensions Act 1975**

Section 31(5)(*e*) provides for regulations to be made for referring to an industrial tribunal any question whether an organisation is an independent trade union recognised to any extent for the purpose of collective bargaining or whether the requirements of regulations made under s. 31 as to consultation have been complied with. The Occupational Pension Schemes (Certification of Employment) Regulations 1975 (S.I. 1975/1927) contain provisions to that effect (regs. 4(2), 4(3) and 10(4)).

(10) **The Employment Protection Act 1975**

By s. 101(1) an "appropriate trade union" (as defined in s. 101(7)) may complain that an employer has dismissed as redundant or is proposing to dismiss as redundant one or more employees and has not complied with any of the requirements of s. 99 (which imposes a duty on employers to consult with trade union representatives in an impending redundancy situation). If the tribunal finds the complaint well-founded it may make a protective award for payment of remuneration to the employees concerned for a specified period (s. 101(3) and (4)).

Section 103(1) provides that an employee may complain that he is an employee of a description to which a protective award relates and that his employer has failed, wholly or in part, to pay him remuneration under that award.

By s. 104(3) an employer may appeal to an industrial tribunal where the Secretary of State reduces a redundancy rebate in pursuance of s. 104(1) (which applies where an employer has failed to give notice to the Secretary of State in accordance with s. 100 of his proposal to dismiss certain numbers of employees within stated periods).

(11) The Race Relations Act 1976

Section 54(1) provides that a complaint of unlawful discrimination by virtue of Pt. II of the Act (which deals with discrimination in the employment field), or by virtue of an act which is to be treated as such discrimination by virtue of ss. 32 or 33 (which create vicarious liabilities of various kinds), may be presented to an industrial tribunal. But by s. 57(1) and (2) proceedings for discrimination in other fields, as specified in Pt. III, or by virtue of an act which is to be treated as such discrimination by virtue of s. 32 and s. 33, may in Scotland only be taken in the sheriff court.

By s. 59(1) a person may appeal against any requirement of a non-discrimination notice, so far as the requirement relates to acts which are within the jurisdiction of the tribunal, or to a sheriff court so far as the requirement relates to acts which are within the jurisdiction of the court and are not within the jurisdiction of an industrial tribunal.

The acts referred to in s. 59(1) are those specified in the notice appealed against, so far as within the jurisdiction of the tribunal, *i.e.* by virtue of s. 54(1).

Sections 63(2) and 63(3) make provision for an application to an industrial tribunal by the Commission for Racial Equality *inter alia* for a decision on a contravention of ss. 29, 30 or 31 (relating to discriminatory advertisements, instructions to discriminate and pressure to discriminate), in a case based on any provision of Pt. II of the Act; in any other case the application must be made to the sheriff court.

Section 64(1) provides that with a view to making an application to the sheriff court under ss. 62(1) or 63(4) (which enable the Commission to apply for an order restraining a person from repeated contraventions of the Act) the Commission may complain to an industrial tribunal that the person concerned has done an unlawful act within the jurisdiction of an industrial tribunal. Section 64(3) defines "an act within the jurisdiction of an industrial tribunal" for the purposes of ss. 62 to 64 as being those in respect of which jurisdiction is conferred by ss. 54 and 63, *i.e.* discriminating acts in the employment field.

(12) The Employment Act 1980

Section 2(4)[16] provides that a trade union may present a complaint to an industrial tribunal that it has made a request to an employer (under s. 2(1)) to permit premises of his to be used for the purpose of giving workers employed by him who are members of the union an opportunity of voting in a ballot which satisfies the requirements of a scheme under s. 1 of the Act as to the purpose of the question (or one of the

---

[16] Effective from October 1, 1980 (The Employment Act 1980 (Commencement No. 1) Order 1980 (S.I. 1980/1170)).

questions) to be voted upon,[17] and that it was reasonably practicable for the employer to comply with it, but that he has failed to do so. But s. 2(1) does not apply where, at the time the request was made, the union is not recognised by the employer to any extent for the purpose of collective bargaining, or the number of workers employed by the employer, added to the number employed by any associated employer, does not exceed twenty (s. 2(3)).

Section 4(4)[18] provides that a complaint may be presented to an industrial tribunal against a trade union by a person that an application by him for membership of the union has been unreasonably refused, or that he has been unreasonably expelled from the union, in contravention of s. 4(2).[19]

If a complaint under s. 4 is declared to be well-founded, s. 5(1) provides that the complainant may make a further (and separate) application for an award of compensation to be paid to him by the union. If at the time when the application is made[20] the applicant has been admitted or re-admitted to the union, the application is to be made to an industrial tribunal, but if not, to the Employment Appeal Tribunal (s. 5(2)).

---

[17] *I.e.* (as provided in s. 1(3)):—
(*a*) for obtaining a decision or ascertaining the views of members of a trade union as to the taking or ending of a strike or other industrial action;
(*b*) carrying out an election provided for by the rules of a trade union;
(*c*) electing a worker who is a member of a trade union to be a representative of other workers also employed by his employer;
(*d*) amending the rules of a trade union;
(*e*) obtaining a decision in accordance with the Trade Union (Amalgamations etc.) Act 1964 on a resolution to approve an instrument of amalgamation or transfer;
and such other purposes as the Secretary of State may by order specify.

[18] Sections 4 and 5 are effective from September 8, 1980 (The Employment Act 1980 (Commencement No. 1) Order 1980).

[19] Which confers on every person who is, or is seeking to be, in employment to which s. 4 applies (*i.e.* that with respect to which it is the practice, in accordance with a union membership agreement, for the employee to belong to a specified trade union—in ordinary language, a closed shop) the right—
(a) not to have an application for membership of a specified trade union unreasonably refused;
(b) not to be unreasonably expelled from a specified trade union.

[20] It must be between four weeks and six months from the date of the declaration that the complaint was well-founded (s. 5(3)).

CHAPTER 2

REGULATIONS AND RULES OF PROCEDURE

ENABLING ENACTMENTS

Section 12 of the Industrial Training Act 1964 enabled regulations to be made for the establishment of tribunals to determine appeals against assessments to levy, including the procedure to be followed on such appeals. Similar enabling provisions, but expressed in increasingly detailed terms, which reflect the expansion in the scope and importance of industrial tribunals, have been enacted and re-enacted in various successive statutes passed since then. The current enabling provisions are those in s. 128 of the Employment Protection (Consolidation) Act 1978, and Sched. 9.

Sections 128(1) and 128(2) of the 1978 Act are in the following terms:

> "128—(1) The Secretary of State may by regulations make provision for the establishment of tribunals, to be known as industrial tribunals, to exercise the jurisdiction conferred on them by or under this Act or any other Act, whether passed before or after this Act.
>
> (2) Regulations made wholly or partly under section 12 of the Industrial Training Act 1964 and in force immediately before the date on which this section comes into force shall, so far as so made, continue to have effect as if they had been made under subsection (1), and tribunals established in accordance with such regulations shall continue to be known as industrial tribunals."

Paragraph 1(1) of Sched. 9 to the 1978 Act empowers the Secretary of State by regulations to make such provision as appears to him to be necessary or expedient with respect to proceedings before industrial tribunals. The succeeding subparagraphs (2) to (7) prescribe what provisions may, and in some cases must, be included in such regulations. It is not necessary to set them out in detail, since they are reflected in the rules of procedure which are discussed in detail in succeeding chapters. In terms of s. 10 of the Tribunals and Inquiries Act 1971 the power of the Secretary of State to make procedural rules cannot be exercised except after consultation with the Council on Tribunals.[1]

All the regulations currently in force relating to the establishment and proceedings of industrial tribunals were made before the passing of the

---

[1] For the role of the Council on Tribunals in relation to industrial tribunals, see Chap. 3, at p. 18.

1978 Act. In so far as made under s. 12 of the Industrial Training Act 1964, they remain in force by virtue of s. 128(2) of the 1978 Act. In so far as made under subsequent Acts they are preserved by para. 1 of Sched. 15 to the 1978 Act, which is in the following terms:

> "So far as anything done or treated as done under or for the purposes of any enactment repealed by this Act could have been done under a corresponding provision of this Act it shall not be invalidated by the repeal but shall have effect as if done under or for the purposes of that provision."

As regards the construction of the regulations, para. 4 of Sched. 15 to the 1978 Act provides as follows:

> "Any reference in an enactment or document, whether express or implied, to—
>
> (*a*) an enactment which is re-enacted in a corresponding provision of this Act;
>
> (*b*) an enactment replaced or amended by a provision of the Employment Protection Act 1975 which is re-enacted in a corresponding provision of this Act;
>
> (*c*) an enactment in the Industrial Relations Act 1971 which was re-enacted with or without amendment in a corresponding provision in Schedule 1 to the Trade Union and Labour Relations Act 1974 and that corresponding provision is re-enacted by a corresponding provision of this Act;
>
> shall, except so far as the context otherwise requires, be construed as, or as including, a reference to the corresponding provision of this Act."[2]

As regards legal proceedings before industrial tribunals, para. 18 of Sched. 15 to the 1978 Act provides that notwithstanding the repeal of any enactment by the 1978 Act, industrial tribunals may continue to exercise the jurisdiction conferred on them by or under any enactment which is repealed by the 1978 Act with respect to matters arising out of or in connection with the repealed enactments.

REGULATIONS RELATING TO THE ESTABLISHMENT AND CONSTITUTION OF INDUSTRIAL TRIBUNALS

The regulations which provide for the establishment of industrial tribunals in Scotland are the Industrial Tribunals (Scotland) Regulations 1965 (S.I. 1965/1157), made under s. 12 of the Industrial Training Act

---

[2] These provisions were relied on in *White* v. *Pressed Steel Fisher* [1980] I.R.L.R. 176 in upholding the validity of the jurisdiction of industrial tribunals under the Safety Representatives and Safety Committees Regulations 1977 (See Chap. 1, p. 10).

1964, as amended (substantially) by the Industrial Tribunals (Scotland) (Amendment) Regulations 1967 (S.I. 1967/302), and by the Industrial Tribunals (Scotland) (Amendment) Regulations 1972 (S.I. 1972/638) and 1977 (S.I. 1977/1474).

The regulations (as so amended) contain provisions regarding the President of the Industrial Tribunals (Scotland) (reg. 3), as to the establishment of tribunals (reg. 4), and as to Chairmen and members of tribunals (reg. 5). These provisions are discussed in detail elsewhere.[3]

The equivalent regulations relating to the establishment and constitution of Industrial Tribunals in England and Wales, which do not differ significantly, are the Industrial Tribunals (England and Wales) Regulations 1965 (S.I. 1965/1101) as amended by the Industrial Tribunals (England and Wales) (Amendment) Regulations 1967 (S.I. 1967/301), the Industrial Tribunals (England and Wales) (Amendment) Regulations 1970 (S.I. 1970/941), and the Industrial Tribunals (Amendment) Regulations 1977 (S.I. 1977/1473).

RULES OF PROCEDURE

The main regulations governing the procedure of industrial tribunals in Scotland are the Industrial Tribunals (Rules of Procedure) (Scotland) Regulations 1980 (S.I. 1980/885) made under para. 1 of Sched. 9 to the Employment Protection (Consolidation) Act 1978. They replace the Industrial Tribunals (Labour Relations) (Scotland) Regulations 1974 (S.I. 1974/1387) which had been amended by various subsequent regulations.

Regulation 3 provides that except where separate rules of procedure, made under the provisions of any enactment, are applicable, the rules of procedure contained in the Schedule to the regulations shall have effect in relation to all proceedings before a tribunal where various other requirements are satisfied, which are specified and discussed in Chapter 4 at pp. 29 and 30.

The regulations came into operation on October 1, 1980, except in relation to proceedings instituted before that date. The rules of procedure in the Schedule are called the Industrial Tribunals Rules of Procedure (Scotland) 1980.[4]

The equivalent rules of procedure in England and Wales are those in the Schedule to the Industrial Tribunals (Rules of Procedure) Regulations 1980 (S.I. 1980/884) replacing those in the Schedule to the Industrial Tribunals (Labour Relations) Regulations 1974 (S.I. 1974/1386)

---

[3] Mainly in Chap. 3.

[4] See Appendix 1, pp. 277 to 290.

as amended. They reflect differences between Scottish and English litigation procedures which for the most part are only terminological, but in some respects go deeper.[5] Otherwise they are in identical terms to the Scottish rules.

Separate rules of procedure[6] have been made, and continue to have effect, in relation to the following proceedings.

(1) For appeals under the Industrial Training Act 1964, the rules in Scheds. 1 and 2 to the Industrial Tribunals (Scotland) Regulations 1965 (S.I. 1965/1157), Sched. 2 having been added by the Industrial Tribunals (Scotland) (Amendment) Regulations 1967 (S.I. 1967/302).[7] The rules in Sched. 1 apply to levy orders coming into operation before March 13, 1967, and those in Sched. 2 to orders coming into operation on or after that date.

(2) For appeals under s. 24 of the Health and Safety at Work etc. Act 1974, the rules in the Schedule to the Industrial Tribunals (Improvement and Prohibition Notices Appeals) (Scotland) Regulations 1974 (S.I. 1974/1926).[8]

(3) For appeals against non-discrimination notices under s. 68 of the Sex Discrimination Act 1975 and s. 59 of the Race Relations Act 1976, the rules in the Schedule to the Industrial Tribunals (Non-Discrimination Notices Appeals) (Scotland) Regulations 1977 (S.I. 1977/1095). In a case under the equivalent rules in England and Wales[9], the rules were considered to be defective in various respects, and the tribunal had to construct its own procedure to remedy the deficiency *(Amari Plastics Ltd* v. *CRE* (1980) COIT 1024/226).

Apart from these, the Industrial Tribunals Rules of Procedure (Scotland) 1980 govern all other proceedings at present within the jurisdiction of industrial tribunals in Scotland. These four sets of rules are discussed in detail in succeeding chapters, with the exception of those in Sched. 1 to the Industrial Tribunals (Scotland) Regulations 1965, which are on similar lines to those in Sched. 2, but less detailed.

---

[5] *E.g.* In relation to recovery and production of documents, the Scottish r. 4(1)(*b*) is based on the commission and diligence granted in the Scottish courts, whereas the English r. 4(1)(*b*) is based on the English practice of discovery.

[6] Printed in *Encyclopaedia of Labour Relations Law*, vol. 3, Pt. 4A.

[7] The equivalent rules in England and Wales are those in the Industrial Tribunals (England and Wales) Regulations 1965, referred to above, as amended by those in the Schedule to the Industrial Tribunals (England and Wales) (Amendment) Regulations 1967.

[8] The equivalent rules in England and Wales are in the Schedule to the Industrial Tribunals (Improvement and Prohibition Notices Appeals) Regulations 1974 (S.I. 1974/1925).

[9] The Industrial Tribunals (Non-Discrimination Notices Appeals) Regulations 1977 (S.I. 1977/1094).

CHAPTER 3

THE INDUSTRIAL TRIBUNALS (SCOTLAND)

THE DEPARTMENT OF EMPLOYMENT

The Government department responsible for policy matters in relation to industrial tribunals in Scotland and England and Wales and for their staffing and administration is the Department of Employment. Statutory regulations affecting the constitution and procedure of the tribunals made by the Secretary of State acting under the powers conferred by s. 128(1) and para. 1(1) of Sched. 9 to the Employment Protection (Consolidation) Act 1978 are in practice made by the Secretary of State for Employment.

THE COUNCIL ON TRIBUNALS

By paras. 10 and 38 of Sched. 1 to the Tribunals and Inquiries Act 1971, industrial tribunals in England and Wales and Scotland are under the general supervision of the Council on Tribunals, which was originally constituted by the Tribunals and Inquiries Act 1958, and industrial tribunals in Scotland are also under the supervision of the Scottish Committee of the Council. The functions of the Council, and of its Scottish Committee, so far as relating to industrial tribunals, are defined in s. 1(1) of the Act as being—

(*a*) to keep under review their constitution and working and from time to time to report thereon;

(*b*) to consider and report on such particular matters as may be referred to the Council under the 1971 Act.

Section 4 of the 1971 Act makes provision for reports and references to the Council and its Scottish Committee. Section 5 enables the Council, or its Scottish Committee, to make recommendations to the appropriate Minister as to the making of appointments to membership of tribunals. Section 8 restricts the power of a Minister to terminate a person's membership of a tribunal except with the consent in Scotland of the Lord President of the Court of Session. The requirement in s. 10 that procedural rules for tribunals must be made in consultation with the Council has already been noted.[1]

In cases where a tribunal hearing is in private, a member of the

---

[1] See p. 14.

Council or of its Scottish Committee is entitled to attend the hearing in his capacity as such.[2]

A member of the Council, or of its Scottish Committee, attending a tribunal hearing in an official capacity (whether the hearing is public or private) sits alongside the tribunal, and is identified as such to the parties. But, in Scotland, he is not regarded as being entitled to accompany the tribunal when they retire, and thus to be privy to the tribunal's private discussions.

THE PRESIDENT OF THE INDUSTRIAL TRIBUNALS (SCOTLAND)

The President of the Industrial Tribunals (Scotland) is an advocate or solicitor of not less than seven years' standing, appointed by the Lord President of the Court of Session. He must vacate office at the end of the completed year of service in which he attains the age of 72. He may resign office by notice in writing to the Lord President. His appointment is revocable at the instance of the Lord President if he is incapacitated by infirmity of mind or body from discharging the duties of his office, or if he becomes bankrupt or insolvent. If he is for any reason unable to act or if there is a vacancy in his office, his functions may be discharged by a person nominated for that purpose by the Lord President.[3]

Provisions for the remuneration of and pensions for the President are made in paras. 9 and 11 of Sched. 9 to the Employment Protection (Consolidation) Act 1978.

The President supervises the internal administration of industrial tribunals in Scotland, and also presides as Chairman over sittings of individual tribunals. Under the regulations and rules of procedure relating to industrial tribunals, certain specific functions are assigned to him, which are noted in the appropriate context.

TRIBUNALS

The number of industrial tribunals to be established in Scotland is determined by the President. The times and places at which they sit are also determined by the President or, in relation to any area specified by him in Scotland, by a member of the panel of Chairmen nominated by him to act in that area.[4]

---

[2] The Industrial Tribunals Rules of Procedure (Scotland) 1980, r. 7(2), and equivalent provisions in the other rules.

[3] The Industrial Tribunals (Scotland) Regulations 1965, reg. 3, as amended by the Industrial Tribunals (Scotland) (Amendment) Regulations 1972.

[4] The Industrial Tribunals (Scotland) Regulations 1965, reg. 4, as amended by the Industrial Tribunals (Scotland) (Amendment) Regulations 1967.

Except in respect of the matters specified below, a tribunal consists of a Chairman and two other members but, in the absence of any one member of a tribunal, other than the Chairman, the tribunal may, with the consent of parties, consist of the Chairman and one other member only.[5] For any of the following purposes, however, a tribunal may consist of the President, the Chairman of the tribunal or a member of the panel of Chairmen for the time being nominated for the purpose by the President, sitting alone:

(a) making an order dismissing the proceedings where the appellant or applicant has given written notice of the abandonment of his appeal or application;
(b) making an order allowing the appeal where (in cases under the Industrial Training Act 1964) the appropriate board has given written notice that the appeal is not contested;
(c) deciding an appeal or application in accordance with the written agreement of the parties;
(d) dealing with any interlocutory matter or application;
(e) making an order for expenses in connection with an order or decision mentioned in the foregoing paragraphs.[6]

The meaning of the expression "interlocutory matter or application" is discussed in Chapter 9 (at p. 192). The President or a Chairman may also sit alone to determine an application for interim relief under s. 77 or s. 79 of the Employment Protection (Consolidation) Act 1978.[7]

The various rules of procedure also prescribe what acts may be done by the President or a Chairman alone.[8]

CHAIRMEN

For each hearing the Chairman is the President or a person selected from a panel of Chairmen, who are advocates or solicitors of not less than seven years' standing, appointed by the Lord President of the Court of Session. The selection of a Chairman from the panel is made by the President or a member of the panel who has been nominated by the President for the purpose. The President or the nominated Chairman may select himself.[9] The President or a Chairman nominated by him for

---

[5] The Industrial Tribunals (Scotland) Regulations 1965, reg. 5(1), as amended by the Industrial Tribunals (Scotland) (Amendment) Regulations 1967.

[6] The Industrial Tribunals (Scotland) Regulations 1965, reg. 5(1A), as amended by the Industrial Tribunals (Scotland) (Amendment) Regulations 1967.

[7] 1978 Act, Sched. 9, para. 8.

[8] See Chap. 6, p. 104.

[9] The Industrial Tribunals (Scotland) Regulations 1965, reg. 5(2), as amended by the Industrial Tribunals (Scotland) (Amendment) Regulations 1967.

the purpose may at any time select another Chairman from the panel in substitution for the Chairman previously selected to hear a case.[10]

Chairmen are appointed either on a full-time or part-time basis. They hold and vacate office under the terms of the instruments under which they are appointed (in practice a minute of appointment signed by the Lord President), but may resign office by notice in writing to the Lord President. A Chairman who ceases to hold office is eligible for re-appointment.[11] A Chairman must vacate office at the end of the completed year of service in the course of which he attains the age of 72. The Lord President may suspend or terminate the appointment of a full-time Chairman if in his opinion he becomes unfit to perform the duties of the office by reason of inability, misconduct, or any other cause. A Chairman must also resign if he is adopted as a prospective candidate for Parliament or is nominated as a candidate in a Parliamentary election.[12]

Provision for the remuneration of and pensions for full-time Chairmen is made in paras. 9 and 11 of Sched. 9 to the Employment Protection (Consolidation) Act 1978; the remuneration of part-time Chairmen appears to be covered by para. 10 of Sched. 9. A full-time Chairman can retire on full pension after 15 years' service and attaining the age of 65.

Apart from dealing with interlocutory and other matters under reg. 5(1A) of the 1965 regulations, the function of a Chairman is to preside over tribunal hearings, to rule on procedural matters which arise in the course of the hearing, consulting with his colleagues where appropriate to do so, to advise them on the relevant law, and to intimate their decision to the partries and thereafter to record it in writing.[13]

A Chairman should not participate in a case in which he has any personal, professional or pecuniary interest, unless the interest has been declared and all parties have expressly agreed to its being waived. It follows that a part-time Chairman should not act as such in a case in which any firm of which he is a member in any capacity has such an interest. He should not appear on behalf of a client before a tribunal, at least in an area in which he acts as a Chairman, and, if a solicitor, should not act as Chairman in a case in which a client of his or of his firm is a party, whether represented by a member of his firm or otherwise.[14] Similarly, a full-time Chairman should not sit in any case in which he personally acted for one of the parties while in private practice, although he is not regarded as being debarred from sitting in a case in

---

10 *Ibid* reg. 5(4).

11 The Industrial Tribunals (Scotland) Regulations 1965, reg. 5(5).

12 Memorandum of Conditions of Service of Full-time Chairmen—Department of Employment. The terms of the memorandum are referred to and adopted in the minute of appointment signed by the Lord President.

13 See Chap. 9 as to intimation and promulgation of the decision, and its form and content.

14 Memorandum of conditions of service, *supra*.

which a client of his former firm is a party if he himself did not act for the party concerned.

Full-time Chairmen are appointed to the Central Office or to one of the area offices at Edinburgh, Aberdeen and Dundee, but may be required to sit in another area. Part-time Chairmen are not appointed to any particular office, but in practice those who are solicitors usually sit in the locality in which they practise.

The Chairman and his colleagues have equal votes in arriving at their decision, which may be by a majority. But where the tribunal consists of two members only, the Chairman has a second or casting vote.[15] In fact about 99% of tribunal decisions are unanimous.

THE REGIONAL CHAIRMAN

The Regional Chairman is the Chairman appointed by the President to carry out such functions as the President may designate in connection with the due administration of justice by industrial tribunals in Scotland, or the person nominated by the President or the Regional Chairman to discharge for the time being the functions of the Regional Chairman.[16]

Under the Industrial Tribunals Rules of Procedure (Scotland) 1980 certain specific functions are allocated to the Regional Chairman, in addition to those which may be designated by the President from time to time. These are noted in the appropriate context. In practice, the Regional Chairman also deputises for the President in the absence of the latter.

MEMBERS OF TRIBUNALS

For each hearing the other members of the tribunal are selected by the President (or by a member of the panel of Chairmen nominated by the President for the purpose) from two panels of persons appointed by the Secretary of State, one member being selected from each panel. The members of one panel are appointed after consultation with any organisation or association of organisations representative of employers (in practice, the C.B.I.), and of the other after consultation with any

---

15 The Industrial Tribunals Rules of Procedure (Scotland) 1980, r. 9(1); the Industrial Tribunals (Scotland) Regulations 1965 (as amended), Sched. 2, r. 12 (1); the Industrial Tribunals (Improvement and Prohibition Notices Appeals) (Scotland) Regulations 1974, r. 11(1); the Industrial Tribunals (Non-Discrimination Notices Appeals) (Scotland) Regulations 1977, r. 9(1).

16 The Industrial Tribunals (Rules of Procedure) (Scotland) Regulations 1980, reg. 2.

organisation or association of organisations representative of employed persons (in practice, the T.U.C.).[17]

Provision is made for the payment of fees and allowances to members in para. 10 of Sched. 9 to the Employment Protection (Consolidation) Act 1978.

Wherever possible either the Chairman or one of the members selected to hear cases under the Equal Pay Act 1970 and the Sex Discrimination Act 1975 is a woman. Tribunals convened to hear cases under the Race Relations Act 1976 should include, wherever possible, at least one member with special knowledge or experience of relations between persons of different racial groups in the employment field.[18]

Members should not participate in any case in which they have a personal, professional or pecuniary interest, unless such interest has been declared and expressly waived by both parties. In particular, no member should act as such in a case in which his firm or his employer has such an interest or as a respondent. A member of the employees' panel should not act in a case in which he is a member of the same trade union (or other employees' organisation) as the applicant. Nor should a member of the employer's panel act in a case in which the respondent is a member of the same employers' association related to the same trade, industry or profession as him or his firm. But the fact that both are members of an organisation representative of employers as a whole, and not a particular industry (*e.g.* the C.B.I.) would not debar him from acting. Similarly, a member should not appear as a representative of a party before a tribunal in an area in which he sits as a member.

Where a potential interest becomes apparent to a member before the date of the hearing, the appropriate office of the tribunals should at once be informed, so that arrangements may be made for a replacement. Where the potential interest only becomes apparent as the hearing is about to take place, or during the course of a hearing, the Chairman should be notified at once, so that he may consider whether the matter is one which ought to be disclosed to the parties. Where the disclosure is made, the hearing cannot proceed and has to be adjourned to be heard later by a differently constituted tribunal, unless all parties agree to waive the interest or to the case being decided by the Chairman and the other member only. Any such agreement should be recorded in writing and signed by or on behalf of all parties.

As already noted,[20] the members of the tribunal have equal votes with

---

[17] The Industrial Tribunals (Scotland) Regulations 1965, reg. 5(3), as amended by the Industrial Tribunals (Scotland) (Amendment) Regulations 1977.

[18] An undertaking to that effect was given by Lord Jacques, spokesman for the Department of Employment, during the passage of the Race Relations Bill. (See footnote on p. 24 below).

[19] This is made clear in the letter of appointment by the Secretary of State.

[20] See p. 22.

the Chairman in arriving at the tribunal's decision. The members' function is a judicial one, and an industrial tribunal has been described as "an industrial jury." Accordingly, while they are appointed on the strength of their practical knowledge and experience of their respective sides of industry, and to make use of that knowledge and experience in deciding cases, they act objectively and impartially in arriving at their decision, discarding any extraneous loyalties. They are free to ask questions during the course of the hearing, and should do so for the purpose of resolving any doubts they may have, but in a manner which does not create an impression of partiality of approach. Members are entitled to use their own knowledge and experience to fill in gaps in the evidence, but where the tribunal makes particular use of this in reaching its decision it should be stated. If the practical experience of a member is contrary to that of a witness, the member should indicate this, so that the witness may have the opportunity to comment.[21] In *Hammington* v. *Berker Sportcraft Ltd* [1980] I.C.R. 248 it was held that where a tribunal relied on the personal knowledge and experience of one of their members it was necessary to indicate not only that he was a specialist in the field, but also to bring the facts known by that member to the attention of parties' representatives, so that they could either be dealt with or an adjournment could be asked for.

ASSESSORS

Rule 5(3) of the Industrial Tribunals Rules of Procedure (Scotland) 1980 provides that where in the case of any proceedings it is provided for one or more assessors to be appointed, the President or the Regional Chairman may, if he thinks fit, appoint a person or persons having special knowledge or experience in relation to the subject-matter of the case to sit with the tribunal as assessor or assessors.

The only type of proceedings governed by these rules in which provision is made for appointment of assessors appears to be those under the Local Government (Compensation) (Scotland) Regulations 1975, reg. 42(2). In *Habib* v. *Elkington & Co. Ltd.* (EAT 232/79), a case under the Race Relations Act, a request that a person with specialised knowledge of Indian culture and of community problems should be appointed to sit with the tribunal as an assessor was held to be incompetent, as the Act made no provision for the appointment of an assessor in such cases.[22]

---

21 *Dugdale and Others* v. *Kraft Foods Ltd.* [1977] I.C.R. 48.

22 But the tribunal itself could and perhaps should have included a member experienced in such matters, in view of the recommendation by Lord Jacques, referred to at p. 23 above. The matter has now been referred to the full Employment Appeal Tribunal (EAT 311/80).

The Health and Safety at Work, etc. Act 1974 s. 24(4), however, makes provision for the appointment of assessors in appeals against improvement notices or prohibition notices, and r. 6(3) in the Industrial Tribunals (Improvement and Prohibition Notices Appeals) (Scotland) Regulations 1974 confers power on the President or a nominated Chairman to appoint one or more assessors in such cases. Provision is made in para. 10 of Sched. 9 to the Employment Protection (Consolidation) Act 1978 for the payment of fees and allowances to persons appointed as assessors in industrial tribunal proceedings.

The appointment of assessors is a discretionary matter, and neither party is entitled to insist on such an appointment. If appointed, the assessors(s) sit(s) along with the members of the tribunal. The role of an assessor is not defined in any of the statutory provisions, but it may be assumed that it is to give expert advice and guidance to the tribunal, but not to take part in their decision. As regards nautical assessors in civil proceedings in the courts, it has been held that the assessor is not a judge in the case, and that it is for the sheriff to pronounce upon the trustworthiness of the evidence led before him. Nor can the opinion of the assessor be taken as evidence upon a point upon which no evidence was led.[23] The same principles may be assumed to apply in industrial tribunal proceedings.

THE SECRETARY OF THE TRIBUNALS AND ASSISTANT SECRETARY

The Secretary of the Tribunals and the Assistant Secretary of the Tribunals are respectively the persons acting as the Secretary or as an Assistant Secretary at the Central Office of the Industrial Tribunals (Scotland).[24]

Rule 12(6) of the Industrial Tribunals Rules of Procedure (Scotland) 1980 provides that any functions of the Secretary of the Tribunals, other than that mentioned in r. 1(2),[25] may be performed by an assistant secretary. There are similar provisions in the other rules.

The rules prescribe numerous procedural functions which are to be performed by the Secretary. These are noted in the appropriate context. In practice, subject to directions from the President, he is responsible for the internal administration of the staff and offices of the industrial tribunals in Scotland. Notices and other written communications to parties involved in tribunal proceedings are, with certain exceptions, issued under the name of the Secretary.

---

23 Dobie, *Sheriff Court Practice*, p. 186.

24 The Industrial Tribunals (Rules of Procedure) (Scotland) Regulations 1980, reg. 2. There are similar provisions in the other procedural regulations.

25 Which empowers the Secretary to intimate to an applicant that his application does not appear to entitle him to relief—see p. 91 below.

TRIBUNAL CLERKS

The clerk to a tribunal is the person appointed by the Secretary of the Tribunals or an assistant secretary to act in that capacity at one or more hearings.[26]

Certain specific functions are prescribed in the rules for tribunal clerks with regard to the recording of tribunal decisions and matters associated therewith.[27] Generally, the clerk's function at a hearing is to receive and deal with parties, their representatives and witnesses, usher in the tribunal and the witnesses when they come to give their evidence, and take charge of productions, listing and numbering them. When not occupied at a hearing, tribunal clerks perform administrative duties in connection with the processing of case papers and files, arrange hearings and record tribunal decisions. They also deal with enquiries from parties and their representatives, and other members of the public, and as such comprise the link for the purpose of communications between parties and the tribunal before and after the hearing. Any such communications should be noted in the case file. They answer, so far as they can, enquiries about tribunal procedure in general, but it is not part of their function to give advice about the merits of, or the procedure to be adopted in, individual cases.

TRIBUNAL OFFICES

The Central Office of the Industrial Tribunals (Scotland) is at St Andrew House, 141 West Nile Street, Glasgow, G1 2RU. This is the administrative headquarters of the industrial tribunals in Scotland. Area offices, staffed by tribunal clerks and other staff, are located in Edinburgh, Aberdeen and Dundee, where cases arising in those areas are heard. The staff at those offices deal with those parts of the administrative procedures relating to such cases which are not dealt with centrally in Glasgow.[28] There are also unstaffed offices in Dumfries and Inverness where cases arising in those areas are heard, the administration of such cases being dealt with in Glasgow and (as regards Inverness cases) partly in Aberdeen. But in the various procedural regulations the expression "the Office of the Tribunals" means the Central Office,[29] and there are no offices designated as regional offices, as in England and Wales.

---

26 The Industrial Tribunals (Rules of Procedure) (Scotland) Regulations 1980, reg. 2. There are similar provisions in the other regulations.

27 See Chap. 9 at p. 221.

28 See Chap. 5 at p. 102.

29 Regulation 2 of each of the regulations. But see p. 125 below as to delivery of documents directed to the Secretary.

The addresses of the area offices are:—

11 Melville Crescent,
Edinburgh.

252 Union Street,
Aberdeen.

13 Albert Square,
Dundee.

CHAPTER 4

JURISDICTION

GENERAL

In any proceedings the first question is whether the tribunal has jurisdiction to entertain them. Jurisdiction is a fundamental point, which must be taken by the tribunal itself, even if none of the parties has raised it.[1] Once a question of jurisdiction has become apparent, enquiry into the merits of the case will normally be precluded until it has been investigated and resolved, usually at a preliminary hearing, at which any evidence necessary for a decision on the point will be heard. But where the facts relevant to the question cannot be separated from those relevant to the merits of the case, the jurisdictional question will be reserved for decision after all the facts have been investigated.[2]

Industrial tribunals in Scotland may, generally speaking, entertain an application or appeal at the instance of any person, whether resident in Scotland or elsewhere, and irrespective of nationality, who is qualified to bring the proceedings under the statutory provisions governing the grounds on which the application or appeal is based, provided that he is not affected by any other personal disability of a wider nature; that the person against whom the proceedings are brought is the person against whom they should properly be directed and is amenable to the jurisdiction of industrial tribunals in Scotland; and that there is no impediment by statute or at common law to such proceedings being taken.

Apart from the limits on jurisdiction in the procedural regulations and the regulations relating to offshore employment, the jurisdiction of an industrial tribunal may be excluded or affected by limitations arising either by the operation of the general law or from the provisions of the particular legislation governing the proceedings, or by considerations which are special to the parties themselves. And the tribunal's jurisdiction cannot operate beyond the limits by which it has been defined by statute. Thus it has been held that a tribunal cannot award a redundancy payment based on a longer period of continuous employment than the Act would allow, on the strength of an agreement between employer and employee providing for employment under a previous employer to count, where it would not count under the

---

1 *British Midlands Airways Ltd.* v. *Lewis* [1978] I.C.R. 782 at p. 784.

2 See Chap. 7 at pp. 160 to 162.

statutory provisions relating to computation of continuous employment.[3]

While any obvious jurisdictional points will be raised by the Central Office of the Tribunals at the commencement of the proceedings, parties and their representatives should always give consideration to, and raise at the outset by way of preliminary point, any question of jurisdiction which may appear to apply. It is only possible here to comment in detail on those matters which are generally treated in practice as raising preliminary questions of jurisdiction. Many of the statutory rights have other exceptions to the general rule which, if they apply, will defeat an applicant's claim to the remedy he seeks, but which are not referred to here, because in practice they are regarded as going to the merits rather than to jurisdiction. Reference should always therefore be made to the actual statutory provisions governing the proceedings in question. It should also be kept in mind that under ss. 7 and 149(1) of the Employment Protection (Consolidation) Act 1978 the Secretary of State has power to reduce the weekly hours of employment necessary to qualify for rights, and to extend or limit the classes of persons or classes of employment to which certain of the provisions of the Act are to apply, as well as to vary or exclude the operation of a number of the provisions which exclude jurisdiction. Other Acts of Parliament also contain powers enabling their provisions to be varied or amended, which may have the effect of extending or limiting the jurisdiction of industrial tribunals, and particularly ss. 106 and 107 of the Employment Protection Act 1975, s. 80 of the Sex Discrimination Act 1975, and s. 73 of the Race Relations Act 1976.

LIMITS OF JURISDICTION UNDER PROCEDURAL REGULATIONS

The Industrial Tribunals (Rules of Procedure) (Scotland) Regulations 1980, which govern most industrial tribunal proceedings in Scotland, provide (reg. 3) that the Industrial Tribunals Rules of Procedure (Scotland) 1980 shall have effect in relation to all proceedings before a tribunal which fall under the regulations where:

(*a*) the respondent or one of the respondents resides or carries on business in Scotland;[4] or

(*b*) the proceedings relate to a contract of employment the place of execution or performance of which is in Scotland[4]; or

---

[3] *Secretary of State for Employment* v. *Globe Elastic Thread Co. Ltd.* [1979] I.C.R. 706; see also under "Personal Bar" at p. 39 below.

[4] While there is no jurisdiction under (*a*) if a respondent has ceased to reside or carry on business, such a respondent will in most cases be amenable to the jurisdiction of the tribunal by virtue of (*b*).

(*c*) the proceedings are to determine a question which has been referred to the tribunal by a sheriff in Scotland; or
(*d*) in proceedings under the Docks and Harbours Act 1966, they are in relation to a port in Scotland.

The Industrial Tribunals (Scotland) Regulations 1965 (as amended by the Industrial Tribunals (Scotland) Regulations 1967), which govern appeals against assessments to levy under the Industrial Training Act 1964, do not specify any territorial limits on the jurisdiction of Scottish industrial tribunals. Regulation 6 provides that the rules of procedure in Sched. 2 shall have effect in relation to appeals by persons assessed to levy under a levy order coming into operation on or after March 13, 1967. (As explained in Chapter 2 (at p. 17), appeals under levy orders which came into operation prior to that date are governed by the rules in Sched. 1 to the regulations).

An appeal against an improvement or prohibition notice under s. 24 of the Health and Safety at Work etc. Act 1974, is governed by the Industrial Tribunals (Improvement and Prohibition Notices Appeals) (Scotland) Regulations 1974, and an appeal against a non-discrimination notice under s. 68 of the Sex Discrimination Act 1975 or s. 59 of the Race Relations Act 1976 is governed by the Industrial Tribunals (Non-Discrimination Notices Appeals) (Scotland) Regulations 1977 if it relates to "a matter arising in Scotland" (reg. 3 in each of the regulations).

The equivalent regulations for England and Wales[5] are all in identical terms, *mutatis mutandis*.

Thus, provided the proceedings are otherwise properly directed against him, a respondent is not exempt from the jurisdiction of the industrial tribunals either in Scotland or in England and Wales merely by virtue of the fact that he is not resident in the country in which the proceedings are brought. But if the respondent neither resides nor carries on business in either of the two countries, there may be little or no practical value in bringing proceedings against him, because so long as that situation persists, it might be very difficult, if not impossible, to enforce any award which a tribunal might make against him.[6]

Circumstances may arise, however, where proceedings could properly be brought either in Scotland or in England and Wales, *e.g.* where the respondent resides in Scotland but also carries on business in England and Wales, or *vice versa*. In these circumstances, an applicant can pick the country in which he chooses to bring the proceedings, but to avoid the problem which arose in *Odeco (UK)* v. *Peacham* [1979] I.C.R. 823, r. 16(1) of the Industrial Tribunals Rules of Pro-

---

[5] See Chap. 2 at p. 17.

[6] As to service on respondents furth of Scotland, see Chap. 6 at p. 126. As to enforcement of a tribunal award, see Chap. 9, pp. 226 to 231.

cedure (Scotland) 1980 provides that where it appears to the President or the Regional Chairman that the proceedings could be determined in England and Wales, and that it would be more convenient to do so, he may, on the application of a party or of his own motion, and with the consent of the President of the Industrial Tribunals (England and Wales), direct that the proceedings be transferred to the Office of the Industrial Tribunals (England and Wales); but no such directions may be made unless notice has been sent to all parties concerned giving them an opportunity to show cause why such a direction should not be made. There are equivalent and reciprocal provisions in r. 16(1) of the Industrial Tribunals Rules of Procedure 1980. Any such question will be decided in the light of all relevant circumstances, but chiefly according to where the witnesses on each side are situated. There are no equivalent provisions in any of the other rules of procedure governing industrial tribunal proceedings.

OFFSHORE EMPLOYMENT

The Employment Protection (Offshore Employment) Order 1976 (S.I. 1976/766), (as amended by the Employment Protection (Offshore Employment) (Amendment) Orders 1977 (S.I. 1977/588), and 1981 (S.I. 1981/208), applies (by art. 2(1)) to employment for the purposes of—

(*a*) any activities (other than activities connected with a ship which is in the course of navigation or is a survey ship or is engaged in dredging[7] or fishing) in "the territorial waters"[8];

(*b*) any activities connected with the exploration of the seabed or subsoil or the exploitation of their natural resources in any "designated area"[9] (other than an area in which the law of Northern Ireland applies) being activities carried out on or from an offshore installation in any such designated area;[10]

(*c*) any activities in the foreign sector of the continental shelf (as defined in s. 137 of the Employment Protection (Consolidation) Act 1978) connected with the exploration or exploitation of the Frigg Gas Field (but only where the employer is within the classes specified in art. 3 of the amending Order of 1981).

Article 3 applies the provisions of the following Acts—

(*a*) The Industrial Training Act 1964;

(*b*) The Trade Union and Labour Relations Act 1974;

---

7 Which does not include the excavation of the seabed or its subsoil in the course of pipe-laying.

8 *I.e.* the territorial waters of the United Kingdom other than those adjacent to Northern Ireland (art. 1(2)).

9/10 *I.e.* any area designated by order under s. 1(7) of the Continental Shelf Act 1964.

(*c*) The Employment Protection Act 1975;
(*d*) The Employment Protection (Consolidation) Act 1978;
(*e*) The Wages Council Act 1979;
(*f*) The Employment Act 1980,

to the extent and for the purposes (and subject to the modifications) specified in the Schedule to the amending order of 1981 to or in relation to persons in employment to which the order applies.

In the Schedule to the amending order of 1981 the provisions of the foregoing Acts, except s. 29 of the Employment Protection (Consolidation) Act 1978, (which relates to time off for public duties) are, in effect, applied in their entirety so far as relevant to or in relation to persons in employment to which the principal order (as amended) applies, but the following modifications may be noted (the others being only of a minor nature).

(1) The expression "Great Britain" is expanded to include the areas specified in art. 2(1) of the principal order (referred to above) for the purposes of—

(*a*) s. 141 of the 1978 Act and s. 119(5) of the Employment Protection Act 1975 (which have the general effect of excluding employment outside Great Britain from most of the rights conferred by those Acts); and

(*b*) para. 14(1)(*a*) of Sched. 13 to the 1978 Act, (which has the effect of excluding certain employment outside Great Britain from qualifying service for entitlement to and computation of a redundancy payment),

the result being to stop these exclusions applying to relevant offshore employment.

(2) The application of s. 144(1)(*a*) of the 1978 Act, which excludes certain mariners from some of the provisions of the Act, is not restricted to employment on a British ship, so that the exclusion applies to any employment of the type specified in s. 144(1)(*a*) falling within art. 2(1) of the order, whether on a British ship or otherwise.

Articles 6(1) and 6(2) of the order provide that industrial tribunals in England and Wales and in Scotland shall respectively have jurisdiction in respect of matters arising in connection with employment to which the order applies from acts or omissions occurring in the English or Scottish areas as they would have if those acts or omissions had occurred respectively in England and Wales or in Scotland. The English and Scottish areas are defined in art. 1(4) as having the same meanings as in the Continental Shelf (Jurisdiction) Order 1968 (S.I. 1968/892), as amended. The amending instruments are specified in art. 1(4). The geographical limits of the areas are too complicated to be summarised conveniently here. This division of jurisdiction is probably now of little significance in proceedings governed by the 1980 rules of procedure, which enable cases to be transferred between the two countries. Article 6(3) of the order (as amended by the 1981 order) confers concurrent jurisdiction on tribunals in both countries in matters arising in connection with employment wholly or mainly for the purposes of activities connected with the Frigg Gas Field.

An offshore installation is any structure (whether fixed or otherwise) which is for use offshore for purposes connected with the exploration of the seabed or its subsoil or the exploitation of their natural resources, notwithstanding that it is not in operation or is undergoing construction, maintenance, repair, demolition, or any similar works (art. 1(3)(*a*) and (*b*)). A ship (whether registered in the United Kingdom or elsewhere) is a structure, but is not treated as an offshore installation while engaged in navigation or dredging for purposes other than those specified in art. 1(3)(*a*), or if it is a survey ship. The purposes in art. 1(3)(*a*) do not include fishing (art. 1(3)(*d*)). The order does not apply to any employment to which any provision of the legislation applied by art. 3 would apply regardless of the order (art. 2(1A)), or to employment wholly or mainly for the purpose of activities connected with the Ekofisk Field (art. 2(2)). Subject to the provisions of art. 3 of the amending order of 1981, it applies to individuals whether or not they are British subjects, and bodies corporate whether or not they are incorporated under the law of any part of the United Kingdom, notwithstanding that such application may affect their activities outside the United Kingdom (art. 4).

As to the position regarding Consular Conventions which may affect certain proceedings arising from offshore employment, see below at pp. 36 to 37.

Section 10(5) of the Sex Discrimination Act 1975 and s. 8(5) of the Race Relations Act 1976 enable employment concerned with exploration of the seabed or subsoil or the exploitation of their natural resources in any area for the time being designated under s. 1(7) of the Continental Shelf Act 1964 (except one in which the law of Northern Ireland applies) to be treated as employment in Great Britain for the purposes of Pt. II of those Acts, which deal with discrimination in the employment field. No order has as yet been made applying these provisions.

LIMITATIONS UNDER GENERAL LAW

(1) **Foreign and commonwealth states**

Section 1(1) of the State Immunity Act 1978, taken with s. 14(1), affirms the general immunity of foreign and commonwealth states from the jurisdiction of the courts of the United Kingdom, except where the Act provides otherwise. The definition of "court" in s. 22(1) includes any tribunal or body exercising judicial functions, and is therefore applicable to industrial tribunals. But a "separate entity" which is distinct from the executive organs of the government of the state, and is capable of suing or being sued (*e.g.* a state bank), is not counted as a department of a state, and is only immune if the proceedings relate to anything done by it in the exercise of sovereign authority, in a situation in which the state itself would be immune.[11]

The tribunal must give effect to any such immunity even though the state does not appear in the proceedings (s. 1(2)), a certificate by the Secretary of State being conclusive evidence on any question whether a country is a state (s. 21). But by s. 2 immunity is lost if the state has agreed in writing to submit to the jurisdiction, or itself initiates or intervenes in the proceedings (other than to claim immunity).

The exceptions from the general immunity thus conferred include, by s. 4(1) (taken with s. 23(3)), proceedings in relation to contracts of employment entered into before the Act came into force[12] and either made in the United Kingdom or where the work is to be wholly or partly performed there. But there are a number of exceptions to the general rule in s. 4(1), an important one being proceedings relating to the employment of members of diplomatic missions and consular posts (s. 16(1)(*a*)).[13]

The effect of this exception is that industrial tribunals potentially have jurisdiction only where the employment is with some other agency or organisation of the state, being either a "separate entity" (unless the case falls within the limited immunity noted above) or, if it is not, where the other exceptions in s. 4(2) to the application of s. 4(1) do not apply. One of these exceptions is that parties may contract out of s. 4(1) by agreement in writing: but by s. 4(4) this exception does not apply where United Kingdom law requires the proceedings to be brought before a court or tribunal of the United Kingdom, a provision which applies to much of the employment legislation, under which exclusive jurisdiction is conferred on industrial tribunals.[14] Apart from this exception, the question whether an industrial tribunal has jurisdiction by virtue of s. 4(1) depends next on whether the agency or organisation for which the work is performed is maintained for commercial purposes. If it is, the state concerned will only be immune if the individual was habitually resident in the state when the contract was made (s. 4(3)): if it is not, the state will be immune if—

---

11 Section 14(1) and (2). This distinction flows from problems discussed in *Trendtex Trading Corporation Ltd.* v. *Central Bank of Nigeria* [1977] Q.B. 529.

12 November 22, 1978 (State Immunity Act Commencement Order 1978 (S.I. 1978/1572)).

13 These expressions being used as defined in the Conventions scheduled to the Diplomatic Privileges Act 1964 and the Consular Relations Act 1968.

14 The Employment Protection (Consolidation) Act 1978, s. 129; the Employment Protection Act 1975, s. 108(1); the Employment Act 1980, s. 2(8).

(a) *at the time when the proceedings are brought* the individual is a national of the state concerned, or

(b) *at the time when the contract was made* the individual was neither a national of the United Kingdom nor habitually resident there.

Finally, while a state may not be immune, the proceedings may be affected by the other jurisdictional bars referred to in this chapter, particularly if the work was not to be performed wholly or mainly in Great Britain.[15]

A state which is subject to the jurisdiction of a tribunal is entitled to various procedural privileges in the course of the proceedings, which are noted in context elsewhere.[16]

(2) **Diplomatic and consular immunities**

The Diplomatic Privileges Act 1964 and the Consular Relations Act 1968 confer various immunities from civil proceedings in the United Kingdom on the officials and staffs of diplomatic missions and consular posts and on their families and servants. Where such an immunity is available, it applies in industrial tribunal proceedings (see *Omerri* v. *Uganda High Commission* (1973) 8 I.T.R. 14). The immunity may be waived in the manner provided, but until then any proceedings against the person enjoying immunity are void and cannot proceed.[17] In a question whether a person is entitled to immunity, a certificate by the Secretary of State stating a fact is conclusive evidence of that fact (1964 Act, s. 4; 1968 Act, s. 11). But the interpretation of that fact is for the court or tribunal.

The immunities are set out in the Conventions scheduled to the Acts, and vary according to the rank of the official concerned (higher rank conferring greater immunity) and whether the act which is in issue was performed in an official or a private capacity. As far as consular posts are concerned there are also differences according to whether the head of the post is a "career" officer or an honorary officer. And, generally speaking, members of the family of a diplomatic or consular officer are not immune if they are United Kingdom nationals or habitually resident in the United Kingdom.

As noted above, in proceedings relating to the employment of a member of a diplomatic mission or consular post the state which employs him would enjoy immunity by virtue of s. 16(1)(*a*) of the State Immunity Act 1978, unless it were waived. But the question whether such a person himself enjoys immunity from proceedings relating to the

[15] See below p. 71 to 74.

[16] See Chap. 5, p. 97; Chap. 6, p. 109; Chap. 9, p. 228.

[17] *Reg.* v. *Madan* [1961] 2 Q.B. 61.

employment of an individual by him in a private capacity would not be affected by s. 16(1) of the 1978 Act, and would depend on the provisions of whichever of the Acts of 1964 or 1968 was applicable.

Diplomatic and consular officials also enjoy certain privileges in relation to giving evidence and enforcement of judgment, and these are noted in context.[18]

(3) **Foreign vessels and aircraft**

Section 4 of the Consular Relations Act 1968 provides that by Order in Council the jurisdiction of any court in the United Kingdom to entertain proceedings relating to the remuneration or any contract of service of the master or commander or a member of the crew of any ship or aircraft belonging to a state specified in such order may be excluded or limited, except where a consular officer of that state has been notified of the intention to invoke the jurisdiction of the court and has not objected within a specified time.

In terms of these provisions Conventions have been concluded with the various countries listed below. They provide that jurisdiction in such cases is excluded unless the appropriate consular officer has been notified and has not objected within a period of two weeks; and that a statement to that effect must be included in the details of the claim when the proceedings are commenced.

The countries concerned are as follows:

List of Consular Conventions

State	*Text of Convention*	*Relevant Article*	*Statutory Instrument*
Austria	Cmnd. 2278	41(1)	1903 (1970)
Belgium	Cmnd. 2559	39(1)	1904 (1970)
Bulgaria[19]	Cmnd. 3920	52(1)	1918 (1970)
Czechoslovakia[19]	Cmnd. 6096	45(1)	768 (1976)
Denmark	Cmnd. 2033	27(1)	1905 (1970)
German Democratic Republic[19]	Cmnd. 6501	49	1152 (1976)
Germany, Federal Republic of	Cmnd. 607	32(1)	1907 (1970)
Greece	Cmnd. 525	28(1)	1908 (1970)
Hungary[19]	Cmnd. 4848	55(1)	1846 (1971)
Italy	Cmnd. 1135	29(1)	1909 (1970)
Japan	Cmnd. 2833	34(1)	1910 (1970)

[18] See Chap. 8, p. 180; Chap. 9, p. 228.

[19] Extends also to commanders or crew members of aircraft.

State	*Text of Convention*	*Relevant Article*	*Statutory Instrument*
Mexico	Cmnd. 633	29(1) and Second Agreed Minute	1911 (1970)
Norway	Cmnd. 590	27(1)	1912 (1970)
Poland[19]	Cmnd. 4790	63(1)	1919 (1970)
Romania[19]	Cmnd. 4663	25(10)	1920 (1970)
Soviet Union (Merchant Navigation Treaty)	Cmnd. 5008	16(1)	1916 (1970)
Spain	Cmnd. 2016	47(1)	1913 (1970)
Sweden	Cmnd. 9340	27(1)	1914 (1970)
Yugoslavia	Cmnd. 3147	41(1)	1917 (1970)

In the case of Mexico, the requirement does not apply if the proceedings are instituted by a British national.[20]

It would appear that these orders are not overridden by the provisions of s. 4 of the State Immunity Act 1978, referred to above, since they are the subject of separate bilateral treaties with the countries concerned, and in any event s. 16(1) of the 1978 Act provides that none of the immunities and privileges conferred by the Consular Relations Act 1968 are to be affected. The orders should therefore be taken to apply to proceedings before industrial tribunals. They are perhaps most likely to occur in the context of offshore employment. If therefore any application is received in respect of proceedings to which any of the foregoing orders apply, it would seem that it would have to be refused unless and until accompanied by a statement to the required effect from the appropriate consular officer.

(4) **Res judicata**

The plea of *res judicata* means that the question raised has been decided already in an action between the same party, or between parties in the same interest.[21] The plea will be sustained if there is identity of the parties, of subject-matter and of *media concludendi* (which, roughly translated, means grounds of action). The plea is available in civil litigation in Scotland and in England and Wales (where it is

---

[19] Extends also to commanders or crew members of aircraft.

[20] *I.e.* a citizen of the United Kingdom and Colonies or a British subject by virtue of ss. 2, 13 or 16 of the British Nationality Act 1948 or of the British Nationality Act 1965, or a British protected person within the meaning of the Act of 1948.

[21] Gloag and Henderson, *Introduction to the Law of Scotland*, 8th ed., p. 13.

termed "issue estoppel"), although its development and application in practice in the two countries may not be identical.[22]

The plea has been applied in industrial tribunal proceedings in relation to previous tribunal proceedings.[23] It was also sustained in substance, if not in form, in *Jowett* v. *Earl of Bradford* [1977] I.C.R. 342, where a second application had been entertained by an industrial tribunal but there had been a previous decision of a different tribunal on the same question, announced orally, which had not yet been perfected by being put in writing, owing to the illness of the Chairman. It was held that the second tribunal had no jurisdiction to hear the complaint, and that the first decision should be put in writing and should stand.

A plea of *res judicata* has also been sustained in the High Court in England in relation to previous industrial tribunal proceedings,[24] and if a similar situation were to arise in proceedings in the Court of Session or sheriff court in Scotland, it may be thought that a similar view would be taken.

In the civil courts in Scotland distinctions are drawn in practice between decrees in absence and decrees *in foro,* and between decrees of dismissal on grounds of irrelevancy or incompetency on the one hand and decrees of absolvitor on the other. It would be a question of circumstances as to whether it would be appropriate for an industrial tribunal to apply equivalent distinctions in considering a plea of *res judicata,* and in practice, considering the simpler concepts of tribunal procedures, it will probably be inappropriate to do so.

(5) **Personal bar**

It is a principle of Scottish law that the assertion of a right may conflict with ordinary concepts of justice, either owing to the method by which the right was acquired or the conduct of the party vested with it. The principle is known as personal bar, the equivalent English principle being called estoppel.

The principle was invoked in England by the Court of Appeal in *Evenden* v. *Guildford City Association Football Club Ltd.* [1975] I.C.R. 367 in deciding that where an employee had accepted employment on

---

22 For the tests applicable in Scotland, see *Grahame* v. *Secretary of State for Scotland,* 1951 S.L.T. 312 and *Weissenbruch* v. *Weissenbruch,* 1965 S.L.T. 139.

23 *Curtis* v. *James Paterson (Darlington) Ltd.* [1974] I.R.L.R. 88; *McLoughlin* v. *Gordons (Stockport) Ltd.* [1978] I.C.R. 561.

24 *Green and Anr.* v. *Hampshire County Council* [1979] I.C.R. 861. The plaintiffs' complaints of unfair dismissal were dismissed by an industrial tribunal in May 1973; a subsequent appeal to the National Industrial Relations Court was refused as being time-barred; in November 1977 they commenced proceedings in the Chancery Division seeking declarations that their dismissals were illegal, and that the procedure adopted by the defendants was contrary to the rules of natural justice. It was held that the decision of the industrial tribunal in 1973 was a judicial decision by a judicial tribunal giving rise to an issue estoppel, since it involved investigation, analysis and findings of fact, and an application of law to those findings.

the basis of an assurance by the employer that a period of employment with a previous employer would be counted as continuous, the employer was estopped from disputing the employee's claim to a redundancy payment based on both periods of employment. But in *Secretary of State for Employment* v. *Globe Elastic Thread Co. Ltd.* [1979] I.C.R. 706, the House of Lords held that *Evenden* had been wrongly decided, and that nothing in the nature of an estoppel between employer and employee could confer on an industrial tribunal a jurisdiction beyond that given by the Redundancy Payments Act so as to make a payment agreed between them, based on a longer period of service than the House had decided that the Act permitted, a redundancy payment under the Act for the purpose of calculating the rebate to be paid by the Secretary of State to the employer. The view was expressed that in so far as the agreement conferred on the employee the right to a larger redundancy payment than the Act allowed, his right to the excess over the statutory payment could only be enforced in the courts, and not before a tribunal unless and until the jurisdiction conferred by section 131 of the Employment Protection (Consolidation) Act 1978 came into effect.[25]

While, therefore, there can be no question of the doctrine of personal bar being invoked so as to enlarge a tribunal's jurisdiction beyond its statutory limits, there seems no reason in principle why, within those limits, the doctrine should not operate in tribunal proceedings, at least in one of its main applications, namely personal bar by representation (the English equivalent being, it is understood, promissory estoppel[26]), which has been defined as follows: "Where A has by his words or conduct justified B in believing that a certain state of facts exists, and B has acted on such belief to his prejudice, A is not permitted to affirm against B that a different set of facts existed at the same time."[27] That view was expressed by Lord McDonald in *Murphy* v. *A. Birrell & Sons Ltd.* [1978] I.R.L.R. 458. It will be noted first, that the definition refers to representations of fact and not of law, and secondly, that for the doctrine to operate, the person to whom the representation is made, and who pleads the operation of the doctrine, must have acted on the representation to his prejudice.[28]

(6) **Illegal contracts**

It is a general principle of Scottish and English law that rights and obligations which arise from a contract which is illegal cannot be en-

---

25 See Chap. 1, p. 7.

26 See *Secretary of State* v. *Globe Elastic Thread Co. Ltd.*, *supra*.

27 *Per* Lord Chancellor Birkenhead in *Gatty* v. *Maclaine*, 1921 S.C. (H.L.) 1.

28 For other conditions for the operation of the doctrine, see Gloag and Henderson, *op. cit.*, p. 39.

forced.[29] The principle has been applied in proceedings before industrial tribunals, so as to debar an employee remunerated, wholly or partly, in such a way as is intended to defraud the Inland Revenue from claiming a redundancy payment or complaining that he has been unfairly dismissed. The principle would seem to apply, however, to any other claim based on a contract of employment which is tainted in this way. A typical example is where an employee is given a bonus payment in cash out of the till without PAYE tax being deducted and paid by the employer.

As far as industrial tribunal proceedings are concerned, the first authority was *Tomlinson* v. *Dick Evans "U" Drive Ltd.* [1978] I.C.R. 639, in which Bristow J said (at page 642): "We take it to be clear law that someone who tries to assert in the courts an illegal contract will not succeed". The suggestion that the principle did not apply because the right which the employee was seeking to enforce (*i.e.* in that case, the right not to be unfairly dismissed) was conferred by statute, and could be enforced irrespective of the illegality of the contract from which it arose, because the effect of the employment legislation was said to be to give the employee a protected status, was firmly rejected, on the view that: "it is the employee's situation as party to a contract of employment which is the subject of protection by the legislation which it did not enjoy under the common law. Unless he was a party to a contract of employment,[30] the statute cannot and does not give him a right not to be unfairly dismissed, or the right to receive a redundancy payment". In *Tomlinson's* case the illegal part of the contract lay in the payment of a bonus. The industrial tribunal adopted the principle stated in *Napier* v. *National Business Agency Ltd.* [1951] 2 All E.R. 264 that where a part of a contract is illegal, the legal part cannot be severed from the illegal part and enforced, and the whole agreement is unenforceable. This view was not expressly approved by the appeal tribunal, but as the appeal failed, it is to be inferred that it was. The views expressed in *Napier's* case may appear to conflict, however, with the view expressed in certain other contexts that the mere fact that a contract contains an illegal provision does not necessarily involve the consequence that it is completely unenforceable.[31] But these views themselves contrast with the general rule that an agreement to defraud a third party is an unlawful contract on which no action can be based,[32]

---

29 Gloag and Henderson, *op. cit.*, Chap. IX, p. 88.

30 Meaning of course, a legal contract which can be enforced (author's note).

31 See Gloag on *Contract*, 2nd ed., p. 589, and Gloag and Henderson, *op. cit.*, pp. 89-90, where it is stated (citing opinion of Lord Dunedin in *Farmers Mart* v. *Milne*, 1914 S.C. (H.L.) 84), that the general test is whether the pursuer can maintain his case without founding on the illegal provision.

32 Gloag, *op. cit.*, p. 560, citing *Laughland* v. *Millar, Laughland & Co.* (1904) 6 F. 413. With specific reference to fraud on the Revenue, see also *Miller* v. *Karlinski* [1945] 62 T.L.R. 85, per Du Parcq LJ.

and it is thought that they would not be regarded as applying in the present context. Moreover the "severance" line of argument has subsequently been expressly rejected by the Employment Appeal Tribunal.[33]

A contract of employment may at some stage become tainted with illegality although previously it had been legal. In *Attridge* v. *Jaydees Newsagents Ltd.* (EAT 11.3.1980) it was held that a period during which a contract had been temporarily illegal could not count as a period of continuous employment for the purpose of the statutory provisions relating to the computation of continuous employment.

Problems have arisen over the relevance of the employee's knowledge of and participation in the illegal arrangement. The following statement in Chitty on *Contracts* (at para. 909) was approved in *Davidson* v. *Pillay* [1979] I.R.L.R. 275: "When the contract does not necessarily involve the commission of a legally objectionable act, and the legally objectionable intention or purpose of one party is unknown to the other, the latter is not precluded from enforcing the contract". But the comment was made that the passage indicates that if one party knows of the illegality, then he must not participate further but do all he reasonably can to avoid any further illegal performance of the contract. Accordingly it was held that the state of knowledge of the employee of the illegality of the arrangement was a matter which must be considered by the industrial tribunal. However in *Corby* v. *Morrison* [1980] I.R.L.R. 218 another division of the appeal tribunal took an apparently different view, relying on a later passage in Chitty (at para. 910): "Where a contract is to do a thing which cannot be performed without a violation of the law, it is void whether the parties knew the law or not", and on a passage on the judgment of Du Parcq LJ in *Miller* v. *Karlinski, supra:*" . . . it makes no difference whether or not the parties knew that what they were doing was illegal. Ignorance of the law cannot excuse them. The question is: ought the agreement to be enforced by the court?" The division of the appeal tribunal which decided *Attridge* v. *Jaydees Newsagents Ltd., supra,* on the other hand (which does not appear to have considered *Corby* v. *Morrison*), accepted the submission that for the contract to be tainted with illegality the employee must have known about it: *Davidson* v. *Pillay* and *Tomlinson* v. *Evans* (in which it was said that "the evil lies in the dishonesty in which the employee knowingly participated") were approved.

Thus the judicial view seems to be divided, and the difference remains to be resolved. The opinion of Sir Raymond Evershed MR in *Napier's* case may reconcile the apparent difference: "If those were the facts, what is the inference? It must surely be that by making an agreement in that form the parties to it were doing that which they must be

[33] In *Corby* v. *Morrison* [1980] I.R.L.R. 219, relying on *Miller* v. *Karlinski, supra.*

taken to know[34] would be liable to defeat the proper claims of the Inland Revenue . . .". This view seems consistent with reality, in that nowadays there can be few employees who are unaware of the obligation on their employer to deduct tax and national insurance contributions, and knowledge whether or not these obligations were being complied with must be relatively easy to infer if the employee has been provided, as the law requires, with an itemised pay statement.

This, however, illustrates another aspect of the matter, namely the question whether the contract of employment is unenforceable if the employee is not *in pari delicto* (*i.e.* is less blameworthy) with the employer in the commission of the illegality. This rule has a limited application in Scottish law, in situations where one of the parties was able to compel the other to concur in the illegal act, the reported cases being all concerned with collusive agreements in bankruptcy.[35] But stated in this general way, the rule could be relevant in an employment situation, if the employer has been in the stronger position to insist on an illegal method of performance, or by failure to provide an itemised pay statement has concealed the illegality in the performance of the contract from the employee (which of course raises again the question of the significance of the employee's knowledge of the illegality). The appeal tribunal were faced with the argument in *Attridge's* case, but did not find it necessary to decide the question, so it remains open.

It is for the court or tribunal to take notice of the illegality of a contract even if it has not been pleaded by the parties.[36] Moreover, as pointed out in *Corby* v. *Morrison, supra,* a tribunal could send the case papers to the appropriate office of the Inland Revenue.

It is not only contracts which are designed to evade tax which are illegal but also contracts for the commission of any crime or for immoral purposes, and those which are contrary to public policy, and a contract or a term of a contract may be illegal by virtue of statutory provisions.[37] The most pertinent examples of the latter type are the restrictions on contracting-out of the provisions of the employment legislation.[38] The extent to which other illegal contracts could be recognised, founded upon or enforced in industrial tribunal proceedings would depend on the nature of the illegality and the application of the ordinary principles of law on the subject.

---

34 (Author's italics).

35 Gloag and Henderson, *op. cit.* p. 89; Gloag, *op. cit.* p. 587.

36 *Per* Lord McLaren in *McDougall* v. *Bremner* (1907) 15 S.L.T. 193.

37 For illustrations see Gloag and Henderson, *op. cit.* pp. 91-92.

38 Employment Protection (Consolidation) Act, s. 140; Employment Protection Act 1975, s. 118; Employment Act 1980, ss. 4(11); Sex Discrimination Act 1975, s. 77; Race Relations Act 1976, s. 72. See also Chap. 6, p. 131.

LIMITATIONS UNDER EMPLOYMENT LEGISLATION

(1) **Time limits**

(a) *General*

In most cases time limits are prescribed for the initiation of industrial tribunal proceedings in the Act or regulations governing the proceedings. When a time-bar question arises it is always for the applicant or appellant to prove the facts required to bring himself within the tribunal's jurisdiction.

Time limits are reckoned by the calendar. So if the stated period begins on January 3 and is three months, it expires on April 2, not April 3. In most cases the legislation requires the application to be "presented" on or before a certain day. The meaning of this expression is discussed below in the context of unfair dismissal.

(b) *The Employment Protection (Consolidation) Act 1978*

(i) **General: Cases with no time limit.** The basic time limit is three months for most of the grounds of complaint, including unfair dismissal, apart from applications for interim relief pending determination of a complaint of unfair dismissal, where it is only seven days (see (iii) below), and redundancy payment cases, where it is six months. And in the following cases *no* time limit is prescribed:

> Section 11. While the employment subsists, a reference relating to written statements of terms of employment or an itemised pay statement may be made at any time. The time limit of three months referred to below only applies once the employment has terminated.
>
> Section 108. References and appeals relating to employer's payments in redundancy situations.
>
> Section 112. References regarding equivalent payments to civil servants, etc.
>
> Section 131. Claims for damages etc. for breach of contract of employment—but s. 131(5) enables provision to be made for time limits when s. 131 is brought into operation.
>
> Section 139(6). Applications regarding proceedings against the House of Commons Commission or Mr Speaker.

As regards cases under s. 130 (jurisdiction formerly exercisable by statutory referees), reference should be made to the relevant statutes, which are listed in Sched. 10.

Where the limit is three months, in every case but one (references under s. 11) the formula used states that a tribunal shall not entertain the complaint unless it is presented before the end of that period, beginning with the happening of a specified event, or within such period as the tribunal considers reasonable in a case where it is satisfied that it was not reasonably practicable for the complaint to be presented before the end of the period of three months, or some equivalent wording. The way in which this formula is to be broken down is discussed in the context of unfair dismissal complaints (see (ii) below), the law relating to which governs the other grounds of complaint to which the formula applies.

(ii) **Unfair dismissal complaints.** With two exceptions, the three months' period in the formula referred to under (i) above begins with the effective date of termination of the contract of employment (see s. 67(2)). The first exception (see s. 67(3)) is where s. 62(3) applies, *i.e.* where the employee was dismissed during a lock-out, strike or other industrial action and another employee also so dismissed has been offered re-engagement, but the complainant has not; in that case the commencing date is the first date on which any relevant employee was offered re-engagement. The second exception is where the employer has failed to permit the employee to return to work after pregnancy or confinement, in which case the period begins on the notified day of return (see Sched. 2, para. 2(3)).

The tribunal has to make an enquiry into the following matters.

(1) Apart from those cases where s. 67(3) applies, what was the effective date of termination or (as the case may be) the notified day of return?

The *effective date of termination* is defined in s. 55(4). Where the contract is determined by notice (whether given by the employer or the employee) it is the date on which the notice expires; where the contract is terminated without notice, it is the date on which the termination takes effect; and where the employee is on a fixed term contract which expires without being renewed, it is the date on which that term expires.[39] Once notice has been given, a complaint may be presented before the effective date of termination (see s. 67(4)), but a complaint presented before any act of dismissal has occurred is premature and cannot be entertained.

Section 67(2) is not one of the provisions affected by s. 55(5), by virtue of which the effective date of termination may be deemed to be on a later date than as defined by s. 55(4). Thus if an employer dismisses an employee summarily, or on short notice, even if the employer is in breach of contract in doing so, the effective date of termination is that on which the employee is told to leave, even if longer notice had previously been given.[40] (But a dismissal by letter does not take effect

---

39 As to what is a fixed term contract, see below, p. 71.

40 See *Dedman* v. *British Building and Engineering Appliances Ltd.* [1974] I.C.R. 53, *per* Lord Denning MR.

until the date on which the employee reads the letter, or has a reasonable opportunity of doing so.[41]) Thus if the termination of employment is immediate, a payment of wages in lieu of notice is regarded as compensation or damages for the breach of contract, and the employment does not continue,[42] even if the payment is not made until after the date on which the employee is told to leave.[43] But if the employer purports to dismiss on notice, while at the same time telling the employee not to work the notice, the effective date of termination is the date when the notice expires,[44] even if at the time when the notice is given the employee is given full payment in advance of the wages due to him.[45] If, however, the employee leaves against the wishes of the employer before the expiry of a notice which is still running, or before an agreed date for leaving, the effective date of termination will be the date on which he leaves.[46] And where an employee appeals against dismissal under a domestic appeals procedure, the employment does not continue until the appeal has been decided[47] (unless, of course, the contract so provides). Where the contract provided that an employee was to be treated as suspended without pay pending the determination of an appeal, but that, if reinstated, he would receive back pay for the period of suspension, and the employee's appeal was unsuccessful, the effective date of termination was held to be the original date on which his employment was summarily terminated (*J. Sainsbury Ltd.* v. *Savage* [1981] I.C.R. 1).

The meaning of *the notified day of return* is found in s. 47(1) (as amended by s. 11(3) of the Employment Act 1980) and s. 47(8) (see s. 153(1)). By s. 47(1) it is the date on which the employee proposes to return to work, of which at least 21 days prior notice must be given to the employer in writing. The employee must, of course, be entitled to return to work in terms of s. 33, as amended by s. 11 of the 1980 Act. But s. 47(8) provides that if the day of return is postponed or deferred to a later day in the circumstances provided for in subsections (2) (3)(*a*) and (5)(*q.v.*), that later day shall be treated as the notified day of return.

(2) Was the complaint presented before the expiry of the period of three months beginning with the effective date of termination (or whichever other date is relevant)?

---

41 *Brown* v. *Southall & Knight* [1980] I.C.R. 617.

42 *Dixon* v. *Stenor Ltd.* [1973] I.C.R. 157; *Brindle* v. *H. W. Smith (Cabinets) Ltd.* [1972] I.R.L.R. 125.

43 Ackerman, *Law of Unfair Dismissal*, p. 23 (approved in *Kevworth Ltd.* v. *Cameron* EAT 27/6/80).

44 *Lees* v. *A. Greaves (Lees) Ltd.* (1973) 8 I.T.R. 144.

45 *Adams* v. *GKN (Sankey) Ltd.* [1980] I.R.L.R. 416.

46 *Lees* v. *A. Greaves (Lees) Ltd., supra.*

47 *MacDonald* v. *South Cambridgeshire Rural D.C.* [1973] I.C.R. 611.

An application is presented on the day on which it is received at the appropriate office of the tribunals, not the day on which it is posted (see *Hammond* v. *Haigh, Castle and Co. Ltd.* (1973) 8 I.T.R. 199). By r. 17(2) of the Industrial Tribunals Rules of Procedure 1980 the appropriate office is the Central Office, unless the Secretary of the Tribunals has notified the parties that it should be some other office. But if the period expires on a day on which the Central Office is closed, an application received there on the next day on which it is open is treated as being in time (see *Anglo-Continental School of English (Bournemouth) Ltd.* v. *Gardner* (1973) 8 I.T.R. 251). And although a local office of the tribunals will accept an application and pass it on to the Central Office, unless the local office has been previously notified by the Secretary as the office to which the application should be presented (which will only be in exceptional circumstances), it is not treated as presented until the day it is received at the latter. (*Bengey* v. *North Devon District Council* (1976) I.T.R. 211 is not applicable to Scotland, where the local tribunal offices are not classified as regional offices).

(3) If the complaint was not presented before the expiry of the period of three months, was it reasonably practicable for this to have been done?

This is a subject on which there is a volume of case law, the proliferation of which was deprecated by Lord Denning MR in the leading case of *Walls Meat Co. Ltd.* v. *Khan* [1979] I.C.R. 52 (at p. 57). It was emphasised in that case that the question whether it is reasonably practicable for a complaint to be presented on time is essentially one of fact for the industrial tribunal. The Court of Appeal did, however, prescribe certain tests, making use of earlier authority on the subject, to which the court added in *Riley* v. *Tesco Stores Ltd.* [1980] I.C.R. 323.

(*aa*) The question has to be determined subjectively, by reference to the particular complainant, and all material circumstances affecting his position, "not in vacuo on some ideal or theoretical basis but in the world of practical affairs" (*per* Shaw LJ in *Walls Meat Co.* at p. 58).

(*bb*) Shortly put, as by Lord Denning in *Walls Meat Co.* (at p. 56), the question is: Was there just cause or excuse for not presenting the complaint in time?

(*cc*) Presentation of a complaint will not be reasonably practicable if there is some impediment which reasonably prevents, or interferes with, or inhibits such performance. The impediment may be physical (*e.g.* the illness or unavoidable absence abroad of the complainant) or mental, *i.e.* ignorance or mistaken belief on the complainant's part as to essential matters (*per* Shaw LJ and Brandon LJ in *Walls Meat Co.* at pp. 59 and

60). (The maxim "ignorance of the law is no excuse" is not rigorously applied in this area). Whether there is ignorance or mistaken belief, and how long it persisted, is a question of fact for the tribunal. But the ignorance or mistake must have been reasonable (*per* Lord Denning and Brandon LJ in *Walls Meat Co.* at pp. 56 and 60). It may be easier to infer ignorance of one of the lesser known rights than of the right to complain of unfair dismissal, which by now can almost be regarded as common knowledge (see the judgment of Stephenson LJ in *Riley* v. *Tesco Stores* at p. 328).

(*dd*) If the failure to present the claim in time results from fault or wrong advice on the part of an adviser, this will not of itself excuse the complainant, and he must take the consequences, unless the adviser could not reasonably have been expected to have been aware of the employee's rights (*per* Lord Denning MR in *Walls Meat Co.* at p. 56, following *Dedman* v. *British Building and Engineering Appliances Ltd., supra*). It makes no difference whether the adviser is a solicitor or some other less skilled person, such as a trade union official or one of the staff of a citizens' advice bureau.[48] But an adviser is not at fault if he fails to advise about a right concerning which he has not been consulted.

While the foregoing principles are clear enough, there are certain areas in which their application may cause difficulty. First, the situation where other forms of proceedings also arise from the same circumstances—*e.g.* a criminal investigation or charge following a dismissal for alleged theft, or the prosecution of a domestic appeal or an appeal to a national insurance tribunal. Each of these cases will be judged on its own circumstances, but unless the tribunal is satisfied that the complainant has laboured under a genuine belief or misunderstanding that the matter precluded him from presenting the complaint, or made it unnecessary to do so, and that the belief was reasonably held, this kind of matter will not generally excuse a complaint to an industrial tribunal not being presented in time, because in appropriate cases the hearing of the complaint will always be deferred to await the outcome of the other proceedings.[49] Complaints should never therefore be left to await the outcome of other proceedings.

Secondly, there is the question whether ignorance of how a complaint should be made, and of the time limit for presenting it, will excuse a complainant who is aware of his right to complain. This depends on whether the ignorance was reasonable (*per* Brandon LJ in *Walls Meat Co. Ltd., supra* at p. 61), which is a question of fact for the

48 *Riley* v. *Tesco Stores Ltd., supra.*

49 See Chap. 6, p. 121.

tribunal to decide in the light of all the relevant circumstances (but Shaw LJ in the same case said that it would not of itself make it not reasonably practicable to present the claim on time). The extent to which enquiries have been made is a relevant factor. Once an individual knows that he has the right to complain, he should waste no time in finding out how to pursue it.

The third problem relates to the complainant who is aware of his rights, and how and within what time to pursue them, but defers lodging his complaint until so late that it is received out of time. In the absence of the kind of genuine impediment referred to in *Walls Meat Co.* v. *Khan, supra,* strict logic might suggest that an applicant would have to show that it was not *reasonably* practicable to present the complaint during *any* part of the stated period in which he was aware of his rights. It would then be a question of fact whether delay which was attributable to tactical factors, or to such reasons as sheer inertia, was reasonable. This approach, however, was disapproved by Lord Denning MR in *Dedman's* case, *supra,* and in *Burton* v. *Field Sons & Co. Ltd.* [1977] I.C.R. 106 it was held that a dismissed employee is entitled, if he so wishes, to wait until towards the end of the three months' period, and that the question whether it was reasonably practicable for the complaint to be presented on time should be determined by reference to whether at the time the application was posted it was reasonable to expect that in normal course of post it would arrive in time. However, in a recent Scottish case (*Craig* v. *Associated Dairies Ltd.,* EAT 12/1980), the Employment Appeal Tribunal decided against an employee on the ground *inter alia* that for some time prior to the expiry of the three months' period it had been reasonably practicable for his complaint to have been presented, in that he had been warned by a trade union official to get his complaint in. On any showing, as emphasised in *Beanstalk Shelving Ltd.* v. *Horn* [1980] I.C.R. 273, with the risk of delays in the post it is dangerous to leave the posting of an application until the last moment, and wherever it is practicable to do so a complaint should be posted well before the expiry of the stated period.

(4) If it was not reasonably practicable for the complaint to be presented within the period of three months, was it presented within such further period as was reasonable?

The previous questions have to be considered strictly by reference to the dates concerned and the "reasonably practicable" test. If the applicant fails to surmount the hurdle they present, the tribunal cannot entertain the application, even if it is only presented one day late. But if the applicant passes the test, this fourth question arises, in relation to which the tribunal has a rather wider discretion, to be exercised by reference to what it considers reasonable in the circumstances of the particular case. If there was some impediment which made it not reasonably practicable for the application to be presented in time, the answer to the question will depend on when the impediment was removed, and whether the applicant acted with reasonable expedition thereafter.

(iii) **Applications for interim relief.** These must be presented before the end of the period of seven days immediately following the effective date of termination of the applicant's employment. The application may be presented before the effective date of termination has arrived. Before the end of the prescribed period a certificate in writing must also be presented, signed by an authorised official of the employee's trade union, or intended trade union, stating that the employee was, or proposed to become, a member of the union, and that there appear to be reasonable grounds for supposing that the reason for his dismissal was the one alleged in the complaint (s. 77(2)).

An application for revocation of an order under s. 77 may be made at any time between the making of the order and the determination of the complaint of unfair dismissal to which it relates (s. 79(1)).

(iv) **Other three months' time limits.** Except where otherwise stated, the formula is in wording of similar intent to that of s. 67(2) relating to unfair dismissal, and the same considerations apply, *mutatis mutandis*.

Section 11 (References relating to written statements of terms of employment and itemised pay statements). The period of three months begins with "the date on which the employment ceased", not the "effective date of termination" (s. 11(9)). As explained above, no time limit operates while the employment subsists. Note that in this case the tribunal has no power at all to entertain an application for a reference "made" (not "presented") after the end of the three months' period.

Section 17 (Guarantee payments). The period begins with any day to which the complaint relates (s. 17(2)). If therefore an application is presented on May 1, it is in time as respects the previous February 2 and any day thereafter, but no claim can be entertained relating to February 1 or any earlier date.

Section 22 (Suspension on medical grounds). The period is defined in the same way as in s. 17(2) (s. 22(2)).

Section 24 (Trade union membership and activities). The period begins with the date of the action complained of, or the last of such actions, where there is a series (s. 24(2)).

Sections 27, 28 and 29 (Time off for trade union duties and activities and public duties). The period begins on the date when the failure to give permission occurs (see s. 30(1)).

Section 31 (Time off to look for work). The period begins with the date on which time off should have been allowed (s. 31(7)).

Section 31A (Time off for ante-natal care). The period begins with the date of the appointment concerned (s. 31A(7)—see Employment Act 1980, s. 13).

Section 36 (Maternity pay). The period begins with the last day of the payment period or payment periods, as the case may be (s. 36(2)).

Section 43 (Complaints and appeals relating to maternity pay and rebates). The period begins with the date on which the decision of the Secretary of State was communicated to the complainant or appellant.

Section 53 (Written reasons for dismissal). The complaint must be presented at such a time that the tribunal would entertain a complaint of unfair dismissal in respect of the same dismissal, presented at the same time (s. 53(5)).

Section 124 (Payments by the Secretary of State on employer's insolvency). The period begins with the date on which the decision of the Secretary of State is communicated to the applicant.

(v) **Redundancy payments.** Unless, before the end of the period of six months beginning with "the relevant date" (as to which see below) or (in cases under s. 86, where failure to permit a woman to return to work after pregnancy or confinement is treated as dismissal) the notified day of return[50]—

(*a*) the payment has been agreed and paid, or

(*b*) the employee has made a claim for the payment by notice in writing given to the employer,[51] or

(*c*) a question as to the right of the employee to the payment, or as to the amount of the payment, has been referred to an industrial tribunal, or

(*d*) a complaint of unfair dismissal has been presented by the employee,

the employee is not entitled to a redundancy payment (s. 101(1)). But the employee does not lose his right to a redundancy payment if, during the period of six months immediately following, he takes any of the steps specified in (*b*), (*c*), or (*d*) above, and it appears to the tribunal to be just and equitable that he should receive a redundancy payment, having regard to the reason which he shows for his failure to take such steps within the first period of six months, and to all the other relevant circumstances (s. 101(2)).

Thus after the first six months the absolute right to the payment (assuming the employee is qualified in the first place) is lost, and it is within the tribunal's discretion whether the employee should receive a redundancy payment. But if the requisite action is not taken within the period of twelve months commencing on the relevant date, the right to the payment is then lost absolutely. Note, however, that the time bar

50 Sched. 2, para. 4(1)(*a*). As to the notified day of return, see above, p. 45.

51 As to what constitutes such notice see *Hetherington* v. *Dependable Products Ltd.* (1971) 6 I.T.R. 1; *Price* v. *Smithfield & Zwanenberg Group Ltd.* [1978] I.C.R. 93.

refers only to entitlement to a redundancy payment: in *Bentley Engineering Co. Ltd.* v. *Crown* [1976] I.R.L.R. 146 an employee who claimed, after the expiry of the six months' period, a larger redundancy payment than he had been given was held to be entitled to do so, because he had made his original claim to the payment within the prescribed period. If, however, the employee dies within either of the periods of six months referred to in s. 101, the period in question is extended to one year (Sched. 12, Pt. IV, para. 27).

"The relevant date" is defined in s. 90. Section 90(1) relates to the dismissal of an employee. Paragraphs (*a*), (*b*) and (*c*) are in effect identical with the definition of "the effective date of termination" in s. 55(4), which applies to the unfair dismissal provisions of the Act (*q.v.* above, pp. 44 to 45). Paragraph (*d*) deals with the case where a contract of employment has been renewed and under the provisions of s. 84(6) the employee is treated as having been dismissed on the termination of his employment under the previous contract: for the purposes of the time limits in s. 101 the relevant date is as defined by para. (*a*), (*b*) or (*c*) above in relation to the renewed, or new, contract or (where there has been more than one trial period under s. 84), the last such contract, and not the date of termination of the previous contract. Paragraph (*e*) deals with the case where the employee gives notice within a period of notice given by his employer, but is taken to be dismissed by virtue of s. 85(2): here the relevant date is that on which the employee's notice of termination expires. Section 90(2) relates both to a notice of intention to claim a redundancy payment following a period of lay-off or short-time (the giving of which is an essential prerequisite to a redundancy payment under para. (*b*) of s. 81(1)), and also to entitlement to a redundancy payment on that ground. Where the case falls within s. 88(1)(*a*)(*q.v.*), it is the date on which the last of the four or more consecutive weeks before the service of the notice of intention to claim came to an end; where the case falls within s. 88(1)(*b*), it means the date on which the last of the series of six or more weeks before the service of the notice of intention to claim came to an end. Note that for the purposes of s. 101, the relevant date as defined by s. 90(1) and (2) is not affected by the provisions of s. 90(3), by virtue of which a later date may be treated as the relevant date for certain other purposes. Note also, however, that Pt. IV of Sched. 12 contains various provisions which may affect the calculation of the relevant date for the purposes of s. 101 where the employee dies: if he dies during a period of notice given by the employer, the effect of para. 22(1) on s. 90(1)(*a*) is that the relevant date is the date of the employee's death; while para. 24 has a similar effect for the purposes of s. 84(6) and para. (*d*) of s. 90(1) in a case where an employee dies during a period of notice given by him in a trial period. (But there is no equivalent modification to para. (*e*) of s. 90(1)).

(c) *The Employment Protection Act 1975*

The time limit for complaints under ss. 101, 103 and 104 is three months beginning with the date on which the dismissal takes effect (s. 101(6)) or, as the case may be, the day or the last of the days in respect of which failure to pay remuneration under a protective award is alleged (s. 103(2)), or the date on which the decision of the Secretary of State reducing the amount of redundancy rebate is communicated to the employer (s. 104(3)).

In each case the formula used is similar in intent to that of s. 67(2) of the Employment Protection (Consolidation) Act 1978 (see above pp. 43 to 49), so that the tribunal has a discretion to admit a claim presented after the limit has expired if satisfied that it was not reasonably practicable for the complaint to have been presented before the limit expired.

(d) *The Employment Act 1980*

(i) For complaints under s. 2(4) and s. 4(4), the time limits are three months (beginning with the date of the employer's failure to permit his premises to be used for a ballot) and six months (beginning with the date of the refusal of the employee's application to join the trade union concerned, or his expulsion from it, as the case may be), respectively (ss. 2(5) and 4(6)).

Again the formula used is similar in intent to that for unfair dismissal complaints (see above, pp. 43 to 49), and the tribunal has a discretion to admit a claim presented late if satisfied that it was not reasonably practicable for it to be presented in time.

(ii) Applications for compensation following a successful complaint under s. 4(4) cannot be made before the end of the period of four weeks beginning with the date of the tribunal's declaration under s. 4, or after the end of the period of six months beginning with that date (s. 5(3)). The tribunal has no power to extend these limits.

(e) *The Industrial Training Act 1964*

The various levy orders made under s. 12 of the Act prescribe the time within which appeals may be taken, which is generally one month.

For further information, see Chapter 5, p. 92.

(f) *The Docks and Harbours Act 1966*

No time limit is specified for a referral to a tribunal.

(g) *The Equal Pay Act 1970*

No claim in respect of an equality clause may be referred to an industrial tribunal (except by a court under s. 2(3)) if the employee has not been in the employment of the employer within the six months preceding the date of the reference (s. 2(4)). Even if the proceedings are not barred by s. 2(4), their usefulness may also be limited in practice by the provisions in s. 2(5) that a woman shall not be entitled to be awarded any arrears of remuneration or damages in respect of a time earlier than two years before the date on which the proceedings were instituted.

(h) *The Health and Safety at Work etc. Act 1974*

(i) An appeal against an improvement notice or a prohibition notice under s. 24(2) must be initiated within 21 days from the date of service of the notice (the Industrial Tribunals (Improvement and Prohibition Notices Appeals) (Scotland) Regulations 1974, r. 2(1)). For further information, see Chapter 5, p. 92.

(ii) Complaints under reg. 11 of the Safety Representatives and Safety Committee Regulations 1977 must be presented within three months of the date when the employer's failure to permit the safety representative to take time off (or to pay him for doing so, as the case may be) occurred (reg. 11(2)). As with complaints of unfair dismissal (see above, pp. 43 to 49), the tribunal has a discretion to admit a complaint presented late, if satisfied that it was not reasonably practicable to have presented it in time.

(i) *The Social Security Pensions Act 1975*

No time limits as such are specified for referrals to a tribunal under regs. 4(2) and (3) and 10(4) of the Occupational Pension Schemes (Certification of Employment) Regulations 1975. But time limits prescribed in the regulations for other matters impose practical limits on the time within which proceedings may usefully be commenced.

(j) *The Sex Discrimination Act 1975 and the Race Relations Act 1976*

(i) Complaints of unlawful discrimination under s. 63 of the Sex Discrimination Act 1975 and s. 54 of the Race Relations Act 1976 must be presented before the end of the period of three months beginning when the act complained of was done, subject to the discretion conferred on the tribunal referred to below (1975 Act, s. 76(1); 1976 Act, s. 68(1)).

An application by the Equal Opportunities Commission under s. 72(2)(*a*) of the 1975 Act for a decision whether an alleged contravention of ss. 38 to 40 occurred, or by the Commission for Racial Equality under s. 63(2)(*a*) of the 1976 Act for a decision whether an alleged contravention of ss. 29 to 31 of that Act occurred, must in each case be made before the end of the period of six months beginning with the act to which it relates was done (1975 Act, s. 76(3);[52] 1976 Act, s. 68(4)). A similar time limit is imposed for complaints by either of the Commissions under s. 73(1) of the 1975 Act and s. 64(1) of the 1976 Act (complaints of unlawful acts of discrimination within the jurisdiction of an industrial tribunal with a view to further proceedings). The period begins when the act complained of was done (1975 Act, s. 76(4); 1976 Act, s. 68(5)).

In relation to each of the above cases, however, it is provided that the tribunal may consider any such complaint, claim or application which is out of time if, in all the circumstances of the case, it considers it just and equitable to do so (1975 Act, s. 76(5); 1976 Act, s. 68(6)). The discretion thereby conferred is framed in wider terms than that conferred by the "reasonably practicable" formula discussed under the heading of unfair dismissal (see above, pp. 43 to 49), and gives the tribunal virtually a complete discretion (which must of course be exercised in a judicial manner) whether or not to admit a late application.

(ii) Appeals against non-discrimination notices under s. 68 of the 1975 Act and s. 59 of the 1976 Act must be taken not later than six weeks after the notice is served. The Acts do not confer any power to enable a late appeal to be entertained. For further information, see Chapter 5, p. 93.

(2) **No employment involved**

As will be inferred from the way in which the various grounds of jurisdiction are stated in Chapter 1 (*q.v.*), it is fundamental to nearly all of them (either expressly or by implication) that they arise from an employment situation, actual or potential, present or past. In most cases the matter arises directly, in the sense that the statutory provisions confer the right to complaint or to refer to a tribunal on an employee or an employer, or less directly because they are framed with reference to employment. But even where the right to complain is conferred on someone else (*e.g.* the trustees of an occupational pension scheme under s. 124(2) of the Employment Protection (Consolidation) Act 1978, or a trade union under s. 101 of the Employment Protection Act 1975), the plea may still be available that a tribunal does not have jurisdiction because the claim does not have its origins in an employment situation.

In most of the relevant Acts employment and the related expressions "employee", "employer" and "employed" are *generally* defined as meaning work under a contract of employment, which in turn is defined as a contract of service or apprenticeship, which (as specifically stated in certain of the definitions) may be oral or written, express or implied.[53]

52 As amended by the Race Relations Act 1976, Sched. 4, para. 8(*b*).

53 The Employment Protection (Consolidation) Act 1978, s. 153(1); Employment Protection Act 1975, s. 126(1), and Employment Act 1980, s. 2(9), both adopting the meaning in the Trade Union and Labour Relations Act 1974 (s. 30(1)).

But in the Equal Pay Act 1970 (s. 1(6)), the Sex Discrimination Act 1975 (s. 82(1)), and the Race Relations Act 1976 (s. 78(1)), the expression is given the additional meaning "a contract personally to execute any work or labour".

In the vast majority of cases there will be no difficulty in determining whether the status or relationship in question is that of employer and employee (or, in older legal language, master and servant) stemming from a contract of service or apprenticeship, or is some different relationship, either consisting of partnership, or the holding of an office, or depending on a contract for services, the latter of which is the basis of the relationship between a self-employed person, or an independent contractor, and the person or persons for whom he works.[54] But there are cases in which the distinction is not apparent, or is blurred, and these can give rise to difficulty. The position of the "salaried partner" has not, so far as is known, been tested. The boundaries of the category of officeholder cannot be regarded as settled.[55] It includes persons in police service (see below, p. 57). Ministers of religion are accepted as generally falling within the category. A director of a company is, as such, the holder of an office. But he may also be employed by the company under a contract of service.[56] And the view has been expressed that teachers in Scotland are officeholders (in *Malloch* v. *Aberdeen Corporation,* 1971 S.L.T. 245). But it seems now to be generally accepted that they work under a contract of employment, since so far as is known the point has never been taken that they are excluded from the statutory rights conferred upon employees (see also s. 80 of the Employment Protection (Consolidation) Act 1978).

Various tests have been propounded for establishing whether a contract of service exists, but there is no single comprehensive one. What is clear is that "the question whether the relation between the parties is that of master and servant or otherwise is a conclusion of law, dependent on the rights conferred and the duties imposed by the contract" (*per* McKenna J in *Ready Mixed Concrete (South East) Ltd.* v. *Minister of Pensions and National Insurance* [1968] 2 Q.B. 497). It is therefore necessary to consider each case by reference to its own facts (including the terms, express or implied, of any agreement between the parties, and their conduct one to another) so as to decide from an objective consideration of the whole circumstances to what conclusion

---

[54] For a detailed exposition of this topic, see Grunfeld, *The Law of Redundancy,* 2nd ed. Chap. 3, pp. 69 to 87.

[55] See *Encyclopaedia of Labour Relations Law,* Vol. 1, 1-53; Rideout, *Principles of Labour Law, pp. 13-14.*

[56] See *Ferguson* v. *Telford, Grier, Mackay Ltd.* (1967) 2 I.T.R. 387 and other cases cited in Grunfeld, *op. cit.* pp. 80-82.

they point, balancing those pointing one way against those pointing the other.[57]

In *Ready Mixed Concrete Ltd., supra* McKenna J put forward a multiple test which has been constantly quoted with approval and followed. He stated that a contract of service exists if three conditions are fulfilled: an agreement, in consideration of a wage or other remuneration, to provide work and skill in the performance of some service for another; an agreement, express or implied, to be subject in the performance of that service to the other's control in a sufficient degree to make that other master; and that the other provisions of the contract are consistent with its being a contract of service. In Scotland, where there is no rule against a gratuitous obligation to work as an employee,[58] the first of these conditions may not be essential, providing the contract is onerous. Where a consideration is paid or given for the service performed, which does not take the form of a salary or wage in the conventional sense, questions may arise as to whether it is consistent with a contract of service or a more independent relationship. Remuneration by commission only, while indicative of independence (*per* McKenna J in *Ready Mixed Concrete Ltd., supra*) is not necessarily inconsistent with a contract of service (*Tyne & Clyde Warehouses Ltd.* v. *Hamerton, supra*). As to the second element, namely control, as McKenna J made clear, it is a matter of degree, involving a number of different considerations. Even where there is a substantial degree of control, other factors may combine to defeat this particular factor from being conclusive (see *Hitchcock* v. *Post Office* [1980] I.C.R. 100). The third condition is a negative one, in that if the other provisions of the contract are inconsistent with a contract of service, the test is not satisfied, notwithstanding the existence of the elements necessary to the first two conditions. But to some extent it begs its own question, inasmuch that, as pointed out in *Construction Industry Training Board* v. *Labour Force Ltd., supra,* there is no "magic formula" for determining, in a given case, which factors should be treated as conclusive of a contract of service. For instance, assessment to income tax under Schedule D, and payment of national insurance contributions on a self-employed basis are not inconsistent with such a contract (*Global Plant Ltd.* v. *Secretary of State for Health and Social Security* [1971] 3 All E.R. 385; *Tyne & Clyde Warehouses Ltd.* v. *Hamerton, supra*). Nor is the fact that both parties to the relationship have described it as being self-employed.[59] But although the true nature

---

57 *Davis* v. *New England College of Arundel* [1977] I.C.R. 6 at p. 10; *Tyne & Clyde Warehouses Ltd.* v. *Hamerton* (1978) I.C.R. 661 at p. 664; *Construction Industry Training Board* v. *Labour Force Ltd.* [1970] 3 All E.R. 220 at p. 226.

58 Gloag & Henderson, *Introduction to the Law of Scotland,* 8th ed. p. 261.

59 *Ready Mixed Concrete Ltd., supra; Davis* v. *New England College of Arundel, supra; Tyne & Clyde Warehouses, supra.*

of a relationship cannot be altered by putting a different label on it, when a situation is in doubt or ambiguous, an agreement between the parties as to how it is to be described can be conclusive in determining the nature of the relationship (*Massey* v. *Crown Life Insurance Co.* [1978] I.C.R. 590). More recently, in *Young & Woods Ltd.* v. *West* [1980] I.R.L.R. 201, the Court of Appeal held that the true legal relationship between the parties was that of employer and employee in spite of explicit agreement and actings consistent with self-employment. They pointed out that to hold parties to such an agreement would, in effect, be to permit them to contract out of the legislation.

Another test has also been used, which is useful in deciding whether the third element of the *Ready Mixed Concrete* test is satisfied. It originated with the judgment of Denning LJ (as he then was) in *Stevenson, Jordan & Harrison Ltd.* v. *McDonald* [1952] 1 T.L.R. (at p. 111): " . . . under a contract of service a man is employed as part of the business, and his work is done as an integral part of the business; whereas under a contract for services, his work, although done for the business . . . is only accessory to it." A similar test was propounded in *Market Investigations Ltd.* v. *Ministry of Social Security* [1969] 2 Q.B. 173 (at p. 184): " 'Is the person who has engaged himself to perform these services performing them as a person in business on his own account?' If the answer to that question is 'Yes' then the contract is a contract for services. If the answer is 'No' then the contract is a contract of service."

Persons in Crown service and some other forms of public service (including members of the staff of the House of Commons) are in a rather anomalous position. They are generally referred to in the legislation as being in employment, but the authorities are not unanimous as to whether or not they work under a contract of service, because their appointments are terminable at pleasure without notice.[60] Special provisions are therefore made in respect of such persons in employment legislation, and in respect of persons in police service, who are in a special position, and fall to be regarded as officeholders,[61] specifically including or excluding them within or from the rights conferred, as noted below (see pp. 76 to 77).[62]

However, redundancy payment rights may (with certain exceptions)

---

[60] See Gloag and Henderson, *op. cit.*, p. 278; *Encyclopaedia of Labour Relations Law*, Vol. 1, 1-049 to 1-052; Rideout, *op. cit.*, p. 14.

[61] *Attorney General for New South Wales* v. *Perpetual Trustee Co. Ltd.* [1955] A.C. 457, *per* Viscount Simonds at p. 489; *Wiltshire Police Authority* v. *Wynn* [1980] I.C.R. 649; *per* Lord Denning MR at p. 657. In the latter case it was held that a police cadet was not in police service, but was neither an apprentice nor a servant, and was therefore not an employee within the definition in s. 153(1) of the Employment Protection (Consolidation) Act 1978.

[62] See also the Redundancy Payments (Scotland) Regulations 1966 (S.I. 1966/1436), which apply to chief constables, constables of the British Airports Authority constabulary, and medical inspectors of aliens and immigrants.

be extended to persons in employment not under a contract of service or apprenticeship (1978 Act, s. 115).

It should be noted, however, that the definitions of "employed" in the Equal Pay Act 1970 (s. 1(6)) and of "employment" in the Sex Discrimination Act 1975 (s. 82(1)) and the Race Relations Act 1976 (s. 78(1)), which extend to cover "a contract personally to execute any work or labour", would appear to embrace most of those other categories of contractual relationship excluded under the narrower definition discussed above.

(3) **No dismissal**

In the Employment Protection (Consolidation) Act 1978, dismissal (or being treated as dismissed) is essential to the right to receive a written statement of reasons for dismissal under s. 53, to complain of unfair dismissal, to apply for interim relief under s. 77, and to qualify for a redundancy payment. Dismissal (or being treated as such) is separately defined in s. 53(1) for the purposes of that section, in s. 55(2) and s. 56 for purposes of unfair dismissal, and in ss. 83 to 86 and 93 for redundancy payment purposes. Where dismissal is in issue, however, the facts relevant to that issue usually also relate to the merits of the case. Accordingly in such cases the usual practice of industrial tribunals in Scotland is not to deal with such questions by way of preliminary hearing, but as part of the merits of the case.

(4) **Age limits**

(a) *Unfair dismissal*

The right not to be unfairly dismissed does not apply to an employee who on or before the effective date of termination (as to which see pp. 44 to 45) attained the age which, in the undertaking in which he was employed, was the normal retiring age for an employee holding the position which he held, or, if a man, attained the age of 65, or, if a woman, attained the age of 60 (Employment Protection (Consolidation) Act 1978, s. 64(1)(*b*)). But by s. 64(3) this exclusion does not apply if the reason for dismissal was an inadmissible reason within the meaning of s. 58(5), *i.e.* one relating to trade union membership or activities.

In the important case of *Nothman* v. *Barnet London Borough Council* [1979] I.C.R. 111 the House of Lords held that the provisions of what is now s. 64(1)(*b*) do not erect several barriers to be surmounted in turn, but one barrier for an employee whose terms of employment specify a normal retiring age, and a different barrier for an employee whose terms of employment do not specify a retiring age. Thus, as in that case, a woman whose terms of employment specify a normal retiring age of 65, and who is dismissed at an age between 60 and 65, is entitled to complain that her dismissal was unfair, and is not barred by the age limit of 60 which would apply if no retiring age is specified. The corollary to this rule would seem to be that if a normal retiring age earlier than 65 for a man, or 60 for a woman, were specified, the employee would be barred from the right to complain if dismissed after he or she has passed the retiring age, but before attaining 65 or 60, as the case may be.

In *Nothman's* case the Court of Appeal held ([1978] I.C.R. 336, *per* Lawton LJ at p. 346) that "normal retiring age" is the age at which an employee must or should retire, unless his service is extended by mutual agreement. Where there is a question whether the normal retiring age has been changed, the question depends on whether the contractual position between the parties has been changed by a clear understanding on the part of both parties.[63] It is not necessary to find or imply a normal retiring age where none exists: this was decided in the case of an employee whose employment with a firm in which there was no normal retiring age began after he had attained 65.[64] In the same case it was also held that the word "attained" in s. 64(1)(*b*) does not mean that age 65 (or 60, as the case may be) must be reached in the course of the particular employment from which the employee is dismissed. If the barrier applies, it comes into play once the specified age is attained.

(b) *Redundancy payments*

An employee is not entitled to a redundancy payment if "immediately before" (but not "on") the relevant date, the employee has attained the age of 65 if a man, or 60, if a woman (s. 82(1)). There is also a lower age limit, since s. 81(4) provides that any week which began before the employee attained the age of 18 is to be excluded in calculating the minimum period of two years' continuous employment required to qualify for a redundancy payment. This in effect excludes any employee dismissed in any week up to and including that in which he attains the age of 20.

"The relevant date" is discussed above (see p. 51). Note, however, that in a case where s. 84(6) applies, the provisions of s. 90(1)(*d*) are slightly different from those which apply for time limit purposes: by subpara. (ii) the relevant date is determined by reference to the previous contract, or, where there has been more than one trial period, the original contract, and not by reference to the new, or the latest of the new, contracts. In a case to which s. 81(4) applies (*i.e.* the lower age limit), note also that s. 90(3) applies, so that if the employee was dismissed without notice or on short notice, the date which is to be treated as the relevant date is that on which the correct statutory notice

---

63 *B.P. Chemicals Ltd.* v. *Joseph* [1980] I.R.L.R. 55.

64 *Dixon* v. *London Production Tools Ltd. & Anr.* [1980] I.R.L.R. 385.

in terms of s. 49(1) would expire if given on the date of termination, or on the date on which notice was given, as the case may be.

(5) **Qualifying service: continuous employment**

(*a*) *General*

For most of the statutory rights under the Employment Protection (Consolidation) Act 1978 a minimum period of employment is an essential qualification, and in most cases the employment has to be "continuous" (within the meaning of the Act) for the required period. As to what constitutes continuous employment, see (f) below. Certain of the rights which do not require a minimum period of service to qualify do not nevertheless apply to employment for less than 16 hours weekly (see (e) below).

(*b*) *Unfair dismissal*

The period is generally 52 weeks' continuous employment ending with the effective date of termination (s. 64(1)(*a*))[65] or, in maternity cases to which s. 56 applies (*i.e.* complaints of failure to permit an employee to return to work after pregnancy or confinement), the notified day of return (Sched. 2, para. 2(3)).[66] But there are the following exceptions:

(i) The period is reduced to four weeks if the employee is dismissed on medical grounds by reason of any requirement or recommendation as mentioned in s. 19(1) (*q.v.*) (see s. 64(2)).

(ii) Section 64(1) does not apply if the reason, or principal reason, for the dismissal was an inadmissible reason in terms of s. 58(5), *i.e.* one relating to trade union membership. In such cases (and, by the same token, in application for interim relief under s. 77), there is no minimum period of service (see s. 64(3)).

(iii) Section 64(1) does not apply to maternity cases to which s. 56 applies (*i.e.* failure to permit the woman to return to work after confinement), and s. 64 as a whole does not apply to an employee who is dismissed while absent from work on account of pregnancy or confinement.[67] But of course the right to return

---

65 As varied by the Employment Protection (Variation of Qualifying Period) Order 1979 (S.I. 1979/959). The previous period was 26 weeks, and an employee employed for more than that period but dismissed after less than 52 weeks is "caught" by the increase in the order. (*Capon* v. *Rees Motors* [1980] I.R.L.R. 294).

66 As to effective date of termination and notified day of return, see above, pp. 44 to 45. Note that if the contract of employment is terminated by the employer s. 55(5) applies, by virtue of which, if the requisite statutory notice is not given, the effective date of termination is deemed to be the date on which it would have expired if given on the date of termination or (as the case may be), the date on which notice was given. See also Sched. 13, para. 11(1).

67 Sched. 2, paras. 2(4) and 6(3).

to work depends on two years' continuous service—see s. 33(3) and (4)—but see s. 56A and 1980 Act, s. 12.

(iv) By s. 64A(1) (added by the Employment Act 1980, s. 8(1)), the minimum qualifying period of continuous employment is two years if at no time during that period did the number of employees employed by the employer *for the time being*[68] of the dismissed employee, added to the number employed by any associated employer[69], exceed 20. These provisions do not apply, however, if the reason for dismissal falls within (i) or (ii) above (s. 64A(2)). Nor do they apply where the period of employment began before October 1, 1980.[70] Thus s. 64A(1) will not be of practical significance until October 1981 (because dismissal from any employment beginning on or after October 1, 1980 occurring within 52 weeks will already be caught by s. 64(1)). Note that there is no requirement as to how long any of the other employees has been employed. It therefore seems that provided the employee has survived the basic qualifying period of 52 weeks, the position then has in effect to be considered retrospectively on a daily basis throughout the relevant period of up to two years, and that one day in that period in which the specified number of employees was exceeded will be sufficient to "knock out" this exclusion.

(c) *Redundancy payments*

The requisite period in s. 81(4) is two years (*i.e.* 104 weeks'—see Sched. 13, para. 1(1)—continuous employment, which must be with the dismissing employer, except where the Act provides for service with a previous employer to be treated as continuous[71]), subject to the exclusion, already noted under (4) above (at p. 59), of weeks which began before the employee attained the age of 18.

Under s. 81(4) the period is calculated retrospectively from and including "the relevant date", but in a case to which s. 86 applies from the "notified day of return".[72] The "relevant date" is discussed above (see p. 51). The notified day of return is discussed at p. 45. Note that if the contract of employment is terminated by the employer, and the dismissal is without notice, or on shorter notice than that required by s. 49(1), the provisions of s. 90(3) apply, so that the date which is treated as the relevant date is that on which notice under s. 49(1) would

68 Author's italics. These words "catch" any change of employer during the qualifying period.

69 For the meaning of "associated employer" see s. 153(4) of the 1978 Act and below, p. 69.

70 The Employment Act 1980 (Commencement No. 1) Order 1980 (S.I. 1980/1170), Sched. 3.

71 See *Secretary of State for Employment* v. *Globe Elastic Thread Co. Ltd.* [1979] I.C.R. 706.

72 Sched. 2, para. 4(1)(a).

expire if given on the date of termination or on the date when notice was given, as the case may be (see also Sched. 13, para. 11(3)). Note also that para. 14(1) of Sched. 13 provides that if in any week an employee[73] was employed outside Great Britain, the week will not count for the purposes of s. 81(4) unless the conditions in para. 14(1)(*b*) (*q.v.*) are satisfied. On the other hand, while such weeks do not count for computing the period in s. 81(4), by para. 14(3) they do not break the continuity of the requisite period; the effect is that the commencement of the period is thrown back by the equivalent number of weeks.

(d) *Other rights*

(i) **Written particulars of terms of employment.** An employee cannot demand a reference to a tribunal under s. 11, based on failure to provide a written statement as required by s. 1 or 4(1), until he has the right to such a statement. In the case of s. 1, the right does not arise until 13 weeks of employment after the employment begins (s. 1(1)), but except where s. 3(4) applies, as mentioned below, the employment does not require to be continuous, and discontinuous weeks which count may be aggregated.

Section 3(1) specifies what is not to count for the purposes of s. 1, namely any period when the hours of employment are normally less than 16 hours weekly. But by s. 3(2) an employee is treated as if his normal weekly hours are 16 *either* after 26 weeks' employment (computed in accordance with s. 3(3), (*q.v.*)) with normal hours between 8 and 16 weekly, if those hours had previously been sixteen or more weekly, *or* after five years' *continuous* employment with normal hours between 8 and 16 weekly (s. 3(4)). Where (because the conditions of s. 5 are fulfilled) the employer is not bound to provide a statement under s. 1, but becomes bound to do so because those conditions have ceased to be fulfilled, s. 5 requires a statement under s. 1 to be provided within one month thereafter. The same period is required by s. 4(1) for the written notification of any change in the terms included in a statement provided under s. 1. Note that in addition to excluding from the computation of a period of employment for these purposes any period during which the exception in s. 3(1) applies, s. 147 also excludes from the computation any period during which the employee may be within any of the exclusions provided by or under ss. 143 to 146 and s. 149 (which are discussed below at pp. 70 to 79).

(ii) **Guarantee payments and remuneration while suspended on medical grounds.** An employee is not entitled to a guarantee payment under s. 12 or to remuneration under s. 19 unless he has been continuously

---

73 Other than a master or seaman in a British ship who is ordinarily resident in Great Britain (para. 14(6)). See also p. 32 above regarding offshore employment.

employed for a period of four weeks ending (as the case may be) with the last complete week before the day for which the guarantee payment is claimed, or on the day on which the suspension begins (s. 143(1) and (2)).

(iii) **Time off to look for work.** An employee under notice of dismissal for redundancy is not entitled to complain that he has been unreasonably refused time off in terms of s. 31(1) unless he was or, as the case may be, would have been, continuously employed for two years on the date on which the notice was due to expire, or would have expired if correctly given under s. 49(1), whichever was the later (s. 31(2)).

(iv) **Maternity rights.** An employee is not entitled to maternity pay, or, as already noted, to return to work after pregnancy or confinement unless *inter alia* at the beginning of the eleventh week before the expected week of confinement she had been or (if dismissed earlier for a reason not to be regarded as automatically unfair under s. 60(1), and not re-engaged) would have been continuously employed for a period of not less than two years (s. 33(3)(*b*) and (4)). (See also s. 56A).

(v) **Written statement of reasons for dismissal.** An employee is not entitled to a statement under s. 53 unless on the effective date of termination he has been, or will have been, continuously employed for a period of 26 weeks ending with the last complete week before that date (s. 53(2)). Thus while an employee dismissed after 26 weeks but before 52 weeks' employment cannot usually complain of unfair dismissal, he is entitled to a statement under s. 53, and can complain to a tribunal if the employer does not comply with his request. As to the effective date of termination, see above, pp. 44 to 45. Note however that in determining that date s. 55(5) applies (see also p. 44 above) in cases where the requisite statutory notice has not been given.

(e) *Itemised pay statements (s. 8) and time off under ss. 27 to 29*

While these rights do not require a minimum period of service as such, they do not apply to employment under a contract which normally involves employment for less than sixteen hours weekly (s. 146(4)). But subss. (5) to (7) of s. 146 contain provisions similar to those of s. 3(2) to (4) (as to which see p. 62 above), under which in certain circumstances employment under a contract normally involving between eight and sixteen hours may count for this purpose.

(f) *"Continuous employment"*

By s. 151(1), the length of an employee's employment, and whether it has been continuous, is determined[74] by reference to Sched. 13 (as

---

[74] Not only for computing qualifying service but also for calculating the amount of a redundancy payment or a basic award for unfair dismissal, the amount of notice required by s. 49 to terminate employment, and the amount of pay in lieu of notice.

amended by the Employment Act 1980, Sched. 1, paras. 31 and 32). Section 151(2) provides that for the purposes of any proceedings, except for a breach of ss. 1, 2 or 4 (relating to the provision of written particulars or terms of employment) or s. 49 (relating to written notice), a person's employment during any period shall, unless the contrary is shown, be presumed to have been continuous.[75] While therefore an employee must aver a sufficient period of continuous employment to qualify for the relief sought, if he does so, it is for the employer (other than in the excepted cases) to prove the contrary. But in the *Globe Elastic Thread* case [1979] I.C.R. 706 it was held that, except as stated on p. 68, the presumption applies only to the dismissing employer. Moreover, if the employer shows a break in continuity, it would appear from the speech of Lord Upjohn in *Fitzgerald* v. *Hall, Russell & Co. Ltd.* (1970) 5 I.T.R. 1 (at p. 14) that the burden shifts to the employee to show that the broken periods are to be treated as continuous.[76]

The provisions of Sched. 13 are complex, and can only be summarised here.[77] The employment is computed in weeks,[78] and a year means 52 weeks (whether continuous or discontinuous) which count for computing a period of employment (para. 1(1)). A week which does not count under the provisions of Sched. 13 will normally break the continuity of the employment, except where otherwise provided (para. 2); the exceptions are noted in context elsewhere.

In order to count, the week must be one in which a valid contract of employment subsists. Thus if during the required period, or any week or weeks thereof, the contract of employment is illegal, the necessary qualifying service cannot be attained.[79] On the other hand, the fact that (subject in redundancy payment cases to para. 14, noted above at p. 62) an employee was engaged to work wholly or mainly outside Great Britain or was otherwise excluded from the right concerned by any other provision of the Act does not affect the application of the Schedule for the purpose of computing an employee's period of employment (para. 1(2)).

These provisions apart, the question whether a week counts depends primarily either on the number of hours in the week which the

---

[75] The reason for the excepted cases, where the onus of establishing continuity, where that is required, lies with the employee, is that under the Contracts of Employment Act 1972 there was no presumption of continuity in the employee's favour, and, as already pointed out, for most purposes under ss. 1, 2 and 4 employment does not require to be continuous.

[76] "But the whole issue in this case is whether the appellant can show that notwithstanding the legal break . . . the provisions of . . . [the Act] entitle him to claim that . . . the period of his employment was continuous from the earlier date."

[77] For a detailed exposition of the subject, see Grunfeld, *op. cit.*, Chap. 9, pp. 336-362.

[78] Ending with Saturday (para. 24(1)).

[79] See above under "illegal contracts", pp. 39 to 42, and *Attridge* v. *Jaydees Newsagents Ltd.* (EAT 11/3/80).

employee actually works (irrespective of the number provided for in his contract, or of the fact that the contract is silent on the matter), or on those for which he is employed to work (irrespective of the number actually worked[80]). Thus so long as a contract for the required number of hours subsists, absence from work does not prevent the week from counting. And if the contract provides for the required number of hours, the fact that it only subsisted for part of the week in question does not matter, so that the weeks in which it begins or terminates will each count, although not in themselves complete.[81] The required number of hours can be reduced by the Secretary of State by an order under s. 7.

A week will count if during that week the employee is actually employed for 16 hours or more (para. 3), *or* his relations with his employer are governed by a contract of employment which normally involves employment for 16 hours or more weekly (para. 4). But where the number of weekly hours normally involved under the contract is reduced from 16 or more weekly to 8 hours or more weekly, weeks at the reduced rate (up to a maximum of 26 between any two periods) will count and will not break the continuity if otherwise they would have counted or would not have broken continuity (para. 5). And even if the hours involved under the contract have never involved as much as 16 or more, if the employee is continuously employed for five years or more under a contract normally involving 8 or more hours weekly at all times during that period, he is then treated as if the contract normally involved employment for 16 hours or more weekly (para. 6), and will thus have sufficient qualifying service for all the statutory rights under the Act. And if an employee is continuously employed in accordance with the provisions of the Schedule for a period required to qualify for a statutory right, he is regarded as continuing to satisfy the required condition notwithstanding any subsequent reduction in hours, unless and until in any subsequent week his contract of employment normally involves employment for less than 8 hours weekly *and* he is *actually* employed in that week for less than 16 hours (para. 7). As already stated, the number of hours specified in paras. 3 to 7 can be reduced by an order by the Secretary of State under s. 7.

Where the contract does not specify the normal number of weekly hours, they have to be implied from any agreement or custom and practice in the industry or firm or, in a "one-off" situation, the actings of the parties.[82] Only hours involved in the contract will count. This

---

80 *Parkes Classic Confectionery Ltd.* v. *Ashcroft* (1973) 8 I.T.R. 43 (at p. 44).

81 *Coulson* v. *City of London Polytechnic* [1976] I.C.R. 433.

82 See *Dean* v. *Eastbourne Fisherman's etc. Club* [1977] I.R.L.R. 143.

excludes meal breaks and voluntary hours.[83] If an employee is required to live on the premises where he works, his hours are those during which he is on duty or his services may be required (para. 24(2)), and if an employee is "on call" at certain hours, these may count.[84]

Reference must now be made to various other provisions of Sched. 13, which admit or exclude weeks which do not fall within those referred to above, so far as they may be relevant in computing qualifying service and are not noted in context elsewhere.

(i) Paragraph 9 is headed "Periods in which there is no contract of employment." By subpara. (1) a week which does not fall under para. 3, 4 or 5 shall nevertheless count as a period of employment if for the whole or part of that week the employee is—

(*a*) incapable of work in consequence of sickness or injury, or
(*b*) absent from work on account of a temporary cessation of work, or
(*c*) absent from work in circumstances such that, by arrangement or custom, he is regarded as continuing in the employment of his employer for all or any purposes, or
(*d*) absent from work wholly or partly because of pregnancy or confinement.

Not more than 26 weeks may count under para. (*a*) or, subject to para. 10, under para. (*d*) of para. 9(1) between any periods falling under paras. 3, 4 or 5. (Paragraph 10 provides that where an employee returns to work after a period of absence caused by pregnancy or confinement the whole of the period of absence shall count under paras. 3, 4 or 5). There are no such restrictions on periods of absence falling under paras. (*b*) or (*c*) of para. 9(1).

On the construction of para. 9(1) as a whole, and the operation of (*b*) in particular, the leading case is *Fitzgerald* v. *Hall, Russell & Co. Ltd.* (1970) 5 I.T.R. 1. There it was held, in relation to para. 9(1)(*b*), that the position must be viewed retrospectively from the point of view of the workman concerned, asking first whether his absence was due to a cessation of work for him, and if so, whether the cessation falls to be regarded as temporary. It is a question of fact and degree whether an absence is temporary: even two years has been held to count (see *Seymour* v. *Barber & Heron Ltd.* (1970) 5 I.T.R. 65 (at p. 68) and *Bentley Engineering* v. *Crown & Anr.* [1976] I.C.R. 225). Paragraph 9(1)(*b*) can apply notwithstanding that the employee takes other employment in the interval between being laid off and re-engaged,[85] but was held not

---

83 *Kincey* v. *Pardey & Johnston Ltd.* (1966) 1 I.T.R. 182; *ITT Components (Europe) Ltd.* v. *Kolak* [1977] I.R.L.R. 53.

84 *Bullock* v. *Merseyside County Council* [1979] I.C.R. 79 (part-time fireman); but contrast *Lake* v. *Essex C.C.* [1979] I.C.R. 577 (teacher working at home in preparation and marking).

85 *Thompson* v. *Bristol Channel Ship Repairers and Engineers Ltd.* (1970) 5 I.T.R. 85.

to apply to a supply teacher whose job began and finished in each term.[86] But the retrospective approach does not apply to para. 9(1)(*c*), on which it was held in *Murphy* v. *A. Birrell & Sons Ltd.* [1978] I.R.L.R. 458 that the arrangement or custom must exist at the time the absence began. As to para. 9(1)(*a*), the sickness or injury must be of a kind which renders the employee incapable of work. The dividing line between absence for sickness and absence because of pregnancy, and hence whether a case falls within para. 9(1)(*a*) or 9(1)(*d*), may sometimes be a narrow one. For a case where para. 9(1)(*d*) operated to preserve continuity where an employee was dismissed a few days after returning to work after confinement, having resigned before her confinement, see *Mitchell* v. *Royal British Legion Club* [1981] I.C.R. 18.

(ii) Where by virtue of s. 55(5) or s. 90(3) a later date falls to be treated as the effective date of termination or as the relevant date (as the case may be) for unfair dismissal or redundancy payment purposes, the period between the actual ending of the employment and the later date counts as a period of employment for the purposes of Sched. 13, as does (for redundancy payment purposes) the interval between the ending of the original contract and the commencement of a new one as referred to in s. 84(1) (para. 11). But the payment of a redundancy payment by the employer or by the Secretary of State under s. 106, or of an equivalent payment under s. 111(3), or s. 1 of the Superannuation Act 1972, is treated as breaking continuity between the period of the employment to which the payment relates and subsequent employment (whether with the same or a different employer) for redundancy payment purposes (para. 12).[87]

(iii) Any weeks during the qualifying period in which the employee takes part in a strike do not count under paras. 3, 4, 5, 9 or 10 (para. 15(1)). But continuity is not broken by such weeks,[88] or by any weeks in which the employee is absent from work because of a lock-out (see paras. 15(2) and (4)): the effect is to throw back the commencement of the qualifying period by the equivalent number of weeks. "Strike" and "lock-out" are defined in para. 24(1).

(iv) Apart from the cases discussed above, continuity will normally be broken by dismissal or resignation if the employer re-employs the employee after an interval, even of only one week.[89] But if there is no such break, continuity is maintained, even where the original employment was terminated by the employee (see *Loggie* v. *Alexander Hall & Sons (Builders) Ltd.* (1969) 4 I.T.R. 390).

---

86 *Rashid* v. *Inner London Education Authority* (1976) 11 I.T.R. 215.

87 But see pp. 69 to 70 below where the payment is repaid.

88 See *Hanson* v. *Fashion Industries (Hartlepool) Ltd.* [1981] I.C.R. 35.

89 But see pp. 69 to 70 below where the re-employment is in consequence of unfair dismissal proceedings or action by a conciliation officer (see also at p. 133).

(v) The provisions of Sched. 13 discussed above relate only to employment by the one employer. Paragraphs 17 and 18 provide for continuity of employment between one employer and the other in various situations (provided, of course, there is no break for some other reason), the onus being on the employer (Grunfeld, *op. cit.* p. 341).

(*a*) If a trade or business or an undertaking is transferred from one person to another (para. 17(2)). "Business" includes a trade or profession, and any activity carried on by a body of persons, whether corporate or unincorporate (s. 153(1)). Most of the reported cases were decided in the context of s. 94(1)[90] and its predecessor, s. 13(1) of the Redundancy Payments Act 1965, but they are also relevant in this context.[91] The difference between the two is that s. 94(1) makes no reference to an undertaking but refers to a change in the ownership of a business or part of a business. In *Newlin Oil Co. Ltd.* v. *Trafford* (1974) 9 I.T.R. 324 it was held that the difference was not significant, and that the ancestor of para. 17(2) (para. 10(2) of Sched. 1 to the Contracts of Employment Act 1963) applied to the transfer of a self-contained part of a business (see also Grunfeld, *op. cit.*, p. 316). The question whether a business has been transferred is one of law, based on the relevant facts, in connection with which many factors are relevant, *e.g.* premises, stock, goodwill, fixtures, employees, capital, and name. The transaction has to be decided by its substance rather than its form, on a broad view of all the circumstances. The test is whether the effect of the transaction is to put the transferee in possession of a going concern, the activities of which he could carry on without interruption,[92] so that the business remains the same business but in different hands,[93] as opposed to a mere transfer of assets. A change in the ownership of part of a business will seldom occur, except when that part is to some extent separate and severable from the rest of the business, either geographically, or by reference to the products, or in some other way (*per* Lord Fraser of Tullybelton in *Melon & Ors.* v. *Hector Powe Ltd., supra,* at p. 50). Paragraph 17(2) also applies on a transfer by two partners to one of those partners (*Allen & Son* v. *Coventry* [1979] I.R.L.R. 399).

(*b*) If by or under an Act of Parliament, public or local, a body

---

90 Which relates to entitlement to a redundancy payment when employment is terminated on a change in the ownership of a business.

91 See Grunfeld, *op. cit.* pp. 311-334 for a full review of the cases on the subject.

92 *Kenmir Ltd.* v. *Frizzell* [1968] 1 All E.R. 414; (1968) 3 I.T.R. 159.

93 *Lloyd* v. *Brassey* [1969] 2 Q.B. 98; (1969) 4 I.T.R. 100. (Approved by the House of Lords in the Scottish case of *Melon & Ors.* v. *Hector Powe Ltd.* [1981] I.C.R. 43).

corporate is substituted as employer in place of another body corporate (para. 17(3)).

(*c*) If on the death of an employer the employee is taken into the employment of the personal representative or trustees of the deceased employer (para. 17(4)). In *Rowley Holmes & Co.* v. *Barber* [1977] I.C.R. 387 an employee who was the executor of his employer and sold the business in that capacity, and was subsequently dismissed by the purchasers, was held not to have lost continuity as between them and the original employer.

(*d*) If there is a change in the partners, personal representatives or trustees who employ any person (para. 17(5)). These provisions have been held not to apply when a person ceases to be employed by a partnership and is then employed by one of the partners (*Harold Fielding Ltd.* v. *Mansi* [1974] I.R.L.R. 79—but para. 17(2), referred to above, may apply).

(*e*) If an employee is taken into employment by an associated employer of his previous employer (para. 18). Any two employers are to be treated as associated if one is a company of which the other (directly or indirectly) has control, or if both are companies of which a third person (directly or indirectly) has control (s. 153(4)). In *Southwood Hostel Management Committee* v. *Taylor* [1979] I.C.R. 813 it was held that "company" in this context means body corporate, and the view was expressed that control connotes something by way of direction of the operation and not simply making the conduct of an operation (*e.g.* by provision of public funds) possible or impossible. In *Merton London Borough Council* v. *Gardiner* [1980] I.R.L.R. 302, this decision was followed (in preference to *Hillingdon Area Health Authority* v. *Kauders* [1979] I.C.R. 472). It was held that the definition in s. 153(4) was exhaustive, and as neither employer was a company they could not be associated. This decision was upheld in the Court of Appeal [1980] I.R.L.R. 472, but the court construed "company" as meaning a limited liability company, and not any body corporate.

Two further specialties remain to be mentioned—

(aa) Paragraph 19 (*q.v.*), which applies the provisions of the Schedule to Crown employment, as defined in subpara. (2).

(bb) The Labour Relations (Continuity of Employment) Regulations 1976 (S.I. 1976/660), made under the predecessor to para. 20, preserve continuity of employment where a dismissed employee is reinstated or re-engaged in consequence of the presentation of a complaint of unfair dismissal, or of action taken by a conciliation officer prior to the presentation of such a complaint. The regulations also preserve continuity where, as a result of re-employment, the employee repays a redundancy payment or an equivalent payment, the payment of which would otherwise break continuity by virtue of para. 12 (see (ii) above, at p. 67). While therefore continuity is automatically preserved if the re-employment takes place once industrial tribunal proceedings have been commenced, or a claim has been made under a dismissals procedure agreement, it would not be automatically preserved by a voluntary reinstatement or re-engagement by the employer before such action has been taken, unless as the result of action by a conciliation officer. If no such action has been taken, it would seem to follow from the decisions in *Secretary of State* v. *Globe Elastic Thread Co. Ltd., supra* and *Murphy* v. *A. Birrell & Sons Ltd., supra* that an industrial tribunal could not hold that continuity was preserved in an interval between dismissal and reinstatement or re-engagement by virtue of an agreement between the employer and the employee to that effect, since such an agreement would by its very nature be retrospective in character and therefore para. 9(1)(*c*) of Sched. 13 would not apply (see above, p. 67). For the implications of this with regard to settlement of proceedings, see Chapter 6, at p. 133. Note also that an interim relief order preserves continuity (see s. 78(1)).

(6) **Certain fixed-term and short-term contracts**

(a) By s. 142(1)[94] and (2) of the Employment Protection (Consolidation) Act 1978, employees on fixed-term contracts who would otherwise have sufficient qualifying service are generally excluded from the right to complain of unfair dismissal where the dismissal consists only of the expiry of the term of the contract without its being renewed, and from the right to a redundancy payment in respect of the expiry of that term without its being renewed (whether by the employer or an associated employer[95] of his) if *before the term so expires* the employee has agreed in writing to exclude his rights in these respects. The agreement may be in the contract itself or in a separate document (s. 142(3)). If an agreement to exclude redundancy rights is made during the currency of the term, it does not apply to the term as renewed, but a further agreement may be made in respect of that term. As regards unfair dismissal rights, s. 142(1) (as amended by the Employment Act 1980, s. 8(2)), applies to contracts for a term of two years or more made before October 1, 1980, and to contracts for a term of one year or more entered into on or after that date.[96] As regards redundancy payment rights, s. 142(2) applies to

---

94 Which does not apply to maternity cases falling under s. 56 (Sched. 2, para. 2(4)).

95 For the definition of "associated employer" see s. 153(4) and above, p. 69.

96 See the Employment Act 1980 (Commencement No. 1) Order 1980, Sched. 3.

contracts for a term of two years or more entered into after December 5, 1965.[97]

As to the meaning of fixed-term contract, see *Dixon* v. *BBC* [1979] I.C.R. 281 (distinguishing *BBC* v. *Ioannou* [1975] I.C.R. 267) and *Wiltshire County Council* v. *National Association of Teachers in Further and Higher Education* [1980] I.C.R. 455. In the latter case Lawton LJ said (at p. 462) that a fixed-term contract is one which has a defined beginning and a defined end. Lord Denning MR pointed out (at p. 459) that under what is now s. 2(2) of the 1978 Act, a written statement of terms of employment must state the date when a fixed-term contract expires, and stated (at p. 460) that a contract terminable on a completely uncertain event, such as the duration of the government, or on the discharge of a particular task, is not a fixed-term contract. But a contract is for a fixed-term if it is for a stated period, although it may be terminable by notice within that period (see *Dixon* v. *BBC, supra* at p. 285).

(b) By s. 143(3) of the Employment Protection (Consolidation) Act 1978 and s. 119(7) of the Employment Protection Act 1975, the right to a guarantee payment, and to remuneration if suspended on medical grounds in terms of s. 19 of the 1978 Act, and the redundancy consultation requirements of ss. 99 and 100 of the 1975 Act, do not apply to employment under a fixed-term contract for twelve weeks or less, or to employment under a contract made in contemplation of a specific task which is not expected to last for more than twelve weeks, in the latter case the right to statutory notice being also excluded unless the employee has actually been continuously employed for more than twelve weeks.

(7) **Employment outside Great Britain**

(a) *General*

Subject to the regulations relating to offshore employment (see above pp. 31 to 33) employment outside Great Britain (*i.e.* England and Wales and Scotland, but not including Northern Ireland, the Isle of Man or the Channel Islands) is generally excluded from the rights conferred by the employment legislation. But the statutory provisions abound with exceptions and qualifications, and require to be considered with care. They divide into two groups: first, the Employment Protection (Consolidation) Act 1978 (s. 141) and the Employment Protection Act 1975 (s. 119(5) and (6)), where the main test is whether the employee "ordinarily works" inside or outside Great Britain, and secondly the Equal Pay Act 1970, the Sex Discrimination Act 1975 and the Race

---

[97] But not where the employee is master or seaman in a British ship and is ordinarily resident in Great Britain (s. 144(3)).

Relations Act 1976, which strike at discrimination in relation to employment "at an establishment in Great Britain".

The leading case on the first question is *Wilson* v. *Maynard Shipbuilding Consultants AB* [1978] I.C.R. 376, where it was held (1) that a person could not, in respect of the whole period of the contract or any given period within it, during the self-same period, be ordinarily working under his contract of employment both in and outside Great Britain; and (2) that in order to ascertain whether an employee ordinarily works inside or outside Great Britain, a tribunal has to look at the relevant terms of the contract, express or implied, over the whole period of the contract, and not at what had happened during the period of employment before termination took place; but that where the times and places of work are left to the employer's discretion, the correct approach is to ascertain from the terms of the contract where the employee's base was to be; and that, in the absence of special factors leading to a contrary conclusion, the country where his base was to be is likely to be the place where the employee is to be treated as ordinarily working. Note the word "likely": the locality of the base is not necessarily conclusive. Furthermore, if the facts were to show that the base was mobile, such as a ship or an oil rig, it might be difficult to apply the test (for instance, the port of registration would hardly be relevant if the ship was on charter, except where s. 141(5) of the 1978 Act and s. 119(6) of the 1975 Act apply, as to which see (b) below).

(*b*) *The Employment Protection (Consolidation) Act 1978 and the Employment Protection Act 1975*

The largest group of exclusions is in s. 141(2) of the 1978 Act,[98] relating to ss. 8 (right to an itemised pay statement) and 53 (right to written reasons for dismissal), Pt. II (Guarantee payments, remuneration on suspension from work on medical grounds, discriminatory action relating to trade union membership, and rights to time off work), Pt. III (maternity rights), Pt. V (unfair dismissal rights), and Pt. VII (rights on employer's insolvency), and in s. 119(5) of the 1975 Act, relating to the rights under s. 99 and s. 100 of that Act. Here the right is excluded if under his contract of employment the employee ordinarily works outside Great Britain. But, by s. 141(5) of the 1978 Act and s. 119(6) of the 1975 Act, a person employed to work on board a ship registered in the United Kingdom, other than one registered at a port outside Great Britain (this exception would therefore apply if the ship were registered at a port in Northern Ireland), is to be regarded as a person who ordinarily works in Great Britain unless—

[98] Which does not, however, apply to maternity cases falling within s. 56 or a dismissal while absent on that account (Sched. 2, paras. 2(4) and 6(3).

(*a*) the employment is wholly outside Great Britain, or
(*b*) he is not ordinarily resident in Great Britain.

The right to a redundancy payment is excluded if on the relevant date (as to which see above, p. 51) the employee is outside Great Britain unless under his contract he ordinarily worked in Great Britain. The right is also excluded if the employee ordinarily works outside Great Britain, unless on the relevant date he is in Great Britain in accordance with instructions given to him by his employer (which would presumably include a visit for business purposes, but not one on leave). (1978 Act, s. 141(3) and (4)[99]).

The test is different with regard to the right to written particulars of terms of employment under ss. 1 and 4 and notice rights under ss. 49 to 51 of the 1978 Act. By s. 141(1), these do not apply during any period when the employee is engaged in work "wholly or mainly" outside Great Britain unless the employee "ordinarily" works in Great Britain and the work outside Great Britain is for the same employer.

(c) *Equal Pay Act 1970, Sex Discrimination Act 1975 and Race Relations Act 1976*

As indicated in (*a*) above, s. 1 of the 1970 Act, s. 6 of the 1975 Act and s. 4 of the 1976 Act prohibit discrimination by employers in relation to employment at "an establishment in Great Britain".

The meaning of this expression is defined in s. 10(1) of the 1975 Act (for the purposes of the Equal Pay Act as well) and s. 8(1) of the 1976 Act. Employment is to be regarded as being at an establishment in Great Britain unless the employee does his work "wholly or mainly" outside Great Britain. By a very complicated qualification in s. 10(2) of the 1975 Act and s. 8(2) of the 1978 Act, if the employment is on board a ship registered at a port in Great Britain, or is on an aircraft or hovercraft registered in the United Kingdom (*i.e.* including Northern Ireland) and operated by a person who has his principal place of business, or is ordinarily resident, in *Great Britain* (*i.e.* not including Northern Ireland), it is regarded as being at an establishment in Great Britain unless the work is done *wholly* outside Great Britain: but if the aircraft or hovercraft is operated under a contract with a person who has his principal place of business, or is ordinarily resident outside the *United Kingdom* (note the difference), the work must be performed "wholly or mainly" outside Great Britain to be excluded from the anti-discriminatory provisions.[1]

---

[99] Not applicable to employment as master or seaman in a British ship if the employee is ordinarily resident in Great Britain (s. 144(3)—but see (11) below, p. 77).

[1] But for ships, aircraft and hovercraft in government ownership see s. 85(7) of the 1975 Act and s. 75(4) of the 1976 Act.

The word "establishment" is not defined as such, and it would be for the tribunal to decide whether on the facts the word applies, but s. 10(4) of the 1975 Act and s. 8(4) of the 1976 Act provide that where work is not done *at* an establishment it shall be treated as done at the establishment *from* which it is done or, if not done from any establishment, at that with which it has the closest connection. And as a corollary to the provisions quoted above, in the case of employment on board a ship registered at a port in Great Britain the ship is deemed to be the establishment, except where the employee does his work wholly outside Great Britain (1975 Act, s. 10(3), 1976 Act, s. 8(3)).

(8) **Crown employment**

(a) The general position of Crown servants, and the reason why employment legislation makes special provision for them, has been explained above (see p. 57). Apart from the armed services, who are in a special position, not being employees and being subject to their own disciplinary regulations, the distinctive position of the Crown as an employer at common law accounts for the exclusion of those provisions which are not applied to Crown employees.

(b) *The Employment Protection (Consolidation) Act 1978*

Section 138(1) applies the following provisions of the Act to Crown employment and most Crown employees—

Part I (so far as it relates to itemised pay statements, *i.e.* excluding the provisions which relate to the right to written particulars of terms of employment);
Part II (guarantee payments, remuneration for suspension from work on medical grounds, action short of dismissal based on trade union membership, and time off work);
Part III (maternity rights) except s. 44 (which does not affect industrial tribunal proceedings);
s. 53 (written statement of reasons for dismissal);
Part V (unfair dismissal);
Part VIII (providing for the resolution of disputes relating to employment);
Part IX (miscellaneous and supplemental).

The rest of Parts I and IV (*i.e.* the provisions which relate to the rights to written particulars of employment and notice of termination of employment) and the whole of Parts VI (redundancy payments) and VII (relating to insolvent employers) are omitted altogether[2] and do not therefore apply to Crown employees (except for the limited purposes of s.

[2] But there may be entitlement under other regulations to an equivalent payment to a redundancy payment, which is referable to an industrial tribunal under s. 112.

112). Section 99 extends the exclusion of Crown employees from the right to a redundancy payment under s. 81 to various other public service employees, including employees of the National Health Service bodies specified in Sched. 5, and employees of Governments of overseas territories.

Crown employment is defined in s. 138(2) as employment under or for the purposes of a Government department or any officer or body exercising on behalf of the Crown functions conferred by any enactment. But s. 138 does not apply to service as a member of the armed services (which include women's services, but does not include employment by an auxiliary force association) (s. 138(3)), nor to any employment which is certified by a Minister as requiring to be excepted for the purpose of safeguarding national security (s. 138(4)), and persons falling within these categories do not have any rights under the Act. And where a Crown employee's terms of employment restrict his right to take part in political activities or activities which may conflict with his official functions, he cannot claim time off work under s. 29 for public duties connected with any such activities (s. 138(8). By s. 138(5), however, employees of the National Health Service bodies listed in Sched. 5, on the other hand, are not regarded as Crown employees for the purposes of most parts of the Act specified in s. 138(1) (with certain minor variations which do not affect industrial tribunal proceedings), and for those purposes (but not of course for the purposes omitted from s. 138(1), as noted above) are regarded as ordinary employees.

(c) *The Employment Protection Act 1975*

Sections 99, 101 and 103 do not apply to Crown employment (s. 121(1)), which is defined in subsections (2) to (6) of s. 121 (as amended by the 1978 Act) in a manner identical to that in the 1978 Act (see (b) above).

(d) *The Equal Pay Act 1970, the Sex Discrimination Act 1975 and the Race Relations Act 1976*

With certain exceptions, these Acts apply to the Crown, with particular inclusions in relation to—

- (i) service for the purposes of a Minister of the Crown or Government department, other than service of a person holding a statutory office, and
- (ii) service on behalf of the Crown for purposes of a person holding a statutory office or for purposes of a statutory office.[3]

[3] 1970 Act, s. 1(8), 1975 Act, s. 85(1) and (2), 1976 Act, s. 75(1) and (2). For definitions of "statutory office" and "service for the purposes of a Minister of the Crown or government department" see subs. (10) of each section.

Service in the armed forces (including the women's services) is also included in Crown employment in s. 75(2) of the 1976 Act, but by ss. 54(2) and 75(8) and (9), industrial tribunals are precluded from considering complaints under ss. 4, 32 and 33 about an act relating to service in the forces, which must be dealt with through service channels. Service in the forces is excluded, however, from s. 1(8) of the 1970 Act[4] and s. 85(2) of the 1975 Act (1970 Act, s. 1(9); 1975 Act, s. 85(4)). Moreover discrimination on grounds of sex in relation to cadet forces is not unlawful under the 1975 Act (s. 85(5)), and the 1975 Act does not apply to employment which may be required to be in support of the armed forces (s. 85(6)).

(9) **House of Commons staff**

Members of the staff of the House of Commons are in an identical position to Crown employees for the purposes of all the Acts discussed in (8) above (Employment Protection (Consolidation) Act 1978, s. 139(1) and (2); Employment Protection Act 1975, s. 122(1) and (2) (as amended by the 1978 Act)), and there are further provisions in s. 139 of the 1978 Act and s. 122 of the 1975 Act to determine against whom proceedings brought by such persons should be directed.

(10) **Police**

(*a*) *The Employment Protection (Consolidation) Act 1978*

By s. 146(2) the following provisions do not apply to employment under a contract of employment in police service or to persons engaged in such employment: ss. 8 and 9 (itemised pay statements), Pts. II (rights arising in course of employment) and III (maternity rights), s. 53 (written statement of reasons for dismissal), Pt. V (unfair dismissal), s. 86 (redundancy rights on not being permitted to return to work after confinement) and Pt. VII (rights on insolvency of employer). This leaves only the rights to written particulars of terms of employment, to statutory notice and to a redundancy payment (apart from cases under s. 86). But the position of persons in police service with regard to these remaining rights is anomalous: since the other rights are expressly included, it might be thought that by inference they enjoy those which are not: moreover s. 146(2) applies to employment under "a contract of employment in police service", while the definition of "employee" in s. 153(1) does not, as did its predecessor in s. 30(1) of the Trade Union and Labour Relations Act 1974, specifically exclude a contract of employment in police service. But it seems settled that a police constable is an officeholder, and thus is not an employee (*Wiltshire Police Authority* v. *Wynn* [1980] I.C.R. 649. See above, p. 57). While therefore the whole

[4] But see s. 7 of the Act.

matter seems to be in doubt, *Wynn's* case at least establishes that a police cadet is not regarded as being in police service or as an employee.

(b) The Employment Protection Act 1975

Part IV (which includes ss. 99, 101 and 103) applies to every employment except where otherwise provided (s. 119(1)). But the definition of "employee" is that in s. 30(1) of the Trade Union and Labour Relations Act 1974, which specifically excludes police service. Thus those sections would appear not to apply to persons in police service.

(c) The Equal Pay Act 1970, the Sex Discrimination Act 1975, the Race Relations Act 1976

No problems of construction arise from these Acts. For Pt. II of the 1975 Act (which by virtue of s. 8(1) also embraces the 1970 Act) and of the 1976 Act, the holding of the office of constable and appointment as a police cadet are treated as employment, (1975 Act, s. 17(1) and (6), 1976 Act, s. 16(1) and (4)). In both sections, provision is expressly made for bringing proceedings against the appropriate chief officer of police (1975 Act, s. 17(5); 1976 Act, s. 16(3)).

(11) **Mariners and fishermen**

Apart from the cases of employment on ships, aircraft and hovercraft which have been noted elsewhere in context, there are particular exclusions relating to mariners and fishermen in the Employment Protection (Consolidation) Act 1978, the Employment Protection Act 1975, and the Race Relations Act 1976.

(a) The largest exclusion relates to those employed as share fishermen, *i.e.* masters or crew members of fishing vessels where the employee is remunerated only by a share in the profits or gross earnings of a vessel. They are excluded (by s. 144(2))[5] from all rights under the 1978 Act except those to written particulars of terms of employment and to statutory notice of termination of employment, and (by s. 119(4)) from s. 99 (and, by implication, ss. 101 and 103) of the 1975 Act. But if he falls within (b) below, a share fisherman will also be excluded from the rights not affected by s. 144(2).

(b) The master of or a seaman on a sea-going British ship of 80 tons or more (including such a seaman who is shore-bound) and the skipper of or seaman on a fishing boat registrable under the Merchant Shipping Act 1894 are excluded from the right to a written statement of particulars

---

[5] Which, somewhat understandably, does not apply to maternity cases (Sched. 2, paras. 2(4), 4(3) and 6(3)).

of employment and to statutory notice of termination of employment (1978 Act, s. 144(1)).

(c) By s. 144(4) of the 1978 Act, merchant seamen are excluded from the right to an itemised pay statement (s. 8), the right to time off for public duties (s. 29) and to look for work under s. 31, and from the rights under ss. 122 and 123 on the employer's insolvency. Employment as a merchant seaman is defined in s. 144(5) (*q.v.*). Merchant seamen are also excluded (by s. 119(12)) from s. 99 of the Employment Protection Act 1975 (and by implication from ss. 101 and 103). The definition of merchant seaman for this purpose in s. 119(14) is simpler than that in s. 144(5) of the 1978 Act. There is also an order excluding merchant seamen from redundancy payment rights (The Redundancy Payments (Merchant Seamen Exclusion) Order 1973 (S.I. 1973/1281)).

(d) Seamen recruited abroad do not enjoy protection against discrimination on grounds of race, whether as direct employees under s. 4 or as contract workers under s. 7 (Race Relations Act 1976, s. 9(1)[6] and (2).

(12) **Dock workers**

Under the Employment Protection (Consolidation) Act 1978 dock workers who are registered as such under the statutory schemes for dock work[7] are excluded from the right to written particulars of terms of employment (ss. 1 to 6) and to statutory notice, except when not engaged in dock work (s. 145(1)). Unless their employment is wholly or mainly in other work they are also excluded by s. 145(2)[8] and (3) from the rights to a guarantee payment (s. 12), to remuneration on suspension on medical grounds (s. 19), to time off to look for work (s. 31), and to a written statement of reasons for dismissal (s. 53), from unfair dismissal rights (s. 54), from the right to a redundancy payment (s. 81)[9] and from the rights on the employer's insolvency under ss. 122 and 123, and, by s. 119(3) of the Employment Protection Act 1975, from s. 99 (and by implication ss. 101 and 103) of that Act.

(13) **Spouses and domestic servants**

Where the employer is the husband or wife of the employee, by s. 146 (1) of the Employment Protection (Consolidation) Act 1978[10] the following provisions of the Act do not apply: ss. 1 and 4 (written particulars of

---

[6] Does not apply to offshore employment (see s. 9(3)).

[7] Defined in s. 145(5).

[8] Which does not apply in maternity cases falling under s. 56; s. 145 as a whole does not apply to dismissals while attempting to return to work (Sched. 2, paras. 2(4) and 6(3)).

[9] Except in the circumstances set forth in s. 145(4) (*q.v.*).

[10] Which does not apply in maternity cases (Sched. 2, paras. 2(4), 4(3) and 6(3)).

employment), s. 8 (itemised pay statements), Pt. II (rights arising in course of employment), Pt. III (maternity rights), s. 53 (written statement of reasons for dismissal), Pt. V (unfair dismissal), Pt. VI (redundancy payments) and ss. 122 and 123 (rights on employer's insolvency). Thus a spouse is left only with the right to statutory notice and notice pay.

In addition, by s. 100(2), a domestic servant in a private household is not entitled to a redundancy payment if related to the employer by parentage, grandparentage, brotherhood or sisterhood, step-parentage, half-brotherhood or half-sisterhood.

(14) **National security**

Complaints under s. 24 of the Employment Protection (Consolidation) Act 1978 (action short of dismissal taken against an employee for reasons connected with trade union membership and activities) and s. 67 (unfair dismissal) must be dismissed if it is shown that the action complained of was taken for the purpose of safeguarding national security (Sched. 9, para. 2(1)). A certificate by a Minister of the Crown certifying that the action was taken for that purpose is conclusive evidence of that fact (para. 2(2)).

(15) **Exclusions by statutory order**

(a) *Unfair dismissal*

If the Secretary of State makes an order designating a dismissal procedures agreement for the purposes of s. 65 of the Employment Protection (Consolidation) Act 1978, by s. 65(3) and (4) the provisions of the agreement replace the right not to be unfairly dismissed in s. 54 and, in consequence, the right to complain to an industrial tribunal, except where the dismissal falls under s. 60(1), *i.e.* is connected with pregnancy. Such an order is revocable under the provisions of s. 66.

(b) *Redundancy payments*

An exemption order under s. 96 of the 1978 Act cannot exclude the jurisdiction of an industrial tribunal under s. 91 (s. 96(2) and (3)). By implication, the same would seem to apply to any regulations made under s. 98 for the exclusion or reduction of redundancy payments on account of pension rights.

(c) *Collective agreements on redundancies and guarantee payments*

An order under s. 107 of the Employment Protection Act 1975 which excludes the operation of s. 99 must either provide for a complaint to an industrial tribunal for a breach of the provisions of the agreement or for an equivalent procedure, as must an order under s. 18 of the 1978 Act.

(16) **Exclusions by agreement**

There are general restrictions on contracting out of the employment legislation (see Chapter 6, pp. 131 to 132), and therefore any agreement to exclude the jurisdiction of an industrial tribunal, except in so far as expressly permitted in the legislation[11], is null and void, and unenforceable.

(17) **Other exclusions**

Many of the provisions of the employment legislation include provisions which, if satisfied, have the effect of excluding the right in question. Unless they raise a clearly separable issue which is suitable for a preliminary hearing they are generally regarded as going to the merits. For this reason, and because of their variety and complexity, no attempt can be made to discuss them here. But where such a point arises, a respondent should raise it in specific terms in his notice of appearance. A "border-line" case in this category is s. 62 of the Employment Protection (Consolidation) Act 1978, which precludes a determination whether a dismissal was fair or unfair if it took place during a lock-out or industrial action unless a fellow-worker has been offered re-engagement but the complainant has not. Here the jurisdiction of the tribunal, if initially precluded, will be revived if at any time a relevant re-engagement takes place.

SPECIAL CASES

(1) **Minors**

In the courts a minor, *i.e.* a male between the ages of 14 and 18, and a female between the ages of 12 and 18, can only sue with the consent of a curator, being either his or her legal guardian or a *curator ad litem* specially appointed for the purpose. There being no such limitation in any of the statutory provisions governing industrial tribunal proceedings, an application by a minor is entertained without the participation or concurrence of his curator.[12]

Similarly, when a minor is sued in the courts, his curator (if he has one) must be called as a party to the proceedings, failing which a curator *ad litem* is appointed. While it is not beyond the bounds of possibility, the likelihood of a minor being involved in tribunal proceedings as a respondent will be remote. No such situation ever seems to have occurred in practice, but if it did, it is thought that the tribunal would

---

11 *E.g.* in relation to certain fixed-term contracts (see above, p. 70).

12 But the minor may be excluded on grounds of age in redundancy payment proceedings (see above, p. 59).

have to take such steps as might seem appropriate to protect the minor's interest, and for that matter that of the applicant in the proceedings, looking to the issues involved. Questions might for instance arise as to whether the contract of employment to which the proceedings related was one which was enforceable in law. Where the minor has a legal guardian, intimation of the proceedings would probably be made to him, if considered appropriate. Under each of the rules of procedure a tribunal has power to regulate its own procedure, subject to the provisions of the rules. In addition, in cases under the Industrial Tribunals Rules of Procedure (Scotland) 1980 (r. 14(1)) and under the Industrial Tribunals (Improvement and Prohibition Notices Appeals) Scotland Regulations 1974 (r. 14(2)) there is express power to join an additional respondent. It is thought that these rules would enable the guardian to be conjoined as a party in the proceedings.[13] But where there is no legal guardian, it is doubtful whether the general power of a tribunal to regulate its procedure could extend to the appointment of a *curator ad litem*.

(2) **Persons of unsound mind**

In the courts an insane person (an *"incapax"*) cannot sue, and any action on his behalf must be at the instance of a *curator bonis* acting on his behalf. Likewise in proceedings against such a person a *curator bonis* has to be appointed.[14] Again there are no statutory provisions bearing on the matter in relation to industrial tribunal proceedings, and so far as is known no case has occurred in which the sanity of a party has been in issue. But if it were shown to the tribunal that a party was *incapax*, the tribunal would have to take cognisance of the matter, as it would be fundamental to the ability of the party in question to take or defend the proceedings, and, depending on the circumstances, might also be an issue affecting the merits of the case itself. Intimation of the proceedings would be ordered to the *curator bonis* of the *incapax*, if he had one. The competence of the *curator* being allowed to enter the proceedings or to be joined as additional respondent would have to be considered in the light of the same rules as are referred to under (1) above, but it would appear that any question of the appointment of a *curator bonis* to an *incapax* would have to be dealt with in the courts. If the alleged incapacity were to be challenged, an enquiry might have to be made into the matter by way of preliminary hearing. That apart, it must be regarded as an open question where the matter would go from there. There could be so many practical difficulties in the conduct of proceedings in a situation of this kind that in practice the tribunal might

---

[13] As to joinder of additional respondents generally, see Chap. 6, p. 122.

[14] Dobie, *Sheriff Court Practice*, p. 83.

be left with no alternative but to adjourn them indefinitely for so long as the state of legal incapacity persisted.

It happens from time to time that a party who is not legally insane exhibits apparent signs of paranoia, or irrationality regarding the subject-matter of the case. In such unfortunate cases (in which the party is often unrepresented), all the tribunal can do is to hear him with as much patience and understanding as possible. A preliminary hearing may be necessary to ascertain what ground of complaint, if any, there may be.

(3) **Bankrupts and insolvent parties**

In the courts a bankrupt (*i.e.* an insolvent person whose estate has been sequestrated under the provisions of the Bankruptcy (Scotland) Act 1913) has only limited rights to litigate personally.[15] There is no provision in the legislation relating to industrial tribunals which limits the right of a bankrupt to apply or appeal to a tribunal, however. But his trustee may be interested in the result of the application, to the extent that a decision favourable to the bankrupt may produce a payment which would vest in the trustee, by the operation of law, as an asset of the bankrupt's estate. Likewise a decision in favour of a bankrupt respondent may avoid his estate incurring financial obligations. The case of a bankrupt appellant or applicant is another situation which does not appear to have occurred in practice, but it is thought that if it were to do so (whether bankruptcy had taken place before or after the proceedings had commenced), the proceedings would have to be intimated to the applicant's trustee to enable him to state his position, and similarly that where a company which was an appellant or an applicant, under any of the provisions which enable an employer to apply to an industrial tribunal,[16] had gone into liquidation or had had a receiver or provisional liquidator appointed, the proceedings would be intimated to the liquidator, receiver or provisional liquidator. The question of allowing the trustee, receiver or liquidator to enter the proceedings would have to be considered under the rules referred to under (1) above. Section 231 of the Companies Act (see the succeeding paragraph) may also require to be considered. It may be of some significance in this connection that while the assets of a bankrupt are transferred to and vested in his trustee by the provisions of the Bankruptcy (Scotland) Act 1913, this does not apply to the assets of a company in receivership or liquidation.[17] Nevertheless the receiver's or

---

[15] See Dobie, *op. cit.*, p. 79; Goudy, *Bankruptcy*, 4th ed. pp. 365-6.

[16] See Chap. 1.

[17] See *Smith* v. *Lord Advocate*, 1979 S.L.T. 233; Companies (Floating Charges and Receivers) (Scotland) Act 1972, ss. 13(7) and 14(7).

liquidator's position would give him an undoubted interest in the outcome of the proceedings.

The case of the insolvent employer[18] is not an uncommon one, however. Any sum which a tribunal may order him to pay is a charge on his assets, and his trustee in bankruptcy, or the liquidator, receiver or provisional liquidator of such a company, has a potential interest in the outcome of industrial tribunal proceedings against the employer. Furthermore, while most awards which industrial tribunals make will rank only as ordinary claims, certain debts fall to be treated as wages, and as such to be ranked in priority for the purposes of s. 33 of the Bankruptcy Act 1914, s. 118 of the Bankruptcy (Scotland) Act 1913, and s. 319 of the Companies Act 1948.[19] Those debts, together with certain others specified in s. 122(3) (including a basic award of compensation for unfair dismissal), and certain pension fund contributions and redundancy payments enjoy further protection where the employer is insolvent, in that they may be paid in full by the Secretary of State, who then becomes vested in the right to claim from the employer any amount so paid.[20]

If therefore it comes to the notice of a tribunal that a respondent is in such a position (and either party should bring it to the tribunal's notice at the earliest opportunity), the proceedings will be intimated to the trustee, receiver or liquidator (if appointed) to enable him to state his position, and under the rules referred to under (1) above the tribunal may join him as an additional respondent. In the case of a company in liquidation, it is not always apparent at first sight whether the liquidation is by order of the court or is voluntary. For this reason the practice in Scotland is for proceedings against the company to continue, subject to the liquidator's right to enter the proceedings. If the liquidator or provisional liquidator were to ask for the proceedings to be sisted (*i.e.* suspended) on the ground that s. 231 of the Companies Act 1948[21]

---

[18] By ss. 106(5) and 127(2) of the Employment Protection (Consolidation) Act 1978 an employer is taken to be insolvent for the purposes of ss. 106 and 122 to 126 if:

(*a*) an award of sequestration has been made on his estate or he has executed a trust deed for his creditors or entered into a composition contract;

(*b*) he has died and a judicial factor appointed under s. 163 of the Bankruptcy (Scotland) Act 1913 is required by the provisions of that section to divide his insolvent estate among his creditors; or

(*c*) where the employee is a company, a winding-up order has been made or a resolution for voluntary winding-up is passed with respect to it or a receiver of its undertaking is duly appointed.

[19] *I.e.* guarantee payments, remuneration on suspension on medical grounds under s. 19 of the Employment Protection (Consolidation) Act 1978, payments for time off under ss. 27(3), 31(3) or 31A(4) of the 1978 Act, and remuneration under a protective award under s. 101 of the Employment Protection Act 1975. (See 1978 Act, s. 121(2).

[20] 1978 Act, s. 106 and 125.

[21] "When a winding up order has been made or a provisional liquidator has been appointed, no action or proceedings shall be proceeded with or commenced against the company, except by leave of the court and subject to such terms as the court may impose".

applied, the matter would then be considered. The point has never arisen in Scotland, and there does not appear to be any judicial authority on the application of s. 231 to industrial tribunal proceedings.

If the fact that an employer is bankrupt or in receivership or liquidation only emerges at a hearing, to avoid the necessity of adjournment the usual practice, in cases under rules of procedure which permit a tribunal to review its decisions,[22] is for the tribunal to hear the case, and for the trustee, receiver or liquidator to be informed, and advised that if on receipt of the decision he wishes to object to it, he may do so by way of review. Where the rules do not admit of review, the proceedings would have to be adjourned to enable him to state his position if he had not already come forward to do so. Where a situation of this kind only comes to light very shortly prior to a hearing, the practice is to get in touch with the trustee, receiver or liquidator, by telephone if necessary, and ascertain what position he wishes to take up; if advised that he may apply for an adverse decision to be reviewed, he may agree that the hearing may proceed without any formal appearance on his part.

As to the position where the employer dies insolvent, without having been sequestrated during his lifetime, see (4) below, at pp. 86 to 87.

(4) **Deceased parties**

Schedule 12 to the Employment Protection (Consolidation) Act 1978 supplements and modifies various provisions of the Act as respects the death of an employee or employer.[23] Part I deals with *inter alia* the institution or continuance of tribunal proceedings. The remaining parts adapt the unfair dismissal provisions and the redundancy payment provisions of the Act to the death of the employee or employer. Paragraph 17(4) of Sched. 13 preserves continuity of employment between a deceased employer and his personal representatives or trustees, if an employee is taken into their employment.

Paragraph 2 of Sched. 12 provides that where an employee or employer has died, tribunal proceedings arising under any of "the relevant provisions" may be instituted or continued by a personal representative of the deceased employee or, as the case may be, defended by a personal representative of the deceased employer. The relevant provisions (defined in para. 1) are:

Part I (so far as it relates to itemised pay statements);
Part II (rights arising in course of employment);
Part III (maternity);

---

[22] *I.e.* each of the rules of procedure except those in Sched. 2 to the Industrial Tribunals (Scotland) Regulations 1965, as amended.

[23] By virtue of s. 150, which does not however apply to cases falling under s. 86 (employee not permitted to return to work after confinement treated as dismissed for redundancy payment purposes).

Part IV—s. 53 (written statement of reasons for dismissal);
Part V (unfair dismissal);
Part VI (redundancy payments);
Part VII (insolvency of employer); and
Schedule 12 itself.

Paragraph 4 provides that the relevant provisions are to be construed, in relation to an employee or an employer who has died, by substituting reference to a personal representative of the deceased employee or employer where appropriate or necessary, and similarly by including a reference to a personal representative of the deceased employer in provisions referring to the successor of an employer.

As regards the statutory rights and obligations under "the relevant provisions" which provide grounds for industrial tribunal proceedings, paras. 5 and 6 of Sched. 12 provide in effect that they shall devolve and transmit as if they had accrued prior to the death.

Paragraph 3(1) of Sched. 12 deals with the situation where there is no personal representative of the deceased employee, by providing that tribunal proceedings under any of the relevant provisions (or proceedings to enforce a tribunal award made in such proceedings) may be instituted or continued on behalf of the estate of the deceased employee by such other person as the tribunal may appoint, being either—

(*a*) a person authorised by the employee to act in connection with the proceedings before the employee's death; or
(*b*) the widower, widow, child, father, mother, brother or sister of the deceased employee.

In such a case any award made by the tribunal shall be in such terms and shall be enforceable in such manner as may be provided by regulations (para. 3(2)).

The Industrial Tribunals Awards (Enforcement in case of Death) Regulations 1976 (S.I. 1976/663) provide that where a person has been so appointed, or if an employee dies before the tribunal's award is made, any award shall be made in favour of the estate of the deceased employee. A person appointed under the foregoing provisions may enforce the award on behalf of the estate of the deceased without confirmation, and the receipt of that person is a sufficient discharge to the employer for any sum payable to the estate (reg. 5). Where no such person has been appointed, an award in favour of the estate or the deceased employee is enforceable on behalf of his estate by the person to whom a grant of confirmation has been made (reg. 6).

Beyond a provision in para. 3(1) of Sched. 12, that references in the Schedule to a personal representative shall be construed as including a person appointed by a tribunal to institute or continue proceedings, and a further provision in para. 21 that for redundancy payment purposes in relation to a domestic servant the expression shall be construed as including a reference to any person to whom the management of the household has passed in consequence of the employer's death (other than in pursuance of a sale), the expression "personal representative" is not defined in the 1978 Act. The meaning can vary according to the context, but is generally synonymous with legal representatives[24] *i.e.* in Scotland an executor to whom confirmation has been granted, as opposed to a beneficiary under a will or an heir in intestacy. This could give rise to difficulty if the deceased had died insolvent, and a judicial factor had been appointed on his estate under s. 163 of the Bankruptcy (Scotland) Act 1913. The judicial factor would have a prior right to the assets of the deceased's estate over an executor, whose right is only to the surplus assets, if any, after the claims of creditors have been satisfied. Thus it would seem logical for practical purposes to construe the expression "personal representative" in the context of Pt. I of Sched. 12 as including a judicial factor, more especially since the definition of an insolvent employer in ss. 106(6) and 127(2) includes the situation where a judicial factor has been appointed.

Since an order under para. 3(1) of Sched. 12 appointing a person to institute or continue proceedings on behalf of the estate of a deceased employee can only be made if there is no personal representative, where a question of making such an order arises, the tribunal will require to be satisfied that there is no legal personal representative, and that the person seeking appointment is qualified for appointment under subparas. (*a*) or (*b*) of para. 3(1). Since the making of such an order is not an act required or authorised to be done under the rules of procedure, it would appear that it is not competent for an order to be made by a Chairman alone, and that the matter must be referred to a full tribunal.[25] That being so, it may be necessary for the person seeking appointment to appear before the tribunal and testify to his or her qualifications, but if sufficient documentary evidence is available this may not be necessary. Any hearing in matters of this kind would usually take place on an *ex parte* basis. Any originating application by a person purporting to make a claim on behalf of the estate of a deceased employee would therefore be referred to a Chairman for directions as to how the matter should be dealt with, unless the application bears to be by a legal personal representative. So too, if the application reveals that the employer has died, or if at any stage after proceedings have been commenced it emerges that either of the parties has died.

As pointed out above, para. 3(1) of Sched. 12 applies only to a deceased employee, and not to a deceased employer. This could create

---

[24] Stroud's *Judicial Dictionary*, 3rd ed. vol. 3, p. 2186.

[25] See the Industrial Tribunals Rules of Procedure (Scotland) 1980, r. 12(4).

practical difficulties where an employee seeks to institute or continue proceedings after the death of the employer, but no personal representative (executor or, if applicable, judicial factor if the employer died bankrupt) has been appointed, or where the identity of the personal representative is not known to the applicant. In that case, all that could be done would be to serve the application on the nearest known relative of the deceased, as a "personal representative" in the broadest sense of the expression, leaving it to such person to enter appearance and state the position: this could lead to an application for some more appropriate representative to be substituted as respondent. It is impracticable to attempt to define hard and fast procedures for such situations, which would have to be dealt with in the light of their own particular circumstances. Generally speaking, the widow or widower of the deceased would be the most appropriate person on whom to serve the application in the first place.

Schedule 12 to the Employment Protection Act 1975 contains provisions in identical terms *mutatis mutandis* to the provisions of Sched. 12 to the 1978 Act discussed above, and those provisions apply to tribunal proceedings arising under ss. 99 to 107 of that Act.

But it may be inferred from the fact that it was considered necessary to make special provision for the situation arising on the death of an employee or an employer in the 1975 and 1978 Acts that as regards other grounds of jurisdiction to which those provisions do not extend, tribunal proceedings may neither be instituted or continued by or in the name of the representatives of a deceased party, and that the statutory rights and obligations giving rise to those grounds fall with the death of the employee or the employer. The most significant grounds of jurisdiction which seem to be thus excluded are those under the Equal Pay Act 1970, the Sex Discrimination Act 1975 and the Race Relations Act 1976.

(5) **Assignees and representatives**

As has already emerged from the points discussed under (4) above, complaints to industrial tribunals are of a personal nature. While a person may be able to assign to a third party any financial sum which may be awarded to him by a tribunal, or take a third party bound in respect of a financial obligation which he may incur as the result of tribunal proceedings (in so far as he is not prohibited by statute from so doing), there are no statutory provisions which require a tribunal to recognise the interest of an assignee, and in practice such an interest would not be recognised. Where, however, an agent acts for an undisclosed employer (a situation which seems to arise sometimes when foreigners buy land in Scotland but are reluctant to disclose their identity) the agent is liable under the ordinary operation of law for the actings of his principal, and on that principle would be amenable to the jurisdiction of the tribunal in place of the true employer for so long as he chose not to disclose his principal's identity.

As regards interests which are or may be transferred by the operation of law[26], the position has been discussed under (3) and (4) above.

(6) **Firms, corporations, associations and other public bodies**

In court procedures there are rules governing how firms, corporations and other bodies are to sue and be sued.[27] These relate mainly to the way in which they are to be designated in the proceedings, however, rather than to their ability to enter into or defend them, which is not restricted either in courts or tribunals.

In tribunal proceedings, which are frequently initiated by persons who do not have legal training, to require such nicety of designation would be impracticable, and any application against parties of this type is accepted which gives a sufficient indication of their identity to enable intimation to be made to them. Often respondents themselves correct any faulty descriptions in their notices of appearance, in which case the applications are treated as amended accordingly.[28]

Where the applicant is legally represented, it is for his solicitor to ensure that such a respondent is sufficiently identified in all formal documents to enable enforcement procedures to be operated if the application is successful.[29] In all cases, however, the Chairman should take the matter into consideration, with a view to ensuring adequate identification. Those in which such problems can particularly arise are in relation to persons and firms trading under a trade name, both nominate and descriptive, unincorporated associations such as clubs, and public or corporate bodies for which there are statutory provisions directing how citation is to be made.

---

26 *I.e.* on bankruptcy or death.

27 See Dobie, *Sheriff Court Practice*, p. 85 *et seq.*

28 See Chap. 5 at p. 98 below.

29 See Chap. 9 below, pp. 228 to 229.

CHAPTER 5

INITIAL PROCEDURE

GENERAL

This chapter is concerned with the procedure involved in the commencing stages of industrial tribunal proceedings, *i.e.* down to the point at which the hearing is arranged, and in particular with the documents which require to be completed for that purpose by both parties. Since, as already noted, tribunal procedures are intended to be simple and informal, these documents are intended to supply merely essential information as to the nature of the case which the party seeks to make, and not as formal written pleadings, as required in civil proceedings in the courts. They are nevertheless of considerable importance, and should be completed with care, as the omission of, or a subsequent change in, the line taken on a matter of substance may be considered significant by the tribunal.

Each of the rules of procedure provide that subject to the provisions of the rules themselves, a tribunal may regulate its own procedure. Except where otherwise noted, any of the acts which are required or authorised to be done by a tribunal under the rules which are discussed in this chapter may be done by or on the direction of the President or a Chairman.[1]

INITIATION OF PROCEEDINGS

(1) Cases under the Industrial Tribunals Rules of Procedure (Scotland) 1980

Proceedings are initiated by the applicant or (where applicable) by a sheriff presenting to the Secretary of the Tribunals an application in writing (called an originating application) which must set out:

(*a*) the name and address of the applicant;

(*b*) the names and addresses of the person or persons against whom relief is sought or of the parties to the proceedings before the sheriff (as the case may be);

(*c*) the grounds, with particulars thereof, on which that relief is sought; or in proceedings under s. 51 of the Docks and Harbours

---

[1] The Industrial Tribunals Rules of Procedure (Scotland) 1980, r. 12(1) and (4); the Industrial Tribunals (Scotland) Regulations 1965 (as amended), Sched. 2, r. 14(3) and (4); the Industrial Tribunals (Improvement and Prohibition Notices Appeals) (Scotland) Regulations 1974, r. 14(1) and (3); the Industrial Tribunals (Non-Discrimination Notices Appeals) (Scotland) Regulations 1977, r. 12(1) and (3).

Act 1966 the question for determination and (except where the question is referred by a sheriff) the grounds on which relief is sought. (Rule 1(1)).

No time limit is specified in the rules, as the various statutory provisions governing the grounds of jurisdiction under which proceedings may be brought specify different time limits for the initiation of the proceedings (see Chapter 4, pp. 43 to 54). As to what constitutes "presentation", and where the originating application should be sent, see under (5) below.

A printed form I.T.1[2] should be used for the originating application, but an application is not incompetent if the form is not used, provided that the basic information specified in r. 1(1) is given.[3] In *Gosport Working Mens' and Trade Union Club Ltd.* v. *Taylor and Anr.* (1978) 13 I.T.R. 321, it was held that an application which failed to give the applicant's address but gave his telephone number complied with r. 1(1), and that there was no objection to two applicants making an application in the same document. But neither practice should be resorted to, as considerable administrative inconvenience would result. As the form I.T.1 also provides for important information which is not required by r. 1(1), an applicant whose originating application is not made on form I.T.1 is asked also to complete one.

Notwithstanding the relatively informal nature of the document, full details of the facts giving rise to the application should be stated in the I.T.1. A mere statement like "I was unfairly dismissed", is of no assistance to the tribunal or the employer. For the reasons explained above (at p. 89), careful attention should be given to the questions asked, and the replies should be as full and accurate as possible. The notes for guidance attached to the form should be carefully studied, as should the leaflet on industrial tribunal procedures. If the space provided is insufficient, further information can be given on a separate sheet. Before proceeding with the presentation of the originating application consideration should also be given to whether the applicant has the necessary statutory qualifications for the relief which he seeks, since it is pointless, and may incur liability for expenses, for an applicant to do so if obviously disqualified. (For qualifications and disqualifications see Chapter 4). If more than one statutory complaint is intended, each ground of complaint should be clearly and separately specified in answering question 1, *e.g.* if it is sought to make a complaint of failure to provide written reasons for dismissal as well as one of unfair dismissal, this should be stated: it will not suffice merely to say "I have asked my employer for a letter saying why I was dismissed", when giving reasons for the complaint of unfair dismissal.

---

[2] See Appendix 2.

[3] *Smith* v. *Automobile Proprietary Ltd.* [1973] I.C.R. 306.

Where insufficient information is given the respondent or the tribunal may, under r. 4(1), call for further particulars to be supplied.[4] Furthermore, r. 1(2) provides that where the Secretary of the Tribunals is of the opinion that the originating application does not seek or, on the facts stated therein, cannot entitle the applicant to a relief which a tribunal has power to give, he may give notice to that effect to the applicant (generally called a "Rule 1 letter") stating the reasons for his opinion and informing him that the application will not be registered unless he states in writing that he wishes to proceed with it. The typical case where this is done is where, on the face of it, the applicant is disqualified by age or length of service from the relief which he appears to claim.

Where a Rule 1 letter has to be sent, r. 1(3) provides that the application is not treated as received for the purpose of registration under r. 2 unless the applicant intimates in writing to the Secretary that he wishes to proceed with his application. Upon receipt of such an intimation, however, the Secretary has to proceed in accordance with that rule.

An application which is defective in content (*e.g.* if it is unsigned) is not a nullity if its purpose can be understood by the tribunal staff, and provided such an application is received within the statutory time limits, the defect may be corrected after the time limit has expired.[5] Accordingly all such applications are date-stamped on the day of receipt at the Central Office, thereby establishing the date of presentation (see (5) below). The original is retained and the applicant is sent a photocopy in which to complete deficiencies. Although the case must be registered if the applicant, on being sent a Rule 1 letter, asks for the application to be proceeded with, it is usually put out for a preliminary hearing on the apparent disqualification. In such a situation the respondent is usually informed that it is unnecessary for him to be present at the preliminary hearing.[6]

Tribunals have a wide discretion in the matter of amendment, and provided that the originating application contains the basic information required by r. 1(1) and was presented timeously, the tribunal may make use of this power to enable an applicant to vary or extend the grounds of his claim or bring in or substitute new or additional parties as respondents, with a view to avoiding hardship or injustice.[7]

(2) Cases under the Industrial Tribunals (Scotland) Regulations 1965 (as amended), Sched. 2

An appeal against assessment to levy is instituted by the appellant

4 See Chap. 6 under "Orders for Particulars" at pp. 106 to 108.

5 See *Barley and Ors.* v. *Amey Roadstone Corporation Ltd.* (1976) 11 I.T.R. 283.

6 See Chap. 7 below under "Preliminary Hearings" at pp. 160 to 162.

7 See Chap. 7 below under "Amendments" at pp. 162 to 164.

sending to the board[8], in duplicate, a notice of appeal in the form prescribed in the regulations, setting out the grounds of appeal (rule 1). The various statutory orders relating to the levying of assessments prescribe time limits for appealing. In *Altmiths Ltd.* v. *Construction Industry Training Board* (1966) 1 I.T.R. 42 it was held that the time limit ran from the date on which the notice of assessment to levy was served on the appellants, and not from the actual date of the notice itself. In the earlier statutory orders there was no power to extend the time limit, which led to it being held in a number of cases under those orders[9] that the tribunal's power under r. 10(1) to extend the time for doing any act, notwithstanding that the time appointed may have expired, applied only to a time appointed by the rules, and thus that appeals out of time could not be considered. But the present form of levy order confers power on the industrial training board and the like power on the industrial tribunal "for good cause" to allow an appeal to be taken up to four months after the date of service of the assessment notice, or even longer.[10]

(3) **Cases under the Industrial Tribunals (Improvement and Prohibition Notices Appeals) (Scotland) Regulations 1974**

An appeal is commenced by the applicant sending to the Secretary of the Tribunals a written notice of appeal setting out:

(*a*) the name of the appellant and his address for the service of documents;

(*b*) the date of the improvement notice or prohibition notice appealed against and the address of the premises or place concerned;

(*c*) the name and address of the respondent;

(*d*) particulars of the requirements or directions appealed against; and

(*e*) the grounds of the appeal (rule 1).

The notice must be sent (see (5) below) to the Secretary of the Tribunals within 21 days from the date of the service on the appellant of the notice appealed against (rule 2(1)). But a tribunal may extend the time limit where it is satisfied on an application made in writing to the Secretary, either before or after the expiration of the time limit, that it is not or was not reasonably practicable for an appeal to be brought within that time (rule 2(2))[11]. (For the meaning of "reasonably practicable" see Chapter

---

8 *I.e.* The respondent industrial training board (reg. 2(1)).

9 See *C. & A. Clark (Ossett) Ltd.* v. *Wool Industry Training Board* (1966) 1 I.T.R. 19; *Imperial Engineering Motor Works* v. *Engineering Industry Training Board* (1967) 2 I.T.R. 2; *T. & J. Shaw Ltd.* v. *Road Transport Industry Training Board* (1968) 3 I.T.R. 337.

10 See the Industrial Training Levy (Construction Board) Order 1980 (S.I. 1980/1545).

11 The granting of such an extension cannot be done by the President or a Chairman alone, but must be referred to a full tribunal (see r. 14(3)).

4, p. 46). The bringing of an appeal suspends the operation of an improvement notice, but only suspends the operation of a prohibition notice if the tribunal so directs, on an application by the appellant[12] (Health and Safety at Work etc. Act 1974, s. 24(3)).

(4) Cases under the Industrial Tribunals (Non-Discrimination Notices Appeals) (Scotland) Regulations 1977

An appeal must be commenced not later than six weeks after service of the non-discrimination notice by the appellant sending (see (5) below) to the Secretary of the Tribunals[13] a written notice of appeal setting out:

(*a*) the name of the appellant and his address for the service of documents;
(*b*) the date of the non-discrimination notice appealed against;
(*c*) the name and address of the respondent;
(*d*) particulars of the requirements appealed against; and
(*e*) the grounds of the appeal (rule 1).

In these rules there is no provision enabling a tribunal to extend this time limit. It would seem that if the position is to be compared with that in cases under the Industrial Tribunals (Scotland) Regulations 1965 (as amended) (see under (2) above) the tribunal's general power under r. 12(1) to regulate its own procedure, subject to the provisions of the rules, could not be used to grant such an extension.[14]

(5) General

Whereas in the Industrial Tribunals Rules of Procedure (Scotland) 1980 the originating application requires to be "presented", the date of presentation being the date of receipt by the Secretary, and not the date on which it is sent to the Secretary,[15] in cases under the other rules the notice of appeal is to be "sent" within the prescribed time limit. No doubt with a view to eliminating any doubt as to the date on which the notice was sent, these rules provide that recorded delivery shall be used (unless, in cases under the 1974 or 1977 rules, the notice of appeal is delivered[16]). These provisions are directory and not mandatory, and a

---

12 As to which see Chap. 6, p. 119.

13 For the address to which the notice of appeal should be sent, see (5) below.

14 For the extent to which light may be thrown upon a statutory provision by other statutory provisions, see Craies on *Statute Law*, 7th ed., p. 133 *et seq*. See also Chap. 6, p. 120.

15 See *Hammond* v. *Haigh Castle & Co. Ltd.* [1973] I.C.R. 148, and Chap. 4, p. 46.

16 The Industrial Tribunals Regulations (Scotland) 1965 (as amended) Sched. 2, r. 16(1); the Industrial Tribunals (Improvement and Prohibition Notices Appeals) (Scotland) Regulations 1974, r. 15(3); the Industrial Tribunals (Non-Discrimination Notices Appeals) (Scotland) Regulations 1977, r. 13(3).

notice of appeal received by ordinary post within the time limit would not be incompetent merely on the ground that it had not been sent by recorded delivery. But if the notice of appeal were to go astray, the appellant would be in difficulties if he could not produce evidence that it had been sent by recorded delivery within the prescribed time.[17]

Documents directed to the Secretary of the Tribunals should be sent to "the office of the tribunals" (*i.e.* as defined in reg. 2, the Central Office, and not an area office) unless the Secretary notifies the parties that they should be sent to another office under r. 17(2) of the 1980 rules.[18]

ACTION ON RECEIPT OF ORIGINATING APPLICATION OR NOTICE OF APPEAL

(1) **Cases under the Industrial Tribunals Rules of Procedure (Scotland) 1980**

Rule 2 provides that on receiving an originating application (and subject of course to what is said above about Rule 1 letters) it is the duty of the Secretary to enter the application in the Register[19] and send a copy to the respondent (but where the respondent is a foreign or commonwealth state, to the Ministry of Foreign Affairs of the State through the Foreign and Commonwealth Office—State Immunity Act 1978, s. 12(1)). In reg. 2 of the 1980 regulations "respondent" is defined as meaning a party to the proceedings before the tribunal other than the applicant, and other than the Secretary of State in proceedings under Pts. III and VI of the 1978 Act in which he is not cited as the person against whom relief is sought. In proceedings under s. 51 of the Docks and Harbours Act 1966 the expression "party" means the National Dock Labour Board as reconstituted under the Dock Work Regulation Act 1976, or the licensing authority or any party undernoted.[20]

The Secretary must also inform the parties in writing of the case number of the application entered in the Register (which thereafter constitutes the title of the proceedings) and of the address to which notices and other communications to the Secretary shall be sent. Every copy of the application so sent must be accompanied by a written notice which includes information, as appropriate to the case, about the

---

17 See also Chap. 6 under "Notices etc.", at p. 127.

18 See also Chap. 4, p. 46.

19 *I.e.* The Register of Applications and Decisions (misspelt in reg. 2 of the 1980 regulations).

20 *I.e.* a body having the function of issuing licences under the 1966 Act. The expression also means any person with whom it appears to the applicant that he is in dispute about a question to which that section applies and, in a case where such a question is referred to a tribunal by a sheriff, any party to the proceedings before the court in which the question arose.

means and times for entering appearance, the consequences of failure to do so, and the right to receive a copy of the decision. It has been held that the proceedings were not invalidated by failure on the part of the Central Office of the Tribunals in England to send a copy of an originating application to a respondent.[21]

Rule 2 also provides that in all cases in which the statutory provisions provide for conciliation, the Secretary must also notify the parties that the services of a conciliation officer are available to them. In all such cases he must also send a copy of the originating application to an appropriate conciliation officer, and in proceedings which may involve payments out of the Redundancy Fund or the Maternity Pay Fund, he must also send a copy to the Secretary of State for Employment, notwithstanding the fact that he may not be a party to such proceedings (r. 17(7) and (8)).[22]

Where, without objection by the respondent, an amendment was made at the hearing to include a claim of unfair dismissal in an originating application, an appeal on the ground that the rule in force at the time concerning the sending of documents to a conciliation officer had not been complied with was dismissed on the ground that the omission did not invalidate the proceedings, and that the respondent by consenting to the amendment had waived his right to object.[23]

(2) **Cases under the Industrial Tribunals (Scotland) (Amendment) Regulations 1965 (as amended), Sched. 2**

Rule 2 (1) provides that subject to r. 3, referred to below, and r. 4 (which provides for withdrawal of an appeal at any time), within 21 days from receipt of the notice of appeal the respondent board shall send to the Secretary of the Tribunals:

(*a*) one copy of the notice of appeal;
(*b*) a copy of the assessment notice and of any notice by the board allowing further time for appealing;
(*c*) a notice giving the board's address for service, where that address is different from the address specified in the assessment notice; and
(*d*) any representations in writing relating to the appeal that the board may then desire to submit to the tribunal.

But r. 3(1) to (3) provides that where the board requires further particulars of the grounds on which the appellant intends to rely and of the facts and contentions relative thereto, it must send to the appellant within 21 days from the receipt of the notice of appeal, a notice

21 *Gosport Working Mens and Trade Union Club Ltd.* v. *Taylor, supra.*
22 See also Chap. 6, "Notices, etc" at p. 128.
23 *Sheringham Development Company Ltd.* v. *Browne* [1977] I.C.R. 21.

specifying the further particulars required, which the appellant must supply, in duplicate, within a further period of 21 days, or such longer period as the board may allow.

Rule 3(4) and (5) provides that within 21 days of receiving such further particulars the board must send to the Secretary of the Tribunals:

(*a*) the document specified in r. 2;
(*b*) a copy of the notice requiring the further particulars;
(*c*) such further particulars, and any representations in writing with respect thereto that the board may then desire to submit to the tribunal.

But if the further particulars are not received in time, the board must send the documents mentioned in (*a*) and (*b*) above to the Secretary of the Tribunals not later than the fiftieth day after the receipt of the notice of appeal by the board, or, if the board has allowed a further period of time for delivery of further particulars in terms of r. 3(3), not later than the seventh day after the expiration of such period.

Rule 2(2) provides that failure to comply with any of the foregoing provisions shall not render the appeal or anything done in pursuance thereof invalid.

Rule 5 provides that on receipt of the relevant documents from the board the Secretary of the Tribunals is to enter particulars of the appeal in the Register of Appeals; give notice to the appellant and to the board of the case number of the appeal (which shall thereafter constitute the title of the appeal) and give the address to which notices and other communications to the Secretary shall be sent; give notice to the appellant of the board's address for service under the rules; and send to the appellant a copy of any representations in writing which the board has submitted to the tribunal under r. 2 or 3.

(3) Cases under the Industrial Tribunals (Improvement and Prohibition Notices Appeals) (Scotland) Regulations 1974 and under the Industrial Tribunals (Non-Discrimination Notices Appeals) (Scotland) Regulations 1977

Upon receiving a notice of appeal the Secretary of the Tribunals is to enter particulars of it in the Register,[24] send a copy of the notice to the respondent, and inform the parties in writing of the case number of the appeal (which thereafter constitutes the title of the proceedings) and of the address to which notices and other communications to the Secretary shall be sent (1974 regulations, r. 3; 1977 regulations, r. 2).

---

[24] Defined in reg. 2(2) of each of the regulations as the Register kept in pursuance of the Industrial Tribunals (Labour Relations) (Scotland) Regulations 1974. This is now the Register kept in pursuance of the Industrial Tribunals (Rules of Procedure) (Scotland) Regulations 1980 (see p. 94 above).

APPEARANCE BY RESPONDENT

The provisions referred to below apply only to cases under the Industrial Tribunals Rules of Procedure (Scotland) 1980. Under the other rules of procedure there is no duty on the respondent to enter an appearance, except that under the 1965 regulations the respondent board has to take certain action, as noted above, on receipt of the notice of appeal; that apart, the respondent in such proceedings may submit representations in writing,[25] but is not obliged to do so.

(1) **Entering appearance**

Rule 3(1) of the Industrial Tribunals Rules of Procedure (Scotland) 1980 provides that the respondent must enter appearance within 14 days of receiving a copy of the originating application.[26] This is done by presenting to the Secretary of the Tribunals a written notice of appearance (Form I.T.3)[27] setting out his full name and address and stating whether or not he intends to resist the application, and if so setting out sufficient particulars to show on what grounds. In practice an I.T.3 is forwarded with the copy originating application for completion by the respondent. As in the case of the originating application (see above, p. 94), the notice of appearance should be sent to the Central Office, unless the Secretary of the Tribunals has notified parties that it should be sent to another office (see r. 17(2)), and the date on which the notice of appearance is presented is the date on which it is received at the Central Office or any such other office as the Secretary may have notified.

On receipt of the notice of appearance, the Secretary must send a copy to any other party.[28] As in the case of the I.T.1, when completing a notice of appearance careful attention should be given to the questions asked, and for the reasons explained at p. 89 above, the replies should be as full and accurate as possible. As much detail as possible should be given of the facts and grounds relied on in resisting the application, or on a separate sheet if the space provided is insufficient. In an unfair dismissal case, merely to say "The applicant was dismissed for misconduct and dismissal was reasonable in the circumstances" is of no assistance. It is emphasised that where dismissal is denied, an indica-

---

25 The Industrial Tribunals (Scotland) Regulations 1965 (as amended), Sched. 2, r. 2(1); the Industrial Tribunals (Improvement and Prohibition Notices Appeals) (Scotland) Regulations 1974, r. 8; the Industrial Tribunals (Non-Discrimination Notices Appeals) (Scotland) Regulations 1977, r. 6.

26 But in proceedings against a foreign or commonwealth state the period is two months (State Immunity Act 1978, s. 12(2)).

27 Appendix 3.

28 Rule 3(1).

tion should also be given as to what position the respondent would adopt if the tribunal finds that there has been a dismissal.[29] This is a point which is all too often neglected: it is by no means inevitable that a finding that there was a dismissal will be conclusive of the merits of the case. Similarly, when there is any doubt whether the reason for dismissal falls within the four categories stated in s. 57(2) of the Employment Protection (Consolidation) Act 1978, an alternative case under s. 57(1)(*b*) ("some other substantial reason") should be taken (see *Vickers* v. *Warsop Constitutional Club,* referred to in Chapter 7, at p. 165).

The originating application should be carefully scrutinised and any inaccuracies in it pointed out. Consideration should be given to whether the applicant is qualified for the remedy he seeks, and any points which would exclude the jurisdiction of the tribunal (*e.g.* that the application is time-barred or the applicant disqualified in any other way) should be taken.

Respondents should use the I.T.3 form which is sent to them with the originating application, but any document complying with the basic requirement of r. 3(1) qualifies as a notice of appearance. The requirement to state the ground of resistance has been held in England to be directory and not mandatory.[30] In any event, if the notice is deficient in that respect, the tribunal has power under r. 4(1) to require the respondent to furnish further particulars.[31]

Sometimes the applicant does not correctly designate the employer in the originating application. When that happens most respondents complete the notice of appearance to show the correct designation, in which case the originating application is amended accordingly. Where, however, a respondent on whom an originating application has been served enters appearance in his own name and pleads that he is not the applicant's employer, and should not have been made a party to the proceedings, the Secretary has to take the matter up with the applicant. If it cannot be satisfactorily resolved, a preliminary hearing would have to be arranged to investigate and deal with the point.[32] Tribunals will not give effect to objections of a merely technical nature, however (*e.g.* the omission of "limited" from the title of a company). It has been held in England that the approach to such questions should be similar to that in the High Court, namely to consider if the mistake was genuine and was not misleading or such as to cause any unreasonable doubt as to the identity of the party intended to be sued.[33]

---

29 See Chap. 7, p. 164.

30 *Seldrun Transport Services Ltd.* v. *Baker* [1978] I.C.R. 1035.

31 See Chap. 6, pp. 106 to 108.

32 See Chap. 7 under "Amendments" at p. 164.

33 See *Fellows* v. *Rock Rippers Ltd.* (1973) 8 I.T.R. 348.

(2) **Late appearances**

A notice of appearance received after the expiry of the prescribed period of 14 days can only be received at the discretion of the tribunal. It is deemed to include an application under r. 13(1) for an extension of the time appointed for entering appearance, but the extension is not to be refused without giving the person wishing to enter an appearance an opportunity to show why the extension should be granted. If the tribunal grants the application the Secretary of the Tribunals must then send a copy of the notice of appearance to any other party.[34]

In practice, where a respondent fails to enter appearance within the prescribed time, the Secretary sends him a letter by recorded delivery post, reminding him of the consequences of failure and allowing a further seven days in which to do so. If the respondent sends in a notice of appearance within the extended time stated in the letter, his deemed application for extension of time is granted without further enquiry. If he does not, the case is thereafter treated as one in which no appearance has been entered, with the consequences set out below, and any subsequent attempt on the part of the respondent to enter an appearance is referred to a Chairman for consideration, the respondent being given the opportunity to show cause why the extension should be granted.

In the Scottish case of *Thompson* v. *Davie* (EAT, 14/6/77), where the attempt to enter appearance was not made until the hearing, to which the respondent had been cited to attend as a witness, it was stated that tribunals should be slow to deny a respondent the opportunity to enter appearance. Where (as is more usually the case) the matter arises prior to the hearing, it is for the Chairman to whom it is referred to decide whether or not to allow the notice of appearance to be received. He has to weigh up all the relevant circumstances and considerations. The question of possible prejudice to the applicant is an important factor. In that connection, if the application is made after a hearing has been arranged, which would have to be postponed, it may be granted only on such conditions as to expenses as may be appropriate in terms of r. 11(2).[35] Where the respondent is professionally represented, less latitude may be extended than those in the case of an unrepresented party, and the Chairman will take the conduct of the representative into account, as well as the conduct of the respondent himself. In a case involving over 90 applications, where the respondent (a receiver) applied for leave to enter appearance after five representative cases had been decided against him, and was only given leave in cases where appearance would have been in time if entered on the day the repre-

---

[34] Rule 3(3).

[35] See Chap. 7 below under "Adjournments", at pp. 166 to 167.

sentative cases were heard, the refusal of leave in the other cases was upheld.[36] On the other hand, a case where a wide indulgence was granted is *St Mungo Community Trust* v. *Colleano* [1980] I.C.R. 254, where the respondent did not apply for leave to enter appearance out of time until after the industrial tribunal had actually heard the case and their decision awarding the employee compensation for unfair dismissal had been promulgated. The Chairman refused to consider the application on the ground that having reached a decision the industrial tribunal was *"functus officii"* in the proceedings (*i.e.* its function was completed). It was held that r. 3(3) in the 1974 rules (which in this respect was no different from r. 3(3) of the 1980 rules) contained no restrictions as to time for applying for an extension of time, and that the Chairman's decision to refuse it on that ground was therefore wrong. But, not surprisingly, the qualification was added that there must inevitably be a very heavy burden on a respondent who applies for an extension of time in such circumstances in order to justify his application.

(3) **Respondents who do not enter appearance**

Rule 3(2) provides that a respondent who has not entered appearance is not entitled to take any part in the proceedings except:

- (i) to apply under r. 13(1) for an extension of the time appointed for entering an appearance;
- (ii) to make an application under r. 4(1)(*i*) (*i.e.* for further particulars[37]);
- (iii) to make an application under r. 10(2) in respect of r. 10(1)(*b*) (*i.e.* an application for review of the tribunal's decision on the ground that the respondent did not receive notice of the proceedings leading to the decision[38]);
- (iv) to be called as a witness by any person; and
- (v) to be sent a copy of a decision or specification of reasons or corrected decision or specification in pursuance of r. 9(3), 9(7) or 10(5).[39]

In particular, as was specified in the rules which were in force before the 1980 rules,[40] such a respondent cannot:

---

36 *Ryan Plant International* v. *Price* [1976] I.C.R. 424.

37 This provision is intended to assist the respondent, who, within the time allowed for entering appearance, seeks to obtain further particulars of the grounds on which the originating application is based, to enable him to prepare his defence. It is not intended for use as a delaying tactic by a respondent who has failed to enter appearance within the prescribed period.

38 See Chap. 11, p. 244.

39 See Chap. 9, pp. 194, 224.

40 *I.e.* in the Industrial Tribunals (Labour Relations) (Scotland) Regulations 1974.

(*a*) make an application under r. 4 for recovery of documents or witness orders;
(*b*) submit representations for consideration by the tribunal under r. 7(3);
(*c*) be heard or represented at the hearing under r. 8 (although, of course, he is at liberty to attend it, as a member of the public);
(*d*) apply for directions under r. 13(2) or receive a notice of any extension of time under r. 11(2) and 13(4); or
(*e*) make an application for review under r. 10 except, as noted above, under r. 10(1)(*b*).

ARRANGING THE HEARING

The date, time and place of the hearing are fixed by the President, the Regional Chairman or a nominated Chairman. It is the duty of the Secretary of the Tribunals to send each party a written notice of hearing. In cases under the Industrial Tribunals Rules of Procedure (Scotland) 1980 (rule 5(1)), the Industrial Tribunals (Improvement and Prohibition Notices Appeals) (Scotland) Regulations 1974 (rule 6(1)) and the Industrial Tribunals (Non-Discrimination Notices Appeals) (Scotland) Regulations 1977 (rule 4(1)), the notice must be sent at least 14 days before the date of the hearing, or within such shorter time as may be agreed by the Secretary with the parties, and must include information and guidance as to attendance at the hearing, witnesses and the bringing of documents (if any), representation by another person and written representations. In cases under the Industrial Tribunals (Scotland) Regulations 1965 (as amended), Sched. 2, there is no provision for notice of less than 14 days and the form of notice is prescribed in the rules (rule 8).

The notice of hearing contains detailed instructions to parties about requirements in the way of witnesses and documents and the like and its contents should be carefully noted and complied with.[41]

In order to minimise questions as to whether parties have had due notice of the hearing, the notice of hearing is invariably sent by recorded delivery, and a copy is sent to a respondent who has not entered an appearance for purposes of information only.[42]

In proceedings under the Docks and Harbours Act 1966, the President or the Regional Chairman may direct the Secretary to take any one or more of the following steps, namely—

(*a*) advertise the hearing in the press;

---

[41] See Appendix 4.

[42] See Chap. 6 under "Notices etc.", p. 127, and Chap. 11, p. 244.

(*b*) send notice of the hearing to such persons as may be directed;
(*c*) post notices of the hearing conspicuously in the locality of the port in questions.

The requirements as to the period of notice contained in r. 5(1) do not apply to any such notices (1980 rules, r. 5(2)).

The place appointed for the hearing is usually the Central Office or one of the other offices,[43] but it may be at the home of a witness who is unwell or housebound,[44] or at the respondents' premises if the tribunal considers that an inspection is necessary,[45] or the tribunal may sit in any other locality if this would be more convenient, and particularly if it would result in a saving of expenses to parties or public funds. The type of case in which this may take place is where all the parties, witnesses and representatives are situated in the islands or a part of the mainland which is remote from any office of the tribunals, but such arrangements are rarely made in practice. A party who wishes the hearing to take place at any location other than a tribunal office should make a written request to the Secretary at the earliest possible opportunity.

If the case is to be heard at or in a locality served by one of the area offices, the case file is transferred from the Central Office to the area office concerned after the notice of appearance has been lodged, or the time for doing so has expired. The area office proceeds to make the arrangements for the hearing, and deals with all procedural matters from then until the tribunal's written decision has been signed by the Chairman. The case file is then returned to the Central Office, which deals with the promulgation of the decision,[46] and retains the file. If further procedure is required (*e.g.* if an application for review is made, or if the case is directed by an appellate court to be re-heard), the file is returned to the area office, which deals with it up to the stage of promulgation of the tribunal's further decision.

As regards the date of the hearing, in order to minimise applications for postponement, before the date is fixed a letter (generally called a "date letter") is sent to parties or their representatives stating a period within which it is proposed to bring out the case for hearing, and asking them to reply within 14 days, stating any dates within the period proposed which are not suitable. The letter contains a warning that any applications for postponement after the notice of hearing has been issued will only be granted in exceptional circumstances.

The hearing date is fixed in the light of the reply which is received, and parties are advised by postcard before the notice of hearing is

43 See Chap. 3, pp. 26, 27.

44 See Chap. 7, under "Witnesses who cannot attend", at pp. 154, 155.

45 See Chap. 7 under "Inspection", at p. 160.

46 See Chap. 9, under "Intimation and Promulgation", at pp. 194, 195.

issued. Any application for postponement made after the issue of the postcard is referred to a Chairman. It is therefore of considerable importance to reply to the date letter within the time prescribed, and before doing so to enquire as to the availability not only of the party concerned and his representatives, but also of all potential witnesses, in order to minimise the risk of having to apply for a postponement, which is a matter within the discretion of the Chairman to whom it is referred.[47]

The date letter also asks parties to say if the case is likely to take longer than half a day. Regrettably, this request is all too often ignored, even in cases in which it should be obvious that the hearing may take a full day or longer, with the result that unnecessary adjournments have to take place. When this happens it is seldom that the case can be continued on the next day, and sometimes there has to be a gap of several weeks before the adjourned hearing takes place. This is not conducive to the proper administration of justice, nor does it make for convenience. Parties and their representatives can greatly facilitate the administration of the system by giving the tribunal office an estimate, approximate though it can only be, of the potential extent of their evidence and of the case as a whole when replying to the date letter. In doing so, it is better to over-estimate than under-estimate.

APPOINTMENT OF ASSESSORS

In cases in which provision is made for the appointment of an assessor or assessors,[48] the appointment is made by the President, the Regional Chairman or a nominated Chairman at the stage when the hearing is to be arranged.[49]

---

47 See Chap. 6 under "Extensions of time and postponements" at pp. 120, 121.

48 See Chap. 3 under "Assessors", at pp. 24, 25.

49 The Industrial Tribunals Rules of Procedure (Scotland) 1980, r. 5(3); the Industrial Tribunals (Improvement and Prohibition Notices Appeals) (Scotland) Regulations 1974, r. 6(3).

CHAPTER 6

INCIDENTAL PROCEDURE

GENERAL

This chapter is concerned with incidental procedural matters, other than those already referred to in Chapters 4 and 5, and with the disposal of cases in situations which do not require them to be heard by a tribunal. Many of the orders made on these matters fall within the description "interlocutory", the meaning and significance of which are explained in Chapter 9 (p. 192). But, as explained there, that classification can be anomalous when related to certain aspects of actual practice. Except where otherwise noted, in respect of all the matters mentioned in this chapter the powers of a tribunal can be and normally are exercised by the President or a Chairman sitting alone in chambers (usually a Chairman), unless the matter occurs in the course of a hearing before a full tribunal, or where the rules require them to be exercised by a full tribunal.

The policy of industrial tribunals with regard to interlocutory matters in Scotland and England and Wales was summarised in *Stone* v. *Charrington & Co. Ltd.* (EAT 15/2/77) (unreported) as follows:

> "Having regard to the fact that industrial tribunals are intended to deal with matters, so far as possible, speedily, simply and cheaply, the general policy is to seek to avoid making interlocutory orders, such as orders for discovery, save in so far as they appear to be genuinely necessary in order to do justice between the parties."

This approach was approved by the House of Lords in *Science Research Council* v. *Nassé* [1979] I.C.R. 921.

Incidental orders may be made on the application of a party or, where the rules so provide, by the tribunal of its own motion. The rules require most applications by a party to be made in writing to the Secretary of the Tribunals, and this should in fact be done in every case, except only where, for sufficient reason, an application for postponement or adjournment has to be made on the eve of a hearing, either because of an emergency or a last minute settlement. In that event application may be made by telephone to the tribunal office, but where the reason is a last minute settlement the hearing will not be cancelled until the other side have been contacted to confirm that there has been a settlement. An application in writing should state clearly the nature of the application and the ground upon which it is made; the relevant rules of procedure should also be referred to. Although the rules may allow an incidental application to be made at the hearing itself this should only be done when some unforeseeable development occurs at the hearing. Normally an incidental application should be made as far in advance of the hearing as possible, to allow adequate time for the making of the order and for compliance with it. If an application comes too late for this purpose it may be refused or, if granted, and an adjournment becomes necessary, the party making the application may be found liable in the expenses occasioned by the adjournment.

Certain matters must be intimated to the parties or other persons concerned, so that they may show cause why the proposed order should not be made. In other cases the rules confer a discretion on the tribunal to direct intimation to the opposite party. These provisions are noted in context below. Where opposition is to be taken, it should be made in writing to the Secretary of the Tribunals, stating the grounds in full. Otherwise incidental applications are dealt with *ex parte, i.e.* on the basis of the information supplied and without hearing parties. If the information supplied is inadequate further information may have to be called for.

Most incidental matters are then disposed of by correspondence, taking into account the reasons given for the application, and any reasons submitted for opposing it. But where the Chairman considers that the matter is too complex to be dealt with in this way he may direct an interlocutory hearing on the matter in chambers, either on an *ex parte* basis or (where the application is opposed) with both parties present or represented. In complex or multiple cases an interlocutory hearing may also be directed to discuss and settle procedural points in advance of the hearing.

The decision of the Chairman on an interlocutory matter is communicated to the parties by letter from the Secretary of the Tribunals to those concerned. Where an incidental application is refused *ex parte* only the person making the application is notified. In other cases notification is made in writing to all concerned, who may include third parties. Where orders for particulars and document or witness orders are made, these are signed by the Chairman and sent by the Secretary to the parties or persons against whom the order is made. Where an application is refused, or if an application is granted after opposition, or an order is being made of the tribunal's own motion, the Chairman's reasons for making the order are specified in full, either in the Secretary's letter or in a separate document.[1] Orders disposing of proceedings are signed by the Chairman.

An interlocutory order is, by definition,[2] not a "decision" of a tribunal. While therefore it is recorded in the case file, it is not entered

---

1 See *ASTMS* v. *Mucci* (1973) 8 I.T.R. 118.

2 See reg. 2 of each of the procedural regulations.

in the Register of Decisions, and is not open to review under the rules which empower a tribunal to review its decision (see Chapter 11, p. 244). But there are provisions in the rules, which are noted below in context, enabling orders for particulars and document and witness orders to be varied or set aside on application being made to that effect. And in practice other interlocutory orders made *ex parte* may be recalled or varied by virtue of the general power of tribunals to regulate their own procedure if new or additional facts and circumstances are disclosed which would have affected the making of the order. An interlocutory order is also appealable if it can be said to involve a question of law (see Chapter 12, p. 257).

An order by the President or a Chairman which disposes of proceedings is a decision and as such is entered in the Register of Decisions. It is therefore open to review or appeal.

ORDERS FOR PARTICULARS

(1) **Under the Industrial Tribunals Rules of Procedure (Scotland) 1980**

Rule 4(1) provides that a tribunal may require a party to furnish in writing to "the person specified by the tribunal" (which appears to include the tribunal itself) "further particulars of the grounds on which he or it relies and of any facts and contentions relevant thereto." The order may be made on the application of a party to the proceedings (other than a respondent who has not entered appearance) or of the tribunal's own motion. Where application is made by a party, the tribunal may require him to give notice of the application to the other parties, indicating how objection may be made.

Generally speaking, such applications are not encouraged.[3] In *White* v. *University of Manchester* [1976] I.C.R. 419 the Employment Appeal Tribunal said unnecessary legalism was to be avoided, but a party was entitled to know in reasonable detail what allegations he has to meet. *International Computers Ltd.* v. *Whitley, supra* is an example of a case where an order was upheld: the employers were seeking specification of allegations by the employee that they had condoned the making of fraudulent claims by him. The tribunal's power to make an order for particulars of its own motion will be used where the information disclosed in the originating application or notice of appearance does not give a sufficient indication of the issues and it appears desirable to have them better identified, *e.g.* to enable a view to be formed on an application for a document order or a witness order. But a letter from

---

[3] See *Rajguru* v. *Top Order Ltd.* [1978] I.C.R. 565; *International Computers Ltd.* v. *Whitley* [1978] I.R.L.R. 318.

the Secretary of the Tribunals to the party concerned under the provisions of the rules which empower him to call for further particulars of an originating application or notice of appearance (see Chapter 5, p. 91) will often make it unnecessary to make formal orders for particulars under r. 4.

An order for particulars should not be just an order to supply "further and better particulars". It should specify as precisely as possible what information is to be provided. An application for such an order should state correspondingly precisely what information is required. While some generalisation may be unavoidable, the generality itself should be stated as exactly as possible. The order will also specify within what time limit the information is to be provided.

Rule 4(2) provides that a party on whom an order for particulars has been made on an *ex parte* application, or of the tribunal's own motion, may apply to the tribunal by notice to the Secretary of the Tribunals to vary or set aside the order. The application must be made before the time for compliance, and notice of the application must be given to the other parties and, in proceedings which may involve payments out of the Redundancy Fund or Maternity Pay Fund, to the Secretary of State if not a party. Any such application would be dealt with in the same way as an objection taken in advance to an interlocutory order (see above, p. 105).

Rule 4(4) provides that if an order for particulars is not complied with, the tribunal may dismiss the originating application, or, as the case may be, strike out the whole or part of a notice of appearance, and where appropriate, direct that a respondent shall be debarred from defending altogether. Before such action is taken notice must be given to the party who has not complied with the requirement giving him an opportunity to show cause why such should not be done. This requirement (which was not in the previous rules) reflects the decision in *Morrit* v. *London Borough of Lambeth* (EAT 244/79) that it was "Draconian" to stop a case from being heard on its merits because of a procedural failure where no prior warning has been given, especially where the party was unrepresented. An order to dismiss an originating application on these grounds would dispose of the proceedings and be a decision of the tribunal. But an order to strike out a notice of appearance or debar a respondent from defending would be treated as an interlocutory order.

(2) **Under the Industrial Tribunals (Scotland) Regulations 1965 (as amended), Sched. 2**

Further particulars may be required from the appellant by the respondent industrial training board by r. 3. The provisions of the rule are referred to in Chapter 5 (see pp. 95, 96).

If the appellant fails to send to the board further particulars in accordance with a notice under r. 3, r. 6(1) provides that on application by the board the tribunal may direct the appellant to supply the further particulars called for by the board, which are to be sent in duplicate to the Secretary of the Tribunals, one copy to be sent by him to the board. If the appellant fails to comply with such a direction the tribunal may on the application of the board dismiss the appeal or give such other directions as may seem proper. There is no requirement that notice be given to the appellant before this is done, but the principle in *Morrit* v. *London Borough of Lambeth, supra* would apply.

Rule 6(4) provides that the tribunal may direct the board to furnish particulars relating to the assessment which appear to be requisite for the decision of the appeal, a copy of which must also be sent to the appellant.

(3) **Under other rules**

Under the Industrial Tribunals (Improvement and Prohibition Notices Appeals) (Scotland) Regulations 1974 (r. 5) and the Industrial Tribunals (Non-Discrimination Notices Appeals) (Scotland) Regulations 1977 (r. 3), the tribunal has similar powers to those in the 1980 rules, but there is no express provision for the tribunal to make an order of its own motion. Application may be made to vary or set aside the order, but such an application cannot be entertained unless made before the expiration of the time appointed for compliance. Neither rule lays down any sanction for non-compliance.

DOCUMENT AND WITNESS ORDERS

(1) **General**

The enabling legislation (Employment Protection (Consolidation) Act 1978, Sched. 9, para. 1(2)(*d*) and (*e*)) provides for granting to any person "such recovery or inspection of documents as might be granted by the sheriff" and for requiring persons to attend to give evidence and to produce documents.

Rule 4(1) of the Industrial Tribunals Rules of Procedure (Scotland) 1980 provides that a tribunal may—

(i) [Relates to orders for particulars, discussed above];

(ii) Grant to the person making the application such a commission and diligence for the recovery or inspection (including the taking of copies) of documents as might be granted by a sheriff; and

(iii) Require the attendance of any person (including a party to the proceedings) as a witness or require the production of any document relating to the matter to be determined, wherever such witness may be within Great Britain (N.B. not the U.K.).

An order under r. 4(1)(ii) and (iii) may be made on the application of a party to the proceedings, but there is no provision for one to be made on the tribunal's own motion. The provisions of r. 12(3) as to intimation to other parties applies, as to an application for an order for particulars (see above, p. 105). A party on whom an *ex parte* order has been made under paragraph (ii), and any person on whom an *ex parte* order has been made under paragraph (iii) of r. 4(1), may apply under r. 4(2) to have the order varied or set aside. The provisions of r. 4(2) as to the time in which such application may be made and as to notice to other parties also apply as they do to an application to vary or set aside an order for particulars (see above).

Failure to comply with an order under paragraph (ii) of r. 4(1) may attract the same sanction for non-compliance under r. 4(4) as failure to comply with an order for particulars (see p. 107). In addition, any person who without reasonable cause fails to comply with any witness or document order made under r. 4(1)(ii) or (iii) is liable on summary conviction to a fine not exceeding £100,[4] and this must be stated in any such order (r. 4(3)).

As already explained (see p. 105), document and witness orders are signed by the President or a Chairman. They are served by recorded delivery post, as required by r. 17(5).

The other rules contain provisions in broadly similar terms to those of r. 4 of the 1980 rules. The relevant rules are r. 7 in the Industrial Tribunals (Scotland) Regulations 1965 (as amended), Sched. 2; r. 5 in the Industrial Tribunals (Improvement and Prohibition Notices Appeals) (Scotland) Regulations 1974; and r. 3 in the Industrial Tribunals (Non-Discrimination Notices Appeals) (Scotland) Regulations 1977. There are some minor differences. The right to apply to vary or set aside an order is not confined to orders made *ex parte*, except in the case of a document order under r. 7 in the 1965 rules. Under those rules notice of any such application must be given to the party on whose application the order was made, but not under the 1974 or 1977 rules. Under both of the latter rules production may not be ordered of a document if the Secretary of State certifies that production would be against the interests of national security. There are no other sanctions for non-compliance, apart from the appropriate statutory fine.

(2) **Document orders**

Orders for recovery and inspection of documents are made under para. (ii) of r. 4(1) of the Industrial Tribunals Rules of Procedure (Scot-

4 But a foreign or commonwealth state is immune (State Immunity Act 1978, s. 13(1)).

land) 1980 and its equivalents in the other rules (see (1) above). Orders for production of documents at a hearing or to a diet of commission (see below) are made under para. (iii) of r. 4(1), and its equivalent in the other rules. This reflects the wording of the rules themselves and the enabling provisions of para. 1 of Sched. 9 to the 1978 Act referred to in (1) above.

The documents which a sheriff may order to be recovered by diligence, and recovery of which may therefore be ordered by an industrial tribunal under para. (ii) of r. 4(1), are those founded on by the parties in their pleadings or which are deemed "relevant to the cause" (Sheriff Courts (Scotland) Act 1907 (as amended), Sched. 1, rr. 48 and 62). The documents of which production may be ordered under para. (iii) of r. 4(1) are those "relating to the matter to be determined". Although the terms in which para. (ii) are drawn would enable a tribunal to adopt the court procedure of appointing a commissioner to recover the documents at a diet of commission,[5] it has never been necessary to proceed in this way, and orders under para. (ii) generally require the document to be recovered or inspected to be produced to the tribunal. (It may be noted in this connection that the sheriff may elect to receive the documents himself, although in practice he rarely does so[6]). But, as indicated in *Nassé's* case, it might be appropriate to appoint a commissioner where difficult questions of confidentiality arise (see (4) below). The Chairman could act as commissioner.

An application for a document order must specify clearly what documents or classes of documents are sought, and against whom the order is sought. If the Chairman considers that they are not relevant or admissible, or that the application is too widely framed, or is unnecessary or premature, he may refuse the application in whole or in part, or in granting it may alter the terms in which the documents are specified. It should be kept in mind that a document order is intended to recover actual documents which the party applying for it knows, or has reason to believe, may exist, and be in the hands of the person against whom the order is sought. It is not intended as a means of getting information assembled in a convenient form. Where, in effect, further particulars of the opponent's case are sought, the application should be for particulars. Where information is sought which is of a general nature, the appropriate course may be to apply for a witness order against a suitable person to provide it. It should also be noted that the rules refer only to documents, and therefore there is no statutory warrant for ordering production of analogous evidence of a non-documentary nature, such as photographs and tape-recordings, or of any other moveable article.

---

[5] As indicated by Lord Fraser in *Science Research Council* v. *Nassé* [1979] I.C.R. 921, at pp. 949-950.

[6] Dobie, *Sheriff Court Practice*, p. 197.

As tribunals are not bound by the rules of evidence, a document order for production of an original or principal document is not regarded as necessary where a copy or draft is already available, unless it is alleged that the copy or draft is not identical with the original or principal, and that the difference between them is material. Similarly the rule in court procedure that a document must be properly stamped before it can be looked at by the court is not applied by tribunals.

As regards bankers' books, including those of the Post Office and other savings banks, there are special provisions in the Bankers' Books Evidence Act 1879. In practice, banks are helpful about providing copies of relevant entries. If an order relating to entries in bank books calls for production of excerpts from the account in question certified by the bank, it is unlikely that the bank would stand on the 1879 Act.

As to how far back in time it may be permissible to go in discrimination cases, see *Selvarajan* v. *Inner London Education Authority* [1980] I.R.L.R. 313.

Application for a formal document order should not be made without first endeavouring to obtain voluntary production of the documents sought. If this has not been done, the application for an order may be refused as premature. Where voluntary production has been refused, this should be stated when making the application.

Although the Sheriff Court Rules as to what documents may be the subject of an order for commission and diligence are widely drawn, in court practice their application is circumscribed by judicial decisions on the subject. Such decisions reflect the practice of the court with regard to written pleadings or the rules of evidence in court proceedings, neither of which are applicable to industrial tribunal proceedings,[7] and thus may be difficult to relate to industrial tribunal practice. Similarly, the equivalent rules before industrial tribunals in England and Wales (see Chapter 2) confer on tribunals in that country the powers of the county court in relation to "discovery and inspection of documents". Discovery in England includes "general discovery" which has no exact equivalent in Scotland. While therefore English decisions on this subject are helpful on matters of principle, they have to be considered carefully with these distinctions in view.

In considering an application for a document order the Chairman has to weigh up the object of keeping procedural formalities to the minimum against the entitlement of the party to be put in possession of any documents which are necessary to prove his case. He must be satisfied (if necessary after making further enquiries) that the document is or may be relevant to the case, that production is necessary for the

---

[7] See Chap. 8, p. 169. The rules as to what documents are recoverable by diligence are discussed in Dobie, *Sheriff Court Practice*, at p. 194-5, and more fully in *Walkers, The Law of Evidence in Scotland*, Chap. XXIII.

determination of the issue and that the document cannot be obtained without making an order. An interlocutory hearing may be necessary to ascertain the relevance of the document to the issue between the parties, and if the issue is not sufficiently clearly identified it may be necessary to make an order for further particulars, before deciding whether to grant or refuse the document order. The question whether to make an order must not be approached restrictively, however; production should not be refused on the ground that a document is irrelevant unless it is clear that it is beyond the scope of the proceedings. There is authority for the view that production may not be ordered of a document required only for the purpose of cross-examination, and having no other connection with the proceedings.[8] Where an applicant in a racial discrimination complaint sought discovery of a class of documents potentially as large as 1,600 in number, the Employment Appeal Tribunal agreed that such an order would be oppressive, and restricted the order to a category extending potentially to 78.[9]

Documents produced under an order are made available to the party who called for them, or to his representative. If produced prior to the hearing they are made available for inspection and noting only in the first place. It then becomes a matter for the party to decide whether to put the document in evidence at the hearing. In the meanwhile, he is not entitled to borrow the document for the purpose of making copies. Accordingly, unless allowed to do so by the tribunal, at its discretion and on a suitable receipt in writing (a privilege normally extended only to solicitors), any notes or copies which they desire to make must be taken under a clerk's supervision in the tribunal office. This practice has become necessary because unfortunately attempts have been made to tamper with documents which have been recovered. If business books, diaries and the like have to be produced, which contain entries of no relevance to the proceedings, and which may be required for other purposes in the meanwhile, once the relevant entries have been identified by the party who called for them, photocopies can be made by the tribunal staff, and unless the person calling for the books seeks to found on their general appearance, the originals can be returned. If, however, the possessor of the books were to object on grounds of confidentiality to the non-relevant parts being disclosed, the President or a Chairman would inspect the documents and direct that only copies or excerpts of those entries which appeared to him to be relevant should be disclosed. The position with regard to objections on grounds of confidentiality is discussed in (4) below.

---

8 See *French* v. *Purnell*, 1931 S.L.T. 85; *Gowans* v. *UBM Motors Ltd.* (1978) 13 I.T.R. 163. But for a different view, see Walkers, *op. cit.*, at p. 320.

9 *Perera* v. *Civil Service Commission* [1980] I.R.L.R. 233.

(3) **Documents in the hands of Government departments**

There are special requirements in court proceedings where production is sought of documents in the hands of a Government department. Intimation of the application must be made to the Lord Advocate, and if objection is taken that production would be contrary to the public interest, diligence for recovery will almost certainly be refused.[10] In industrial tribunal proceedings intimation of an application for a document order is not made to the Lord Advocate unless the document sought is in the hands of his department, the Crown Office, or a procurator fiscal, but production would be refused if the document is obviously objectionable on grounds of public interest, the obvious example being documents relating to investigation of crime by the police or the Crown authorities. In a doubtful case, the party making the application could be directed under r. 12(3) of the 1980 rules to intimate the application to the department concerned.Objections on grounds of public policy are discussed further in (4) below.

(4) **Confidentiality and public interest**

Certain communications are regarded as privileged at law. They are referred to in Chapter 8 (p. 188). Although industrial tribunals are not bound by the rules of evidence in courts of law, documents within these categories are regarded as similarly protected in industrial tribunal proceedings, and subject to the exceptions which have been admitted in practice[11] should not be the subject of recovery or production orders. And in Scotland a private diary is confidential and cannot be recovered unless something has occurred to destroy that confidentiality, such as the diary having been abandoned or left about.[12]

As regards objection on grounds of public policy, the types of case and the considerations which have been applied by the courts in Scotland are discussed in Walkers' *Law of Evidence* at para. 295, pp. 325-6. In England, the class of cases in which discovery has been refused because it would be contrary to the public interest to reveal a source of information in matters of public concern is not confined to communications to the police, and has been extended to bodies such as the Gaming Board and the National Society for the Prevention of Cruelty to Children.[13] The categories of public interest are not closed, and must alter as social conditions and legislation develop.[14] In addition to written communications which are protected under common law rules, there are specific

---

10 Walkers, *op. cit.*, p. 325.

11 See Walkers, *Law of Evidence,* Chap. XXXI.

12 *Duke of Argyll* v. *Duchess of Argyll,* 1962 S.C.(H.L.) 88.

13 See the speech of Lord Salmon in *Science Research Council* v. *Nassé* [1979] I.C.R. 921 at p. 935.

14 *Per* Lord Hailsham of St Marylebone in *D.* v. *NSPCC* [1978] A.C. 171 at p. 230.

statutory provisions against the admissibility in evidence of communications to conciliation officers (see Chapter 8, p. 189) and, in appeals against improvement notices, prohibition notices and non-discrimination notices, against the admission of documents production of which is certified by the Secretary of State to be against the interests of national security (see (1) above, p. 109).

Unless it falls within the above rules, a document which has been written or handed over in confidence is not protected from production on grounds of confidentiality alone. This was decided by the House of Lords in *Science Research Council* v. *Nassé, supra* (in terms expressly applying to Scotland[15]) with reference to confidential reports on employees in cases of alleged discrimination on grounds of sex, race or trade union activities. But it was held that the tribunal, in the free exercise of its discretion to order discovery, should have regard to the fact that such documents were confidential and that discovery would be a breach of confidence, so that relevance alone, though a necessary ingredient, does not provide an automatic test for ordering discovery, the ultimate test being whether discovery is necessary for disposing of the proceedings fairly. In the Court of Appeal Lord Denning had suggested that the number of cases of this kind where discovery would be necessary might be very rare, but the House of Lords did not accept this proposition.

It was also held that in order to decide whether discovery is necessary, the tribunal should inspect the documents and, if it decides to order discovery, consider what special procedures might be necessary to protect the interests of the author of the document, such as covering up his identity. Lord Fraser suggested that the Scottish procedure of commission and diligence could be used, enabling excerpts to be made by the commissioner. It was accepted[16] that there could be no hard and fast rule, and it must depend on the circumstances and the issues whether the inspection should take place at the interlocutory stage or at the hearing itself. The observations to that effect of Arnold J in *British Railways Board* v. *Natarajan* [1979] I.C.R. 326 (at p. 333) were approved, as was his statement that before deciding whether an examination of the document is necessary, the Chairman of the tribunal must decide whether it is reasonable to expect that there is any real likelihood of relevant material emerging from the examination, and that if there is not, examination would not be necessary.

Where objection is taken at the interlocutory stage to production of documents on grounds of confidentiality, it will generally be appropriate to convene an interlocutory hearing to deal with the matter. Where

---

[15] See the speech of Lord Fraser of Tullybelton at p. 949.

[16] *Per* Lord Edmund Davies, at p. 941.

objection seems likely from the nature of the document specified in the application it may be desirable to direct the party making the application to give notice of it to the other party or parties in terms of r. 12(3), so that objections may be heard and considered, and the documents may be examined by the Chairman (if he considers it appropriate to do so) before any order is made. As indicated by Lord Fraser in *Nassé's* case, the Chairman could make an order for commission and diligence for recovery, acting himself in the role of commissioner, and directing the documents to be excerpted in such a way as to minimise the breach of confidence involved in production.

In *Crown Agents* v. *Lawal* [1979] I.C.R. 103 the Employment Appeal Tribunal expressed the view that a confidential report on an applicant (in that case a medical report) which is produced in industrial tribunal proceedings should never be permitted to get into the hands of the applicant himself. This observation must, however, be considered in the light of the subsequent observations of the House of Lords in *Nassé's* case. In any event, while it may be possible to rely on professional advisers not disclosing such a document to an applicant, if he is represented, such a restriction would be impracticable if he is not. Lord Fraser appeared to accept in *Nassé* that once a document is produced it will be disclosed to the complainer, but pointed out that production may be refused if the information can be obtained from other sources which do not involve disclosing private information (at pp. 948 and 949). Otherwise the main practical safeguard must be to try to cover up the identity of the author and any third party on whom the document reports.[17]

(5) **Witness orders**

The rules of procedure regarding orders to attend a hearing to give evidence or to produce documents have been explained in (1) above. Provision is made in para. 10 of Sched. 9 to the Employment Protection (Consolidation) Act 1978 for the payment of allowances out of public funds to witnesses for the purposes of, or in connection with, their attendance. It is within the Chairman's discretion whether to sanction the payment of such allowances (see Chapter 10, p. 242).

Applications for witness orders should state clearly the full name and address of the person whose attendance is desired. At the risk of stating the obvious, an order cannot be made for the attendance of the holder of an office or position (*e.g.* "the assistant manager"). The person concerned must be named. Witness orders are not granted as a matter of course, but only if it appears to the Chairman that the witness can give relevant evidence, and that it is necessary to make an order

[17] See also in this connection *Perera* v. *Civil Service Commission, supra*.

because he will not or may not attend, or would find it easier to attend under order.[18] If necessary, the Chairman will cause enquiries to be made on these matters before deciding whether or not to grant an order. He may, under r. 12(3), direct the party applying for the order to give notice of it to the other parties, stating how they may object.

It is not uncommon for parties, particularly unrepresented applicants in unfair dismissal cases, to ask for numerous witnesses, whether fellow employees or representatives of management, to give evidence which the Chairman, from his experience of the issues which are relevant in such cases, will consider to be unlikely to be necessary. If an order is refused for this or any other reason it should be made plain in stating the reasons for refusal that if it should turn out at the hearing that the evidence of the witness would or could have been relevant and necessary for the determination of the issue, the application for a witness order may be renewed.

The witness order, signed by the Chairman, is intimated to the witness by recorded delivery post. The rules which provide for application to be made for a document order to be set aside apply also to witness orders (see above, p. 109). Where a Chairman set aside an order on a witness to produce documents on the strength of views expressed to a tribunal official by a colleague of the witness as to the relevance and necessity for the documents in question, he was held to have acted wrongly.[19] As to willing witnesses who are unable to attend for *bona fide* reasons, see Chapter 7 at pp. 154, 155.

PRE-HEARING ASSESSMENTS

The Industrial Tribunals Rules of Procedure (Scotland) 1980 introduced for the first time a form of procedure called a pre-hearing assessment. There was no equivalent procedure under the preceding rules, and there is none in the other rules. The relevant rule is r. 6.

A pre-hearing assessment provides a method by which a tribunal may consider a case, or some particular aspect of a case, and whether that of an applicant or a respondent, which on paper (*i.e.* in the originating application or notice of appearance) appears to have no, or very little, prospect of success, in order to ascertain whether there may be more in the case than is apparent from the papers; if apparently there is not, the rule provides that the tribunal may indicate to the party concerned that his application is unlikely to succeed or that his contentions (or any particular contention) appear to have no reasonable prospect of success, and that if he persists with the case (or the part of it in question)

---

18 *Dada* v. *Metal Box Co. Ltd.* (1974) 9 I.T.R. 390.

19 *Wilcox* v. *HGS* [1976] I.C.R. 306.

and fails, he may be found liable in expenses (r. 6(2)). The underlying thinking is that such an indication may result in the withdrawal or abandonment of potentially hopeless applications or defences, and save the expense and inconvenience involved to opponents in having to resist them and in convening tribunals to hear them. The procedure is intended for cases which appear to be hopeless on the merits, and a pre-hearing assessment will not be ordered to consider questions of jurisdiction, which are dealt with by way of preliminary hearing (see Chapter 7, p. 160) leading to a formal decision by the tribunal. The type of case which would be suitable for a pre-hearing assessment is where an applicant admits in his originating application to an act of gross misconduct, and complains that his dismissal is unfair solely on the ground that he had not previously received a warning.

A pre-hearing assessment may be held either on the application of a party (other than a respondent who has not entered an appearance) or of the tribunal's own motion. The question whether an assessment should be held will normally be considered at the Central Office, in the course of routine examination of the case file by a Chairman before it is either listed for hearing at the Central Office or sent to a local office for that purpose. In the latter case, the decision will be made in consultation with the Chairman at the local office. Where application for an assessment is made by a party after that stage, it will be dealt with by a Chairman at the office handling the case at the time.

A pre-hearing assessment is made by a fully constituted tribunal and not by a Chairman alone (see r. 12(4)). Notice of the decision to hold an assessment must first be given to the parties (and in cases which may involve payments out of the Redundancy Fund or Maternity Pay Fund, the Secretary of State, if not a party), giving them the opportunity to submit representations in writing and to advance oral argument at the pre-hearing assessment if they so wish (r. 6(2)). But (since one of the objects of the procedure is to minimise the necessity of appearing) the party whose case is not to be assessed is also told that his attendance at the sitting of the tribunal will not be necessary.

An application for a pre-hearing assessment should be made in writing to the Secretary of the Tribunals at the earliest opportunity. If the application is refused, the party who made the application will be informed in writing. The opposite party will not normally be informed unless either it is clear that he is aware that the application has been made or that statements which amount to further particulars of the case to be made by the party making the application (and which therefore ought to be disclosed to the opposite party) are in the written application for the assessment.

No inferences should be drawn by either party as to the prospects of success on either side from the fact that the application has been refused, since the grounds for refusal will usually be that the prospects of success cannot adequately be evaluated without hearing evidence. Similarly, if an assessment takes place, and the tribunal decides not to give an "indication" in terms of r. 6(2) to the party whose case is being assessed, neither he nor his opponent should make the assumption that his prospects of success are good. The only inference which it is proper to draw is that *on the basis of the information before the tribunal* his case does not seem hopeless to the tribunal making the assessment. If the case goes on, the picture presented to the tribunal which eventually hears the evidence may be very different and the degree of success achieved by one party or the other could vary infinitely. By the same token, the giving of an "indication" should not be regarded as a guarantee of success by the opponent of the party whose case is assessed.

In making the assessment the tribunal has to consider the originating application and notice of appearance, any other written representations, and what is said to them by the party whose case is being assessed, and by any other parties who appear. Evidence as such will not be taken. If in the light of all the available information the tribunal considers that the case being assessed has no reasonable prospect of success, it may make an indication under r. 6(2) about potential liability for expenses to the party concerned, as explained above. Such an indication will normally be given orally at the conclusion of the sitting, but in any event it must be recorded in a document signed by the Chairman. A copy must be sent to the parties and made available to the tribunal which ultimately hears the case, if it is not subsequently withdrawn or settled (r. 6(3)). Where the party whose case is being assessed persuades the tribunal that it has a reasonable prospect of success, so that the tribunal decides that no "indication" should be given in terms of r. 6(2), no document requires to be issued, or would be issued, although a record of the view formed by the tribunal would be made in the case file. But if the other parties were not present, they would be notified by the Secretary that the tribunal had decided not to give any such indication.

If a tribunal has made an indication in terms of r. 6(2), and the case eventually proceeds to a hearing, no member of the tribunal which made the pre-hearing assessment may be a member of the tribunal at the hearing (r. 6(4)). At the hearing the tribunal may take into account the indication made at the pre-hearing assessment, but would not be bound by it. As already stated, the case where an "indication" would be given is that which would appear to be hopeless on the merits. A hopeless case is not necessarily a frivolous or vexatious one,[20] but r.

---

20 See Chap. 10, p. 234.

11(1) of the Industrial Tribunals Rules of Procedure (Scotland) 1980 is wider than its predecessor, and empowers a tribunal to award expenses where the conduct of a party, although not frivolous or vexatious, has been otherwise unreasonable. If a party were to carry on with a case in the face of an "indication" given at a pre-hearing assessment and failed, it would be open to the tribunal which decided the case to award expenses on the view that his conduct had been unreasonable. An indication of opinion in terms of r. 6(2) is by definition not a decision of a tribunal,[21] and is not entered in the Register of Decisions. Nor is it open to review under r. 10. But insofar as a question of law may arise in connection with a pre-hearing assessment (or a refusal to hold one) it would be appealable by virtue of s. 136(1) of the Employment Protection (Consolidation) Act 1978.

At the time of writing few pre-hearing assessments have taken place, and apart from what is stated above it is not practicable to give any further forecast as to how this novel form of procedure will be worked out and developed in practice.

APPLICATIONS FOR DIRECTIONS TO SUSPEND PROHIBITION NOTICES

Rule 4 in the Industrial Tribunals (Improvement and Prohibition Notices Appeals) (Scotland) Regulations 1974 makes provision for application to be made for a direction suspending the operation of a prohibition notice until the appeal is finally disposed of or withdrawn, under s. 24(3)(*b*) of the Health and Safety at Work etc. Act 1974. Such applications must be sent in writing to the Secretary, setting out the case number of the appeal, if known, or particulars sufficient to identify the appeal, and the grounds on which the application is made. The application is to be entered in the Register, and a copy sent to the respondent.

A Chairman cannot deal with such an application (r. 14(3)) and it must therefore be the subject of a hearing by a full tribunal. Where the application is made at a sufficiently early stage in the proceedings, a preliminary hearing would be convened. Any evidence would be taken which might be necessary to enable the tribunal to decide it. Although a direction under this rule falls strictly speaking within the definition of an interlocutory order (see Chapter 9, p. 192), nevertheless in reg. 2(2) it is specifically defined as a "decision" of the tribunal, and as such would be entered in the Register of Decisions and would be open to review.

---

[21] See the definition of "decision" in reg. 2 of the Industrial Tribunals Rules of Procedure (Scotland) Regulations 1980.

MISCELLANEOUS INTERLOCUTORY MATTERS

(1) **General**

As noted at p. 138, each of the rules provide that, subject to the provisions of the rules, a tribunal may regulate its own procedure. The power may be used to fill in and remedy any gap in the rules, *e.g.* to order a re-hearing (*Charman* v. *Palmers Scaffolding Ltd.* [1979] I.C.R. 335 at p. 338). But it probably cannot provide a warrant for dispensing with a specific requirement of the rules or for proceeding in a manner inconsistent with such a requirement, except where a dispensatory power is also provided, or where the circumstances are such that the requirement is unworkable or inconsistent with another requirement. For example an application for directions may be made "at any time" (r. 13(2) of the 1980 rules), but must be made in writing to the Secretary (r. 13(3)). It has been held competent under the predecessor to r. 13(2) to ask for directions in the course of a hearing,[22] but if this were to be done it would be pointless to insist on strict compliance with r. 13(3).

(2) **Extensions of time and postponements**

Under r. 12(2)(*a*) of the Industrial Tribunals Rules of Procedure (Scotland) 1980 a tribunal may extend the time appointed for doing any act notwithstanding that it may have expired. Except in the case of applications under r. 4(2) (*i.e.* to vary or set aside an order for particulars or a document or witness order) such an application may be made after the time appointed has expired (r. 13(1)). Before granting an application under r. 13(1) the tribunal may require notice of the application to be given to the other party or parties informing them how they may object (r. 12(3)). A tribunal may also postpone or adjourn a hearing, and is particularly enjoined to do so in cases where an opportunity for conciliation and settlement is desired (r. 12(2)(*b*)).

The other rules all confer the power to postpone or adjourn a hearing (Industrial Tribunals (Scotland) Regulations 1965 (as amended), Sched. 2, r. 14(1)(*c*); the Industrial Tribunals (Improvement and Prohibition Notice Appeals) (Scotland) 1974, r. 14(2)(*a*); the Industrial Tribunals (Non-Discrimination Notices Appeals) (Scotland) Regulations 1977, r. 12(2)(*a*)). But only the 1965 rules (r. 14(1)(*a*)) confer a general power to extend time limits similar to that in the 1980 rules.

Applications of this kind should always be made as soon as possible after it becomes apparent that a postponement or adjournment may be necessary, and should explain the reason for the application as fully and clearly as possible. Unreasonable delay in applying may, depending on the circumstances, result in an award of expenses (see Chapter 7, p.

---

22 See *Charman's* case, *supra*, p. 338.

166). In considering applications of this kind, the Chairman has to assess whether the postponement is necessary in the interests of justice, so that essential issues may be adequately put before the tribunal, against the desirability of avoiding excessive delay. He may cause further enquiries to be made for that purpose. As held in *Jacobs* v. *Norsalta* [1977] I.C.R. 189, the power to postpone must not be used arbitrarily or to defeat the object of the legislation, but subject to this the Chairman has a complete discretion. The Court of Appeal in *Carter* v. *Credit Change Ltd.* [1979] I.C.R. 908 approved the principle stated in *Jacobs* v. *Norsalta, supra* and declined to state any principle other than that the industrial tribunal Chairman should attempt to do justice as best he or she can in each individual case. The view was expressed that expedition, while an important factor to be taken into account, was not to be elevated into a general principle of law.

A Chairman will look less kindly on an application for postponement made by a party or representative who has failed to reply to the "date letter",[23] and will be readier to grant a postponement where the reason advanced is the absence of an essential witness. Parties are warned that once the hearing is fixed postponements will only be granted in exceptional circumstances.

Where the grounds of the application are that court proceedings are pending, whether civil or criminal, arising out of matters which to any extent are related to industrial tribunal proceedings, the practice in Scotland differs from that in England and Wales where, as held by the Court of Appeal in *Carter* v. *Credit Change Ltd., supra,* affirming *Jacobs* v. *Norsalta* (where the proceedings in question were civil) and *Bastick* v. *James Laing (Turf Accountants) Ltd.* [1979] I.C.R. 778 (where they were criminal) the Chairman has a complete discretion, provided that it is properly and judicially exercised. In Scotland the Chairman has a similar discretion where civil proceedings are pending, but not where a criminal prosecution is, or may be, pending. In such cases the invariable practice is to postpone the hearing until the Crown Office or procurator fiscal has decided not to prosecute, or the criminal proceedings have been concluded, to avoid any risk of prejudice to the investigation of the matter by the police and the Crown authorities, and to any subsequent criminal proceedings. The practice reflects the views of the Crown Office in accordance with the principles laid down in *Stirling* v. *Associated Newspapers Ltd.* 1960 J.C. 5 and *Smith* v. *H.M. Advocate* 1952 J.C. 66.

(3) **Applications for directions**

In proceedings under the Industrial Tribunals Rules of Procedure (Scotland) 1980 a party (other than a respondent who has not entered an

[23] See Chap. 5, pp. 102, 103.

appearance) may at any time apply to the tribunal for directions on a matter arising in connection with the proceedings (r. 13(2)). Except where application is made during the hearing[24] a notice must be presented to the Secretary, stating the title of the proceedings and setting out the grounds of the application (r. 13(3)). Before granting the application the tribunal may require notice to be given to the other party or parties stating how they may object (r. 12(3)). In *Charman* v. *Palmers Scaffolding Ltd.* [1979] I.C.R. 335 it was held that under the equivalent rule to r. 13(2) a Chairman could order a case to be re-heard before a differently constituted tribunal.

There are similar provisions in the Industrial Tribunals (Scotland) Regulations 1965 (as amended), Sched. 2 (r. 15(2)-(4)), but not in the other rules.

(4) **Vexatious allegations**

In cases under the Industrial Tribunals Rules of Procedure (Scotland) 1980, a tribunal may order anything in an originating application or notice of appearance to be struck out or amended on the ground that it is vexatious (r. 12(2)(e). Before any order is made notice must be given to the party against whom it is proposed giving him an opportunity to show why it should not be made. (See also at p. 136 below).

(5) **Additional and representative respondents**

Rule 14(1) of the Industrial Tribunals (Rules of Procedure) 1980 provides that a tribunal may at any time either upon the application of any person or of its own motion, direct any person against whom any relief is sought to be joined as a party, and give such consequential directions as it considers necessary.

Rule 14(2) provides that upon application by any person, or of its own motion, a tribunal may order that any respondent named in the originating application or subsequently added, who shall appear to the tribunal not to have been, or to have ceased to be, directly interested in the subject of the originating application, be dismissed from the proceedings.

Rule 14(3) provides that where there are numerous persons having the same interest in an originating application, one or more of them may be cited as the person or persons against whom relief is sought or may be authorised by the tribunal, before or at the hearing, to defend on behalf of all the persons so interested.

It will be noted that r. 14(3) does not apply where there is a multiplicity of applicants. That situation is provided for in r. 15 (see (6) below). Rule 14 enables a tribunal to deal with such situations as that of the applicant

---

24 See above, p. 120.

employed in a group of companies who directs proceedings against the wrong employer, or where (as has happened) the situation is so confused that it is not clear which is the true respondent. The rule will also enable third parties (trade unions or contractors) to be sisted (or joined) into unfair dismissal proceedings by virtue of ss. 76A, 76B, and 76C of the Employment Protection (Consolidation) Act 1978 (added by s. 10 of the Employment Act 1980).

On the other hand, r. 14(1) would not provide a machinery for dealing with the situation where fault is imputed by a party against a body, such as a Citizens' Advice Bureau, against whom it is not competent to seek relief before an industrial tribunal for faulty advice or mishandling of proceedings. The Court of Appeal held in *Riley* v. *Tesco Stores Ltd.* [1980] I.C.R. 323 that it would be unjust for the tribunal to draw a conclusion adverse to such a body without giving it an opportunity to state its case, but recognised that it could only be done by such a procedure as issuing a witness order on the appropriate person to speak to the matter. Similarly, an attempt to bring the Advisory, Conciliation and Arbitration Service (ACAS) into proceedings was refused (under the differently worded equivalent to r. 14(1) in the previous rules of 1974) in *Marshall* v. *Alexander Sloan & Co. Ltd.* [1980] I.C.R. 394.

Rules 14(2)(*c*) in the Industrial Tribunals (Improvement and Prohibition Notices Appeals) (Scotland) Regulations 1974 and 12(2)(*c*) in the Industrial Tribunals (Non-Discrimination Notices Appeals) (Scotland) Regulations 1977 provide that on the application of a party or of its own motion a tribunal may direct any other person to be joined as a party to the appeal, giving such consequential directions as it considers necessary. But the tribunal may only make such a direction after having given to the person proposed to be joined a reasonable opportunity of making a written or oral objection. There are no equivalent provisions in the rules in the Industrial Tribunals (Scotland) Regulations 1965 (as amended), Sched. 2.

(6) **Consolidation of proceedings**

Rule 15 of the Industrial Tribunals Rules of Procedure (Scotland) 1980 provides that where there are pending before the industrial tribunal two or more originating applications, then, if at any time upon the application of a party or of its own motion it appears to a tribunal that—

(*a*) Some common question of law or fact arises in both or all the originating applications, or

(*b*) The relief claimed therein is in respect of or arises out of the same set of facts, or

(*c*) For some other reason it is desirable to make an order under the rule, the tribunal may order that some or all the originating applications shall be considered together, and may give such consequential directions as may be necessary. But such an order may not be made without sending notice to all parties concerned giving them an opportunity to object.

These provisions enable a test case to be selected out of a number of cases arising out of common circumstances. The others will be held over and thereafter decided in the light of the decision in the test case, but taking into account any individual differences of circumstances. The rule also enables the tribunal to require that cases with a common background can be taken together.

There are no equivalent provisions in the other rules.

(7) **Transfer of proceedings**

The provisions of the Industrial Tribunals Rules of Procedure (Scotland) 1980 enabling proceedings to be transferred from Scotland to England and Wales and *vice versa* have been referred to in Chapter 4, (pp. 30, 31).

(8) **Amendments**

Rule 17(4) of the Industrial Tribunals Rules of Procedure (Scotland) 1980 provides that a party may at any time by notice to the Secretary and to the other party or parties (and, where appropriate, to the appropriate conciliation officer) change his address for service. There are similar provisions in the other rules.[25] In addition, under the Industrial Tribunals (Improvement and Prohibition Notices Appeals) (Scotland) Regulations 1974 (r. 14(2)(*d*)) and the Industrial Tribunals (Non-Discrimination Notices Appeals) (Scotland) Regulations 1977 (r. 12(2)(*d*)) a tribunal may make any necessary amendments to the description of a party in the Register, and in any other documents relating to the appeal.

Otherwise there are no express provisions allowing amendment of an originating application, notice of appeal, or notice of appearance. But it is well settled that by virtue of its power to regulate its own procedure, a tribunal has a wide discretion to allow amendments at any stage of the proceedings.

The question of amendment probably arises more commonly at a hearing than before it, and the principles and practice involved are discussed in that context in Chapter 7.[26] Where application to amend is made prior to a hearing the question whether it should be allowed will depend on the nature of the proposed amendment, whether it appears

---

[25] The Industrial Tribunals (Scotland) Regulations 1965 (as amended) Sched. 2, r. 16(2); the Industrial Tribunals (Improvement and Prohibition Notices Appeals) (Scotland) Regulations 1974, r. 15(2); the Industrial Tribunals (Non-Discrimination Notices Appeals) (Scotland) Regulations 1977, r. 13(2).

[26] See p. 162 *et seq.* See also Chap. 5, at p. 91.

to be competent (*e.g.* in the case of an amendment seeking to introduce an additional ground of complaint, whether it is time-barred), and the extent to which the other side may complain of being taken by surprise. But in general, if the amendment appears to be competent it will be allowed, subject to the opposite party being given the opportunity to make any consequential amendments in reply. But if the proposed amendment is substantial and the application to amend comes at a late stage prior to the hearing, so that in consequence the hearing has to be postponed to allow the opposite party to consider it, the party seeking to amend may be found liable for any expenses incurred or allowances paid as a result of the postponement.[27]

Once an amendment has been allowed, it is the duty of the tribunal staff to note it on the originating application or notice of appearance, together with any consequential amendments made by the other parties, and also (where it relates to the name or address of a party) in the case file.

(9) **Notices, etc.**

(a) *General*

Rule 17(1) of the Industrial Tribunals Rules of Procedure (Scotland) 1980 provides that any notices given under the rules shall be in writing. Rule 17(2) states that all notices and documents which require to be presented to the Secretary of the Tribunals may be presented at the Office of the Tribunals (*i.e.* as defined in reg. 2, the Central Office[28]) or such other office as he may notify to the parties. Rule 17(3) provides that all notices and documents required or authorised to be sent or given to any person undermentioned may be sent by post (subject to r. 17(5) referred to below) or delivered to or at—

- (*a*) in the case of the Secretary of State in proceedings to which he is not a party (if he is a party, (d) below will apply), the offices of the Department of Employment, Pentland House, 41 Robb's Loan, Edinburgh EH14 1TW or such other office as may be notified by the Secretary of State;
- (*b*) in the case of the National Dock Labour Board, the principal office of the Board;
- (*c*) in the case of a sheriff, the office of the sheriff clerk;
- (*d*) in the case of a party:—
    - (i) his address for service specified in the originating application or in a notice of appearance or in a notice of a changed address under r. 17(4); or

---

[27] See Chap. 7, p. 166.

[28] The definition is of significance in relation to the question whether an application has been duly presented, or presented timeously, (see Chap. 4, p. 46).

(ii) if no address for service has been so specified, his last known address or place of business in the United Kingdom or, if the party is a corporation, the corporation's registered or principal office in the United Kingdom or, in any case, at such address or place outside the United Kingdom as the President or the Regional Chairman may allow;

(*e*) in the case of a document directed to any other person, his address or place of business in the United Kingdom, or if such a person is a corporation, the corporation's registered or principal office in the United Kingdom.

If sent or given to the authorised representative of a party, the document is deemed to have been sent or given to that party.

There are similar provisions under the other rules, with appropriate differences in the addresses specified.[29]

It will be noted that whereas there is provision under para. (*d*) of r. 17(3) of the 1980 rules for service on a corporation which does not have a registered or principal office in the United Kingdom and which is a party, there is no equivalent provision in para. (*e*) for service on such a corporation if it is not a party. It is thought that the general "long-stop" power in r. 17(6), referred to below, could be used to cover any anomalous situations arising from the wording of r. 17(3) in relation to persons outside the United Kingdom. It should also be noted that any such anomalies are procedural and do not affect jurisdiction.[30]

(b) Recorded delivery: returned notices

The rules prescribe circumstances in which the recorded delivery service is to be used. In the Industrial Tribunals Rules of Procedure (Scotland) 1980 (r. 17(5)) these are:

(*a*) Where a second set of documents or notices is sent to a respondent who has not entered an appearance;

(*b*) Orders under r. 4(1)(*b*)(iii) requiring the attendance of a witness or the production of a document.

By r. 15(3) in the Industrial Tribunals (Improvement and Prohibition Notices Appeals) (Scotland) Regulations 1974 and r. 13(3) in the Industrial Tribunals (Non-Discrimination Notices Appeals) (Scotland) Regulations 1977 a notice of appeal is to be sent by recorded delivery if not delivered. These provisions should be regarded as directory, rather than mandatory.[31]

---

[29] The Industrial Tribunals (Scotland) Regulations 1965 (as amended) Sched. 2, r. 16(1); the Industrial Tribunals (Improvement and Prohibition Notices Appeals) (Scotland) Regulations 1974, r. 15(1); the Industrial Tribunals (Non-Discrimination Appeals) (Scotland) Regulations 1977, r. 13(1).

[30] See *Knulty and Anr.* v. *Eloc Electro-Optiek and Communicatie BV* [1979] I.C.R. 827.

[31] See Chap. 5 above, p. 93.

In practice, however, recorded delivery is also used when issuing orders for particulars and document orders under r. 4(1)(*b*)(ii) of the 1980 rules and its equivalents. It is also used when issuing notices of hearings or notices cancelling hearings, in order to minimise the difficulties if a party fails to appear at a hearing.[32]

The purpose of using recorded delivery is to provide proof of the date of despatch and of delivery so that if the document is not returned, it may be assumed to have been delivered. It was stated by Denning LJ in *R.* v. *London Quarter Sessions (ex p. Rossi)* [1956] 1 All E.R. 670 (at p. 676) that a decision taken in the absence of a party on the faith of such an assumption is regular.[33]

Accordingly, where a notice of hearing sent to an unrepresented applicant is returned, and the applicant cannot be located, the hearing is cancelled, and the proceedings are sisted.[34] Where the applicant is represented, however, the notice will also have been sent to his representative, and the fact that a copy may also be sent to the applicant does not excuse the representative from the obligation to ensure that the applicant is aware of the arrangements for the hearing. If the copy which is sent to the applicant is returned, his representative is normally informed. The hearing will not be cancelled, however, unless and until the tribunal has been informed that he has been unable to make contact with the applicant and is unable to proceed without him. In that event, the proceedings are sisted, as stated above.

Where a notice of hearing sent to a respondent is returned, what further action to be taken will depend on the reason stated by the Post Office for non-delivery. The hearing will not be cancelled, but if the respondent does not appear, the tribunal will enquire what action has been taken, and will only proceed to hear the case if satisfied that everything reasonably requisite has been done to apprise the respondent of the proceedings.[35] If it is considered that the respondent is attempting to evade postal service, arrangements may be made for the notice to be delivered by a sheriff officer. This may also be done where a witness order or an order for particulars or documents is returned.

Rule 17(6) of the Industrial Tribunals Rules of Procedure (Scotland) 1980 applies in this connection. This provides that where for any sufficient reason service of any document or notice cannot be effected in the manner prescribed, the President or the Regional Chairman may make an order for substituted service in such manner as he may deem fit, and such service has the same effect as service in the manner

---

32 See Chap. 7 under "Parties who do not appear", at pp. 141 to 143.

33 See also the Interpretation Act 1978, s. 7, and *Migwain Ltd.* v. *TGWU* [1979] I.C.R. 597.

34 See also below under "Excessive delay", at p. 137.

35 See Chap. 7, p. 142.

prescribed under the rule.[36] In appropriate cases, use could be made of this power to advertise the proceedings in the press, *e.g.* where intimation of an originating application to a respondent has been returned, and his whereabouts are not known.

(c) Special provisions regarding notices

By rr. 17(7) to (9) of the Industrial Tribunals Rules of Procedure (Scotland) 1980 the Secretary is directed to send copies of all documents and notices to an appropriate conciliation officer in proceedings under any enactment providing for conciliation;[37] and to the Secretary of State in proceedings which may involve payments out of the Redundancy Fund or Maternity Pay Fund, notwithstanding the he may not be a party. He is also directed to send copies of the decision of the tribunal, and of any certificate of correction, variation or revocation of the decision under rr. 9 and 10 to the Equal Opportunities Commission in proceedings under the Equal Pay Act 1970 and the Sex Discrimination Act 1975, and to the Commission for Racial Equality in proceedings under the Race Relations Act 1976.

Rule 15(5) of the Industrial Tribunals (Improvement and Prohibition Notices Appeals) (Scotland) Regulations 1974 provides that where the respondent is an inspector appointed otherwise than by the Health and Safety Executive, the Secretary shall send to the Executive copies of the notice of appeal and of the tribunal's written decision on the appeal.

CONCILIATION AND SETTLEMENT

(1) **General**

Provision is made for conciliation by the Advisory, Conciliation and Arbitration Service (ACAS) in the following cases:—
Under the *Employment Protection (Consolidation) Act 1978:*

- (i) Under s. 133(1):—
  - (*a*) Proceedings arising out of a contravention or alleged contravention of the following sections:
    - S. 8 (Itemised pay statements).
    - S. 12 (Guarantee payments).
    - S. 19 (Remuneration on suspension on medical grounds).
    - S. 23 (Trade union membership and activities).
    - Ss. 27, 28, 29, 31 and 31A (Time off work).

---

[36] There are similar provisions in the Industrial Tribunals (Improvement and Prohibition Notices Appeals) (Scotland) Regulations 1974 (r. 15(4)) and in the Industrial Tribunals (Non-Discrimination Notices Appeals) (Scotland) Regulations 1977 (r. 13(4)).

[37] See further below under "Conciliation".

S. 33 (Rights in connection with pregnancy or confinement).

S. 53 (Written statement of reasons for dismissal).

(*b*) Proceedings arising out of any contravention or alleged contravention of ss. 99 and 102 of the Employment Protection Act 1975 (consultation prior to redundancy and protective awards).

(*c*) Proceedings or claims in respect of which an industrial tribunal has jurisdiction by virtue of s. 131 (damages for certain breaches of contracts of employment).

(*d*) Proceedings arising out of a contravention or alleged contravention of s. 4 of the Employment Act 1980.

(The Secretary of State may by order extend the above categories of proceedings by adding others, whether in the 1978 Act itself or in any other Act (s. 133 (7)).

(ii) Under s. 134:—

Complaints of unfair dismissal under s. 67.

Under the *Sex Discrimination Act 1975 (s. 64):*

Complaints of unlawful discrimination in the employment field under s. 63, and complaints under s. 2(1) of the Equal Pay Act 1970.

Under the *Race Relations Act 1976 (s. 55):*

Complaints of unlawful discrimination in the employment field under s. 54.

(2) **Conciliation in relation to industrial tribunal proceedings**

In relation to all of the above cases the Industrial Tribunals Rules of Procedure (Scotland) 1980 require the Secretary of the Tribunals to notify parties that the services of a conciliation officer are available to them, and to send copies of the complaint and of all relevant documents to the appropriate conciliation officer (rr. 2 and 17(7)). But non-compliance with this requirement does not invalidate the proceedings.[38] The statutory provisions above referred to direct that if either party requests a conciliation officer to do so, or if he himself considers that he could act with a reasonable prospect of success, it is his duty to endeavour to promote a settlement without the complaint being determined by an industrial tribunal. Moreover, if a person claims that action has been taken in respect of which a complaint could be presented by him to an industrial tribunal arising out of any of the provisions specified in s. 133(1) of the 1978 Act, or claims that he was unfairly dismissed, before a complaint is presented to a tribunal a conciliation officer may act in the foregoing manner, if so requested by the person

---

[38] *Sheringham Development Co. Ltd.* v. *Browne* [1977] I.C.R. 20.

making the claim or the person against whom the complaint could be made (ss. 133(3) and 134(3)).

Where the complaint is one of unfair dismissal, the conciliation officer may promote a settlement based on reinstatement or re-engagement on terms which appear to him to be equitable,[39] if he considers re-employment to be practicable, and if the complainant wishes it, but otherwise settlement is to be based on a sum to be paid by way of compensation (1978 Act, s. 134(2)).

Where the agreed terms provide for reinstatement or re-engagement, continuity of employment is preserved by the Labour Relations (Continuity of Employment) Regulations 1976 (S.I. 1976/660)[40] in those cases to which the regulations apply, *i.e.* where a complaint of unfair dismissal has been presented, where an equivalent claim has been made under a dismissals procedure agreement, or where a conciliation officer has acted in terms of s. 134(3) before a complaint has been presented.[41]

On receipt of the papers, the conciliation officer will normally contact both parties to see if there is room for a settlement. In the pamphlet issued by ACAS his function is described as to try to help the parties to reach an agreement:

> "He does not act as an arbitrator on the merits of the case, nor does he impose or even recommend a particular settlement. Settlements are the responsibility of the parties concerned."

In *Duport Furniture Products Ltd.* v. *Moore* [1980] I.C.R. 581 it was affirmed that a conciliation officer is not under a duty to ensure that the terms of a settlement are equitable as between the parties. It is also of the greatest importance that parties should appreciate that a conciliation officer is entirely independent of the industrial tribunals and that nothing a conciliation officer says should be regarded as emanating from the tribunal. Moreover anything communicated to a conciliation officer in connection with the performance of his functions is not admissible in evidence before an industrial tribunal, except with the consent of the person who communicated it (1978 Act, ss. 133(6) and 134(5); Sex Discrimination Act 1975, s. 64(4); Race Relations Act 1976, s. 55(4)).

Where a settlement is achieved its terms are recorded by the conciliation officer in a form COT2 or COT3 (usually the latter), which is signed by the parties. This binds the parties to the agreed terms (*Duport Furniture Products Ltd.* v. *Moore, supra*). Where the result of the conciliation officer's action is a withdrawal of the complaint, the

---

39 But see *Duport Furniture Products Ltd.* v. *Moore* [1980] I.C.R. 581, referred to below.

40 The regulations continue to apply by virtue of para. 1 of Sched. 15 to the 1978 Act.

41 But not otherwise (see Chap. 4, pp. 69, 70, and below, p. 133).

applicant signs a form COT4. In either case the form is sent to the industrial tribunal, so that the proceedings may be disposed of in the appropriate manner. (See below, pp. 133 to 136).

(3) **Restrictions on contracting out and on settlements**

Sections 140(1) of the Employment Protection (Consolidation) Act 1978 and 118(1) of the Employment Protection Act 1975 provide that, subject to the specific exemptions provided in ss. 140(2) and 118(2), any provision in an agreement (whether a contract of employment or not) shall be void insofar as it purports to exclude any person from presenting a complaint to or bringing proceedings before an industrial tribunal. There are provisions to the same general effect in s. 77(3) of the Sex Discrimination Act 1975 (applying also to the Equal Pay Act 1970) and s. 72(3) of the Race Relations Act 1976, and s. 4(11) of the Employment Act 1980.

Sections 140(2) of the 1978 Act and 118(2) of the Employment Protection Act 1975 provide three broad classes of exceptions to those provisions. The first two are certain collective agreements recognised by statute or statutory order and agreements relating to dismissal in certain fixed term contracts. The third category comprises agreements to refrain from instituting or continuing proceedings before an industrial tribunal where a conciliation officer has taken action in accordance with his statutory functions under ss. 133 and 134 (see (1) above). The latter category of exception also applies to the equivalent provisions of the Sex Discrimination Act 1975 (by s. 77(4)) and the Race Relations Act 1976 (by s. 72(4)), and in s. 4(11) of the 1980 Act.

At common law an agreement to settle a litigation, or a prospective litigation, properly arrived at, is an enforceable contract, binding on both parties. Once concluded, the pursuer or complainant is not at liberty to resile and seek to continue with the proceedings unless the other party defaults. If that occurs he may take action to enforce compliance with the terms of the settement (which precludes any enquiry into the merits of the dispute) or may continue with the proceedings, provided there is not by then any procedural barrier against doing so. The effect of the above statutory provisions is, however, that unless one of the exceptions applies, an agreement to settle industrial tribunal proceedings, actual or potential, is void and unenforceable. The exception where a conciliation officer has taken action, although applying to many cases, applies only in those cases where a conciliation officer has a statutory function. But conciliation officers do not have statutory functions in relation to all classes of industrial tribunal proceedings: e.g. contraventions of ss. 1 and 4 of the 1978 Act and redundancy payment cases are not within s. 133(1), and are therefore not within that particular class of exception in s. 140(2). Thus an agreement to withdraw or settle by way of compromise any case in which a conciliation officer does not have a statutory function, or in which, having one, he has not exercised it, is bad, unless it falls within one of the other classes of stated exception, which will be rare, and awkward consequences may follow, as explained below.

Where parties have purported to conclude a settlement which is bad in this way, the decision in *Naqui* v. *Stephens Jewellers Ltd.* [1978] I.C.R. 631 shows that it is no bar to a complaint being presented and the proceedings being heard on the merits, even if it means reopening proceedings which have been dismissed following a purported withdrawal of the complaint (see below). In that case the court rejected the possibility that the applicant would be estopped (or in Scottish terminology, barred) from proceeding because of his conduct in purporting to withdraw. But in *Whittaker* v. *British Mail Order Corporation Ltd.* [1973] I.R.L.R. 296 not much in the way of action on the part of a conciliation officer (only a telephone contact with the parties) sufficed to exclude the operation of the statutory bar and validate the settlement.

It is also important to keep in mind the distinction between a unilateral withdrawal and a settlement, which can become blurred. An application which is withdrawn is normally dismissed (see below under "Withdrawals"). But often an applicant will intimate withdrawal in circumstances where his action is not unilateral, in that it results from an agreement between the parties that if the applicant withdraws his application the respondent will reinstate him or pay him a sum of money. Such an agreement is potentially void by virtue of the statutory bar, even if it results in a withdrawal, unless it comes within the exceptions already noted. It follows that, in such cases, unless a conciliation officer has taken action in accordance with the relevant provisions, the settlement is at risk.

Accordingly in every case where a conciliation officer has a statutory function, if parties agree terms of settlement directly and not through the conciliation officer, they will be well advised to arrange for the settlement to be recorded by ACAS on a form COT3. In that way there should be no possible criticism of its validity (see *Duport Furniture Products Ltd.* v. *Moore, supra*). The conciliation officer will probably have been in touch with the parties already at some earlier stage, and although this may be enough to validate the settlement (*Whittaker's* case *supra*), it may be difficult to prove. But a form COT3 would be virtually conclusive. From an employee's point of view it is also of importance that the settlement should be processed through ACAS if it involves reinstatement or re-engagement, in order to preserve continuity of employment under the regulations of 1976 referred to above.[42]

These observations apply as well to settlements arrived at after a hearing has begun as well as to those agreed beforehand. Tribunals will always readily adjourn proceedings to enable settlements to be formally concluded.

As already mentioned, awkward consequences may follow if parties purport to conclude an agreement which is illegal by virtue of the statutory bars referred to. In the first place, as explained, the agreement cannot preclude proceedings being taken before, and the merits of the complaint being considered by, an industrial tribunal. Secondly, any sums paid in implement would be regarded as purely *ex gratia*. A tribunal cannot act outwith its statutory powers, and while in cases where it has power to award compensation or damages (*e.g.* in unfair dismissal and discrimination complaints), it can take an *ex gratia* payment into account as going to diminish loss, it cannot do so in those cases where the limits of the remedy are defined by statute. There a tribunal would have to ignore the *ex gratia* payment and award the statutory compensation, and it is very doubtful if the respondent could claim repayment of the *ex gratia* payment in the civil courts under the law of quasi-contract.[43] Where a payment has been offered in general settlement of all claims following dismissal it falls to be disregarded as an *ex gratia* payment in redundancy payment proceedings. But if a sum has been offered and accepted in specific settlement of the *statutory* right to a redundancy payment, while acceptance cannot preclude the employee from raising proceedings to claim a larger sum, there seems no reason why the sum previously paid should not go towards satisfying the eventual statutory entitlement if it is found to be larger in amount. Lastly, and of considerable importance to an employee where the employer has agreed to reinstate or re-engage him, continuity of employment will not be preserved (see Chapter 4, pp. 69, 70).

(4) **Settlement procedures**

The procedure for disposal of cases which are settled prior to hearing is described below (under "Withdrawals and settlements", p. 134). Where the settlement is reached at the commencement of or during a hearing the proceedings are disposed of by a formal decision of the full tribunal. The form of order to be made is for the tribunal to decide, taking into account whatever parties may have requested or agreed.

42 See also Chap. 4, pp. 69, 70.

43 See Gloag and Henderson, *Introduction to the Law of Scotland*, 8th ed., Chaps. VIII (para. 23), IX and XIV. But see *Chelsea Football Club and Athletic Co. Ltd.* v. *Heath* [1981] I.R.L.R. 73.

The parties should be advised of the problems referred to in (3) above concerning the validity of settlements, because of which it will generally be advisable to adjourn the proceedings to enable them to validate the settlement through ACAS, after which an appropriate formal order can be made. The order made by a Chairman for a settlement or withdrawal prior to hearing will normally suffice, but there may be situations where it is appropriate that the tribunal should be asked, of consent, to make an order on the respondent in specific terms, *e.g.* to pay a sum of money or provide a reference. But if such an order is made the regulations relating to recoupment of unemployment and supplementary benefit will apply, if the order falls within the scope of the regulations (see Chapter 9, pp. 220 to 223).

DISPOSAL OF PROCEEDINGS WITHOUT HEARING

(1) **General**

As already explained (see p. 106), orders by a tribunal Chairman disposing of proceedings where no hearing is required are decisions and not interlocutory orders. They are entered in the Register of Decisions and where a tribunal has power to review its decision, are open to review.

(2) **Withdrawals, settlements and decisions by agreement**

Under r. 12(2)(*c*) of the Industrial Tribunals Rules of Procedure (Scotland) 1980 if an applicant or appellant gives notice of the withdrawal of his originating application or notice of appeal, the tribunal may dismiss the proceedings. There are equivalent powers in the other rules.[44]

The normal procedure is for the tribunal to issue an order recording the withdrawal of the case and dismissing the proceedings. If, however, the notice of withdrawal is not an ACAS form COT4, but comes directly from the applicant or his representative, and it appears to the Chairman from the notice that the withdrawal is not unilateral, but results from a settlement, then because of the problems regarding the validity of settlements explained above (see under "Conciliation and Settlement" (3) at pp. 131 to 133), the order should not state that the proceedings are dismissed, but only record that they are withdrawn. This enables them to be reopened should the necessity arise without the necessity of an

[44] The Industrial Tribunals Regulations (Scotland) 1965 (as amended) Sched. 2, r. 14(1)(*d*) (which also provides that if the board give notice that the appeal is not to be contested, the tribunal may make an order allowing the appeal); the Industrial Tribunals (Improvement and Prohibition Notices Appeals) (Scotland) Regulations 1974, r. 14(2)(*e*); the Industrial Tribunals (Non-Discrimination Notices Appeals) (Scotland) Regulations 1977, r. 12(2)(*e*).

application for review. If however the notice of withdrawal is an ACAS form COT4, no question should arise as to the validity of the withdrawal, and the proceedings will be dismissed.

Rule 12(5) of the 1980 rules provides that r. 11 regarding expenses shall apply to an order dismissing proceedings on a withdrawal. If therefore an application is withdrawn unilaterally in circumstances where unnecessary expense has been occasioned to the other side, an order for expenses may be made if the tribunal considers that the applicant's conduct in failing to withdraw at an earlier stage is frivolous or vexatious or otherwise unreasonable.[45] Withdrawals should therefore be intimated at as early a stage as possible. If a respondent considers that he has been prejudiced in this way an application for expenses should be made immediately the withdrawal is notified, so that it may be considered by the tribunal before any order dismissing the proceedings is pronounced. But an application for expenses after such an order has been pronounced is not incompetent, since the tribunal is not *functus officii* (*i.e.* its functions are not completely discharged) at that stage.[46] Likewise, if a respondent has previously given notice that expenses would be sought, or if a question of expenses has been reserved at an earlier stage of the proceedings, an order dismissing the proceedings should not be made without giving both parties the opportunity to state their position.

As far as settlements are concerned, for the reasons explained above (at p. 132) these should be recorded on ACAS form COT3 to avoid any subsequent question as to validity. When the form COT3 is received, the Chairman signs an order recording that settlement has been reached on the terms set out in the form (which normally are repeated in the order); ordering that the proceedings be indefinitely adjourned; and stating that parties may apply to the tribunal if any further difficulties arise. This enables the proceedings to be reopened should the necessity arise, *e.g.* if a party defaults or reneges on the agreed terms of settlement. In that event the other party could either ask for the merits of the case to be considered or (if an applicant) for an order on the respondent to pay any sum agreed to be paid by way of settlement. An award of expenses would usually be appropriate.

It is understood that when terms of settlement are agreed, some respondents seek to make it a condition of settlement that the proceedings be withdrawn, because under the foregoing procedure where the proceedings are settled, as opposed to withdrawn, the terms of settlement are normally recorded in the order adjourning the proceedings.

---

45 As to the meaning of "frivolous", "vexatious" and "otherwise unreasonable" see Chap. 10, pp. 234, 235.

46 *St. Mungo Community Trust* v. *Colleano* [1980] I.C.R. 254; *Zakia* v. *Home Office* (EAT 28/79).

As the order is entered in the Register of Decisions it is available to public inspection,[47] which the respondent may not wish. On the other hand the terms would not be recorded in the order pronounced on a withdrawal. From an applicant's point of view, on the other hand, it is undesirable for proceedings to be dismissed if agreed terms of settlement still remain to be implemented. The advantage of a COT3 is that it constitutes an enforceable agreement. There seems no reason however to prevent the parties from agreeing in a COT3 that the terms of settlement should not be recorded in the Register, in which case the tribunal's order adjourning the proceedings would merely narrate that parties had agreed terms of settlement, but would not disclose what the terms were. This may provide a solution in any case where the difference between these points of view presents a serious difficulty.

The course suggested would be competent, because each of the rules provide that (except in proceedings under the Docks and Harbours Act 1966) if the parties agree in writing upon the terms of a decision to be made by the tribunal, the tribunal may decide accordingly.[48] The original of the COT3 always remains on the case file, and parties will each also have copies to refer to, so the fact that the terms of settlement are not recorded in the decision in the Register should not present any serious practical difficulties if the proceedings have to be reopened.

(3) **Vexatious cases**

By r. 12(2)(*e*) of the Industrial Tribunals Rules of Procedure (Scotland) 1980 (but not under the other rules) the tribunal may at any stage of the proceedings order to be struck out or amended any originating application or notice of appearance on the ground that it is vexatious. (For the meaning of "Vexatious" see Chapter 10, p. 234).

No such order may be made unless notice has been given to the party concerned giving him an opportunity to show cause why it should not be made.

An order to strike out an originating application disposes of the proceedings and they would be dismissed. But an order to amend or to strike out a notice of appearance would be treated as an interlocutory order, and not a decision.

---

47 See Chap. 9, p. 194.

48 The Industrial Tribunals Rules of Procedure (Scotland) 1980, r. 12(2)(*d*); the Industrial Tribunals (Scotland) Regulations 1965 (as amended), Sched. 2, r. 14(1)(*e*); the Industrial Tribunals (Improvement and Prohibition Notices Appeals) (Scotland) Regulations 1974, r. 14(2)(*f*); the Industrial Tribunals (Non-Discrimination Notices Appeals) (Scotland) Regulations 1977, r. 12(2)(*f*).

(4) **Excessive delay**

By r. 12(2)(*f*) of the Industrial Tribunals Rules of Procedure (Scotland) 1980 the tribunal may, on the application of the respondent, or of its own motion, order an application to be struck out for excessive delay in proceeding with it. There are no equivalent provisions in the other rules.

Most stages in procedure are under the control of the tribunal, whose procedures are designed to minimise delay. An applicant may, however, ask for proceedings to be suspended owing to absence from the country; or the tribunal may have arrived at a decision favourable to the applicant on the merits of the case, without having been able to decide the remedy to be afforded to the applicant. In cases of this kind the initiative for reviving the proceedings rests with the applicant. Or the applicant may have disappeared, and cannot be contacted. This rule enables applications which have gone to sleep in such a way to be finally disposed of. No such order may be made without notice to the applicant giving him an opportunity to show cause why it should not be granted.

The usual procedure is that the application is treated as sisted (stayed) for 12 months, and if no further steps are taken to revive them, after due notice, an order is made dismissing the proceedings. But in the final analysis each case will depend on its own circumstances. In *Rahi* v. *H. M. Land Registry* [1979] I.C.R. 93 a delay of two years was held not to have been inordinate, but the circumstances were somewhat exceptional.

(5) **Failure to comply with orders for particulars and document orders**

The tribunal's powers to dismiss an originating application or strike out the whole or a part of a notice of appearance or debar a respondent from defending for failure to comply with an order for particulars or a document order have been noted at pp. 107 and 109 above.

A dismissal order would be treated as a decision, but any other order would be treated as interlocutory.

CHAPTER 7

THE HEARING

GENERAL: REGULATION OF PROCEDURE

The basic concepts of simplicity and informality, and the power of a tribunal to regulate its own procedure, subject to the provisions of the rules, have already been noted.[1] The latter power has enabled tribunals to regulate the conduct of a hearing without being obliged to follow the rules of practice in the civil courts, and so as to enable justice to be done between the parties in a flexible, informal and expeditious manner. It has thus been the basis of decisions that the ordinary rules of evidence do not apply in proceedings before industrial tribunals,[2] that if some untoward event occurs a tribunal has power to stop a case and order a re-hearing before a differently constituted tribunal,[3] and that there is no set rule for the order in which closing addresses should be made.[4] The power has now been reinforced in specific terms in the Industrial Tribunals Rules of Procedure (Scotland) 1980, rule 8(1) of which states as follows:—

> "The tribunal shall conduct the hearing in such manner as it considers most suitable to the clarification of the issues before it and generally to the just handling of the proceedings; it shall so far as it appears appropriate to it seek to avoid formality in its proceedings and it shall not be bound by any enactment or rule of law relating to the admissibility of evidence in civil proceedings".

While it may be trite to observe that tribunals must conform to the rules of natural justice, and natural justice has been invoked in relation to tribunal proceedings,[5] its rules are so rudimentary (and, to some extent, difficult to reconcile)[6] that they do not constitute an adequate or exhaustive test of the regularity of industrial tribunal proceedings, which have been the subject of much judicial authority. Where the rules of natural justice have been in issue, it has usually been in relation to the question whether a domestic appeal tribunal or committee has acted in conformity with them.

---

[1] See Chap. 1, p. 1 and Chap. 5, p. 89.

[2] *Douglas* v. *Provident Clothing and Supply Company Ltd.* (1969) 4 I.T.R. 15.

[3] *Charman* v. *Palmer's Scaffolding Ltd.* [1979] I.C.R. 335.

[4] *Glencross* v. *Dymoke* [1979] I.C.R. 536; *Peters* v. *Science Museum*, Court of Appeal, Nov. 29, 1979.

[5] *E.g. Haxey Engineering Ltd.* v. *Turner*, referred to at p. 168 below.

[6] See *Khanum* v. *Mid Glamorgan Health Authority* [1979] I.C.R. 40; *Bentley Engineering Co. Ltd.* v. *Mistry* [1979] I.C.R. 47. In *Barrs* v. *British Wool Marketing Board*, 1957 S.C. 72 it was stated that in considering whether a tribunal has contravened the principles of natural justice the question before the court is not whether the tribunal has arrived at a fair result, but whether it has dealt fairly and equally with the parties before it in arriving at that result (*per* the Lord President at p. 82).

The question whether the power of a tribunal to regulate its own procedure extends to enabling it to perform an act not provided for in the rules, or to dispense with a specific requirement in the rules, is discussed in Chapter 6 (at p. 120).

CONSTITUTION OF THE HEARING

In all the regulations and rules of procedure, the hearing is defined as meaning a "sitting of a tribunal duly constituted for the purpose of receiving evidence, hearing addresses and witnesses or doing anything lawfully requisite to enable the tribunal to reach a decision on any question."

The constitution of a tribunal for a hearing has been described in Chapter 3 above (see p. 20), and the method of convening the tribunal has been described in Chapter 5 (at pp. 101 to 103).

PUBLIC AND PRIVATE HEARINGS

In every case except appeals under the Industrial Training Act 1964, tribunal hearings are directed by the rules to be in public unless the tribunal decides that a private hearing would be appropriate. In *Milne and Lyall* v. *Waldren* [1980] I.C.R. 138 the Employment Appeal Tribunal upheld a decision by a Chairman that this was a matter to be decided by the tribunal convened to hear the case, and expressed a tentative opinion that it was not within the powers of a Chairman sitting alone to decide such a matter.

Under the Industrial Tribunals Rules of Procedure (Scotland) 1980 (rule 7(1)) a private hearing may take place where in the opinion of the tribunal it would be against the interests of national security to allow the evidence to be given in public, or where evidence is to be given which in the opinion of the tribunal is likely to consist of—

(*a*) information which could not be disclosed without contravening a prohibition imposed by or under any enactment; or

(*b*) any information which has been communicated in confidence or which has been otherwise obtained in consequence of the confidence reposed in the witness by another person; or

(*c*) information the disclosure of which would cause substantial injury to any undertaking in which the witness works for reasons other than its effect on negotiations with respect to any of the matters mentioned in s. 29(1) of the Trade Union and Labour Relations Act 1974 (*i.e.* a trade dispute).

The equivalent provisions in the Industrial Tribunals (Improvement and Prohibition Notices Appeals) (Scotland) Regulations 1974 (rule 7(1)), and in the Industrial Tribunals (Non-Discrimination Notices Appeals) (Scotland) Regulations 1977 (rule 5(1)), are similar, but grounds (*a*) and (*b*) above do not apply, and under ground (*c*) is included the possibility of prejudice to the undertaking of the appellant. But in appeals under the Industrial Training Act 1964, the hearing is directed to be in private unless the appellant requests that it be in public. (The Industrial Tribunals (Scotland) Regulations 1965, (as amended), Sched. 2, r. 9(1)).

All the rules contain provisions enabling a member of the Council on Tribunals or of its Scottish Committee to be present at a hearing which is in private.

If the tribunal decides to allow a private hearing because some of the evidence falls within the categories specified as appropriate to be heard in private, the whole hearing takes place in private, because it would be impracticable to hold the rest of the hearing in public without jeopardising the confidentiality of the part for which a private hearing is necessary. In *Cahm* v. *Ward and Goldstone Ltd.* [1979] I.C.R. 574, where civil proceedings were also pending, it was held that the industrial tribunal proceedings should be adjourned pending the hearing of the High Court action, in the course of which it would be decided whether the evidence should be heard in public, and that the question whether the adjourned industrial tribunal proceedings should be heard in private should be decided in the light of the views taken in the High Court action. This case should not necessarily be regarded as a precedent for any similar situation which might arise in industrial tribunal proceedings in Scotland.[7]

APPEARANCE AND REPRESENTATION

Each of the rules provide that at the hearing a party who is entitled to be heard (which of course does not include a respondent excluded by r. 3(2) of the Industrial Tribunals Rules of Procedure (Scotland) 1980[8]) may present his case in person or through a representative. In each of the rules, with one exception, the representative may be counsel or a solicitor, or any other person whom the party may desire to represent him; specific reference is made to representatives of trade unions and employers' associations in certain cases, but this seems hardly necessary in view of the wide terms in which the rules are couched.[9] But in *Singh* v. *London Country Bus Services Ltd.* (1976) 11 I.T.R. 131 the view was expressed that it was undesirable that a person who was a member of an appeal body which considered the employee's case should conduct the employers' case before the industrial tribunal.

[7] See Chap. 6 at p. 121.

[8] *I.e.* one who has not entered appearance—see Chap. 5, p. 100.

[9] The Industrial Tribunals Rules of Procedure (Scotland) 1980, r. 7(6); the Industrial Tribunals (Scotland) Regulations 1965 (as amended), Sched. 2, r. 10(1); the Industrial Tribunals (Improvement and Prohibition Notices Appeals) (Scotland) Regulations 1974, r. 9; the Industrial Tribunals (Non-Discrimination Notices Appeals) (Scotland) Regulations 1977, r. 7.

Under the Industrial Tribunals (Scotland) Regulations 1965, as amended (for appeals under the Industrial Training Act 1964), however, the appellant may only be represented by a person other than counsel or a solicitor with leave of the tribunal, and the respondent industrial training board, if not represented by counsel or a solicitor, may only be represented by a member or officer of the board (Sched. 2, r. 10(1) and 10(2)).

In cases under the Industrial Tribunals Rules of Procedure (Scotland) 1980, the Secretary of State may appear and be heard as if he were a party in proceedings which may involve any payments out of the Redundancy Fund or the Maternity Pay Fund (rule 7(5)).

In the courts a case may be presented only by a legal representative or by the litigant in person. Legal representation is the norm, and statutory legal aid is available to litigants who qualify for it. In tribunal proceedings legal aid is only available under the statutory legal advice scheme, which covers pre-hearing procedures, but does not extend to cover the cost of representation at the hearing. This is because, as already stated, tribunal procedures are designed to encourage parties to feel able to avoid expense by presenting their cases without legal representation. In practice, about 45 per cent of employees are unrepresented, about 40 per cent are legally represented, and about 15 per cent by persons who are not legally qualified (mainly trade union officials), while about 40 per cent of employers are not legally represented. Absence of legal representation is not of itself a ground for ordering a case to be re-heard,[10] unless there are other circumstances which make the case exceptional.[11]

During the course of the hearing, parties and their representatives are entitled to be present throughout the proceedings even if they are to give evidence. A party which is a firm or company may, if represented, have one of its members present throughout the hearing to instruct its representative, and that person is not thereby debarred from giving evidence.

PARTIES WHO DO NOT APPEAR: WRITTEN REPRESENTATIONS

Each of the rules provide that if a party fails to appear or be represented at the time and the place fixed for the hearing, the tribunal may dispose of the case in his absence or adjourn it until a later date.[12]

---

10 *Dalton* v. *Burtons Gold Medal Biscuits Ltd.* [1974] I.R.L.R. 45.

11 *Sinclair* v. *SCWS Ltd.* (1972) 7 I.T.R. 185.

12 The Industrial Tribunals Rules of Procedure (Scotland) 1980, r. 8(3); the Industrial Tribunals (Scotland) Regulations 1965 (as amended), Sched. 2, r. 11(3); the Industrial Tribunals (Improvement and Prohibition Notices Appeals) (Scotland) Regulations 1974, r. 10(2); the Industrial Tribunals (Non-Discrimination Notices Appeals) (Scotland) Regulations 1977, r. 8(2).

The rules also provide that parties may submit written representations to the Secretary for consideration by the tribunal. Such representations must be sent not less than seven days before the hearing and a copy must be sent at the same time to the other party.[13] If a party does not appear, the tribunal must not dispose of the application in his absence without considering any such representations.[14]

The Industrial Tribunals Rules of Procedure (Scotland) 1980 provide that where a party fails to appear, the tribunal may treat as written representations the contents of the originating application or notice of appearance (as the case may be), whether or not any other written representations have been submitted (rule 7(4)). In practice this would also be done in cases under the other rules, although there is no specific provision to that effect. While written representations are always helpful in that they assist the tribunal to identify the issues (and to that extent are to be encouraged), it is only appropriate to leave a case to be decided upon them where the facts are not in dispute and only submissions are necessary. In most cases it is inappropriate to do so, and particularly so for either party in proceedings of a contentious nature.

If a party (other than a respondent who is not entitled to be heard under r. 3(2) of the Industrial Tribunals Rules of Procedure (Scotland) 1980 because he has failed to enter appearance) fails to appear, unless the tribunal has been forewarned that he does not intend to be present and is content that it should proceed to dispose of the case in his absence, it must enquire into the circumstances before deciding what action to take, since, notwithstanding the provisions which enable a tribunal to dipose of a case in a party's absence, to proceed to do so may amount to a fundamental nullity if there has been a flaw in the antecedent procedure,[15] entitling the party to appeal against the decision[16] or even to seek to have it reduced in the civil courts[17], and in any event may entitle him to apply to have the decision reviewed by the tribunal.[18]

---

[13] The Industrial Tribunals Rules of Procedure (Scotland) 1980, r. 7(3); the Industrial Tribunals (Scotland) Regulations 1965 (as amended), Sched. 2, r. 9(2); the Industrial Tribunals (Improvement and Prohibition Notices Appeals) (Scotland) Regulations 1974, r. 8; the Industrial Tribunals (Non-Discrimination Notices Appeals) (Scotland) Regulations 1977, r. 6.

[14] The Industrial Tribunals Rules of Procedure (Scotland) 1980, r. 8(3); the Industrial Tribunals (Scotland) Regulations 1965, (as amended), Sched. 2, r. 11(3); the Industrial Tribunals (Improvement and Prohibition Notices Appeals) (Scotland) Regulations 1974, r. 10(2); the Industrial Tribunals (Non-Discrimination Notices Appeals) (Scotland) Regulations 1977, r. 8(2).

[15] See *R.* v. *The Industrial Tribunal* (ex p. *George Green and Thompson Ltd.*) (1967) 2 I.T.R. 360; *R.* v. *London Quarter Sessions* (ex p. *Rossi*) [1956] 1 All E.R. 670; *Priddle* v. *Fisher and Sons* (1968) 3 I.T.R. 358.

[16] See Chap. 12 *supra*.

[17] See Gloag and Henderson, *Introduction to the Law of Scotland*, 8th ed., at p. 18.

[18] See Chap. 11, *supra*.

The tribunal first requires to be satisfied therefore that the party has had sufficient notice of the proceedings, and in particular that the requirements of the rules in that respect have been complied with.[19] If it is possible to contact the party's residence or place of business by telephone, this is done by the tribunal clerk to try to find out the reason for his absence. The tribunal office is also searched to ascertain whether he has arrived but failed to make his presence known or has been misdirected. If it appears that the party intends to come but has been delayed, the tribunal will allow reasonable time for him to arrive. If after the expiry of a reasonable period (usually 30 minutes) after the time appointed the missing party has not arrived and there is no explanation, the tribunal will decide what should be done in the circumstances, taking into account any submissions made by the other party, and such indications as may be available as to the reason for the absence. If there is any indication of an acceptable reason, the case will be adjourned to a later date, but reserving the question of the expense of the abortive hearing until then, to be decided in the light of such explanations as may be tendered. Otherwise, if the absent party is an applicant or appellant, the practice in Scotland is to dismiss the application if the respondent asks for this to be done, with a suitable award of expenses if the circumstances appear to justify it.[20]

If the missing party is a respondent, however, the tribunal will usually proceed to hear and decide the case in his absence. They will hear such evidence from the applicant as is necessary to enable them to decide whether *prima facie* he qualifies for the relief which he claims,[21] and if satisfied on that matter, also to enable them to decide what remedy to afford.

In either case the tribunal's decision is open to review on the ground that it was taken in the absence of a party entitled to be heard,[22] and this is made clear in the written decision which is sent to the absent party at his address for service. In *D. C. Thomson & Co. Ltd.* v. *Alexander* (EAT 158/79) a review granted because the reason for the applicant's non-appearance was failure on the part of his solicitor to note the date of the hearing was upheld by the Employment Appeal Tribunal.

CONDUCT OF THE HEARING

With the exception of the Industrial Tribunals Rules of Procedure (Scotland) 1980, each of the rules provide that at the hearing the parties who

[19] See Chap. 5 at p. 101 and Chap. 6 at p. 127.

[20] See Chap. 10 at pp. 237, 238.

[21] *E.g.* in unfair dismissal and redundancy cases, that he was dismissed and had the requisite period of service.

[22] See Chap. 11 at p. 244.

are entitled to appear shall be entitled to make opening statements, to give evidence, to call witnesses, to cross-examine witnesses and to address the tribunal.[23]

The predecessor to the Industrial Tribunals Rules of Procedure (Scotland) 1980 contained similar provisions,[24] but r. 8(2) of the 1980 rules limits the entitlement of parties who are entitled to appear (including the Secretary of State if, not being a party he elects to appear under r. 7(5), as noted above) to giving evidence, calling witnesses, questioning (as opposed to cross-examining) witnesses, and addressing the tribunal. The changes were made to emphasise the difference between tribunal procedures and those of the courts, especially in relation to the English practice of making opening statements (see further below under that heading), with a view to avoiding any tendency to unnecessary legalism in tribunal proceedings. Each of the rules also provides that the tribunal may require any witness to give evidence on oath or affirmation.[25]

Subject to these provisions and the other provisions of the rules, a tribunal, as already noted,[26] may regulate the procedure of the hearing as it thinks fit. While the interests of justice require the proceedings to be orderly, excessive legal formalism inhibits the average person, who would be daunted by the prospect of appearing before a court, and tribunals therefore try to conduct their proceedings in as informal a manner as is consistent with dignity and fair play. How this is done will vary according to the nature and complexity of the proceedings and whether the parties are represented legally or otherwise. In the courts, where the parties are almost always legally represented and the issues are defined in advance, proceedings are conducted in the "adversarial" manner within a relatively complex setting of procedural rules which vary according to the nature of the proceedings. It is for counsel or solicitors to elicit the evidence which they consider (or hope) sufficient to establish their case or rebut their opponent's, with the judge playing a relatively inactive part, and intervening only if objection is taken to any particular line of evidence, or if there is an obvious breach of the rules of procedure or a point which obviously requires to be clarified.

---

23 The Industrial Tribunals (Scotland) Regulations 1965 (as amended) Sched. 2, r. 11(1); the Industrial Tribunals (Improvement and Prohibition Notices Appeals) (Scotland) Regulations 1974, r. 10(1); the Industrial Tribunals (Non-Discrimination Notices Appeals) (Scotland) Regulations 1977, r. 8(1).

24 The Industrial Tribunals (Labour Relations) (Scotland) Regulations 1974, r. 7(1).

25 The Industrial Tribunals Rules of Procedure (Scotland) 1980, r. 8(4); the Industrial Tribunals (Scotland) Regulations 1965 (as amended), Sched. 2, r. 11(4); the Industrial Tribunals (Improvement and Prohibition Notices Appeals) (Scotland) Regulations 1974, r. 10(3); the Industrial Tribunals (Non-Discrimination Notices Appeals) (Scotland) Regulations 1977, r. 8(3).

26 See above, p. 138.

It has been held that in tribunals it is the duty of parties, whether legally represented or not, to see that the relevant evidence is placed before the tribunal; that there is no duty on the tribunal to act as an investigatory tribunal; and that the system in tribunals as well as courts is an adversarial one (*Craig* v. *British Railways* (1973) 8 I.T.R. 636; *Oakley & Son* v. *Bradford* (EAT 19/2/80)). These cases were decided before the 1980 rules came into operation. Even under the rules in force at the time they would have had to be regarded as not entirely recognising the difficulties which arise if the adversarial system is not, to say the least, in some measure adapted, in proceedings before industrial tribunals. The issues may be just as complex, and sometimes more so, than those in civil litigation, but the deliberately simpler procedural rules and the frequent absence of legal representation on one or both sides, had to dictate a more flexible approach. If the issues have been well defined in advance and the parties are both represented by experienced legal representatives, an adversarial manner of proceeding may be appropriate, and the part played by the tribunal may be little different from that of the judge in court proceedings, except that the chairman may intervene from time to time to clarify issues or avoid unnecessary enquiry. Just as frequently, however, either or both of the parties is unrepresented, ignorant of the legal issues involved in the case, and unversed in the skills of advocacy (to the extent that they are often incapable of framing questions, particularly in cross-examination) and the rules of litigation. An unqualified representative will often labour under similar difficulties. For these very reasons the issues are often ill-defined at the outset and have to be identified. In that situation the adoption of a strictly adversarial approach would be inappropriate, and prevent justice being done. In *Craig* v. *British Railways, supra* it was recognised that a tribunal would give persons who are not legally qualified or are manifestly unversed in legal procedure such assistance as they can in presenting their cases. So while parties and witnesses can be invited and encouraged to recount the facts, and indications can be given to them and their representatives as to what lines of enquiry are relevant, often the only way by which the tribunal can effectively get at the facts which are essential for the determination of the issue is to take the initiative in asking questions which, drawing on their experience, and the information already disclosed, seem appropriate for that purpose.

The primary responsibility for conducting this kind of enquiry lies with the Chairman, who has a delicate balance to maintain in ensuring that where a party lacks skilled representation, the points which are relevant to his case are uncovered and adequately tested, without compromising the impartiality with which he must be seen to conduct the proceedings. This is particularly so when such parties are given the opportunity to cross-examine, which they usually find difficult. Then the Chairman has to try to find out what are the points which the party seeks to make against the witness and suggest how the relevant ones should be put to the witness, or put them himself. The other members also play an important role in asking such questions as seem appropriate in the light of their experience, which they too should be careful to do in as an impartial manner as possible. In *Dugdale* v. *Kraft Foods Ltd.* [1977] I.C.R. 48, however, it was stated that while members are entitled to draw on their knowledge and experience for the purpose of explaining and understanding the evidence, if evidence is given which is contrary to their knowledge and experience, they should put their contrary knowledge and experience to the witness so that he may deal with it. For the part which such matters should play in the tribunal's decision, see also *Hammington* v. *Berker Sportcraft Ltd.* [1980] I.C.R. 248, and Chapter 3 at p. 24.

The adoption of a system of this kind, besides being often inescapable where there is no legal representation, also has advantages where parties are legally represented, by enabling the common ground to be established, unnecessary enquiries to be eliminated, and the essential matters to be more quickly reached. It reflects the different conception of industrial tribunal proceedings, as compared with those of the courts, which has already been commented upon above, and which is now reflected specifically in r. 8(1) of the Industrial Tribunals Rules of Procedure (Scotland) 1980, and its equivalent in England and Wales.[27] Thus while under such a system the duty may (and should, it is submitted) still lie on parties to see that the relevant evidence is put before the tribunal, tribunals could not discharge their functions properly if they were to be precluded from adopting an "investigatory" approach, so far as may be necessary to achieve the ends of justice.

THE ORDER OF PROCEEDING

Apart from any other preliminary points, the first question which has to be settled is which party is to start. Unless parties agree on grounds of convenience to depart from the usual order, the party who leads is the one on whom the primary onus lies in law.[28] For example, in unfair dismissal cases, if dismissal is admitted, the onus is on the employer to show the reason for the dismissal, and his case is heard first; if dismissal is not admitted, however, the primary onus is on the applicant to show that he was dismissed, and he leads. But in *Hawker Siddeley Power Engineering Ltd.* v. *Rump* [1979] I.R.L.R. 425 it was held that there had

---

[27] See above, p. 138 and Chap. 1, p. 1.

[28] See Chap. 8 at pp. 173 to 175.

been no irregularity in asking the employers' representative to open when dismissal was in issue, and there are cases in which this may make for convenience.

OPENING STATEMENTS

As pointed out above (under "Conduct of the hearing"[29]) parties are not entitled to make opening statements in cases under the Industrial Tribunals Rules of Procedure (Scotland) 1980, although the tribunal may permit such a statement to be made. Whether it will do so will usually depend on the amount of information already disclosed. In Scotland, opening statements do not generally form part of civil or criminal court procedures. If an opening statement is made to the tribunal, it usually consists of a short summary of the essential features of the case, and a brief indication of the evidence which it is proposed to lay before the tribunal, without going into the amount of detail which is understood to be customary in England. Lengthy and detailed statements are not usually expected or encouraged. Under the other rules, however, a party is entitled to make an opening statement,[30] but the same principles will apply.

In any event, if the case papers do not adequately indicate the main issues in the case, the tribunal will usually ask either or both of the parties to summarise their respective positions before beginning to hear the evidence. While there is no system of formal written pleadings as in the courts, nevertheless the tribunal's task is considerably eased if, within reasonable limits and without unnecessary prolixity, parties state their respective cases adequately in writing beforehand, because in that way the tribunal will be able to ascertain the common ground and get quicker to the heart of the differences between them. Where the originating application or the notice of appearance does not give details, therefore, it is always of assistance if parties submit statements summarising their respective cases, preferably in writing before the hearing, but failing that at its commencement, either orally or in writing. If there is representation on both sides and a joint statement of admitted facts can be arrived at and put before the tribunal, so much the better.

It should be kept in view that factual statements made in an opening statement will not be regarded as evidence, unless they are a matter of

---

29 See p. 144.

30 The Industrial Tribunals (Scotland) Regulations 1965 (as amended), Sched. 2, r. 11(1); the Industrial Tribunals (Improvement and Prohibition Notices Appeals) (Scotland) Regulations 1974, r. 10(1); the Industrial Tribunals (Non-Discrimination Notices Appeals) (Scotland) Regulations 1977, r. 8(1).

admission, and they have to be proved in evidence. But in an English case where an applicant in an opening statement took up a position which was inconsistent with his having been dismissed, the tribunal's decision to stop the case at that point and hear no evidence was upheld.[31]

PRESENTATION OF EVIDENCE

The usual procedure is for the witnesses for the party leading to give their evidence in turn, followed by those on the other side. Witnesses other than parties themselves (or the representative of a firm or corporate body[32]) stay outside the tribunal room until their turn comes. Once their evidence has been given, they may remain in the tribunal room, and if they do so they are not barred from being recalled to give further evidence at a later stage. Accordingly, they should not leave without the tribunal's permission. While a witness is under examination he should not discuss the case, or his own evidence, with any other person, nor should he be approached on the subject, if his examination is interrupted by an adjournment. If it emerges that any such discussion has taken place, this may be brought to the notice of the tribunal. The witness should, so far as practicable, remain apart from other persons during the adjournment.

A witness may refresh his memory from notes taken at the time, but will not usually be allowed to give his evidence by reading from or handing in a precognition, or other equivalent written statement prepared for the purpose of the hearing.[33] Normally he will give evidence by answering questions from the party who has called him, or his representative, but in cases where the party is unrepresented, or where the representative lacks experience, he may be invited by the tribunal to give his account of the matters on which he is called to give evidence, with the tribunal asking such questions as it may consider appropriate.

Having given his evidence-in-chief, the witness is open to questioning by or on behalf of the opposite party. As already pointed out[34] there is a difference between the wording of the rules in this respect. Under the Industrial Tribunal Rules of Procedure (Scotland) 1980 (rule 8(2)) a party is entitled to *question* a witness, whereas under the other rules he is entitled to *cross-examine*, as was also the case in the rules which preceded the 1980 rules. Inasmuch that cross-examination is the

---

31 *Brennan* v. *C. Lindley and Co. Ltd.* [1974] I.R.L.R. 153.

32 See above, p. 141.

33 See *Hardisty* v. *Lowton Construction Group Ltd.* (1973) 8 I.T.R. 603.

34 Under "Conduct of the hearing" at p. 144.

process of questioning the opposite party's witnesses, the difference in wording is of little practical significance, but the wording of the 1980 rules serves to demonstrate that the rules of the law of evidence in the courts about the conduct of cross-examination, and the effects of failure to cross-examine, do not apply in tribunal proceedings.[35] With that reservation, it remains convenient to call the questioning of the opposite party's witnesses cross-examination, under whichever of the rules the case may fall. The witness may also be questioned by the tribunal.[36]

An opportunity to cross-examine should usually always be given.[37] But where the evidence-in-chief of a party or (where the party is a firm), of its main witness, creates such an adverse impression that he cannot possibly succeed on any issue, cross-examination may be dispensed with as unnecessary. The purposes of cross-examination are to test the credibility of the witness, and the accuracy of his evidence, and to bring out points helpful to the cross-examiner not mentioned in his evidence-in-chief. Its scope will be controlled by the tribunal and incursions into irrelevant, extraneous or peripheral matters will be restrained unless appropriate for the purpose of testing credibility. But to set arbitrary limits, such as a time limit, for purposes of personal convenience is improper.[38] If a new matter emerges from the tribunal's questions, further cross-examination will generally be allowed on that subject.

Finally, the party who has adduced the witness may re-examine. The purpose of re-examination is to clear up any confusion or contradictions which have emerged as a result of cross-examination, and in that way it can be useful, but should be confined to matters which have already arisen. Parties and their representatives should therefore try to ensure that all matters which they regard as significant are brought out in evidence-in-chief, and not as an after-thought when cross-examination and questions by the tribunal are over. If an attempt is made to raise new matter in re-examination, the tribunal may allow such evidence to be led if they consider that this would be in the interests of justice, and will allow more latitude in this respect to a party who is unrepresented or whose representative is inexperienced. But if they do so, the opposite party should be allowed the opportunity to cross-examine on the new matter.

The form and scope of questions in evidence are discussed further in Chapter 8 below (see pp. 185 to 187), where the reasons for the need to

35 See Chap. 8 at p. 178 *et seq*.

36 As to how this should be done, see above ("Conduct of the hearing") at p. 146, and Chap. 3, p.24.

37 *McBride* v. *British Railways Board and Anr.* (1972) 7 I.T.R. 84.

38 *Vickers* v. *Hudson Brothers (Middlesborough) Ltd.* (1970) 5 I.T.R. 259.

interview a witness before the hearing, and note the evidence which he can give, are also pointed out.

In *Barnes and Taylor* v. *BPC (Business Forms) Ltd.* [1975] I.C.R. 390 it was held that a tribunal should not dictate the order in which witnesses are called, but that a procedural irregularity of this kind would not necessarily invalidate the proceedings. This case was decided before the Industrial Tribunals Rules of Procedure (Scotland) 1980 came into operation, however, r. 8(1) of which[39] gives a tribunal a very wide discretion in the way in which the hearing may be conducted. It is thought that the case would now be authoritative only in cases falling under the other rules. It may appear that the evidence of a witness is unlikely to be necessary, or that a change in the intended order of evidence would be of advantage, *e.g.* to enable a witness to be released and so get back to work; to save a witness whose evidence is likely to be of short duration from having to return on another day; or where, having heard the essentials of the case from the main witnesses on one side, the tribunal feel that they wish to hear the main evidence for the opponent, particularly if his position does not seem clear, as can often be the case where there is no representation. In such situations, in cases under the 1980 rules, the tribunal may decide what witnesses are are to be heard, and in what order. In cases falling under the other rules, on the authority of *Barnes and Taylor, supra,* the tribunal may only make suggestions of that kind, leaving it in the final analysis for the parties to agree that the order of calling witnesses may be changed, or for the party concerned to dispense with a witness. But it should not decide that a witness be dispensed with unless it is unanimously satisfied either that the evidence would appear to be irrelevant, or that the evidence so far led on the subject appears to be sufficient. If the tribunal is in any doubt on these matters, the evidence of the witness should be heard.

If a change in the order of witnesses is made or a witness is dispensed with at the tribunal's ruling or suggestion, it should always be made clear that the witnesses who have been held back or dispensed with can be called later if this appears appropriate in the light of subsequent evidence: but the tribunal need not do so where a party on his own initiative elects not to call a witness.

ATTESTATION OF WITNESSES

Normally evidence is given on oath or affirmation, but factual statements made informally may be volunteered or elicited. Such statements should not be accepted as evidence unless admitted by the

---

[39] See above, p. 138.

other side; if disputed or if further elaboration or clarification seems necessary, then evidence on oath should be given on the matter.[40]

The oath is administered by the Chairman in the usual form used in the Scottish courts,

> "I swear by Almighty God that I will tell the truth, the whole truth and nothing but the truth."

Affirmation is appropriate where a person objects to taking the oath on the ground that he has no religious belief, or that taking an oath is contrary to his religious belief,[41] or where it is not reasonably practicable, without inconvenience or delay, to administer an oath in the manner appropriate to the witness's religious belief.[42]

The form of affirmation is,

> "I do solemnly, sincerely and truly declare and affirm that I will tell the truth . . . (etc, as above)."

An affirmation has the same effect as if made on oath.[43] If a witness desires to add to the oath a ceremony peculiar to his faith or country[44] (*e.g.* a Jew may desire to swear on the Pentateuch with his head covered), he may be permitted to do so, but if this would not be reasonably practicable, he may be required, under the Oaths Act 1961, to affirm instead.

Section 7(1)(*a*) of the False Oaths (Scotland) Act 1933 provides that for the purpose of proceedings for making a false statement on oath or for perjury at common law, the forms and ceremonies used in administering an oath shall be immaterial if the person before whom the oath is taken has power to administer an oath for the purpose of verifying the statements in question, and if the oath has been administered in a form and with ceremonies which the person taking the oath has accepted without objection or has declared to be binding on him.

An industrial tribunal does not have the power to punish for contempt of court, and therefore cannot itself impose a sanction on a person who wilfully refuses to take an oath, *i.e.* who does not object on one of the specified grounds for which affirmation may be made instead. It could only deal with such a case by noting in its decision that the witness had so refused, and that this fact had been taken into account in assessing the value of his evidence. But once an oath has been taken or affirmation made, the sanction of prosecution for perjury or for making a false oath is available. If the stringent standards of proof in such cases is to be satisfied, however, it has to be proved that the

---

40 *Dahad* v. *B.V. Circuits Ltd.* (EAT 195/78).

41 Oaths Act 1888, ss. 1 and 2.

42 Oaths Act, 1961, s. 1.

43 False Oaths (Scotland) Act 1933, s. 7(1)(*b*).

44 See Dobie, *Sheriff Court Practice*, p. 190.

oath was administered or affirmation made, and the witness has to be adequately identified. This may pose difficulties in practice.

INTERPRETERS

If a witness, whether a party to the proceedings or not, is deaf and dumb, or unable to speak or understand English, his evidence should be given through a suitably qualified interpreter, who should be sworn honestly and faithfully to perform his duties as such. Where the person under such a disability is a party, the interpreter should be present throughout the hearing to interpret the evidence of other witnesses and the other statements and submissions made during the course of the proceedings.[45]

RECORDING OF EVIDENCE

It is the duty of the Chairman to record the substance of the verbal evidence which is given, but he is under no duty to make a verbatim record.[46] The other members of the tribunal and the tribunal clerk also make notes of the evidence, and parties are of course free to make their own notes.

In the event of a question arising on appeal as to whether material evidence was given which is not referred to in the tribunal's written decision, or that a fact found by the tribunal is contrary to the evidence, the Employment Appeal Tribunal may call for copies of the Chairman's notes to be supplied, but in Scotland will not do so otherwise; in particular the notes will not be provided to enable the appellant's adviser to comb through them in order to find a ground of appeal.[47]

While the tribunal cannot object to parties noting the proceedings for themselves in shorthand, cases have arisen in which attempts have been made to do so on a tape recorder. The practice is considered to be objectionable, on the view that it could inhibit witnesses from giving evidence to a greater degree than if the evidence is being noted in shorthand, and it is generally disapproved of.

---

45 *McGowan* v. *G. S. Thompson Ltd.*, (EAT/780/78).

46 *Archbold Freightage Ltd.* v. *Wilson* [1974] I.R.L.R. 10; *Hector Powe Ltd.* v. *Melon* (EAT 512/1977).

47 *Hector Powe Ltd.* v. *Melon, supra.*

PRODUCTIONS: DOCUMENTARY EVIDENCE

In contrast to the practice of the courts, there are no requirements that productions should be inventoried and lodged prior to the commencement of the hearing, nor as to providing copies of documents, photographs etc. for the tribunal and the opposite side. To impose such a requirement on an unrepresented party would be impracticable. Nevertheless in practice productions are often lodged with the originating application or notice of appearance, or at some intermediate stage prior to the commencement of the hearing. It is of considerable assistance if they are. More frequently, however, they are produced either in a bundle at the beginning of the hearing or separately as the hearing proceeds. Where in an English case a large bundle of documents was produced immediately prior to the commencement of a hearing, the party producing them was found liable for the costs of an adjournment granted to enable them to be considered by the opposite party.[48] At whatever stage documents are lodged, it always helps if they are listed, and copies are provided for the use of the three members of the tribunal and the opposite party.

Productions which have been lodged before the hearing (whether voluntarily or under a document order) do not become part of the evidence in the case until they have been referred to at the hearing and admitted in evidence. This should always be made clear by the Chairman when documents have been lodged beforehand, lest parties assume that prior lodgment is sufficient.

Once referred to and admitted in evidence, the production is numbered with the prefix "A" or "R" according to whether it has been produced by the applicant or appellant, or by the respondent. Normally it remains with the case papers until the period for lodging an appeal has expired. But if required for business or any other reasonable purposes in the meanwhile (as for instance in the case of business books or diaries which are in day-to-day use) the production will be returned on request once the tribunal has arrived at its decision (copies having been made of the passages on which the tribunal have relied in reaching their decision, and of any others which have been referred to in evidence), on the understanding that they will be returned if required at the hearing of the appeal.

If objection is taken at the hearing to a document being admitted in evidence, the decision on the matter is one for the tribunal, but it is for the Chairman to advise his colleagues whether there are any legal considerations which militate against production. He would normally adopt the same approach as when considering an application for a

---

48 *Ladbroke Racing Ltd.* v. *Hickey* [1979] I.C.R. 525.

document order.[49] Generally speaking, documents should be allowed unless clearly inadmissible. Where admissibility may be in doubt, the document may be admitted under reservation of that question. In *Vickers Ltd.* v. *Smith* [1977] I.R.L.R. 11 it was held that a tribunal was wrong in not permitting a doctor's report to be put in as evidence by the employers on grounds that no notice of the report had been given: if the applicant was prejudiced by lack of notice an adjournment could have been allowed. In *Rosedale Mouldings Ltd.* v. *Sibley* [1980] I.C.R. 816 a tribunal was held to have been wrong to exclude on grounds of possible prejudice a document which was admissible at common law and probative of issues before it.

When productions are tendered for admission in evidence, the leading of evidence should stop while they are considered by the tribunal and the other side. Depending on their length and importance, adjournment may be necessary for this purpose, particularly if they raise new matter which may take the other side by surprise.

While photographs, films, tape recordings, items of plant, and the like cannot be made the subject of a document order,[50] they may be admitted in evidence. Questions may arise as to the weight to be given to such evidence, and if not admitted, the identity of the production would have to be proved.[51]

When excerpts of lengthy documents (*e.g.* working rule agreements) are produced, difficulties can arise if the excerpt is not admitted to be what it purports to be, or if objection is taken that the complete document contains other matter which would put the excerpt in a different light. If this happens, the complete document may have to be produced, which may even involve continuing the case for further hearing. Whether the tribunal will be prepared to grant such latitude, or will decide that the matter must rest on the evidence adduced, and according to where the onus lies, will depend on the circumstances. Whenever possible, therefore, such documents should be produced complete, with suitable excerpts for the use of the tribunal and the other side. As explained above, they can be returned once the tribunal has arrived at its decision.

WITNESSES WHO CANNOT ATTEND

If a necessary witness cannot attend the hearing for *bona fide* reasons such as illness, essential business commitments or holiday arrangements made without reason to anticipate that the date of the hearing

---

49 See Chap. 6, p. 112, and Chap. 8, pp. 184, 185.

50 See Chap. 6, p. 110.

51 See Chap. 8, p. 184.

would clash with them, the tribunal, if satisfied as to the genuineness and reasonableness of the reason (a medical certificate may be required where the reason given is illness), and if of the opinion that evidence of the witness is necessary, will usually agree to adjourn the hearing until a date when the witness is available.

The difficulty should be brought to the notice of the tribunal as soon as it is known, however. If this is done in sufficient time before the hearing, the matter will be dealt with by a Chairman on an interlocutory basis;[52] he would usually decide that the hearing as a whole should be postponed. If it arises at or on the eve of the hearing, and the tribunal consider that the evidence of the witness is essential, it may decide to adjourn, or to hear all or part of the rest of the evidence in the meanwhile, in which case a change in the order of witnesses may be required.[53]

Where the reason given for inability to attend is ill-health of indefinite duration, or that the witness is house-bound on account of old age, application may be made for the tribunal to visit the witness to hear his evidence, in which case the tribunal, their clerk, and representatives of both parties would attend at the appropriate location. To hear the evidence of a particular witness in this way would not appear to conflict with the general requirement that tribunal hearings should be in public (on this see also below under "Inspection" at p. 160). So too, if on the likely date of the hearing a witness will be absent abroad permanently or for a lengthy period, arrangements can be made for the hearing to be accelerated or for a special hearing to take the witness's evidence. But any such special arrangements could not take place on less than the 14 days' notice required by the rules for a hearing unless both parties agree.[54]

By contrast with court proceedings, it would be incompetent for the tribunal to grant commission to one of its number to hear evidence, because such evidence would not have been taken at a hearing duly constituted in terms of the rules.[55]

THE SCOPE OF THE HEARING

As already noted,[56] in *Craig* v. *British Railways* (1973) 8 I.T.R. 636 it was held that there was no duty incumbent on the tribunal itself to ensure

---

52 See Chap. 6, pp. 120, 121.

53 See above, p. 150.

54 See Chap. 5, p. 101.

55 See above, p. 139 and Chap. 5, p. 101.

56 See above, p. 145.

that all relevant evidence is before it, even in cases where parties are not legally represented.[57] The tribunal's duties to parties who are not legally represented have been defined as being to ensure that they are aware that they may apply for such orders for further particulars, production of documents or citation of witnesses as they may consider appropriate.[58] There is no *duty* on the tribunal to investigate and consider a possible defence which has not been put in issue, *e.g.* where dismissal is denied, a defence that if there was dismissal it was for a valid reason and was fair in the circumstances.[59] But while the precise way in which it is done may vary, in practice tribunals will at least endeavour to identify the issues, and especially where parties are not legally represented, explain how they may properly be formulated, and where dismissal is denied but no other substantive defence is put forward, the respondent should be given the opportunity to put forward such a case at the commencement of the hearing.[60]

But while the tribunal may give assistance of this kind to parties, so as to ensure that a fair balance is maintained between them, the duty nevertheless remains squarely on them to come to the hearing prepared to lead sufficient evidence on all matters which appear to be in issue.[61] This involves bringing such witnesses as may be appropriate to discharge any onus which lies on a party, and in matters where the onus lies on the opposing party, to refute his case.[62] All relevant documents should also be brought, so that they may be produced or may be available for production if required. But it is not sufficient merely to produce documents, and assume that the tribunal will by themselves analyse or interpret them. Where a document is not self-explanatory, the points which a party seeks to take from it should be explained by a competent witness, and, where appropriate, a written summary, or suitable excerpts, should be provided. Documents relating to the terms and conditions of the applicant's employment should always be produced, as should documents relating to remuneration, as mentioned below. The parties are warned about these matters in the notice of hearing. Unwilling witnesses can be ordered to attend and document orders can be made, as explained in Chapter 6 above.

In *Eaton Ltd.* v. *Nuttall* [1977] I.C.R. 272 it was held that it was the duty of employers in equal pay cases to come to the hearing with the relevant

---

57 See also *Hawker Siddleley Power Engineering Ltd.* v. *Rump* [1979] I.R.L.R. 425 at p. 428.

58 See *Copson* v. *Eversure Accessories Ltd.* [1974] I.C.R. 636.

59 See *Derby City Council* v. *Marshall* [1979] I.C.R. 731 and below under "Amendments" at p. 164.

60 See *Sutcliffe* v. *Hawker Siddeley Aviation Ltd.* [1973] I.C.R. 560 (at p. 565); *Howe* v. *Berridge*, (EAT (Scot.) 788/78).

61 As to sufficiency of evidence, see Chap. 8 below.

62 See Chap. 8 below under "Burden of proof".

information prepared in a comprehensive and readily assimilable form, since they alone were in a position to provide it. There are helpful observations on the sort of evidence which an employer should be prepared to lead in cases where unfair selection for redundancy is in issue in *Bristol Channel Ship Repairers Ltd.* v. *O'Keefe* [1978] I.C.R. 691 (at p. 698) and in *Cox* v. *Wildt Mellor Bromley* [1978] I.C.R. 736 (at p. 742). In *Gordon District Council* v. *Hay,* 1978 S.L.T. 2 it was held that in appeals from decisions on compensation questions under the Local Government (Compensation) (Scotland) Regulations 1975 an industrial tribunal was entitled to consider the whole matter *de novo* and to determine what was fair, equitable and reasonable compensation. This decision was upheld in the Inner House (Second Division—not reported).

While it is better to assume that relevant witnesses or documents will be required, rather than leave the matter to chance, tribunals recognise that attendance at a hearing can be disruptive for businesses, particularly in smaller firms where the number of employees potentially involved in the proceedings is liable to be in inverse proportion to its size. They therefore take into account the practical limitations which this can impose on the conduct of a case, either by making appropriate allowance in assessing the weight of evidence or by granting adjournments if considered appropriate. But any such difficulties should be brought out, and it should not be assumed that the tribunal will take them for granted. If raised in advance of the hearing, the Chairman may be able to suggest ways in which inconvenience can be kept to the minimum. It is also in their own interest for parties, when replying to the "date letter"[63] to indicate the potential length of the hearing, so that enough time may be set aside for it.[64]

In preparing for the hearing there is an understandable tendency to concentrate attention on the merits of the case. But in the interests of expedition and economy, provided time and circumstances permit, Scottish tribunals will not normally restrict the hearing to the merits, and will expect all appropriate evidence to be led on the remedy to be afforded to the applicant if he is successful, so that it can give a complete decision on every aspect of the case without having to recall parties for a further hearing. In this respect their practice differs from tribunals in England, where it is understood that in unfair dismissal cases it is common to confine the initial hearing to a consideration of the merits, and to have a further hearing on the remedy if they are decided in favour of the applicant. It is for the tribunal to raise the possible categories of remedy and of loss, and especially to explain

63 See Chap. 5, p. 103.

64 See also below under "Adjournments", pp. 165, 166.

about reinstatement and re-engagement[65] and to enquire whether loss of pension rights may be involved in compensation for unfair dismissal, but once it is established what the categories are, it is for the employee to produce all necessary evidence about the remedy he seeks,[66] such as (in unfair dismissal cases) wage slips both from employment with the respondents and from any subsequent employment, and benefit statements.[67] As already stated, document and witness orders can be applied for prior to the hearing if necessary. Certain information (particularly relating to loss of pension rights) may be in the employers' hands, and if the applicant is unrepresented it is for the tribunal to ensure that he knows of his rights to ask for particulars and document and witness orders.[68] The passage on "Remedies" in Chapter 9 (pp. 205 to 219) is intended to indicate what evidence will be required on this aspect of a case. Generally speaking, there is no onus on the employer on this aspect of the case, except in unfair dismissal cases to show why it would be impracticable to comply with an order for reinstatement or re-engagement, but it greatly assists the tribunal, and may well avoid an adjournment, with a consequent saving in time and expense, if he comes to the hearing prepared to provide such information as is available to him on those aspects of the remedy which the applicant seeks which are within his knowledge; apart from anything else, he is then in a position to correct any inaccuracies in the applicant's evidence on the subject.

Where the information produced at the hearing on matters relating to remedy is insufficient, in order to minimise the necessity of recalling parties for a further hearing, with attendant delay and expense, the usual practice is for the tribunal to call for any necessary further information to be supplied in documentary form. The information is also made available to the opposite party, who is given the opportunity to comment on it. Generally this is sufficient to enable the tribunal to finalise its award. But if the information supplied is insufficient or controversial, a further hearing, preceded if necessary by applications for and issue of witness and document orders, has to be convened.

It is always helpful if detailed matters such as dates of employment and wage losses can be agreed (preferably in advance), and even better if parties can agree the amount of any financial awards to be made, and

---

65 Employment Protection (Consolidation) Act, 1978, s. 68(1).

66 *Copson* v. *Eversure Accessories Ltd.* [1974] I.C.R. 636; *Tidman* v. *Aveling Marshall Ltd.* [1977] I.C.R. 506.

67 But see Chap. 9 below at pp. 213 and 220 as to the practice in cases to which the Social Security (Unemployment, Sickness and Invalidity Benefit) Regulations 1976 and the Employment Protection (Recoupment of Unemployment Benefit and Supplementary Benefit) Regulations 1977 apply.

68 See *Copson* v. *Eversure Accessories Ltd., supra.*

so avoid enquiry on the subject. Where parties had agreed among themselves as to the amount by which compensation should be reduced on account of the employee's contribution to his dismissal, it was held that although this was a matter for the tribunal to decide it was wrong for them not to hear what agreement had been reached.[69]

THE DUTY TO HEAR BOTH SIDES: STOPPING OF CASES

In *Ridley* v. *G. E. C. Machines Ltd.* (1978) 13 I.T.R. 195, the Employment Appeal Tribunal expressed the opinion that it is generally unsatisfactory if an industrial tribunal stops the case after hearing one side only, and while emphasising that there is no inflexible rule, stated that the ordinary general practice should be to hear both sides, because only by doing so can the whole picture be seen, and in order to avoid leaving parties with a sense of injustice.

This opinion was first expressed in the context of claims of constructive dismissal,[70] but it was re-stated more generally in *Ridley's* case and has also been expressed in the context of claims of discrimination on grounds of sex.[71] It may be regarded as being of general (but not universal) application, particularly to claims of unfair dismissal, where the conduct of both sides is frequently in issue, if not in relation to the merits of the claim, at least to questions relating to the remedy sought (*e.g.* for determining whether the employee has contributed to his dismissal). As stated in *Ridley's* case, there may be cases which are so obviously hopeless that it would be a waste of time for the opposite side to lead evidence (or even the applicant, as in *Brennan* v. *C. Lindley & Co. Ltd.* [1974] I.R.L.R. 153), but they are exceptional.[72] Perhaps rather more common is the unfair dismissal case where the employers having led evidence which appears to justify dismissal, the applicant's evidence-in-chief does nothing to assist him: here if the applicant has no further evidence to lead the tribunal may well indicate to the employer that cross-examination and submissions are not required.

Submissions of "no case to answer" are therefore generally out of place in tribunal proceedings, but if a party makes such a submission unsuccessfully, he should not normally be precluded from leading evidence in support of his own case.[73] Where, however, respondents represented by counsel made such a submission, having been told that they would not be precluded from calling evidence if the submission

69 *Weatherill* v. *Shipton Automation Ltd.* (1977) 12 I.T.R. 123.

70 In *Buskin* v. *Vacutech Successors Ltd.* (1977) 12 I.T.R. 107.

71 *Humphreys* v. *Board of Management of St George's Primary School* [1978] I.C.R. 546.

72 See also *George A. Palmer Ltd.* v. *Beeby* [1978] I.C.R. 196.

73 *Walker* v. *Josiah Wedgwood & Sons Ltd.* [1978] I.C.R. 744.

failed, and counsel elected to make such a submission and to call no evidence as to constructive dismissal, the Employment Appeal Tribunal, having held that the industrial tribunal erred in law in finding the applicant had not been dismissed, refused to remit the case back to the industrial tribunal for the respondents to call evidence and contest the issue of constructive dismissal.[74]

INSPECTION

Sometimes it may be desirable for the tribunal to visit the employer's premises. The types of case in which it is most likely to occur are those under the Equal Pay Act 1970 or appeals under the Health and Safety at Work etc. Act 1974, where a proper understanding of the mechanics of the job or of the physical layout of the premises may be essential. In none of the reported cases on the subject has the point been taken that a visit is incompetent, as infringing the general rule that tribunal hearings must take place in public.

An inspection may take place on the application of either party, or may be initiated by the tribunal. As it is part of the hearing, the usual 14 days' notice would have to be given to both parties in terms of the rules, unless it is arranged for a stated date after the hearing of the evidence. But in *Dorothy Perkins Ltd.* v. *Dance* [1977] I.R.L.R. 226 (an equal pay case) the opinion was expressed that the tribunal should not make an inspection until the persons concerned and the questions in issue had been identified in evidence.

Both parties and their representatives are given the opportunity to be present at an inspection. It has been stated by the Employment Appeal Tribunal[75] that if on the strength of what they have observed at an inspection, the tribunal or any member of it are inclined to a different conclusion than that for which a party is contending, they should indicate accordingly during the hearing, so that the witnesses for the party may have the opportunity to comment. This is consistent with previous similar observations in *Dugdale and Others* v. *Kraft Foods Ltd.* [1977] I.C.R. 48.[76]

PRELIMINARY HEARINGS: JURISDICTIONAL ISSUES

Where an application shows that a tribunal may not have jurisdiction to entertain it on grounds of competency or otherwise, or if a point of

---

74 *Stokes* v. *Hampstead Wine Co. Ltd.* [1979] I.R.L.R. 298.

75 In *Edward Gardner & Sons Ltd.* v. *Cassidy* (EAT 826/1977).

76 See also *Hammington* v. *Berker Sportcraft Ltd.* [1980] I.C.R. 248 and Chap. 3, p. 24.

jurisdiction or competency is taken by the respondent in the notice of appearance, the case will usually be put out for a preliminary hearing on that point alone. Where the preliminary point is taken by the respondent, he should apply for a preliminary hearing. Preliminary hearings are not granted, however, if the preliminary point is one which cannot be decided without examination of the merits, *e.g.* where an employee with less than the requisite service claims unfair dismissal, alleging that the reason for dismissal was that he took part in trade union activities; in such a case it is necessary to enquire into the reason for dismissal in order to decide whether the tribunal has jurisdiction.

Where dismissal is denied, the question whether the applicant was dismissed is not treated as a preliminary point, but one relating to the merits. Likewise, it is not usual to grant a preliminary hearing to discuss the relevancy (as opposed to the competency)[77] of the application. The pre-hearing assessment procedure[78] provides an opportunity for investigating cases which appear to be irrelevant. Generally speaking tribunals should get at the facts before deciding on relevancy.[79]

At a preliminary hearing, evidence will usually have to be heard on the point in issue. The onus usually lies with the applicant, and where the potential bar to jurisdiction is self-evident, and it does not appear that evidence from the respondent will be required, the respondent may be advised that it is not necessary for him to attend if he does not wish to do so, in cases under those rules which contain provisions for review of the tribunal's decision. If both parties have been present and the tribunal decides the preliminary point in the applicant's favour, the case is continued for further hearing on the merits. If the respondent had been told that his attendance was not necessary, and was not present, but the applicant's evidence appears *prima facie* to indicate that the tribunal has jurisdiction, the case should be continued for further hearing on the preliminary point and on the merits, as a decision adverse to the respondent should not be made in his absence. The respondent could however ask for the next hearing to be confined to the preliminary point alone.

Sometimes a point of jurisdiction or competency, actual or potential, emerges during the course of a hearing which has not been previously raised or foreseen. When this happens it is the duty of the tribunal to take notice of it,[80] and make appropriate enquiry into the relevant facts. In that case they should grant an adjournment for such time as may be

---

77 Competency is concerned with whether the relief sought is available under the law; relevancy with whether the facts relied on are sufficient to set up a claim or defence which is otherwise competent.

78 See Chap. 6, pp. 116 to 119.

79 See *Turley* v. *Allders Department Stores Ltd.* [1980] I.C.R. 66.

80 *British Midlands Airways Ltd.* v. *Lewis* [1978] I.C.R. 782 at p. 784.

necessary to enable parties to make their own enquiries into the matter, and, if unrepresented, obtain advice on the subject.[81]

Where a tribunal decides a preliminary point in favour of the applicant, it will depend on the nature of the case and administrative convenience as to whether the same tribunal goes on to take the hearing on the merits. In *Glacier Metal Co. Ltd.* v. *Dyer* [1974] I.R.L.R. 189 an objection to the hearing on the merits being heard by the tribunal which had decided the preliminary point was rejected.

AMENDMENTS

(1) **To the originating application or notice of appeal**

The absence in tribunal procedures of formal written pleadings has the result that questions may emerge at the hearing as to what statutory grounds of complaint are in issue, whether the correct parties have been called as respondents, or whether the grounds on which the application is based have been sufficiently stated. Such questions may lead to an application to amend the originating application or notice of appeal.

In *Chapman and Others* v. *Goonvean and Rostowrack China Clay Company Ltd.* [1973] I.C.R. 50 Sir John Donaldson said (at p. 59),

> "In all circumstances industrial tribunals should make the widest use of their powers to allow amendment of claims and to extend the time limits in order to ensure justice is done not only to the applicant, but to the respondent, who must always be granted any adjournment necessary to enable him to answer a new basis of claim which emerges at a late stage."

It was also stated in *Coates* v. *C. J. Crispin Ltd.* [1973] I.C.R. 413 (at p. 420),

> "But if the ground of complaint is dismissal the tribunal should always be prepared on the facts to consider whether either a redundancy payment or compensation for unfair dismissal, or both, is due unless (a), on the facts, the tribunal has been deprived of jurisdiction in relation to compensation for unfair dismissal by . . . time bar, (b) the validity of one or other claim has been determined in previous proceedings between the same parties, or (c) there has been an unequivocal abandonment of one or other claim in such circumstances that, even if there was an adjournment of the hearing, consideration of the abandoned claim would be unjust to the respondent employer."

If the proposed amendment involves adding an additional case, which

---

[81] *Burrows* v. *Correna International Ltd.* (EAT 307/79).

the tribunal decides is not barred for any of the reasons stated in *Coates* v. *C. J. Crispin Ltd., supra,* it is a matter within the tribunal's discretion as to whether to allow it. In deciding whether to allow an amendment which will add or substitute a new party, the tribunal should satisfy itself that the mistake sought to be corrected was a genuine one, and was not misleading. In every case the tribunal should have regard to all the circumstances and to where any balance of hardship may lie. Where unnecessary expense is incurred because of the amendment, it may be appropriate to grant the application on condition that the applicant should be liable in expenses,[82] and particular provision is made for such situations in the Industrial Tribunals Rules of Procedure (Scotland) 1980.[83]

Where the matter is simply one of correction or of clarifying doubts which arise from the wording of the originating application or notice of appeal, application of the foregoing principles rarely presents difficulties.Where, by contrast, the applicant seeks by way of amendment to put forward a new, or apparently new, ground of complaint or contention, the tribunal must first decide whether it is time-barred or jurisdiction is excluded for any other reason, hearing evidence on the matter if necessary.[84] Adjournment may be necessary to enable the other side to consider the new point,[85] and would be essential if it is one which would potentially affect the Redundancy Fund or the Maternity Pay Fund, since in that case intimation would have to be made to the Department of Employment before the proceedings could go further. Likewise, if it is one in respect of which ACAS has a statutory conciliatory function to perform, the application, as amended, would have to be intimated to them.[86]

If an applicant is unrepresented, or his representative is plainly inexperienced, and if the facts which emerge disclose an obvious *prima facie* ground of complaint which has not been previously put forward, tribunals generally regard it as incumbent on them to point this out to the applicant, and give him the opportunity to seek leave to add to such a complaint, particularly when it arises in the context of a dismissal. As was stated in *Coates, supra* (at p. 417),

> "An employee may turn to an Industrial Tribunal for assistance on a number of reasons. But by far the most common reason is that he has lost his job and thinks that he must have some claim against his employer. The loss of the job is a fact. After that the problems begin."

---

82 *Cocking* v. *Sandhurst (Stationers) Ltd.* (1975) 10 I.T.R. 6.

83 Rule 11(2) and (3). See also below (under "Adjournments") at p. 166.

84 *Parsons Peebles Ltd.* v. *McGregor and Anr.* (EAT 429/430/78) and *Coates* v. *Crispin, supra.*

85 *W. Devis & Sons Ltd.* v. *Sexton* (EAT 558/29).

86 See Chap. 6, p. 128.

Of course, it does not follow that if the tribunal raises the matter, the applicant will necessarily be allowed to introduce the new ground of complaint. The principles in the cases referred to above have to be followed and applied.

Once an amendment has been allowed, it is the duty of the tribunal clerk to note it on the originating application or notice of appearance, together with any consequential amendments made by the other parties, and also (where it relates to the name or address of a party) in the case file.

(2) **To the notice of appearance**

The above principles and practices are also applied, *vice versa*, to questions of amendment resulting from inadequacies in notices of appearance,[87] and to attempts at the hearing to introduce a further ground of defence not hitherto stated. In particular, it commonly occurs in unfair dismissal and redundancy payment cases that a respondent who denies dismissal fails to go on (as often he could and should do) to state any further ground of defence should the tribunal decide that the applicant was dismissed. In such a situation, while in *Derby City Council* v. *Marshall* [1979] I.C.R. 731 it was indicated that there is no duty on the tribunal to investigate whether there was a valid reason for dismissal where none has been put forward, failure to consider the reason for and fairness of the dismissal has been characterised by the Employment Appeal Tribunal in Scotland as unduly legalistic.[88] The tribunal will generally ask what the respondents' position is, and allow any formal amendment to the notice of appearance which may be appropriate, but subject to such further directions by way of adjournment or otherwise as may be appropriate to protect the applicant from being taken by surprise. In unfair dismissal cases, where there is any doubt whether the reason for dismissal falls within the four categories stated in s. 57(2) of the Employment Protection (Consolidation) Act 1978, an alternative case under s. 57(1)(*b*) ("some other substantial reason") should be added if this has not already been taken in the notice of appearance (see *Vickers* v. *Warsop Constitutional Club*, referred to at p. 165 below).

Likewise, while it is seldom that a respondent in his notice of appearance takes up any position concerning the remedy which the applicant seeks, tribunals in Scotland do not regard any such failure as precluding them from hearing evidence and taking into account any matters which, under the relevant statutory provisions, may go to mitigate or reduce the remedy to be afforded to the applicant.

---

[87] It is of course only in cases under the Industrial Tribunals Rules of Procedure (Scotland) 1980 that a notice of appearance is required (see Chap. 5, p. 97).

[88] In *Strathclyde Regional Council* v. *Syme* (EAT 3/8/79). See also Chap. 5, pp. 97, 98.

Scottish tribunals do not regard their practice in these matters as inconsistent with the decision in *Nelson* v. *BBC* [1977] I.C.R. 649 where, in sending a case back to an industrial tribunal after upholding an appeal by the employee, the Court of Appeal refused to allow the employers at the next hearing before the industrial tribunal to make formal amendments to the documents and submit to trial an issue which had not previously been raised before the industrial tribunal, but had emerged before the Employment Appeal Tribunal; the issue was whether the respondents could show a different statutory reason for dismissal from that which had originally been put forward, but which had been rejected by the Court of Appeal. It was stressed (by Megaw LJ at p. 661) that the decision was based on the special circumstances of that case. It should be contrasted with *Gorman* v. *London Computer Training Centre Ltd.* [1978] I.C.R. 394, where it was considered and distinguished. But in *Vickers* v. *Warsop Constitutional Club Ltd.* (EAT 522/79) where the industrial tribunal found that the reason for dismissal was a statutory reason which had not been canvassed at the hearing (*i.e.* "some other substantial reason" under s. 57(1)(*b*) of the Employment Protection (Consolidation) Act 1978) they were held to have erred.[89]

ADJOURNMENTS: TRANSFER TO OTHER TRIBUNALS

Each of the rules provide that a tribunal may adjourn any hearing.[90] In particular, under the Industrial Tribunals Rules of Procedure (Scotland) 1980, adjournments should be granted where there is provision for conciliation and the opportunity of a settlement being reached.

An adjournment may be granted on the application of either party, or the tribunal itself may decide to adjourn at any stage of the hearing. Apart from *ad hoc* adjournments during the course of a hearing, a case may have to be adjourned until another day if some development during the course of a hearing renders this necessary, and must be adjourned if it cannot be completed in the time set down for it. An adjournment should also be granted where a party has been taken by surprise by the introduction of new matter or a new issue which he could not be expected to have anticipated.[91] When this happens, it may be several weeks before the tribunal can be reconvened. As has already been pointed out, such delays are undesirable, and parties should try to

89 As to pleading a case under s. 57(1)(*b*) as an alternative, see above, p. 164 and Chap. 5, p. 97.

90 The Industrial Tribunals Rules of Procedure (Scotland) 1980, r. 12(2)(*b*); the Industrial Tribunals (Scotland) Regulations 1965, (as amended), Sched. 2, r. 14(1)(*c*); the Industrial Tribunals (Improvement and Prohibition Notices Appeals) (Scotland) Regulations 1974, r. 14(2)(*a*); the Industrial Tribunals (Non-Discrimination Notices Appeals) (Scotland) Regulations 1977, r. 12(2)(*a*).

91 See *Sutcliffe* v. *Hawker Siddeley Aviation Ltd.* [1973] I.C.R. 560, at p. 565.

give the Secretary as realistic an estimate as possible of the length of the hearing when replying to the "date letter".[92]

Under the Industrial Tribunals Rules of Procedure (Scotland) 1980, there are specific provisions regarding expenses resulting from adjournments[93]:

(1) Where on the application of a party to the proceedings the tribunal has postponed or adjourned a hearing, it may make an order for expenses against that party, or, as the case may be, in favour of that party, as respects any expenses incurred or any allowances paid as a result of the postponement or adjournment (rule 11(2)). When a large bundle of documents was produced by the employer immediately prior to the commencement of a hearing an award of costs against him in respect of a consequential adjournment was upheld,[94] but an award against an employee who sought an adjournment to consider new allegations by the employer, on the ground that he should have asked for further particulars of the employer's case, was held to be wrong.[95]

(2) Where in the course of unfair dismissal proceedings the employee has expressed a wish to be re-employed which has been communicated to the employer at least seven days before the hearing of the complaint, or the proceedings arise out of the employer's failure to permit the employee to return to work after an absence due to pregnancy or confinement, and any postponement or adjournment of the hearing has been caused by the respondents' failure, without a special reason, to adduce reasonable evidence as to the availability of the job from which the applicant was dismissed, or, as the case may be, which she held before her absence, or of comparable or suitable employment, the tribunal must make an order for expenses against the respondent as respects any expenses incurred or any allowances paid as a result of the postponement or adjournment (rule 11(3)).

It should be noted firstly that the normal rule under r. 11(1) that expenses are awarded only where a party has acted frivolously or vexatiously or otherwise unreasonably does not apply;[96] and secondly that the mandatory requirement to make an order under r. 11(3) would not apply where the employee has stated in his originating application that he seeks compensation for unfair dismissal, but changes his mind at the hearing to seek re-employment; and it is not regarded as applying if the proceedings had to be adjourned for a reason not relating to the availability of the employee's job. Under each of the above rules (*i.e.* r.

---

92 See p. 157 above, and generally in Chap. 6 under "Extensions of time and postponements" at p. 121.

93 As to expenses generally, see Chap. 10 below.

94 *Ladbroke Racing Ltd.* v. *Hickey* [1979] I.C.R. 525.

95 *Rajguru* v. *Top Order Ltd.* [1978] I.C.R. 565.

96 See *Ladbroke Racing Ltd.* v. *Hickey, supra.*

11(2) and (3)) the orders which the tribunal may make are those specified in r. 11(1)(*a*) and (*b*).[97]

Under the other rules the tribunal has an unfettered discretion in the matter of expenses, which applies when granting an adjournment in a case under any of those rules.[98]

Where an untoward event occurs, such as a member of the tribunal suddenly realising that he has a close relationship to a witness,[99] or a tribunal finding itself so divided that it cannot arrive at an effectual or conclusive decision,[1] a tribunal has the power, either under its powers to regulate its own procedure and to give directions,[2] or inherently,[3] to decide that the proceedings should be re-heard by another tribunal. But where a re-hearing was granted at the request of a party who said that he had "lost confidence" in the impartiality of the tribunal, this was held not to have been a sufficient ground, taken by itself, for granting the request.[4]

A Regional Chairman also has a similar power (by virtue of his office) in relation to a case heard by a tribunal of which he himself is not Chairman.[5]

CLOSING ADDRESSES

At the conclusion of the evidence parties are entitled to address the tribunal. The purpose of a closing address should be to relate the evidence to the relevant law with a view to persuading the tribunal to decide the case in favour of the party on whose behalf it is being addressed. An address properly directed to these purposes can be of considerable assistance, but it is not uncommon for unrepresented parties, or those whose representatives lack experience, merely to ask

---

97 The provisions of r. 11(1) are discussed in Chap. 10 at pp. 233 to 235. The preceding rule in the 1974 regulations has been held not to extend to enabling a tribunal to order a party to pay to the Secretary of State a sum in respect of the cost of providing a tribunal for a hearing which proves abortive because it has to be adjourned—*Seel Garages Ltd.* v. *Byrne* (EAT 48/80). But see the comments on that case at p. 237.

98 See Chap. 10 at pp. 235, 236.

99 *Charman* v. *Palmer's Scaffolding Ltd.* [1979] I.C.R. 335.

1 *R* v. *Industrial Tribunal* ex p. *Cotswold Collotype Co. Ltd.* [1979] I.C.R. 190.

2 As held in *Charman's* case, *supra.*

3 As held in *R.* v. *Industrial Tribunal, supra.*

4 *Automobile Proprietary Ltd.* v. *Healey* (EAT 781/78).

5 *Jones* v. *Marks & Spencer Ltd.* (EAT 356/79).

the tribunal to decide the case on the evidence, in the light of its knowledge of the law and its practical experience, or for them to make speeches of a perfunctory nature. For this reason tribunals do not regard themselves as necessarily precluded from considering any subsidiary issues on which relevant evidence has been led but which have not been the subject of a submission. But if an issue of substance occurs to the tribunal which has not been canvassed during the course of the hearing, it should recall parties to give them an opportunity to make submissions, and if necessary lead additional evidence on the subject.[6] But issues which relate only to the remedy sought by the applicant (*e.g.* questions as to whether he has contributed to his dismissal or failed to mitigate his loss) are usually foreseeable by both sides: where, as is normally the case, sufficient evidence is before the tribunal to enable it to decide them, it will do so in the absence of specific submissions on the subject, unless they are of exceptional complexity.

In Scotland, following the usual procedure in civil cases, closing addresses are normally made in the order in which the evidence has been led, in contrast to the English practice of allowing the party on whom the onus lies to have "the last word". In *Glencross* v. *Dymoke* [1979] I.C.R. 536, however, the Employment Appeal Tribunal in England declined to make any ruling as to the order in which closing addresses should be made, and in *Peters* v. *Science Museum* (Court of Appeal, Nov. 29, 1979) an objection that the usual order in civil cases had been departed from was rejected.

---

[6] As was done in *Hanks* v. *Ace High Productions Ltd.* [1978] I.C.R. 1155. In *Haxey Engineering Ltd.* v. *Turner* (EAT 268/78) a tribunal which decided the merits of an unfair dismissal complaint against an unrepresented employer on a ground which had not been canvassed at the hearing was held to have transgressed natural justice. See also *Vickers* v. *Warsop Constitutional Club*, referred to at p. 165 above.

CHAPTER 8

EVIDENCE

GENERAL

The decision of a court or tribunal must be arrived at on the basis that facts which are relevant to support it are either admitted or have been proved by sufficient evidence, or can be inferred. In the courts there are strict rules governing the weight of evidence required to prove a fact, and to discharge the burden of proof incumbent upon a party, and the admissibility of the evidence which may be adduced for these purposes.[1]

Industrial tribunals are not bound by these rules. This was decided by the Court of Session in *Douglas* v. *Provident Clothing and Supply Co. Ltd.* (1969) 4 I.T.R. 15. The ratio of the decision was that as the rules of procedure in force at the time gave a tribunal the power to regulate its own procedure, to admit evidence which has not been given on oath or affirmation, and to decide a case on written representations and in the absence of a party, they were intended to be much looser in relation to evidence than those in an action in a court of law, and conferred a wide discretion which would not be available to an ordinary court. Thus the decision was couched in general terms, and did not turn on the particular question in issue in the case, which was whether a fact could be proved on the uncorroborated evidence of a single witness. All of the rules of procedure at present in force contain provisions of the kind on which the court relied in *Douglas,* and the decision therefore remains of general and binding authority.

English judicial authority is not so clear, however. In *Lawrence* v. *Newham London Borough Council* [1978] I.C.R. 10 a division of the Employment Appeal Tribunal appeared to take the view that the strict rules of the English law of evidence applied in industrial tribunal proceedings, but subsequently the President of the Appeal Tribunal stated that the decision was not intended to mean that industrial tribunals were bound in all circumstances to apply the strict rules of evidence, or to require industrial tribunals to change their settled and established practice as to the admissibility of evidence. Subsequent appeal tribunal decisions in England have proceeded on that basis. But in *Rosedale Mouldings Ltd.* v. *Sibley* [1980] I.C.R. 816 the Employment Appeal Tribunal in England held that although industrial tribunals were not bound by the strict rules of evidence they had no discretion to

[1] For the law of evidence in the courts, reference should be made to Walkers, *The Law of Evidence in Scotland*.

refuse to admit a document which was admissible at common law and probative of one or more of the issues before them. As far as cases governed by the 1980 rules of procedure are concerned, which comprise the bulk of industrial tribunal proceedings (but were not in force when the *Rosedale* case was decided), the position has now been put beyond doubt by r. 8(1) of the rules in both countries, which expressly states that a tribunal shall not be bound by any enactment or rule of law relating to the admissibility of evidence in proceedings before the courts of law, thereby affirming the wide discretion referred to in *Douglas, supra*. As regards proceedings under other rules, *Douglas* remains the binding authority in Scotland. (See also below under "Admissibility of Evidence" at pp. 178 to 180).

Although the decision in *Douglas* turned on the provisions of the rules of procedure, there are other practical reasons why industrial tribunals should not be circumscribed by a strict application of the rules of evidence in courts of law. Perhaps the most fundamental is that, as has been pointed out in previous chapters, industrial tribunals were intended as a forum where parties could conduct their own cases, and in practice a substantial proportion of cases are conducted by parties themselves or by representatives who are not legally trained. To expect such persons to understand and have regard to the rules of evidence in the preparation and conduct of their cases would be quite unrealistic. One of the main differences flowing from this concept is the much simpler nature of the originating application (or notice of appeal) and notice of appearance in industrial tribunal proceedings, by comparison with the written pleadings used in the courts, the preparation of which requires a technical skill which could not be expected of persons without legal training. Written pleadings set out all the legal issues between the parties, and the principal facts relied on to support their respective positions. From these it is apparent which facts are admitted and which are disputed and have to be proved. The rules of evidence reflect this method of conducting proceedings, which is adversarial in nature, and depends on cases being conducted by skilled advocates who know the rules of litigation. But the issues and the relevant facts are seldom identified in this way in industrial tribunal case papers, and it is often only once the hearing gets under way that they emerge, and the tribunal can discover how much common ground there is between the parties. For these reasons, as already explained in Chapter 7 (p. 144), their proceedings have to be more flexible and may have to be "inquisitorial". It follows from such an approach that to apply rules of evidence which assume a system of written pleadings and knowledge of the rules on the part of the pleader could operate against the interests of justice. Furthermore, as will be seen below (see under "corroboration" and "hearsay evidence"), the issues between the parties are often of such a nature as to militate against an application of the strict rules of evidence.

But while tribunals are not bound to apply the rules of evidence in courts of law, this does not mean that they ignore them. Tribunals must always be concerned with the quality and sufficiency of the evidence they hear. While many of the rules of the law of evidence in the courts relate to the particular way in which court proceedings are conducted, others are of more general application, and reflect general concepts of fairness. Tribunals have regard to them, but adapt their application to the particular way in which their proceedings are conducted. If, for instance, it is ascertained that the contents of a document are common ground, there is no need to take up unnecessary time in proving the document. But if the contents are disputed, sufficient proof will be necessary. What is sufficient will depend on the evidence as a whole, however, rather than on the application of the rules of evidence in court proceedings. So also with facts spoken to in evidence: corroboration becomes unnecessary if it emerges that a fact is common ground (and the tribunal will intervene to find out if it is); as held in *Douglas* v. *Provident Clothing and Supply Co. Ltd., supra,* corroboration is not essential, but where it is available it may be important, where credibility is in issue, to provide the weight of evidence required to satisfy the tribunal. Likewise hearsay evidence is admissible, as discussed below, but its quality may be questionable. This will be taken into account in assessing its sufficiency, as will the extent to which matters in dispute have been tested in cross-examination.

Such examples may serve to demonstrate that while tribunals are not bound by the rules of evidence in the courts, they strive to maintain fundamental standards of justice and fair play in their approach to the admission and assessment of evidence. The corollary of flexibility is apt to be uncertainty, however. Before any court or tribunal it can always be difficult to assess in advance what evidence should be adduced, but the broader approach to evidence adopted by tribunals and the absence of formal pleadings can aggravate the problem. The following summary may be helpful:

(1) It will be rare for there to be sufficient common ground to enable a tribunal to arrive at a decision on the basis of written submissions and without considering evidence. Normally the relevant facts and circumstances must be proved by evidence, oral, documentary or real. Inferences may be taken, but only from facts and circumstances which have been proved. If no facts, or insufficient facts, are proved to yield a reasonable basis for an inference, the deficiency cannot be remedied by speculation.

(2) Accordingly in preparing a case, each of the issues which it will raise, including the remedy to be sought, should be considered against the wording of the relevant legislation and the question asked, "What do I

need to prove, and what evidence do I have, or can I obtain, to prove it?". The most direct or original evidence is always the best, but the tribunal has a discretion to indicate and, if appropriate, limit the extent to which corroboration of such evidence is required.

(3) Where a party seeks to prove matters by evidence which is not "best evidence", or the admissibility of which may be in doubt for some other reason, it is within the tribunal's discretion whether to allow it or not, whether or not a formal objection has been taken by the opposite party. How the discretion will be exercised will depend entirely on the circumstances, but the following matters will be taken into account:

(a) whether "best evidence" is reasonably available, and if it is, why it has not been led; and
(b) whether either party would suffer substantial injustice by the admission or exclusion of the evidence.

Oral "second-best" evidence, *i.e.* hearsay, will generally be admitted, subject to reservations as to its weight. Documentary evidence tendered in place of a witness is more problematical (see p. 185 below).

(4) Where the tribunal decides to exclude second-best evidence because better evidence could have been led, but was not, it may decide, in the light of the circumstances, and again taking into account where the interests of justice lie, to afford an opportunity to lead the better evidence. But such cases should be regarded as exceptional. It is the duty of parties to present all relevant evidence to the tribunal,[2] and tribunals will not normally be indulgent to a party who has not come prepared with adequate evidence.

(5) If, however, evidence is given which the opposite party can reasonably claim has taken him by surprise, or which may affect the credibility of his own witnesses, but was not tested with them, then if the tribunal considers that it materially affects the issue between the parties, it may allow the opposite party the opportunity to rebut the evidence by recalling a witness or leading further evidence. Again it will depend on the circumstances how the discretion will be exercised.

(6) In exercising their discretion in the above matters, the tribunal will take into account the relative qualifications and experience in tribunal proceedings of parties and their representatives, but in the last analysis their decision will depend on what they consider to be in the interests of justice.

Although the rules do not require it, it is normal for evidence to be given on oath or affirmation. Less formal statements may be accepted, but if not admitted, or if needing further elaboration or clarification, sworn evidence on the subject will be taken.

---

[2] *Craig* v. *British Railways* (1973) 8 I.T.R. 636.

THE BURDEN OF PROOF: PRESUMPTIONS

As regards most matters which tribunals have to consider, there are burdens of proof (the "onus") which have to be discharged by one party or the other. In *GEC Telecommunications Ltd.* v. *McAllister* [1975] I.R.L.R. 346 a distinction was drawn between the legal burden of proof of establishing an issue and the evidential burden of proof which may fluctuate and move from one side to the other in the course of a case. The burden of proof is significant in deciding who is to lead at the hearing, and in assessing the evidence led. The general effect is that if on an issue of fact no evidence is led, or the evidence leaves the matter in doubt, the party on whom the onus lies does not discharge it, and accordingly fails on that issue.[3]

The relevant legislation may provide expressly where the legal burden of proof lies. This is the case in the following matters:

(1) **Unfair dismissal**

It is for the employer to show what was the reason for dismissal, and that it was a reason falling within one of the potentially valid categories of reasons for dismissal (Employment Protection (Consolidation) Act 1978, s. 57(1)). Section 57(3) formerly provided that the determination of the question whether the dismissal was fair or unfair should depend on whether "the employer can satisfy the tribunal that in the circumstances (having regard to equity and the substantial merits of the case) he acted reasonably in treating it as a sufficient reason for dismissing the employee". The Employment Act 1980 (s. 6) amends the words quoted by reverting to the formula originally used in s. 24(6) of the Industrial Relations Act 1971, so that the question now depends on whether "in the circumstances (including the size and administrative resources of the employer's undertaking) the employer acted reasonably or unreasonably in treating it as a sufficient reason for dismissing the employee; and that question shall be determined in accordance with equity and the substantial merits of the case". Thus there is no longer a specific legal burden on the employer, but an evidential burden remains on both parties to show facts and circumstances from which the tribunal can decide whether the employer acted reasonably or unreasonably. Section 56A (added by s. 12 of the Employment Act 1980) provides various exclusions from the operation of s. 56 (by which failure to permit a woman to return to work after confinement is treated as dismissal), and subs. (4) provides that it is for the employer to show that the exclusions apply. It is also for the employer to show that it would be impracticable to reinstate a dismissed employee because he has been

---

[3] Walkers, *op. cit.* p. 65. See also *Ford* v. *Westfield Autocar Co.* (1967) 2 I.T.R. 404.

replaced, and to satisfy the tribunal that it was impracticable to comply with an order for reinstatement (ss. 70(1) and 71(2)).

(2) **Action short of dismissal for trade union membership and activities**

It is for the employer to show the purpose for which action was taken against the complainant (s. 25(1)).

(3) **Redundancy**

In proceedings arising out of a failure to permit an employee to return to work after pregnancy or confinement, it is for the employer to show that the reason for the failure or dismissal was redundancy (Sched. 2, para. 5).

(4) **Consultation in redundancy**

By s. 101(2) of the Employment Protection Act 1975 it is for the employer to show that there were special circumstances for not consulting with a trade union in terms of s. 99, and that he took all steps towards compliance which were reasonably practicable.

(5) **Appeals against levy orders**

By s. 12(2) of the Industrial Training Act 1964 it is for the appellant to show that he was wrongly assessed to levy.

(6) **Equal pay**

By s. 1(3) of the Equal Pay Act 1970 it is for the employer to prove that the variation between a woman's contract and a man's contract of employment is genuinely due to a material difference other than one of sex.

(7) **Sex and racial discrimination**

By s. 15(5) of the Sex Discrimination Act 1975 and s. 14(5) of the Race Relations Act 1976 an employment agency escapes liability if it proves that it was reasonable for it to rely on certain statements made by an employer. By s. 57(3) of the 1976 Act a respondent escapes liability for damages if he proves that he did not intend to treat the complainant unfavourably on racial grounds.

More commonly, the legal burden of proof is to be inferred from the terms of the legislation, which may be expressed in various ways:

(1) Certain matters are stated to be presumed unless the contrary is proved. The most important of these provisions are the presumptions in s. 151(2) of the 1978 Act that for the purpose of any proceedings under the Act (with certain exceptions) a person's employment during any period was continuous, and in s. 91(2) that for the purpose of any reference to a tribunal under Pt. VI (*i.e.* relating to redundancy payments) an employee who is dismissed shall be presumed to have been so dismissed by reason of redundancy. Here the burden falls by implication on the party in whose interest it is to rebut the presumption, *i.e.* the employer.

(2) Without saying where the onus lies, it may be provided that where or unless the tribunal is satisfied on a matter, or that where or unless certain facts are found, certain consequences shall follow or shall be regarded as following. Such provisions occur so frequently that it is impracticable to list them. One example may suffice. Section 59 of the 1978 Act provides that where the reason for dismissal is redundancy it must be regarded as unfair if the selection for dismissal was based on the applicant having been a member of a trade union or taken part in its activities, or if it is in breach of an agreed procedure or customary arrangement relating to redundancy: in such a case the more general enquiry under s. 57(3) as to whether the dismissal was reasonable in all the circumstances is excluded. Where the statutory provisions are framed in this way, or where nothing is said one way or the other, the burden will fall on the party in whose interest lies the consequences which flow from the facts, if established. In the example given the employee obtains an automatic award of unfair dismissal if the facts fall within s. 59, so the onus is on him to establish them. If at the same time, however, the employer is asserting that the employee was dismissed for some valid reason other than redundancy, the onus in that respect lies with him. Thus different burdens of proof can be operating at the same time, as a result of which, as pointed out in *GEC Telecommunications* v. *McAllister, supra,* the onus can shift from one party to another. But the party who leads at the hearing is the one on whom the primary onus lies, *i.e.* in the foregoing example the employer, on whom lies the express burden of showing a potentially valid reason for dismissal.

Unless facts are admitted which throw the primary onus on the respondent (such as an admission of dismissal in unfair dismissal and redundancy payment cases) the primary onus lies with the applicant or appellant, because it is for him in the first place to satisfy the tribunal that it has jurisdiction to entertain the application,[4] that he qualifies for the relief which he seeks, and that in the particular circumstances of the case he is entitled to that relief. Thus in relation to the remedy to be afforded, the burden is on the applicant to establish what loss he has sustained. In view of the informal nature of tribunal proceedings, however, precise and detailed proof of every item of loss is not expected.[5] But in addition to those matters mentioned above where the legislation imposes an express burden on the respondent, the burden is also on him to establish facts relating to mitigation of loss (at least so far as they are, or can reasonably be expected to be, within his knowledge) or reduction of compensation on account of contributory fault, where those matters are relevant. (See Chap. 9 under "Remedies" pp. 205 to 219 for an indication of the evidence which may be necessary or relevant

[4] See *H. Goodwin* v. *Fitzmaurice and Ors.* [1977] I R.L.R. 393.

[5] *Norton Tool Co. Ltd.* v. *Tewson* (1972) I.C.R. 501 at pp. 504-5.

with regard to remedy). And where the facts in issue are more within the knowledge or in the hands of the employer rather than the employee, it may occasionally make for convenience if the employer leads on that issue, even although the onus in law may remain with the employee, *e.g.* in any enquiry relating to loss of pension rights as an element in compensation for unfair dismissal, where the legal burden lies on the employee, but evidence of his position under the employer's pension fund must for practical purposes come from the employer.

Irrespective of where the legal burden of proof lies, each party has the evidential burden of proving by sufficient evidence the facts on which he relies to support his case and to refute his opponent's, on the principle that "he who asserts must prove". Whether the burden will be discharged will depend on the tribunal's view of the weight of the evidence adduced, based on the standard of proof which applies. At common law and by statute there are certain presumptions which, if the requisite facts are established, may either be so strong as to exclude any proof by way of rebuttal, or which may apply unless rebutted by sufficient evidence.[6] Insofar as the situations in which they apply may form part of the matters in issue in industrial tribunal proceedings, it is thought that an industrial tribunal ought to have regard to them, at least so far as irrebuttable presumptions are concerned, since they are rules of the substantive law to which they relate rather than of the law of evidence.[7] Legislation may also provide that a certificate by a Minister of the Crown shall be conclusive evidence of the matters stated therein. And s. 73(3) of the Sex Discrimination Act 1975 and s. 69(1) of the Race Relations Act 1976 contain similar provisions with regard to findings by an industrial tribunal, and (in s. 69(1) of the 1976 Act) a court, under those Acts.

The irrebuttable presumptions which might be significant in tribunal proceedings are the long negative prescription of twenty years, on the expiry of which a right is treated as abandoned or satisfied, and the presumptions under s. 15(1) and s. 141(3) of the Companies Act (*q.v.*) and in s. 89(1) of the Employment Protection (Consolidation) Act 1978 (*q.v.*). Most other presumptions in the employment legislation are rebuttable by proof of the contrary. Of the other rebuttable presumptions, the ones which may be of practical significance are those relating to the regularity and validity of actings and records, both official and commercial, the presumption of sanity, the presumption against a transfer of moveable property being a gift, the presumptions arising from payment and receipt of money, and the presumption that a

---

6 See Walkers, *op. cit.*, Chap. VI, where the various types of presumptions are discussed and examples are given.

7 Walkers, *op. cit.*, p. 51.

servant in the general employment of a party continues in that employment and against his having become the servant of another.[8]

STANDARD OF PROOF: WEIGHT OF EVIDENCE

The standard by which parties have to prove matters in proceedings before industrial tribunals is usually the general standard of proof in civil litigation, *i.e.* the balance of probabilities.[9] The question never seems to have arisen as to whether a statutory provision requiring a tribunal to be "satisfied" on a matter implies a higher standard of proof than one which requires a matter to be "shown to" or "found by" a tribunal. The criminal standard of proof beyond reasonable doubt has been expressly disapproved in equal pay cases,[10] and in cases where dishonesty is alleged. In the latter situation it has even been doubted whether the standard of the balance of probabilities is not too high,[11] and there is no particular rule of evidence as to what standard of proof is required or evidence is to be produced to establish redundancy.[12]

The meaning of the balance of probability is that where various inferences arise from the facts, that which is preponderantly the more probable will prevail. If all the inferences are equally consistent, nothing has been proved and the party on whom the onus lies will fail.[13] The tribunal's conclusion must be based on the facts brought out in evidence, however, and not on speculation.[14] As to the extent to which members of the tribunal may draw on their own knowledge and experience, see Chapter 3 at p. 24.

Assessment of the weight of the evidence is a matter for the commonsense of the court, jury or tribunal,[15] in the light of the evidence as a whole, and their view of the reliability and credibility of the witnesses. This may be arrived at intuitively.[16] While the volume of the evidence may be of some significance, a tribunal should not assess evidence merely on the number of witnesses called. Credibility is the essential factor which will determine whether it is accepted. Demeanour,

---

[8] Walkers, *op. cit.*, pp. 51 to 64.

[9] *W. Gimber & Sons Ltd.* v. *Spurrett* (1967) 2 I.T.R. 308 at p. 310; *Hindle* v. *Percival Boats Ltd.* (1969) 4 I.T.R. 86 at p. 92.

[10] *National Vulcan Engineering Group Ltd.* v. *Wade* [1978] I.C.R. 800.

[11] *Lees* v. *The Orchard* [1978] I.R.L.R. 20.

[12] *H. Goodwin Ltd.* v. *Fitzmaurice, supra.*

[13] Walkers, *op. cit.*, p. 79.

[14] *Wolverhampton Die Casting Ltd.* v. *Kitson* (1967) 2 I.T.R. 362; *A. W. Champion Ltd.* v. *Scoble* (1967) 2 I.T.R. 411, at p. 413.

[15] *Lord Advocate* v. *Lord Blantyre* (1879) 6 R.(H.L.) 72, *per* Lord Blackburn at p. 85; *Gill* v. *Harold Andrews Sheepbridge Ltd.* [1974] I.C.R. 294 at p. 296.

[16] *Long and Hambly* v. *Bryan* [1975] I.C.R. 200 at p. 203.

apparent intelligence, motive and the witness's means of knowledge are all matters to be taken into account, as are the coherence of his testimony with regard to facts otherwise established and the extent to which it may have been elicited by leading questions.[17] If an apparently credible witness gives evidence which is inherently more probable than that of a number of opposing witnesses who create an impression of unreliability, either because they are inconsistent on essential matters or because they speak with suspicious unanimity, the evidence of the single witness may be sufficient, especially if there are surrounding facts and circumstances to support his evidence. But failure to call an obvious witness will be taken into account. Failure to cross-examine on a material matter may also be taken into account, more especially if a party is legally represented, but will seldom be fatal, because the deficiency may be remedied by the tribunal themselves asking appropriate questions, or by recalling the witness who should have been asked about it (see also Chapter 7 at pp. 145, 146 and 148 to 150).

There is one particular type of case, however, in which the legislation specifies the standard by which the evidence is to be judged. In applications for interim relief under s. 77 of the Employment Protection (Consolidation) Act 1978 the tribunal has to consider whether it is "likely" that the complaint of unfair dismissal to which the proceedings relate will succeed. This has been interpreted as meaning more than probable, or more than just a reasonable prospect of success.[18] The standard is therefore higher than that of the balance of probabilities.

If in assessing the evidence the tribunal considers that there are factual matters which ought to be cleared up in order that justice may be done between the parties, it may ask for further evidence to be led on the subject, irrespective of where the onus lies; if this is considered necessary, it will usually take place before parties have dispersed, but if the matter is considered to be of sufficient importance, parties may be even recalled for the purpose.[19]

ADMISSIBILITY OF EVIDENCE: GENERAL

It follows from the decision in *Douglas* v. *Provident Clothing and Supply Co. Ltd., supra* and from r. 8(1) of the Industrial Tribunals Rules of Procedure (Scotland) 1980 that there will be few restrictions on the admissibility of evidence, oral or documentary, before an industrial tribunal, provided that it is relevant to the issues before the tribunal.

---

17 Walkers, *op. cit.*, p. 402.

18 *Taplin* v. *C. Shipham Ltd.* [1978] I.R.L.R. 450.

19 *Cf.* Chap. 7 "Closing Addresses", pp. 167, 168.

Evidence which may not be relevant to the main issue may nevertheless be relevant to a subsidiary issue (*e.g.* in unfair dismissal complaints evidence of matters coming to the knowledge of the employer after he has dismissed the employee are not relevant to the fairness of the dismissal, but may well be relevant to compensation[20]). But a tribunal may be expressly directed not to take account of certain matters. Examples of this are to be found in ss. 25, 26, 63 and 74(5) of the Employment Protection (Consolidation) Act 1978, where a tribunal is directed to take no account, either in determining the merits of a complaint or for assessing compensation, of any pressure by industrial action, actual or threatened, which was exercised on the employer to dismiss an employee or take action against him short of dismissal for reasons related to trade union membership and activities. Where a direction of this kind is given, evidence of the matters of which account is not to be taken would generally be inadmissible unless it is relevant in another context. For example, in the examples quoted, ss. 10 and 15(4) of the Employment Act 1980 introduce additional sections (26A and 76A to 76C) into the 1978 Act which have the effect of providing that where an employer claims that he was induced to dismiss an employee by industrial pressure because the complainant was not a trade union member, the trade union or other person who is claimed to have exercised the pressure may be made a party to the proceedings and liable to contribute to any compensation payable to the complainant. In that situation the evidence of pressure which would be inadmissible by virtue of ss. 25, 63 and 74(5) would be admissible for the purposes of ss. 26A and 76A to 76C.

Evidence may be excluded on general grounds of fairness by reason of confidentiality or privilege, or by virtue of other statutory provisions, and certain persons are not compellable as witnesses. These are noted below (pp. 180, 181).

In Scots law there are restrictions on proving alterations in written contracts by extrinsic evidence. Reference should be made to text-books on the subject for the relevant law.[21] Inasmuch that these restrictions may be said to be embodied in the substantive law of contract they may be said to be more than just rules of evidence, and the admissibility of such evidence may be beyond the ambit of the decision in *Douglas* v. *Provident Clothing and Supply Co. Ltd., supra* and r. 8(1) of the 1980 rules. This is a matter which has been raised in the context of constructive dismissal, the test for which, as laid down in *Western Excavating (ECC) Ltd.* v. *Sharp* [1978] I.C.R. 221, depends on the terms of the employee's contract of employment. It could also arise in any other

---

20 *W. Devis & Sons Ltd.* v. *Atkins* [1977] I.C.R. 662.

21 Gloag, *Contract*, 2nd ed., Gloag and Henderson, *op. cit.*, Walkers, *op. cit.*

situation in which the terms of a written contract of employment (or for that matter any other written contract) are in issue. The reported cases on the subject turn to a large extent on their own facts, and on how much may or may not be a matter of admission in the written pleadings. As explained above, the latter matter is not always discernible in industrial tribunal proceedings, so that it would usually be impossible to decide whether a particular line of evidence is admissible until all the circumstances are known. Where therefore an objection of this kind is taken to a line of evidence the normal practice in the courts should be followed, namely to allow it to be received under reservation of its admissibility. The same practice should be generally adopted with regard to any objection to a line of evidence, unless there are clear reasons for excluding it from probation.

EVIDENCE ILLEGALLY OBTAINED

Objection has been taken to evidence on the ground that it was obtained illegally. The general rule on the subject in civil cases seems to be that such evidence is admissible,[22] but in *Argyll* v. *Argyll* 1963 S.L.T.(Notes) 42 the opinion was expressed that there is no absolute rule, and that each case should be decided on its own circumstances, on general considerations of fairness. The matter is essentially discretionary and it is thought that the *Argyll* test ought to be applied by industrial tribunals.

WITNESSES: COMPETENCE AND COMPELLABILITY

In civil proceedings in the courts there are few restrictions on the competence and compellability of individuals as witnesses, but they would also be applied in industrial tribunal proceedings.

By Sched. 1 to the Diplomatic Privileges Act 1964, Art. 31, a diplomatic agent is not obliged to give evidence as a witness (although he may agree to do so). The immunity, which is unqualified, extends to his family and to the administrative and technical staff of the mission and their families if they are not U.K. nationals or permamently resident in the U.K. By Sched. 1 to the Consular Relations Act 1968, Art. 44, a consular officer may be called upon to attend as a witness, but he is under no obligation to give evidence or produce documents concerning matters connected with the exercise of his function. Under both Acts a certificate by or under the authority of the Secretary of State is conclusive evidence as to whether any person is entitled to any such privilege or immunity.

---

22 Walkers, *op. cit.*, p. 2.

Apart from these statutory bars, the only problems about the admissibility of witnesses may relate to spouses, children and persons of doubtful mental capacity. As far as the latter two are concerned, the matter would be for the tribunal to decide, according to their impression of the ability of the witness to appreciate the duty to speak the truth. In doubtful cases, the oath could be dispensed with, and the witness could be merely admonished to tell the truth. Questions of privilege apart (see p. 187 below), there is no rule to prevent spouses giving evidence against each other, although doubts might arise as to their compellability.[23]

CORROBORATION

It was specifically held in *Douglas* v. *Provident Clothing and Supply Company Ltd., supra* that in proceedings before industrial tribunals, and contrary to the general law of evidence in the Scottish courts, an essential fact can be proved on the uncorroborated testimony of a single witness. Scots law differs in respect of corroboration from the law of England, under which a court may generally act on the evidence of a single person or a single document,[24] but the decision in *Douglas* has meant that on this matter there has been no difference between the two countries in the standard of proof in industrial tribunal proceedings.

It is also desirable, as a practical matter, that tribunals should be able to act on the evidence of a single witness. Many of the encounters between employers and employees which lie at the heart of the cases coming before them take place with no other person present. In such cases it would be impossible for the onus to be discharged if the tribunals had to apply the ordinary rule in civil cases in Scotland that corroboration is essential.[25] As a matter of convenience also there are many issues, particularly those of a subsidiary nature, such as compensation, in respect of which insistence on corroboration would impose an unnecessary burden on parties.

Uncorroborated evidence can of course only be accepted as proving a fact if the witness is accepted as being reliable, and while corroboration may not be essential to enable the fact to be proved, it may well be important in a question relating to the weight of the evidence. Therefore, as indicated above, where controversy is anticipated on essential

---

23 On these matters generally, see Walkers, *op. cit.*, pp. 374 to 379.

24 Halsbury's *Laws of England*, Vol. 17, para. 289.

25 It may be noted that s. 9 of the Law Reform (Miscellaneous Provisions) (Scotland) Act 1968 abolished the necessity for corroboration in actions of damages for personal injuries in Scotland, because of the restrictive effect of the common law rule.

matters a party should consider leading corroborative evidence to substantiate his version of the dispute, if it is available. If necessary, application should be made for a witness order. But documents or other proved facts and circumstances may corroborate the evidence of a single witness by showing that his narrative is the most probable account of what occurred.[26]

HEARSAY EVIDENCE

As already stated, hearsay evidence is generally admissible. The law of evidence in the courts on the subject of hearsay evidence recognises distinctions, based on the purpose for which the evidence is tendered.[27] Where it is necessary for the determination of an issue to establish that a statement was made, evidence about the making of the statement is generally admissible. It may, for instance, be necessary to prove that a conversation took place between people merely to establish the subject of discussion, or as evidence of the feelings of the person making the statement towards another person.[28] Such evidence is classified in Scotland as primary hearsay, but in England is not hearsay at all.[29] On the other hand, evidence by a witness of a statement made on some other occasion, which is intended as evidence of the truth of what is asserted, is classified in Scotland as secondary hearsay, and is inadmissible in court, except only if the maker of the alleged statement is dead, insane or a prisoner of war.[30] In England it is classified as hearsay, but a further distinction is made between first-hand hearsay, *i.e.* when a witness says what he himself heard someone else say, and second-hand, *i.e.* when he relates what he was told that someone else said. In civil proceedings, first-hand hearsay is admissible to the extent provided by the Civil Evidence Act 1968, or any other statutory provision, or by agreement between parties.[31] The above differences in classification have to be borne in mind in considering English decisions on the subject of hearsay evidence. In *Lawrence* v. *Newham London Borough Council, supra* it was held that it is within the discretion of the tribunal whether hearsay evidence should be admitted. In Scotland that is to be inferred from the decision in *Douglas, supra,* and from r. 8(1) of the Industrial Tribunals Rules of Procedure (Scotland) 1980.

In practical terms, in many situations (especially complaints of unfair dismissal, which comprise tribunals' staple fare) it would be impossible for the tribunal to decide the issue before it if it could not admit

[26] *O'Hara* v. *Central S.M.T. Co. Ltd.* 1941 S.C. 363 at p. 373.

[27] See Walkers, *op. cit.*, Chap. XXIX, p. 394; Halsbury, *op. cit.*, paras. 53 *et seq.*

[28] Walker, *op. cit.*, pp. 396-7.

[29] Halsbury, *op. cit.*, para. 53.

[30] Walkers, *op. cit.*, p. 394.

[31] Halsbury, *op. cit.*, para. 53.

secondary hearsay evidence (in the Scottish classification). Tribunals have to find out why employers and employees behaved towards each other in a particular way. Often this involves finding out on what basis of information the action was taken, and deciding whether it justified it. But employers and employees do not test their information with the refinement of a court of law: they are apt to act on indirect evidence, and it would be unrealistic and unreasonable to expect otherwise. It is by reference to the information available to the employer at the time that the tribunal must decide whether he was entitled to dismiss.[32] The same principle applies in relation to the actions of an employee who claims that he was constructively dismissed, after having resigned on the strength of information received about his employer's conduct towards him, actual or supposed. In both cases the information is the essential ingredient, and often there will be conflict as to what the information was. The tribunal will be concerned to arrive at the truth on that question, but having arrived at a conclusion, it then has to decide whether the party was reasonably entitled, in an employment situation, and not according to the standards of a court of law, to rely on the information which he had, or could reasonably have been expected to have had, before him when deciding to dismiss, or to resign, as the case may be. It follows that often the tribunal is not directly concerned to decide whether the information was actually true or not. For this reason employees dismissed for supposed dishonesty who come to a tribunal hoping that the proceedings will "clear their name" may be disappointed, unless the basis of the decision is that the employer had no evidence on which he could reasonably have concluded that the employee was dishonest.[33]

If therefore the nature of the issue, and the purpose for which the evidence is led, are kept in mind, it will become apparent that much of the hearsay evidence (in the Scottish sense) which tribunals admit, even although it may be of statements received at second-hand or even less directly, falls into the Scottish primary, rather than secondary category. But of course, in considering whether it was reasonable to act on a particular statement the tribunal will be concerned with its quality and authenticity; and where action was not based on the actual observation or knowledge of the person concerned, will be more likely to uphold action taken on first-hand evidence than on that which is second-hand or less remote. There may be exceptional situations, however, in which the mere fact that statements are in circulation or that there is a certain climate of opinion may be sufficient to justify the action taken.[34] The

---

32 *W. Devis & Sons Ltd.* v. *Atkins* (1977) I.C.R. 662.

33 See *British Home Stores Ltd.* v. *Burchell* (1980) I.C.R. 303 (at p. 304).

34 *Jolliffe* v. *P. D. Timber Ltd.* (EAT 27/6/78); *Saunders* v. *Scottish National Camps Association Ltd.* [1980] I.R.L.R. 174 (NB: The latter decision has been appealed, unsuccessfully).

distinction between primary and secondary hearsay can often become blurred in practice, even in court practice,[35] and is therefore one which it would be impracticable to expect unskilled parties and representatives to observe. Tribunals therefore do not exercise their discretion over the admission of hearsay evidence restrictively. But the principal objection to hearsay evidence is that the original maker of the statement is not available for cross-examination; therefore when such evidence is assessed that factor is taken into account, to a greater or lesser degree, according to the nature and importance of the evidence.

DOCUMENTARY AND REAL EVIDENCE

Notwithstanding the general admissibility of documentary evidence,[36] the objection to hearsay evidence just mentioned applies with equal force to circumstantial evidence provided in writing, whether in the form of a formal affidavit, or informally in the shape of letters, certificates or other written statements, rather than by the personal attendance of a witness. While tribunals do not exercise their discretion in regard to the admissibility of such evidence in a restrictive manner, the weight to be attached to it will depend on the nature and content of the document, and how relevant it is to the main issues in proceedings, and this applies as much to formal affidavits as to less formal documents. Testimonials to character are generally admitted, but are usually of limited relevance and value. Medical reports and certificates will usually be admitted and accepted as evidence of what they purport to say, unless the contents, or the interpretation to be placed upon them, are disputed, and the dispute is relevant to the issues which the tribunal have to consider. The same generally applies to wage certificates, certificates regarding state benefits, entitlements under pension schemes, and the like. But any document, plan, photograph, film, taperecording, item of plant or the like, if not agreed, should be proved by a competent witness; if the controversy is sharp, corroborative evidence may be required to provide sufficient weight. In relation to computer statements which are challenged, the tribunal would have regard to the provisions of ss. 13 to 15 of the Law Reform (Miscellaneous Provisions) (Scotland) Act 1968 in assessing such evidence, but with appropriate allowance for the less stringent requirements of tribunal practice in matters of evidence and proof. As to EEC Directives and other EEC documents, see the European Communities Act 1972, s. 3(3) to (5).

---

35 See Walkers, *op. cit.*, pp. 397-401.

36 See Chap. 7, p. 154, *Vickers Ltd.* v. *Smith* [1977] I.R.L.R. 11 and *Rosedale Mouldings Ltd.* v. *Sibley* [1980] I.C.R. 816 there referred to.

Written statements in substitution for oral evidence on issues of substance will be admitted less readily, because of the objection that the witness cannot be cross-examined. As the tribunal has ample power to postpone or adjourn where there is a sufficient reason why the witness cannot attend in person on the day of the hearing, parties should avoid tendering such written evidence. If they feel obliged to do so, and the tribunal accepts it, it will be subjected to the same scrutiny and discount as secondary hearsay evidence.

If points which require clarification arise from any documents after the conclusion of the hearing, and which do not relate to the substantial merits of the case (*e.g.* relating only to compensation), as a matter of convenience, and to avoid having a further hearing, the tribunal may, with agreement of parties, deal with the matter informally, by correspondence between the Secretary and the originator of the document, but if the matter cannot be resolved satisfactorily in this way a further hearing would have to be convened.

Reference is also made to the section on productions in Chapter 7 (pp. 153 to 154).

Real evidence, properly so called, is a term of wide definition.[37] For present purposes it is used as applying to articles as opposed to documents. If relevant to the issue, there is no restriction on the production of these in industrial tribunal proceedings if it is practicable to do so.

QUESTIONS

The following summary, partly drawn from Walkers' *Law of Evidence in Scotland*, may be of assistance.

(1) **General**

Questions should be as clear and unambiguous as possible, each raising a single point and not a multiplicity. They should not be introduced with a long recital of the questioner's version of the facts. In examination-in-chief leading questions (that is, those which suggest the answer) on matters in controversy are objectionable, *e.g.* the witness should be asked, "Who was present?" not "Was Mr X present?" or "What impression did you form?", rather than "Did you form the impression that . . .?". While it may be unavoidable sometimes to call a witness who has not previously been interviewed, the result can be disastrous if his answers do not assist the party who calls him. Wherever possible, therefore, a witness should be interviewed well beforehand

[37] Walkers, *op. cit.*, p. 440.

to ascertain what his evidence will be, which should be noted in a witness statement or precognition, of which the witness should be given a copy. The risk of a witness giving a wrong or unexpected answer can never be eliminated, but if his evidence is known to be potentially unhelpful, it can be decided not to call him, and risk the consequence that failure to do so may have an adverse result. Hypothetical questions may be appropriate in certain situations, *e.g.* as to what the witness would have done if he had known that a certain practice was forbidden. But hypothetical questions unrelated to evidence already given or to be given are usually of little value, and questions should not be asked which usurp the function of the tribunal. Thus while it is appropriate, and often useful, to ask an applicant why he considers his dismissal to have been unfair or an employer why he considers the dismissal was fair (because that can assist the tribunal to discover the true basis of the complaint or defence), or what impression a witness formed from his own observation, a witness should not be asked such a question as whether in his opinion an employee was redundant, because that is a legal question for the tribunal to decide on the relevant facts: in such a situation the witness should generally be asked only about facts which are relevant to infer redundancy (although for certain purposes it may be relevant to ask whether the employee was *treated* as redundant).

(2) **Cross-examination**

This is one of the most difficult aspects of advocacy, the techniques of which can only be touched on here. Cross-examination has two main purposes: to test the credibility of the witness, and the accuracy of his evidence; and to obtain his evidence on matters which he has not been asked about in evidence-in-chief, and which may form part of or help the cross-examiner's case. Unless a question serves either of these purposes, it should not be asked. As with evidence-in-chief, the questioner should avoid lengthy preambles, and multiple questions, but leading questions may be asked. "Blind" questions may sometimes have to be asked, but should be avoided wherever possible, because if the cross-examiner does not himself know the answer, he will be unable to test it by an appropriate "follow-up" question. The cross-examiner should generally confine himself to questions about matters which are within the scope of the enquiry, although suggestions about interest, relationship, motive or prejudice are permissible to test credibility, provided that they are legitimate.[38] But if they are refuted by the witness in an apparently credible manner, and are not backed up by subsequent evidence (and the tribunal will not

38 See below under "Privilege" and "Rehabilitation of Offenders Act 1974".

permit a subsidiary enquiry on an extraneous matter merely to determine credibility) they will achieve little or nothing. Any such questions which reflect on third parties should usually not be put. An exact reiteration of questions already asked in evidence-in-chief should be avoided: it is tedious, and generally produces the same answers. Where the accuracy of evidence previously given is to be tested, it is preferable merely to refer to it by way of introduction to further and more detailed questions designed to make inroads into it. Where there is no conflict between the witness' evidence-in-chief and the evidence already led or to be led by the cross-examiner or where the evidence-in-chief has not damaged the cross-examiner's case in any other way, cross-examination is unnecessary. Where there is conflict, the cross-examiner should always put his own version of the matter in dispute to the witness, whether it has previously been spoken about in his own witnesses' evidence, or to lay a foundation for new matter which the cross-examiner will be raising in the course of his own case. This is particularly important if the matter in question is one in which the onus lies on the cross-examiner.[39] If evidence is subsequently given by the cross-examiner's witnesses which he has not tested with his opponent's witnesses, the latter may be recalled to give their version of the matter, but evidence given in these circumstances is usually less valuable because the recalled witness (if by this time present in the tribunal room, as he usually will be) will have had the opportunity to consider his position. The effects of failure to cross-examine, have been considered above under "Weight of evidence".

(3) **Re-examination**

This has already been discussed in Chapter 7 (at p. 149).

PRIVILEGE

In the courts a witness is entitled to refuse to answer a question if a true answer may lead to his conviction for a crime or involves an admission of adultery.[40] This principle is applied in industrial tribunal proceedings. The Chairman should explain to the witness that he is not bound to answer such a question. If, notwithstanding this, the witness remains willing to answer, the evidence is competent. But where an issue arises as to whether the proceedings may be barred on grounds of illegality,[41] it may be necessary to ask the witness enough questions (*e.g.* about

---

39 See above under "Burden of proof".

40 Walkers, *op. cit.*, pp. 369-71.

41 See Chap. 4, pp. 39 to 42.

deduction of PAYE) as may be necessary to enable the tribunal to form a view as to whether the contract of employment is illegal.

CONFIDENTIALITY

By the law of evidence certain communications may be excluded from proof on the grounds that they were confidential. On general grounds of fairness they should normally be regarded as similarly protected in industrial tribunal proceedings. The objection mainly arises in connection with the recovery of written communications, but the same considerations apply in relation to oral evidence.

The main categories, to each of which there are exceptions,[42] are:
(1) Communications between husband and wife (but not where the proceedings are concerned with the conduct of the spouses towards each other).
(2) Communications between partners.
(3) Professional communications between solicitor and client.
As regards industrial tribunal proceedings, this was extended in *M. & W. Grazebrook Ltd.* v. *Wallens* [1973] I.C.R. 256 to communications with "other agents" (which would include lay representatives) with a view to the proceedings themselves.
(4) Communications between other persons in connection with the preparation and conduct of the proceeedings, or in the course of conciliation. Thus once an employee has given notice of his intention to raise proceedings for unfair dismissal, internal communications within the firm regarding the circumstances of his dismissal, prepared with a view to resisting the claim, should be protected, but not internal communications about the case prior and subsequent to dismissal. Similarly, correspondence between parties conducted on a "without prejudice" basis will normally be protected. As regards statements made to a conciliation officer, see below.
(5) Where disclosure of the facts would be contrary to public policy, *e.g.* disclosure of a source of information to the police.

Confidentiality in relation to documentary evidence is also discussed under "Document and witness orders" (Chapter 6, pp. 113 to 115), as are objections on grounds of public policy).

Apart from the above categories, communications stated or generally understood to be confidential (*e.g.* financial reports) are not protected. Neither are statements made to clergymen. A doctor must give evidence about a patient if required to do so.

Confidentiality may be waived either expressly or by implication, *e.g.* where a solicitor (or other representative) gives evidence, or if a confidential document is left about (See *Argyll* v. *Argyll* 1962 S.C.(H.L.) 88.

[42] See Walkers, *op. cit.*, Chap. XXXI, pp. 413-421.

Sections 133(6) and 134(5) of the Employment Protection (Consolidation) Act 1978 provide that anything communicated to a conciliation officer in connection with the performance of his functions under those sections shall not be admissible in evidence in any proceedings before an industrial tribunal, except with the consent of the person who communicated it to that officer. There are similar provisions in ss. 64(4) of the Sex Discrimination Act 1975, and 55(4) of the Race Relations Act 1976. In *M. & W. Grazebrook Ltd.* v. *Wallens, supra* it was held that these provisions were not intended to render inadmissible evidence which could have been given if there had been no communication to the conciliation officer: otherwise a party could conceal inconvenient evidence by simply communicating it to a conciliation officer.

REHABILITATION OF OFFENDERS ACT 1974

This Act provides that after certain rehabilitation periods, which vary between 5 and 10 years according to the sentence imposed, but lesser periods in the case of young offenders, a conviction resulting in a non-custodial sentence, or a custodial sentence of not more than 30 months, must be treated in law as spent, and the convicted person must be treated as rehabilitated, provided that he has not meanwhile been convicted of anything more serious than a summary offence.

Section 4(1) provides that, subject to ss. 7 and 8, notwithstanding any other enactment or rule of law to the contrary—

(*a*) no evidence shall be admissible in any proceedings before a judicial authority to prove that a rehabilitated person has been committed, or been charged with, or prosecuted for, or convicted of, or sentenced for any offence which was the subject of a spent conviction; and

(*b*) a person shall not, in any such proceedings, be asked, and if asked, shall not be required to answer, any question relating to his past which cannot be answered without acknowledging or referring to a spent conviction or spent convictions or any circumstances ancillary thereto.

Proceedings before a judicial authority are defined in s. 4(6) as including any tribunal having power by virtue of any enactment to determine any question affecting the rights, privileges, obligations or liabilities of any person, or to receive evidence affecting termination of any such questions. Industrial tribunals fall within this definition. Three exceptions are stated in s. 7:

(i) Section 7(2)(*f*) provides that such an issue may be determined or evidence regarding the spent conviction may be given with consent of the rehabilitated person.

(ii) Section 7(3) allows for the determination of an issue or the admission of evidence of a spent conviction if the judicial authority is satisfied, in the light of any considerations which may appear to it to be relevant (including any evidence which has been or thereafter may be put before it), that justice cannot be done except by admitting or requiring evidence relating to a person's spent convictions or to circumstances ancillary thereto.

(iii) Section 7(4) provides that the Secretary of State may by order exclude the application of s. 4(1) to any proceedings to such extent and for such purposes as may be so specified. The Rehabilitation of Offenders Act 1974 (Exceptions) Order 1975 (S.I. 1975/1023) so designates certain professional persons and offices and employment involving a particularly high degree of risk or responsibility.

QUESTIONS IN SEX DISCRIMINATION AND RACIAL DISCRIMINATION PROCEEDINGS

Section 74(1) of the Sex Discrimination Act 1975 provides that with a view to helping a person (called "the person aggrieved") who considers that he may have been discriminated against in contravention of the Act to decide whether to institute proceedings, and to formulate and present his case in the most effective manner, forms may be prescribed by which the person aggrieved may question the respondent on his reasons for doing any relevant act, or on any other matter which is or may be relevant, and by which the respondent may reply. By subs. (2) any such question and reply (whether in accordance with an order under subs. (1) or not) shall be admissible as evidence, and if it appears to the tribunal that the respondent deliberately, and without reasonable excuse, omitted to reply within a reasonable period or that his reply is evasive or equivocal, the tribunal may draw any inference from that fact that it considers it just and equitable to draw, including an inference that he committed an unlawful act.

The Sex Discrimination (Questions and Replies) Order 1975 (S.I. 1975/2048), which applies to Scotland and to England and Wales, sets out forms by which a person aggrieved may question a respondent under s. 74(1) and by which a respondent may reply. Article 5 provides that in proceedings before an industrial tribunal a question shall only be admissible as evidence in pursuance of s. 74(2) if it was served within certain time limits: if served before a complaint is presented to a tribunal, it must have been served within the period of three months beginning when the act complained of was done; if served when a complaint has been presented to a tribunal, it must be served either within the period of 21 days beginning with the day on which the complaint was presented or if later with leave given, and within a period specified, by a tribunal. Article 6 prescribes the method of service.

Section 65 of the Race Relations Act 1976 and the Race Relations (Questions and Replies) Order 1977 (S.I. 1977/842) are in the same terms (*mutatis mutandis*) as s. 74 of the Sex Discrimination Act 1975 and the Sex Discrimination (Questions and Replies) Order 1975.[43]

In the questionnaire the aggrieved person must state the date and time and give a factual description of the treatment received and of the circumstances leading up to the treatment, and may state the reasons why he or she thinks the treatment unlawful. The person aggrieved may add any further questions which he or she may wish to ask, and must provide an address for the reply. The respondent or potential respondent is asked whether he agrees that the statement given is accurate, and if he does not, is asked to say in what respect he disagrees or to give his version of what happened. He is also asked to state whether he accepts that the alleged treatment was unlawful discrimination, and if not, to say why not; for what reason the alleged treatment was accorded; and how far it was affected by the sex or marital status of the person aggrieved or (as the case may be) by considerations of colour, race, nationality (including citizenship) or ethnic or national origins.

---

43 Both orders are printed in *The Encyclopaedia of Labour Relations Law*, Vol. 3, Pt. 4A.

CHAPTER 9

THE DECISION

GENERAL

In the Industrial Tribunals (Rules of Procedure) (Scotland) Regulations 1980 (reg. 2), the expression "decision" includes a declaration, an order (other than an interlocutory order), recommendation or an award of the tribunal, but not an opinion given in the course of a pre-hearing assessment under r. 6 (as to which see Chapter 6, pp. 116 to 119). In the Industrial Tribunals (Improvement and Prohibition Notices Appeals) (Scotland) Regulations 1974, the expression includes a direction under r. 4 suspending the operation of a prohibition notice and any other order which is not an interlocutory order. In the Industrial Tribunals (Non-Discrimination Notices Appeals) (Scotland) Regulations 1977, the expression includes a direction under s. 68 of the Sex Discrimination Act 1975 or s. 59 of the Race Relations Act 1976 (*i.e.* a direction substituting different requirements for those of a notice which the tribunal has quashed), and any other order which is not an interlocutory order.

In Scottish legal terminology and practice, any written judgment or order by a court in civil proceedings, whether it exhausts the question at issue or not, is called an interlocutor. But an interlocutory judgment, as distinct from a final judgment, is any judicial order or interlocutor pronounced in the preparation or the disposal of a case, which is not decisive of the whole merits of the suit.[1] (The "whole merits of the suit" would in this context include questions of jurisdiction). The main significance of an interlocutory order and an opinion given at a pre-hearing assessment not being a "decision" of the tribunal is that they are not entered in the Register of Decisions and do not fall within the scope of the rules which enable the decision of a tribunal to be reviewed by the same, or a different tribunal. As will have been noticed, however, an order suspending the operation of a prohibition notice, although interlocutory in character by the foregoing definition, is nevertheless defined as a decision. Similarly, an application for interim relief under s. 77 of the Employment Protection (Consolidation) Act 1978 is an interlocutory matter within the above definition, but is not treated as such. But an order by the President or a Chairman refusing an application for review on the ground that it has no reasonable chance of success is not treated as a decision, but as an interlocutory order.

---

[1] Bell's *Dictionary and Digest of the Law of Scotland,* 7th ed. pp. 577, 578.

As explained elsewhere,[2] interlocutory orders can be made by the President or a Chairman alone, as may decisions in the limited class of situations where a case can be disposed of without a hearing, and in applications for interim relief under s. 77 of the Employment Protection (Consolidation) Act 1978. Apart from these, all decisions are taken by a fully constituted tribunal, following a hearing.

As pointed out in Chapter 3 (at p. 22) all members of the tribunal have an equal vote, but if the tribunal consists of the Chairman and one member only, the Chairman has a casting vote. Where a tribunal was so divided that it could not arrive at a decision, the Chairman decided that it would have to be re-heard by a different tribunal; the High Court held that he had acted within his powers.[3] Where the tribunal are divided on the merits of a case, the dissenting member should take part in the decision on the remedy if the majority sustain the complaint, since, given the decision of the majority, unanimity on the remedy may be achieved.[4]

In order to arrive at their decision the tribunal must consider the evidence and contentions on both sides, and having concluded which version of the facts they prefer, where there is any conflict of evidence, should then decide how the relevant law should be applied. Reference is made to what is said in Chapters 3 (p. 24) and 8 (pp. 173 to 178), and below (under "Form and Content" and "Sources of Law" pp. 195 to 205) concerning the decision-making process. In particular, cases must be decided on the evidence placed before the tribunal and not on a basis of speculation. Facts of every day life within common knowledge are assumed to be known, however,[5] and within limits[6] tribunal members are entitled to draw on their own knowledge and experience of industry in arriving at their decision. As to the extent to which a tribunal may take into consideration issues which have not been canvassed at the hearing, see Chapter 7 (under "Closing Addresses"), at p. 168.

It is for the Chairman to advise his colleagues on the relevant law, and record the tribunal's decision in a written document. Usually he will agree with them the broad outlines of the tribunal's findings and reasoning, and they will agree to his filling in details. In difficult cases, however, the draft of the written decision may be submitted for their approval and, if necessary, further discussion. If a member dissents, both members are sent copies of the decision when it is promulgated, but unless the reason for doing so is very succinct, the Chairman will

---

[2] See Chap. 3, p. 20; Chap. 6, p. 104.

[3] *R.* v. *Industrial Tribunal* ex. p. *Cotswold Collotype Co. Ltd.* [1979] I.C.R. 190.

[4] *Morris* v. *Gestetner Ltd.* [1973] I.C.R. 587.

[5] For the limits of judicial knowledge in the rules of evidence in the courts, see Walkers' *Law of Evidence in Scotland*, pp. 47 to 49.

[6] See Chap. 3, p. 24.

first either show the dissenting member his own draft of the reasons for the dissent or (if these have not been sufficiently clearly stated) ask the dissenting member himself to state them in writing for incorporation in the tribunal's written decision.

INTIMATION AND PROMULGATION

The tribunal may announce its decision on all aspects of the case, or some only, before parties have dispersed after the hearing. If so, the announcement will usually confine itself to a brief statement as to who has succeeded, leaving the details to be given in the written decision to follow. But the main reasons for the decision may be indicated. More commonly, however, the tribunal will reserve the decision to be intimated later. This is usually done initially by means of a short "advance notice of decision", signed by the Chairman and stating who has succeeded. But, in terms of each of the rules of procedure, every decision has to be recorded in a written document and signed by the Chairman, containing the reasons for the decision, which is entered in the appropriate Register (see below), a copy being sent to each of the parties, to any other persons entitled to appear who did appear (*e.g.* the Secretary of State) and, where the matter was referred to a tribunal by a sheriff, to that sheriff.[7]

The "advance notice" does not constitute such a document, as it is the equivalent of an oral announcement and does not specify any reasons for the decision.

The Register is the Register of Applications[8] and Decisions kept by the Secretary of the Industrial Tribunals (Scotland) in pursuance of the Industrial Tribunals (Rules of Procedure) (Scotland) Regulations 1980, and under the preceding regulations of 1974, except for cases under the Industrial Tribunals (Scotland) Regulations 1965 (as amended), where it is the Register of Industrial Levy Appeals and Decisions. The Registers are kept at the Central Office and are open to inspection by any person without charge at all reasonable hours. In any case in which evidence has been heard in private, the reasons for the decision are omitted from the Register if the tribunal so directs, but are sent to the parties and to any appellate court in any proceedings relating to the decision.[9] In cases

---

7 The Industrial Tribunals Rules of Procedure (Scotland) 1980 (r. 9(2) and (3)); the Industrial Tribunals (Scotland) (Regulations) 1965 (as amended), Sched. 2, r. 12(2) and (3); the Industrial Tribunals (Improvement and Prohibition Notices Appeals) (Scotland) Regulations 1974, r. 11(2) and (3); the Industrial Tribunals (Non-Discrimination Notices Appeals) (Scotland) Regulations 1977, r. 9(2) and (3).

8 (Misprinted as "Applicants" in the 1980 Regulations).

9 The Industrial Tribunals Rules of Procedure (Scotland) 1980, r. 9(4); the Industrial Tribunals (Improvement and Prohibition Notices Appeals) (Scotland) Regulations 1974, r. 11(4); the Industrial Tribunals (Non-Discrimination Notices Appeals) (Scotland) Regulations 1977, r. 9(4).

under the Industrial Tribunals (Scotland) Regulations 1965 (as amended), Sched. 2, the tribunal may direct that the reasons be omitted from the Register on the ground that disclosure would be contrary to the interests of the appellant (r. 12(3)).

The entry of the decision in the Register and its issue to parties is an important step in procedure known as promulgation. It marks the conclusion of the proceedings leading to the decision, and is the stage at which it becomes complete,[10] and it is from the date of the entry in the Register that the periods for review and appeal are calculated. But the tribunal's function is not entirely exhausted at this point, since it can still entertain an application for review, an application for expenses[11], or even an application for leave to enter a late appearance.[12] Once promulgated, a decision is enforceable by the party in whose favour it is made, subject to limitations while a decision remains open to appeal, or where a review or appeal has been taken (see below under "Enforcement", at p. 228).

If a Chairman becomes seriously ill and is unable to draw up a written decision within a suitable period of time, the decision is prepared by the President, or another Chairman, from the notes taken by the Chairman who heard the case and information supplied by the other members as to the reason for the decision: it is recorded in the decision that this has been done, and it is signed by the two members themselves. There is no need for the case to be reheard (*Jowett* v. *Earl of Bradford* [1977] I.C.R. 342).

PROOF OF DECISIONS

Regulation 4 in each of the regulations provides that the production in any proceedings in any court of a document purporting to be certified by the Secretary of the Tribunals to be a true copy of an entry of a decision in the Register shall, unless the contrary is proved, be sufficient evidence of the document and of the facts stated therein.

FORM AND CONTENT

The written decision consists of two parts: the decision itself (including any orders consequential thereon), and the reasons for it. The first part contains only what is essential for the decision of the issues before the

---

10 *Hanks* v. *Ace High Productions Ltd.* [1978] I.C.R. 1155.

11 *Zakia* v. *Home Office* (EAT 28/79).

12 *St Mungo Community Trust* v. *Colleano* [1980] I.C.R. 254.

tribunal. The findings of fact and of law which lead to the decision are set out in the reasons. In the case of multiple cases, all of them may be covered in one decision, or there may be a full decision on one case, with other shorter decisions in the other cases, referring to and adopting the main decision on matters of common ground, whichever is more convenient.

An application which fails will be said to have been dismissed or refused. The words are used synonymously, and neither has any particular technical significance. Nor are the distinctions in court proceedings between decrees of dismissal and decrees of *absolvitor*, and between decrees in absence and decrees *in foro* of any technical significance in industrial tribunal proceedings (although the absence of a respondent may be of practical significance in the context of an application for review).

In cases where the hearing has been on a preliminary point of jurisdiction, and the respondent has not attended because he has been told that his attendance was not necessary, if the tribunal's *prima facie* view is favourable to the applicant, it should not arrive at a concluded decision on the preliminary point, but should continue the case for further hearing both on the preliminary point and on the merits.

Where the application has succeeded on the merits, a decision to that effect normally incorporates a decision on the remedy on which the tribunal decides. Where the hearing has been confined to the merits, an initial decision on the merits may be issued, continuing the application for further hearing on the remedy. Alternatively, and also in those cases where the evidence on the remedy is incomplete and is provided subsequently in documentary form (see Chapter 7, p. 158), the issue of a written decision may be deferred until the remedy has been considered and decided, so that the tribunal's decision on all aspects of the case may be contained in one document.

The rules of procedure do not contain any requirements as to how the reasons for the decision should be set out. But if the decision does not state findings and facts which are sufficient in law to support the tribunal's decision, or the findings-in-fact do not fairly reflect the evidence given, or if the decision shows that the correct questions of law have not been considered and correctly answered, the decision is liable to be overturned on appeal as having erred in law. What amounts to error of law in this connection is fully discussed in Chapter 12 (pp. 253 to 257). In *Franks Charlesly & Co.* v. *Sothern* (EAT 437/79) May J suggested a "common form" for decisions, setting out:

(1) the nature of the claim before the tribunal, and, if necessary, the issues between the parties;
(2) *seriatim* the facts found by the industrial tribunal on the evidence adduced before it without repeating that evidence;

(3) the submissions made by either side;
(4) what the tribunal considers to be the law applicable to those facts so found; and
(5) their conclusions. (See also *Allders International Ltd.* v. *Parkins* [1981] I.R.L.R. 68).

In *Long and Hambly Ltd.* v. *Bryan* [1975] I.C.R. 200 it was held that a tribunal is only obliged to set out the major issues of fact and its conclusions thereon, and is not obliged to make findings of fact on every peripheral issue between the parties.

Two comments may be made, with respect, on the suggested form. Except for the one type of case in which appeal is open on questions of fact as well as law, where it may be necessary to rehearse in full the evidence of each witness,[13] it is unnecessary (as pointed out in *Franks Charlesly & Co., supra*) to set out all the evidence in detail, and particularly on matters which are common ground. But on matters where there is a conflict of evidence it may help to demonstrate that the two opposing versions have both been taken into account (and thus avoid an appeal on the ground that the findings-in-fact do not reflect the evidence) if both are set down, rather than just the version which the tribunal prefers. But in that event, unless the conflict is not material to the tribunal's decision, it is essential also to make clear which of the two versions is preferred, and what facts are actually held proved.[13] Secondly, as explained in Chapter 7 (p. 167), formal submissions may not be made, or may be perfunctory, in which case it will only be possible to indicate the contentions put forward in the course of the evidence.

In cases where dismissal is a statutory prerequisite[14] there must be a finding that the employee has been dismissed in terms of the relevant statutory definition;[15] otherwise the decision is vitiated.[16] Where a tribunal has to decide whether an employee was redundant, the decision should avoid expressions such as "redundancy situation", except in a broad context; in relation to the employee concerned, the tribunal should relate the relevant facts which it has found proved (or not, as the case may be) to the actual wording in the definition of redundancy in s. 81(2) of the Employment Protection (Consolidation) Act 1978, and decide whether or not they fall within that wording. Likewise in complaints of unfair dismissal, in considering whether in the circumstances it was reasonable to dismiss for the reason found by

---

13 See pp. 259-260 and *Alexander Machinery* v. *Crabtree* at p. 255.

14 *I.e.* in unfair dismissal and redundancy payment cases, and complaints of failure to provide written reasons for dismissal under s. 53 of the Employment Protection (Consolidation) Act 1978.

15 The Employment Protection (Consolidation) Act 1978, ss. 55(2) and 56 for unfair dismissal; ss. 83 to 86 and 93 for redundancy payment purposes; and s. 53(1) for complaints under s. 53.

16 *I.C.I. Ltd.* v. *McCallum* (1969) 4 I.T.R. 24.

the tribunal the facts found should be related to the wording of s. 57(3).[17]

Where compensation is awarded for unfair dismissal, the tribunal should set out the details of the individual heads under which compensation is awarded (which are set out in *Norton Tool Co. Ltd.* v. *Tewson* [1972] I.C.R. 501), the relevant evidence, and the reasoning by which they have arrived at the figures.[18] Where the question whether an employee contributed to his dismissal is in issue, the tribunal must state their conclusion on the issue[19], and the degree of contribution should be expressed in definite terms.[20] As to preservation of continuity of employment where reinstatement or re-engagement, or continuation of employment in an application for interim relief, are ordered, see Chapter 4, pp. 69, 70). As to the application of the regulations relating to recoupment of unemployment and supplementary benefit, see below, pp. 220-223).

Where a decision is by a majority, the respective views and findings of the majority and minority should be clearly stated in the reasons.[21] And in a decision dealing with a number of applications heard together, it should be made clear that each case has received separate consideration: any distinctions between individual cases should be recorded, and it should be made clear which matters the tribunal have found common to all the cases.

SOURCES OF LAW

(1) **General**

An industrial tribunal's decision must be taken with due regard to the rules of law which are applicable to it, so far as binding on the tribunal. These are derived from various sources, as follows.

(2) **Enacted law**

While there are a number of sources of enacted law,[22] industrial tribunals are mainly concerned with public general statutes (as opposed to private Acts) so far as they apply to Scotland, and in particular with those Acts which create the rights and obligations upon which they

---

17 *Elliott* v. *University Computing Co. (Great Britain)* Ltd. [1977] I.C.R. 147.

18 *Fougère* v. *Phoenix Motor Co. Ltd.* [1976] I.C.R. 495; *Green* v. *J. Waterhouse & Sons Ltd.* [1977] I.C.R. 759.

19 *Portsea Island Mutual Co-operative Society Ltd.* v. *Rees* [1980] I.C.R. 260.

20 *Blackwell* v. *G.E.C. Elliott Process Automation Ltd.* [1976] I.R.L.R. 144.

21 *Parkers Bakeries Ltd.* v. *Palmer* [1977] I.R.L.R. 215; see also pp. 193-4 above as to the desirability of the draft decision being approved by the members.

22 See Gloag & Henderson, *Introduction to the Law of Scotland,* 8th ed., Chap. I, p. 1.

adjudicate, and constitute industrial tribunals as the forum before which such rights may be vindicated. An industrial tribunal can only act within the powers conferred upon it by Parliament and cannot invoke a common law principle, such as personal bar or estoppel, so as to enlarge a right beyond the limits set by the Act itself.[23] To Acts of Parliament may be added European Community Law (see (4) below) and subordinate legislation made under powers conferred by Parliament, such as Orders in Council and regulations and orders by Ministers, so far as relevant and applicable.

Most statutes and subordinate legislation contain provisions declaring how various expressions or particular words are to be construed, either generally or for particular purposes. The Interpretation Act 1978 also applies general rules of construction to Acts of Parliament and subordinate legislation made after the commencement of the Act, but only to a limited extent to subordinate legislation made before the commencement of the Act[24]: by contrast, the previous Interpretation Act of 1889 did not apply to subordinate legislation unless the instrument or order itself expressly so provided. Interpretative provisions of a general nature are usually stated to apply "unless the contrary intention appears."

Where the meaning is not defined, or is not clear, tribunals must apply the rules of construction laid down by judicial decision. It is beyond the scope of this work to attempt an exposition of these and references should be made to textbooks on the subject[25]. The general principle is that words and expressions should, where possible, be construed according to their natural and ordinary meaning. If the meaning is ambiguous, a statutory provision may be construed in the least anomalous or unjust way, and there are various rules of construction on the subject.[26] But if the meaning is plain and unambiguous it must be given effect, and it is not permissible to read words into a statutory provision to avoid any injustice or anomaly which would result from applying the literal meaning. The general application of this principle was reaffirmed by the House of Lords in an important decision on the law of unfair dismissal in a strike situation, *Stock* v. *Frank Jones (Tipton) Ltd.* [1978] I.C.R. 347, although Lord Simon of Glaisdale and Lord Scarman accepted the possibility of an exception being made in an extreme case where the anomaly in result would be so gross as to amount to an absurdity, or would frustrate the object of the legislation. The view that the courts have a general power to remedy an injustice

---

[23] *Secretary of State for Employment* v. *Globe Elastic Thread Co. Ltd.* [1979] I.C.R. 706.

[24] Ss. 22(1) and 23(1).

[25] Maxwell, *Interpretation of Statutes;* Craies, *Statute Law.*

[26] They are concisely summarised in Gloag & Henderson, *op. cit.*, Chap. I, pp. 6 to 10.

resulting from the literal construction of a statute by adopting an approach which would promote the underlying "general legislative purpose", which was expressed by Lord Denning MR in *Nothman* v. *Barnet London Borough Council* [1978] I.C.R. 336 (at p. 344), was disclaimed by Lord Russell of Killowen in the House of Lords in that case ([1979] I.C.R. 111 at p. 122), and by implication in *Stock's* case, *supra*. In *Lakhani* v. *Hoover Ltd.* [1978] I.C.R. 1063, the Employment Appeal Tribunal therefore warned industrial tribunals against adopting a "purposive approach" to the construction of a statutory provision, which they said should be left to courts of superior jurisdiction.

(3) **Common law**

Where relevant, common law doctrines and rules are applicable to the issues which industrial tribunals have to consider. They may be imported by express statutory provision, *e.g.* s. 74(4) of the Employment Protection (Consolidation) Act 1978 provides that in calculating loss for the purpose of the compensatory award in unfair dismissal cases, an industrial tribunal shall apply the same rule concerning the duty of a person to mitigate his loss as applies to damages recoverable at common law. The application of common law has also been inferred by judicial decision, *e.g.* the question whether an employee is entitled to terminate his contract of employment by reason of his employer's conduct, and so be treated as dismissed in terms of s. 55(2)(c) of the Employment Protection (Consolidation) Act 1978, has to be interpreted according to the ordinary law of contract and not by applying a general test of unreasonableness to the employer's conduct.[27] Likewise, general principles of common law such as personal bar (called estoppel in England), *res judicata,* and the law relating to illegal contracts, have been recognised as applying in proceedings before industrial tribunals.[28] Where a common law rule is inconsistent with the statutory function of tribunals, it cannot apply, or may apply only to a limited extent, the main example being the rules of evidence in court proceedings.[29]

(4) **European Community law**

Section 2 of the European Communities Act 1972 has the effect that the law of the European Communities (*i.e.* the European Coal and Steel Community, the European Economic Community and the European

---

27 *Western Excavating (E.C.C.) Ltd.* v. *Sharp* [1978] I.C.R. 221.

28 See Chap. 4, pp. 37 to 42.

29 See Chap. 8 and *Douglas* v. *Provident Clothing and Supply Co. Ltd.* (1969) 4 I.T.R. 15.

Atomic Energy Community) which is directly enforceable in member states is part of the law of the United Kingdom, and enforceable there in legal proceedings without the necessity of further legislation by Parliament.

The parts of Community law which are directly enforceable are Treaty Articles which are sufficiently clear, precise and unconditional as not to require any further measure of implementation,[30] and (under Art. 189 of the Treaty of Rome) Community regulations.[31] Article 189 also provides that Directives, while binding on member states as to the result to be achieved, leave to the national authorities the choice of form and methods. Generally they are to be implemented by national legislation.[32] But in *Hugh-Jones* v. *St. John's College, Cambridge* [1979] I.C.R. 848 the Employment Appeal Tribunal explained the effect of the decision of the European Court of Justice in *Van Duyn* v. *Home Office* [1975] 3 All E.R. 190 as being that where a member state has not implemented a Directive it cannot rely on national laws or administrative provisions which are in conflict with it in proceedings between the state and an individual, but that an individual could not rely on such a Directive in proceedings against another individual. Decisions of the Council are entirely binding on those to whom they are addressed and affect relations between them and third parties.[33]

By s. 3(1) of the 1972 Act, any question arising in any legal proceeding as to the meaning or effect of any of the Treaties, or as to the validity, meaning or effect of any Community instrument, is a question of law to be determined by the European Court or in accordance with the principles laid down by its decisions. Section 3(2) requires judicial notice to be taken of the Treaties, of the Journal of the Communities and of any decision or opinion of the European Court. Provision is also made in subss. (3) to (5) for proof of the Treaties and of Community instruments.

The principle that in case of conflict between the law of the Community and the law of a member state, the law of the Community shall prevail was established in *Costa* v. *Ente Nazionale Energia Elletrica* [1964] E.C.R. 585.[34] In *Shields* v. *E. Coomes (Holdings) Ltd.* [1978] I.C.R. 1159, it was held (by Lord Denning at p. 1167) that Community law applies before industrial tribunals, as well as in the superior courts. If a question of Community law is taken, therefore, an industrial tribunal would have to consider it. Under Art. 177 of the Treaty of Rome, any

---

30 As held by the European Court of Justice in *Van Gend en Loos* v. *Nederlandse Administrahie der Belashingen* [1963] E.C.R. 1.

31 *Per* Lord Denning MR in *Shields* v. *E. Coomes (Holdings) Ltd., infra.*

32 *Per* Bridge LJ in *Shields* v. *E. Coomes (Holdings) Ltd.*, at p. 1177.

33 *Franz Grad* v. *Finanzamt Traunstein* [1970] E.C.R. 825.

34 *Per* Lord Denning in *Shield* v. *E. Coomes (Holdings) Ltd.*

court or tribunal of a member state may request the European Court to give preliminary ruling on a question of Community law. On a reference being made, the European Commission and the member states may submit representations on the matter. It would be within the powers of an industrial tribunal to make such a reference, but, doubtless because of the expense and delay which would inevitably be involved, the Employment Appeal Tribunal has indicated (in *Jenkins* v. *Kingsgate (Clothing Productions) Ltd.* (EAT 145/79)) that Art. 177 references should only be made sparingly and that they are probably better left to higher courts.

The cases in which Community law has been held to apply in industrial tribunal proceedings have been almost exclusively concerned with equal pay, where questions have arisen with regard to the interpretation of Art. 119 of the Treaty of Rome, which lays down the principle of equal pay for equal work, and with regard to the validity and interpretation of Directives following upon Article 119.[35] In this field, a number of references have been made to the European Court in appeals from decisions of industrial tribunals.[36]

(5) **Foreign law**

Other foreign law has no binding effect in the United Kingdom, but where comparable, it may be of assistance.[37]

(6) **Codes of practice**

Codes of practice issued by the Advisory, Conciliation and Arbitration Service (ACAS), by definition, contain practical guidance for the purpose of promoting the improvement of industrial relations (The Employment Protection Act 1975, s. 6(1)). Failure on the part of any person to observe any provision of a code of practice does not of itself render him liable to any proceedings: but in any proceedings before an industrial tribunal any code of practice is admissible in evidence, and if relevant, may be taken into account by the tribunal in arriving at the decision.[38] While, in appropriate cases, industrial tribunals and

[35] Community law was held not to apply to certain particular issues in sex discrimination cases in *Amies* v. *Inner London Education Authority* [1977] I.C.R. 308 and *Hugh-Jones* v. *St. John's College, supra,* but other issues may arise in such cases which may be affected by Community law on the equal treatment of men and women.

[36] *E.g. Macarthys Ltd.* v. *Smith* [1979] I.C.R. 785, where the question was whether the principle of equal pay could apply between workers not employed contemporaneously; *Worringham & Anr.* v. *Lloyds Bank Ltd.* [1979] I.R.L.R. 440, where the complaint was of unequal treatment in a pension scheme; and *Jenkins* v. *Kingsgate (Clothing Productions) Ltd., supra,* where the question was whether there must be equality of hourly rates between full-time and part-time workers.

[37] For example US law in equal pay legislation—see *Shields* v. *E. Coomes (Holdings) Ltd., supra* (at p. 1167).

[38] The Employment Protection Act 1975, s. 6(11).

appellate courts regularly take into account the provisions of the codes of practice, it has been emphasised in judgments of superior courts that they are not mandatory, and do not themselves have the force of law.[39] Thus a tribunal's decision is not vitiated by a failure to refer to a relevant code.

(7) Judicial precedent: authoritative writers

In applying the canons of statutory construction, and common law principles and rules, industrial tribunals are bound by judicial precedent and authoritative writers, in the same way as are the courts.[40] Industrial tribunals in Scotland are bound by decisions of the Employment Appeal Tribunal (which has jurisdiction in both countries), with the probable exception of decisions in English cases where the ratio is based on rules of English law which do not apply, or have no exact equivalent, in Scotland; decisions of the Inner House of the Court of Session and of the House of Lords in Scottish appeals are also binding on them. An industrial tribunal would also be bound by a decision in the Outer House of the Court of Session, especially in a case decided on appeal from an industrial tribunal in one of those classes of case in which appeal lies direct to the Court of Session and not to the Employment Appeal Tribunal (see Chapter 12, p. 251). An industrial tribunal may derive assistance from, but is not bound by, a decision of another industrial tribunal or a decision of a sheriff. Decisions of the Court of Appeal and of the divisional courts in England and of the House of Lords in English appeals are probably technically not binding on industrial tribunals in Scotland, in which case they are only of "high persuasive authority", but in practice such decisions are followed where they are in point and do not conflict with any rule of Scottish law or Scottish judicial decision of equivalent status. Decisions of the former National Industrial Relations Court are regarded as authoritative unless they have since been over-ruled by higher appellate courts or departed from by the Employment Appeal Tribunal, or the relevant statutory provisions have been so amended that the decision is no longer in point.

There have been regular warnings from appellate courts, however, against rigid adherence to precedent in the field of industrial legislation, beginning with *Chapman and Others* v. *Goonvean and Rostowrack China Clay Company Ltd.* [1973] I.C.R. 50, where Sir John Donaldson said (at p. 58) that it may lead to injustice in a particular case

---

39 *Connely* v. *Liverpool Corporation* (1974) 9 I.T.R. 51; *The Lewis Shops Group* v. *Wiggins* [1973] I.R.L.R. 205.

40 For an exposition of these matters in Scots law, see Gloag and Henderson, *op. cit.*, Chap. 1.

and also unduly restrict the proper development of industrial law. He therefore said that the court would consider itself free to depart from its own decisions when it appeared right to do so, bearing in mind the danger of disturbing retrospectively decisions which had formed the general basis of industrial relations agreements and practices. This approach has been generally followed by the Employment Appeal Tribunal. In *Jowett* v. *Earl of Bradford* (No. 2) [1978] I.C.R. 431 a contrast was made between, on the one hand, decisions of appellate courts on the interpretation of unclear or ambiguous statutory provisions, which become binding precedents, and, on the other hand, tests, methods of approach or guidelines suggested for the operation of statutory provisions, such as para. 6(8) of Sched. 1 to the Trade Union and Labour Relations Act 1974 (now s. 57(3) of the Employment Protection (Consolidation) Act 1978) where the meaning of the statute is clear and unambiguous, and the tribunal's task is to relate the facts to the statutory provisions. In that situation it was said that not to follow a test suggested by the Employment Appeal Tribunal did not in itself amount to an error of law, as such tests are not intended as rules of law or binding precedents. It has to be observed, however, that in practice the Employment Appeal Tribunal uses its own "guidelines" as a yardstick by which to assess whether industrial tribunals have erred in law, although the Court of Appeal has subsequently (in *Bailey* v. *B.P. Oil Kent Refinery Ltd.* [1980] I.R.L.R. 287) gone so far as to doubt the wisdom of appellate courts laying down any guidelines on matters which are essentially for the decision of the industrial tribunal. In practice industrial tribunals do not disregard such guidelines, but generally regard themselves as entitled to *distinguish* them if they do not appear applicable to the facts of a particular case.

In *Walls Meat Company Ltd.* v. *Khan* [1979] I.C.R. 52 Lord Denning MR deprecated excessive reporting of cases on time limits in these terms,

"Let principles be reported, but not particular instances".

In the vast majority of cases which industrial tribunals have to consider, the point for decision is circumstantial and does not raise any new point of principle; it should therefore turn on the weight attached by the tribunal to the evidence taken as a whole, related to the statutory provisions under consideration, and to established principles. Reliance on a decision in another case bearing a superficial factual resemblance can be dangerously misleading, unless treated only as an illustration of the application of the principles in issue.

An expression of opinion by a judge on a point which is not necessary for determining a point in issue is called an *obiter dictum*. Although not strictly binding, *obiter dicta* are treated as authoritative in proportion to the standing of the judge and the relevance of the *dictum*, and in fact (and inevitably) in a developing field much of the law applied by industrial tribunals is based on *obiter dicta*.

A decision which is in point may be challenged on various grounds: that it is inconsistent with prior authority which was not brought to the notice of the court or tribunal; that a statutory amendment of the law has altered the basis on which the previous decision rested; or that it proceeded upon views of morality, political economy or religious observance no longer held in esteem or a scientific theory which has since been proved valueless[41]. But it is thought that, as a tribunal of first instance, an industrial tribunal would only be entitled not to follow such a decision on the first two of those grounds, and would have to leave it to an appellate court to proceed on any of the latter grounds.

REMEDIES

(1) **General**

The remedies which may be granted by an industrial tribunal to a successful applicant or appellant can be broadly classified under four heads:

(a) Declarations, which may be accompanied by a financial award or order, or (in sex and race discrimination cases[42]) by a recommendation;

(b) Orders for payments of sums of money, the amount of which in some cases may be regulated by the statute and in other cases may be for the tribunal to assess;

(c) In unfair dismissal cases, orders for continuation or restoration of employment, which will usually be accompanied by a financial award;[43]

(d) In appeals, orders affirming, cancelling or altering the order or notice appealed against.

It is not possible to discuss each form of remedy in detail here, and this part of the chapter is concerned only to state in general terms what considerations apply to the quantification of financial awards, so as to indicate what evidence a tribunal needs in order to arrive at a decision. For more detailed information, reference must be made to textbooks on employment law, but it should be borne in mind that, unless otherwise provided, in matters relating to remedy, the burden of proof is on the complainant to provide the tribunal with the evidence on which to determine and quantify the remedy to be granted. But in view of the less formal nature of tribunal proceedings, and of the absence of professional representation in many cases, precise and detailed proof of every

41 Gloag & Henderson, *op. cit.*, p. 13.

42 The Sex Discrimination Act 1975, s. 65(1)(c); the Race Relations Act 1976, s. 56(1)(c).

43 The Employment Protection (Consolidation) Act 1978, ss. 68 to 71 and 77 to 79.

item of loss is not expected.[44] And while the burden of proof is not on the employer, he can assist greatly by coming prepared with information on matters within his knowledge.

(2) **Calculation of pay and quantification of other benefits and losses**

(a) *"A week's pay"*

Where, under the Employment Protection (Consolidation) Act 1978 and the Employment Protection Act 1975, the remedy is defined in terms of a week's pay, the pay is calculated in the manner set out in Sched. 14 to the 1978 Act.[45] Broadly speaking, it consists of the gross weekly remuneration within the limits in the Schedule, as opposed to net or take-home pay.[46] The method of calculation varies according to whether or not there are normal working hours and, whether the work is carried out on a time or piece basis, or on a rota basis. Where there are normal hours, overtime is not reckonable unless the contract obliges the employer to provide it, or pay in lieu, and obliges the employee to work it.[47] The calculation for piece and rota workers whose weekly remuneration varies according to the amount of work done, or the number of hours worked, is based on the average of each of the last weeks ending on or in the week prior to "the calculation date" in which remuneration was actually payable. If the employee was not employed for a sufficient period, the tribunal has to decide what amount fairly represents a week's pay, taking various factors into account (see para. 9).

What the calculation date is depends on the statutory purpose for which the calculation is made (see para. 7(1)). Note that the effect of the somewhat obscure provisions of subparas. (*h*) and (*i*) and (*k*) and (*l*) of para. 7(1) (which establish the calculation date for a week's pay for a basic award for unfair dismissal and a redundancy payment respectively[48]), when taken together with para. 7(2), is that the calculation date will be earlier than the "effective date of termination" or the "relevant date" which applies to the computation of the length of service factor in the calculation of the amount of a basic award (s. 73(3))

---

44 *Norton Tool Co. Ltd.* v. *Tewson* [1972] I.C.R. 501 (at pp. 504-5).

45 The operation of Sched. 14 is discussed fully in Grunfeld, The Law of Redundancy, 2nd ed., Chap. 10, pp. 363-393.

46 The dictum to the opposite effect in *Secretary of State for Employment* v. *Jobling* [1980] I.C.R. 380 is *obiter* and as such not strictly binding, and, with respect, is wrong. Remuneration is that to which an employee is entitled before the incidence of compulsory deductions is taken into account (see Grunfeld, *op. cit.*, p. 377).

47 *Tarmac Roadstone Holdings Ltd.* v. *Peacock* [1973] I.C.R. 273.

48 Except in maternity cases to which ss. 56 or 86 apply, where it is the last day on which the employee worked under the original contract of employment (Sched. 2, paras. 2(4) and (5) and 4(3) and (4).

or a redundancy payment (Sched. 4, para. 2): if, by virtue of s. 55(5) or 90(3) the effective date of termination or the relevant date falls after the actual ending of the employment (*i.e.* in cases where the employer has dismissed on no notice, or on inadequate notice) the calculation date will be the date on which the employment actually ended, which is the effective date of termination, or the relevant date, as defined in s. 55(4) and s. 90(1) respectively; where, on the other hand, s. 55(5) or s. 90(3), as the case may be, does not apply, the calculation date is the date on which statutory notice in terms of s. 49 was, or would previously have had to have been, given by the employer in order to terminate the contract on the date on which the employment actually ended, assuming the contract to be terminable by notice, and irrespective of whether such notice was actually given or not. (These assumptions cover the case where the contract of employment is terminated by the employee, or is a fixed term contract which expires without being renewed, neither of which are affected by s. 55(5) or s. 90(3)). The question whether an increase in remuneration under a pay settlement made after the calculation date, but back-dated to a date prior to the calculation date, should be counted was raised in *Reston and Ors.* v. *Leyland Vehicles Ltd.* [1980] I.R.L.R. 376. The industrial tribunal held that it should, but the Employment Appeal Tribunal subsequently disagreed. Every such case will turn on its own particular facts and circumstances.

Pay is calculated in Sched. 14 by reference to remuneration paid under the contract of employment in force on the calculation date, including commission. It does not include the money value of perquisites,[49] or holiday stamps under the National Agreement for the Building Industry,[50] or a lodging allowance.[51] It hardly needs to be said that where an employee's pay period is longer than a week, the remuneration has to be reduced to a weekly figure, and wages statements prepared for lodging at the hearing should be prepared on that basis.

A week's pay is the unit of calculation for basic and additional awards of compensation for unfair dismissal and for redundancy payments, but for these purposes there is a limit (reviewable by the Secretary of State) on the amount which, with effect from February 1, 1981, was £130.[52] A week's pay is also the base from which the guaranteed hourly rate for a guarantee payment is calculated, in accordance with the formulae set out in s. 14 of the 1978 Act (*q.v.*), subject to the (reviewable) limits set by

---

49 Grunfeld, *op. cit.*, p. 377.

50 *Secretary of State for Employment* v. *Haynes* [1980] I.R.L.R. 270.

51 *A. M. Carmichael Ltd.* v. *Laing* (1972) 7 I.T.R. 1.

52 1978 Act, Sched. 14, para. 8; Employment Protection (Variation of Limits) Order 1980 (S.I. 1980/2019).

s. 15;[53] for calculating remuneration for suspension from work on statutory medical grounds (see s. 21); for time off to look for new employment or make arrangements for training (see s. 31(9)) and for ante-natal care (see s. 31A(5)), and for maternity pay (see s. 35(1)), and it is the basis of an award for contravention of the requirements of s. 53 as to supplying written reasons for dismissal. It is also the basis of remuneration payable under a protective award under s. 101 of the Employment Protection Act 1975 (see s. 102(2) and s. 106(3)[54]). Moreover, the formula for determining the amount payable for time off for trade union duties also reflects Sched. 14 in simpler terms (see s. 27(3) and (4) and s. 30(3) of the 1978 Act).

(b) *Arrears of remuneration*

The tribunal has a wider discretion where it is empowered to order remuneration for arrears of pay, in whole or in part (as when ordering reinstatement or re-engagement after an unfair dismissal, or in respect of a contravention of an equality clause in an equal pay case, and in making an order for continuation of a contract of employment, on an application for interim relief under s. 77 of the Employment Protection (Consolidation) Act, 1978). The amount specified in the order should be quantified by reference to the gross remuneration which the employee could have been expected to have earned or to earn in the future (as the case may be), including an estimate for overtime or bonus earnings where these could be expected. But liability for tax and national insurance contributions will arise, and the order will normally direct payment to be made under deduction of P.A.Y.E. and national insurance, and any other normal deductions, such as pension fund contributions. It is not necessary to express the order in terms of weekly pay if the actual pay period is longer. This is expressly provided in s. 78(2) of the 1978 Act. As to perquisites, see (d)(ii) below.

(c) *Compensation and damages*

For the compensatory award which forms part of the statutory compensation for unfair dismissal under s. 74 of the 1978 Act, and for compensation for failure fully to comply with an order for reinstatement or re-engagement under s. 71(1), and in cases of action short of dismissal on account of trade union membership or activity (see s. 26(1)) or failure to permit time off from work in connection with trade union duties or activities or for public duties (see s. 30(2)), the tribunal assesses compensation on a just and equitable basis, having regard to the loss sustained by the complainant. The same formula is used to compensate a trade union for an employer's failure to permit a ballot to

---

[53] £8.75 per day (s. 15(1) as varied by the Employment Protection (Variation of Limits) Order 1980, with further restrictions on the number of days in respect of which a payment may be made).

[54] As amended by Sched. 16 to the 1978 Act, para. 23(6).

be held under s. 2 of the Employment Act 1980. As regards compensation for failure to admit or re-admit an employee to trade union membership under s. 5 of the 1980 Act, the formula also has regard to the loss sustained by the complainant, but here the tribunal is to award such sum as it considers "appropriate" to compensate him for it.

By contrast, damages at common law are the measure of compensation under s. 2(1) of the Equal Pay Act 1970, s. 65(1) of the Sex Discrimination Act 1975 and s. 56(1) of the Race Relations Act 1976. But under the latter Acts no award of damages is to be made for certain acts of unlawful discrimination if the respondent proves that he did not act with the intention of treating the claimant unfavourably.[55]

In all of these cases, the compensation is assessed under various categories or heads of loss. Most of them are common to statutory compensation under the Employment Protection (Consolidation) Act 1978 and the Employment Act 1980 and the common law of damages, but there are differences. Damages are assessed on the principle that the wrongdoer is liable to make good all loss caused naturally and directly by his unlawful act.[56] The statutory law, on the other hand (and it remains to be seen whether the slight difference in the formula in s. 5(4) of the Employment Act 1980 will be considered significant) was held in *Norton Tool Co. Ltd.* v. *Tewson* [1972] I.C.R. 501 to be designed not to make good all such loss, but to compensate the complainant by awarding such amount as the tribunal considers just and equitable in the circumstances *having regard to* the loss sustained by him. The tribunal therefore has a wider discretion than when awarding damages. One particular difference is that while, in the law of damages, injury to feelings may be admissible, with physical pain and suffering also, under the general heading of "solatium", it is not an admissible head of loss under the law of statutory compensation.[57] Further comparison with, and discussion of, the common law of damages cannot be attempted here,[58] and the rest of this passage is concerned only with the quantification of statutory compensation. It should also be made clear that the statutory compensation to which reference is made here does not include compensation for loss of office, which is assessed in the manner provided in the relevant regulations. And, of course, statutory compensation for unfair dismissal should not be confused with damages awarded for the common law wrong of wrongful dismissal, for which action lies before the court and not before an industrial tribunal.

---

55 The Sex Discrimination Act 1975, s. 66(3) (relates to an unlawful requirement or condition falling within s. 1(1)(*b*) or, where applicable, s. 3(1)(*b*)); the Race Relations Act 1976, s. 57(3) (relates to an unlawful requirement or condition falling within s. 1(1)(*b*)).

56 Gloag and Henderson, *op. cit.*, p. 525.

57 *Norton Tool Co. Ltd.* v. *Tewson*, *supra* at p. 504.

58 Reference may be made to Walker, *Damages* and Mayne & Macgregor, *Damages*.

But if such an action is raised, any compensation for unfair dismissal would go towards mitigating, or even extinguishing, any equivalent loss in proceedings for wrongful dismissal, and *vice versa* in the case of damages awarded by the court.

In assessing loss for a compensatory award for unfair dismissal and in complaints under s. 24 of the 1978 Act, the loss sustained by the complainant is expressly stated to include any expenses reasonably incurred by him in consequence of the action complained of, and loss of any benefit which he might reasonably be expected to have had but for that action (s. 26(2) and s. 74(2)).

(d) *Heads of loss for compensation*

The following heads of loss may occur in statutory compensation,[59] although these categories should not be regarded as exhaustive:—

(i) **Loss of pay down to the date of hearing.** This is quantified by reference to net pay, *i.e.* the amount of the "take-home" pay after deduction of income tax and national insurance. Where other deductions, such as pension fund contributions, are made, it will be a question of circumstances whether these should be taken into account. Take-home pay reflects all the gross pay and may therefore exceed the amount of the statutory "week's pay" if there are substantial overtime earnings and if, as explained in (a) above, the latter are not reckonable under Sched. 14, as is commonly the case. Where no records are available to show the difference between gross and net pay, a party, or his adviser, should be able to estimate what it would be by recourse to tax tables, leaflets about national insurance rates, and the like.[60]

The pay will be averaged over whatever period is considered appropriate in the circumstances, *e.g.* allowance may have to be made for substantial periods of absence or the point at which a change in pay took, or would have taken, effect. The average will be worked out on a weekly basis, and wage statements prepared for the tribunal should be made up in that way, even if the pay period is longer. The tribunal will also take into account any increase (or for that matter, any decrease, *e.g.* due to loss of piecework) which the employee would have obtained, and an estimate of the effect of this factor on the take-home pay should be provided, where applicable.

But since the statutory provisions usually state that the loss to be assessed is that which is "attributable to action taken by the employer"[61] or words to the like effect, the assessment must therefore be made by reference to the position in which the employee would have been but for that action. This may lead to the conclusion that while

---

59 See *Norton Tool Co. Ltd.* v. *Tewson, supra.*

60 *Cf. Scott* v. *Creager* [1979] I.C.R. 403.

61 See the Employment Protection (Consolidation) Act 1978, s. 74(1).

loss may have been sustained, it is not relevant for the purpose. If, for instance, in an unfair dismissal case, the tribunal considers that the applicant would have been validly dismissed, e.g. for redundancy, at some time during the period of assessment, this may limit, or even extinguish, the period over which loss is assessed.[62] Similarly, net remuneration from any employment received during the period of assessment (temporary or permanent) must be taken into account and may have the same effect, as should any payment by the employer on account of dismissal. The latter will include any payment of wages in lieu of notice, the excess of any payment, statutory or *ex gratia*, on account of redundancy (where dismissal was for that reason) over the amount of the basic award for unfair dismissal,[63] and any other *ex gratia* payment; but any wages or holiday pay which the employee claims to have been due at the date of dismissal but to be unpaid, are not admissible items of loss, as they are contractual debts upon which it is not within the jurisdiction of the tribunal to adjudicate, since jurisdiction under s. 131 of the Employment Protection (Consolidation) Act 1978 has not yet been brought into operation. But it was held in *Vaughan* v. *Weighpack Ltd.* [1974] I.C.R. 261 that where dismissal is without notice or payment of wages in lieu, the employee is entitled as an "irreducible minimum" to the net amount of wages which ought to have been paid in lieu of notice, and that earnings from other employment during the period over which notice should have been given should not be deducted.

If the employee was unfit for work during any part of the period of assessment, the tribunal will have to consider how much, if any, of the pay lost during the period of unfitness is chargeable against the employer. If, under the contract of employment, there is no entitlement to pay during a period of absence, the employee is not entitled to be compensated for loss of wages during the period of unfitness, unless the ill-health is itself attributable to the employer's action in dismissing the employee, which the employee would have to prove. Where, on the other hand, the employee is entitled under his contract to full pay for a period of absence without deduction of sickness or equivalent state benefit, his loss will include the pay receivable during the relevant period without the deduction of benefit received: but where (as is more common) the contractual entitlement is to the difference between his normal pay and the benefit received, his loss for the relevant period should be assessed on that basis.[64] In the latter case, the tribunal should be provided with information as to the amount of benefit actually

62 *Clarkson International Tools Ltd.* v. *Short* [1973] I.C.R. 191; *Lifeguard Assurance Ltd.* v. *Zadrozny* [1977] I.R.L.R. 56.

63 1978 Act, s. 74(7); *Chelsea Football Club and Athletic Co. Ltd.* v. *Heath* [1981] I.R.L.R. 73.

64 *Sun & Sand Ltd.* v. *Fitzjohn* [1979] I.C.R. 268.

received, if any. (Unemployment or supplementary benefit is not deductible, however, because this will be recouped,[65] and information as to the amount of any such benefit is not required.)

(ii) **Loss of fringe benefits and perquisites.** These have to be quantified in money terms, either on a lump sum or on a weekly basis, as may be appropriate. Such benefits may be of substantial value. Each case turns on its own circumstances, and there are few guiding principles other than the broad formulae laid down in the legislation. The most common items are tips, cars and free housing and associated perquisites, but clothing, school fees and medical expenses are other possible items. With cars, the tribunal needs to be told on what basis the perquisite was given: was it the applicant's own car for expenditure on which he was reimbursed, or was it the employer's car supplied to the applicant? What did the employers pay for such items as licence, insurance, fuel, tyres and maintenance? What outlays does the employee now have to meet which he did not have while enjoying the perquisite? If the employer provided the car and paid for all outgoings on it, the tribunal will assess the cost to the applicant of providing and maintaining a car for private motoring at his own expense over whatever period of time may be appropriate. The same approach will apply to loss of housing, *e.g.* what rent, rates and heating and lighting costs is the employee now faced with by comparison with when he was employed? The fuller the information provided (preferably with supporting documents) without the tribunal having to ask for it, the more realistic the tribunal's asssessment is likely to be.

(iii) **Out-of-pocket expenses.** These may include removal expenses if the employee has had to move as a result of dismissal, and travelling, and postal and telephone expenses incurred in looking for another employment. Records should be kept and produced along with any relative vouchers. If new employment has been found which involves extra travelling to work, not balanced by an increase in take-home pay, a lump sum may be awarded to compensate for this. But the expenses of presenting the case to the tribunal are not allowable.[66]

(iv) **Loss of future earnings.** This has to be assessed broadly on a subjective estimate of how long it will take the employee in question[67] to obtain suitable employment, arrived at by inference from evidence given as to his efforts to find employment, the results so far obtained and the tribunal's knowledge of the employment situation in the area,[68] for the type of employment for which the employee is suited. The award

---

65 See below under "Recoupment of Benefits" pp. 220 to 223.

66 *Nohar* v. *Granitstone (Galloway) Ltd.* (1974) 9 I.T.R. 155 (at p. 156).

67 See *Fougère* v. *Phoenix Motor Co. Ltd.* [1976] I.C.R. 495; *Green* v. *J. Waterhouse & Sons Ltd.* [1977] I.C.R. 759.

68 *Donnelly* v. *Feniger & Blackburn Ltd.* [1973] I.R.L.R. 26.

should be quantified by reference to what the employee would have earned with the respondents over the estimated period of unemployment from the conclusion of the proceedings onwards, but no deduction should be made for unemployment benefit, since it is understood to be the practice of the Department of Employment not to allow benefit for any period of unemployment between the conclusion of the proceedings and one year from the date on which employment ended, in respect of which a tribunal has made an award for loss of remuneration.[69] If the employee has already taken permanent employment at a better rate of take-home pay, there will normally be no admissible loss, but if the employment obtained is shown to be only temporary, a claim for future loss on its cessation would be admissible. And if the new employment is at less take-home pay, an award should be made to cover the difference over a reasonable period for the future.

(v) **Manner of dismissal.** For the reasons explained above, injury to feelings arising out of an unfair dismissal is not an admissible head of loss in itself, but the manner in which a dismissal was effected may affect a tribunal's award for loss of earnings down to the date of hearing or in the future, if there is clear evidence that it has made it more difficult for the employee to find employment.[70]

(vi) **Loss of pension rights.** This is the most troublesome head of loss which tribunals have to consider, and the one on which unfortunately, but understandably, they all too often have little or no evidence or submissions. The fundamental principle is that there is no one right way of assessing this head of loss to the exclusion of others, and a broad common sense approach has to be adopted.[71] This was affirmed in *Copson* v. *Eversure Accessories Ltd.* [1974] I.C.R. 636 (at p. 640) where more detailed guidance was given, and various possible methods of, and factors in, such an assessment were indicated. Since then, the "contracting out" provisions of the Social Security Pensions Act 1975, and the "guaranteed minimum pension" introduced by that Act have added a further element which it may be relevant to consider.

Where the employment of a member of a "contracted out" scheme terminates prematurely, his and his employers' contributions to the fund are normally retained in the fund and a deferred pension is payable to him at retiring age, which is usually of a fixed initial amount (although it may increase thereafter), and may also be coupled with a lump sum payment. Alternatively, if he finds new employment with an

69 Under the Social Security (Unemployment, Sickness and Invalidity Benefit) Amendment Regulations 1976 (S.I. 1976/328), as amended by amending regulations (S.I. 1976/677). Loss of remuneration down to the conclusion of the proceedings comes under the recoupment regulations, referred to at (i) above, and pp. 220 to 223 below.

70 *Youngs of Gosport Ltd.* v. *Kendell* [1977] I.C.R. 907; *Brittains Arborfield Ltd.* v. *van Uden* [1977] I.C.R. 211.

71 *S.C.W.S. Ltd.* v. *Lloyd* [1973] I.C.R. 137, at p. 142.

equivalent scheme, he may be able to transfer to that scheme the current value of his rights, valued actuarially. Or he may be entitled to a refund of his contributions to the scheme, but by virtue of the operation of the Social Security Act 1973 this now applies only to employees with less than 5 years' pensionable service. The first of these alternatives is likely to involve the employee in loss when he comes to retiral, because if he had remained in the employer's service, his pension at retiral age would have been related to his final salary, and due to pay increases in the meanwhile, that pension would have likely been larger than the deferred pension which he will in fact receive. The second alternative (transfer of benefits) will usually be based on the immediate purchase price of a deferred annuity of the amount of the deferred pension and will also be likely to result in loss. Where a refund of contributions is made, the benefits secured by the employers' contribution to the fund are lost altogether. Whichever of these forms it takes, there is thus a loss of the benefits secured by the contributions made to the fund at the date of dismissal (called the "loss for past service") which may be valued by reference to the amount contributed to the fund by the employer down to the date of dismissal. The view has been expressed by the Government Actuary, however, that the "contribution" method of valuation is usually only appropriate in cases of employees with less than five years' service, where contributions are refundable, and that in other cases a valuation based on actuarial principles is preferable, especially where the benefits received are a deferred pension.[72]

Unless the employee immediately finds other pensionable employment, the premature termination of his employment will result in loss of the pension entitlement which would otherwise have been built up by contributions to the fund made after the date of his dismissal. This element is usually valued by reference to the contributions which his employers would have made to the scheme, had he not been dismissed, over the period (actual or estimated) between the date of dismissal and the time when he becomes a member of another "contracted out" pension scheme (as to which an estimate may have to be made by the tribunal if no such employment has been found by the date of the hearing). If the employee has taken new employment without an occupational pension scheme, and the former employer's scheme was contracted out, the former employer's rate of contribution should be reduced, the reduction recommended by the Government Actuary being 3%.[73] If the employee is faced with additional cost in contributing

---

[72] See an article in the *Journal of the Law Society of Scotland*, April 1980, based on the views and recommendations of the Government Actuary. The article illustrates the problems involved in this kind of assessment, and gives tables of valuation factors, and examples of the way in which loss of pension rights may be assessed in a variety of different situations.

[73] See article in the *Journal of the Law Society of Scotland* referred to above.

to his new employer's pension scheme, this is a factor which may also be taken into account (see *Powrmatic Ltd.* v. *Bull* [1977] I.C.R. 469). If the employer has also provided life insurance cover to produce a capital sum payable to the employee's dependents if he dies before attaining retiring age, loss of this cover will also be admissible.

The total loss should be discounted by a "withdrawal factor" to allow for the possibility that for some other reason or another in the future the employee might have ceased to be a member of the employers' scheme before attaining retiral age.[74]

In order to assess these losses, a tribunal needs the following information:

(1) The age and sex of the employee.
(2) The length of *pensionable* service.
(3) Pensionable salary at the effective date of termination.
(4) The employers' contribution rate to the scheme, either in relation to the employee himself or the fund as a whole.[75]
(5) Benefits actually received by the employee, *i.e.* deferred pension, "transfer value" (where the transfer option has been taken), or the amount of contributions refunded, including any premiums paid by the employer to secure the guaranteed minimum pension under the 1975 Act.
(6) Accrued pension entitlement, based on salary and effective date of termination, including any lump sum payable.[76]
(7) Widow's pension entitlement, corresponding to (6) above.[76]

The rules of the employer's pension scheme and (if the employee has found other pensionable employment) of the new pension scheme should also be produced. If the above information is provided, actuarial evidence should not be necessary, nor (having regard to expense) will it be generally desirable, but if the tribunal proposes to adopt the actuarial method referred to above, the Chairman should inform the parties to that effect, and direct their attention to the article in the *Journal of the Law Society of Scotland* referred to on p. 214, so that if they so wish, they may produce actuarial evidence (oral or documentary), and make submissions on the matter. Generally, however, parties are content to agree to leave to the tribunal the whole matter of the valuation of loss of pension rights, including the method to be used.

Loss of life insurance cover can be assessed if a quotation is provided for the cost of obtaining equivalent cover privately.

An employee who was a member of a scheme which is not "contracted-out" under the 1975 Act would lose the benefits by which it "tops up" the state additional pension: this loss may be valued in the

74 See *Powrmatic Ltd.* v. *Bull, supra.*

75 See *Willment Brothers Ltd.* v. *Oliver* [1979] I.C.R. 378.

76 Not required if the "contribution" method of assessment is used.

same way as the loss of benefits under a "contracted-out" scheme, but taking into account the employer's contributions to the state scheme. Further, an employee who was not a member of a "contracted-out" scheme (whether or not he was a member of a "non-contracted-out" scheme) may possibly, in certain circumstances, be able to show that his unfair dismissal has adversely affected the build-up of 20 "best years" under the state scheme.

(vii) **Loss of statutory rights.** Since the basic award for unfair dismissal was introduced in the Employment Protection Act 1975, it has ceased to be the normal practice of industrial tribunals in Scotland to make an award for loss of the accrued right to a redundancy payment or for loss of protection against unfair dismissal.

(3) **Other factors affecting compensation**

Various other considerations affecting the quantification of losses and awards, mainly affecting unfair dismissals, should also be referred to. As already pointed out, the loss which is relevant is that sustained in consequence of, and so far as attributable to, the employer's default. Loss falls to be calculated in the light of the situation at the time of the tribunal's original decision. Accordingly, evidence of subsequent matters will only be admissible to a limited extent on a re-hearing following a review or an appeal.[77] But the amount awarded is to be what the tribunal considers just and equitable in all the circumstances. Where it is shown that the employee was guilty of misconduct unknown to the employer at the time of dismissal, it is open to the tribunal to conclude that in all the circumstances, it would not be just and equitable for him to be compensated at all, or to reduce compensation on that account.[78]

In determining whether the employee's loss is attributable to action taken by the employer, no account is to be taken of pressure on the employer by way of industrial action, or the threat of such action (Employment Protection (Consolidation) Act 1978, s. 74(5)). But if the employer claims that the pressure was exerted because the employee would not join a closed shop and, in terms of the provisions of ss. 76A to 76C[79], the trade union or other persons who exerted such pressure (and, where applicable, a contractor who refused to have the employee working on the contract because of the operation of a closed shop) have been sisted into the proceedings, the tribunal may make such orders in favour of the employer, and if need be, against the contractor (and, if

[77] *Studio Press (Birmingham) Ltd.* v. *Davies* (1977) 12 I.T.R. 93 (review); *Qualcast (Wolverhampton) Ltd.* v. *Ross* [1979] I.C.R. 386 (appeal). See also Chap. 11, p. 250 and Chap. 12, p. 252.

[78] *W. Devis & Sons Ltd.* v. *Atkins* [1977] I.C.R. 662.

[79] Added by the Employment Act 1980, s. 10.

similar pressure had been exerted on the contractor, may also make similar orders in the contractor's favour by way of relief), as it considers to be a just and equitable contribution by the trade union or other persons concerned to the compensation payable by the employer to the applicant, even up to a complete indemnity. There are similar provisions in cases of discriminatory action against an employee on account of trade union membership or activities (1978 Act, ss. 25(2) and 26A[80]). Where an employee is unfairly dismissed while absent from work on account of pregnancy or confinement, compensation is to be assessed without regard to her right to return to work, but may have to be repaid if she exercises the right (1978 Act, Sched. 2, para. 6(4)).

The common law rule that a person is bound to mitigate his loss applies in ascertaining the employee's loss for unfair dismissal (1978 Act, s. 74(4)), for discriminatory action short of dismissal for trade union reasons (s. 26(3)), and for unreasonable exclusion or expulsion from trade union membership (Employment Act, 1980 s. 5(5)). In unfair dismissal cases, the fact that the employee has unreasonably prevented an order for reinstatement or re-engagement from being complied with, is also a factor to be taken into account in this connection (1978 Act, s. 71(5)). Unreasonable refusal of an offer of reinstatement or re-engagement by the employer, or of a job with another employer,[81] at any time after dismissal, may also eliminate compensation for any loss after the offer is made. And if the tribunal considers that the employee has been dilatory in seeking further employment, it may limit the period over which compensation is to be awarded to that which it considers would have been reasonable. But an employee is not bound in mitigation of loss to take a deferred pension rather than an alternative option which may be available to him under a pension scheme.[82]

In cases of unfair dismissal, (1978 Act, s. 74(6)), discriminatory action short of dismissal for trade union reasons (s. 26(5)), and unreasonable exclusion or expulsion from trade union membership (Employment Act, 1980, s. 5(6)), where the tribunal finds that the action complained of was to any extent caused or contributed to by any action of the complainant, it may reduce the award by such an amount as it considers just and equitable, having regard to that finding. This is a matter very much within the discretion of the tribunal, with the exercise of which appellate courts do not readily interfere, but in unfair dismissal cases questions have arisen as to how far the rule extends. In *Kraft Foods Ltd.*

[80] Added by the Employment Act 1980, s. 15(4).

[81] The test applicable to which was stated in *Bessenden Properties Ltd.* v. *Corness* [1973] I.R.L.R. 365 as being, "If the complainant had no hope of recovering compensation from anybody else, and if he had consulted merely his own interests and acted reasonably in the circumstances, would he have accepted the job in mitigation of the loss which he had suffered?"

[82] *Sturdy Finance Ltd.* v. *Bardsley* [1979] I.C.R. 249.

v. *Fox* [1977] I.R.L.R. 431, it was held that it implied conduct on the part of an employee over which he had control and not mere incompetence. This view has been doubted as a proposition of law.[83] But in *Nelson* v. *BBC (No. 2)* [1980] I.C.R. 110 the Court of Appeal held that the conduct had to be culpable or blameworthy, *i.e.* foolish or perverse or unreasonable. Where there is fault, the extent of the contribution may extend as high as 100% in an extreme case, so as to extinguish the award altogether.[84] However, as already pointed out, facts not within the employer's knowledge at the time of the action complained of cannot be founded on in this particular connection, although they may lead to the conclusion that to award compensation would not be just and equitable.

In *Parker & Farr Ltd.* v. *Shelvey* [1979] I.C.R. 896, it was held that the contribution factor should be applied to the net loss ascertained after deducting any payments made by the employer (*e.g.* pay in lieu of notice or any *ex gratia* payment on account of dismissal) from the earnings lost. This decision reflects the previous practice of tribunals and should, it is submitted with respect, be followed in preference to the apparently contrary view expressed in *Clement-Clarke International Ltd.* v. *Manley* [1979] I.C.R. 74. A tribunal has no power to award interest on an award of compensation.[85]

(4) **Statutory limits on compensation**

(a) *Unfair dismissal*

Section 75(1) of the Employment Protection (Consolidation) Act 1978 imposes a limit, reviewable by the Secretary of State, which at December 31, 1980 was £6,250,[86] on the amount of compensation under s. 71(1) for an employer's failure to comply in full with an order for reinstatement or re-engagement, and on the amount of a compensatory award, to which the award must be reduced if it exceeds the limit, after taking into account any payments made by the employer to the employee in respect of the dismissal (*e.g.* a payment in lieu of notice or an *ex gratia* payment) and any of the reductions which are required by law (*e.g.* on account of contributory fault) (see s. 75(3)). The maximum basic award under s. 73(3) is one and a half weeks' pay for a period of 20 years at the limit of £130 per week (see above, p. 207), *i.e.* £3,900. Where no additional award falls to be made under s. 71(2) for failure to reinstate or re-engage, the maximum compensation is therefore £10,150. The

83 *Moncur* v. *International Paint Co. Ltd.* [1978] I.R.L.R. 223; see also *Robert Whiting Designs Ltd. v. Lamb* [1978] I.C.R. 89.

84 *Redpath* v. *Domestic Electrical Rentals Ltd.* (1977) 12 I.T.R. 366; *Sulemanji* v. *Toughened Glass Ltd.* [1979] I.C.R. 799.

85 *Nelson* v. *BBC (No. 2), supra.*

86 The Unfair Dismissal (Increase of Compensation Limit) Order 1979 (S.I. 1979/1723).

maximum additional award is 26 weeks' pay at £130, *i.e.* £3,380, (minimum 13 weeks), but 52 weeks' pay at £130, *i.e.* £6,760 (minimum 26 weeks), if the dismissal is for a reason relating to trade union membership, or an act of discrimination on grounds of sex or race (s. 71(3)). Thus the maximum possible compensation is £16, 910.

(b) *Equal pay*

A tribunal may not award arrears of remuneration for damages for a contravention of an equality clause further back than two years from the commencement of the proceedings (Equal Pay Act 1970, s. 2(5)).

(c) *Sex and racial discrimination cases*

The limit under s. 75(1) of the 1978 Act also applies to compensation for discrimination on grounds of sex or race (Sex Discrimination Act 1975, s. 65(2), Race Relations Act 1976, s. 56(2)). The same limit applies in aggregate where compensation is awarded on both these grounds (1976 Act, s. 56(3)), and also where it is awarded on all three grounds (1978 Act, s. 76(2)). In the latter case, the unfair dismissal compensation which is aggregated is either that awarded under s. 71(1) (on failure to comply in full with a reinstatement or re-engagement order) or, as the case may be, a compensatory award calculated under s. 74. (But failure to comply with a reinstatement or re-engagement order would also attract an additional award in the higher category under s. 71(2) and (3) of the 1978 Act.)

Any compensation, or increase in compensation, awarded by a tribunal for failure to comply with a recommendation made by it is subject to the above limits (1975 Act, s. 65 (2) and (3), 1976 Act, s. 56 (2) and (4)).

(d) *Unreasonable exclusion or expulsion from trade union membership*

The maximum amount of compensation that may be awarded by an industrial tribunal is the aggregate of 30 weeks' pay under para. 8(1)(*b*) of Sched. 14 of the 1978 Act, *i.e.* £3,900 (see (a) above), and the maximum compensatory award for unfair dismissal, *i.e.* £6,250 (Employment Act 1980, s. 5(7)). Thus, where the applicant's loss is assessed at an amount higher than the limit for a compensatory award for unfair dismissal, the excess may be awarded, up to the maximum limit. The maximum award would therefore be £10,150. (But the Employment Appeal Tribunal may award a further sum equal to 52 weeks' pay, *i.e.* £6,760 (see s. 5(8))).

RECOUPMENT OF BENEFITS

(1) **General**

The Employment Protection (Recoupment of Unemployment and Supplementary Benefit) Regulations 1977 (S.I. 1977/674) apply to awards by industrial tribunals in proceedings under various provisions of the Employment Protection Act 1975 which were re-enacted in the Employment Protection (Consolidation) Act 1978, and in proceedings under ss. 101 and 103 of the 1975 Act. The object of the legislation under which the regulations were made is to enable any unemployment or supplementary benefit paid to the recipient of an award to be recouped from the employer out of the award, wholly or in part, for payment into the National Insurance Fund.[87]

The regulations apply (see reg. 3) to :

(i) Payments under a "monetary award" to an amount not exceeding the "prescribed element",[88] which, broadly speaking, consists of that part of the award relating to loss of remuneration down to the conclusion of the proceedings. The various payments and types of proceedings and the matters to which the prescribed element is attributable are set out in the Schedule to the regulations.[89] Where the tribunal announces the effect of the decision to the parties, the conclusion of the proceedings is the date on which the announcement is made; in any other case, it is the date on which the decision is sent to the parties (*i.e.* the date of promulgation) (reg. 2(4)). But the prescribed procedure in relation to monetary awards does not apply where the tribunal is satisfied that the employee has neither received nor claimed benefit during any of the period to which the prescribed element relates (reg. 5(8)). The tribunal will therefore enquire whether benefit has been claimed or received, in order to decide whether the regulations apply, but will not concern itself with the amount of benefit actually received.

Where the award is reduced on account of contributory fault or on account of the statutory limit on the compensatory award under s. 75(1) of the 1978 Act, a proportionate reduction must be made in arriving at the amount of the prescribed element (reg. 5(2)).

(ii) Protective awards under s. 101 of the Employment Protection Act 1975. Here there is no subdivision into the prescribed element, and the whole award is affected by the regulations. An order for payment made in the course of an employee's complaint under s. 103 (on the ground that the employer has failed to pay remuneration under a protective

---

87 The Employment Protection (Consolidation) Act 1978, s. 132 (formerly s. 112 of the Employment Protection Act 1975) as amended by s. 16 of the Social Security (Miscellaneous Provisions) Act 1977; the Social Security Act 1975, s. 114.

88 For the definition of these expressions, see the 1978 Act, s. 132(6).

89 See Appendix 5, p. 299.

award), is classified as a monetary award, however, and reg. 3(2) prevents any overlap in the operation of the regulations between the protective award and the subsequent monetary award.

(2) **Monetary awards**

In any proceedings which would result in payment of a monetary award, the tribunal will find out whether any unemployment or supplementary benefit has been received and, unless satisfied to the contrary, will proceed in the manner prescribed in the regulations. The tribunal clerk will find out which office dealt with the claim for, or payment of, benefit. If a monetary award is made, the tribunal must tell the parties the amount of the prescribed element and explain the effect of the regulations (reg. 5(4)).

If the award is announced, this must be done at the time; but where the tribunal reserves its decision on the amount of the award, the explanation is made in the written decision. The Department of Employment is notified of the amount of the prescribed element by the Secretary of the Tribunals. Payment of the prescribed element is "sisted"[90] under reg. 8(2) until in terms of reg. 9 the Department of Employment has either served a recoupment notice on the employer (with a copy to the employee) or notified the employer that it is not intended to serve one. This must be done within 21 days from the conclusion of the hearing (where the award is announced) or within nine days after the decision is promulgated (where the award is reserved), or as soon as practicable thereafter (reg. 9(5) to (7)). In the meanwhile the employer can pay to the employee only the excess of the award over the prescribed element. The recoupable amount is the amount of the prescribed element (less any tax or social security contributions which fall to be deducted therefrom by the employer) or the amount actually paid in respect of benefit for the period to which the prescribed element relates, whichever is the less (reg. 9(2)). The amount to be recouped, as specified in the notice, is then payable by the employer to the Secretary of State and recoverable as a debt (reg. 9(8) to (11)). The balance of the prescribed element, if any, or the whole of it if no notice is served, is then payable to the employee (reg. 9(8) to (11)). Because of these requirements, the usual practice is to reserve any decision on the amount of compensation in cases to which the regulations apply.

The employee may object to the amount recouped by notice in writing to the Secretary of State given within 21 days of receipt of the recoupment notice or later, if allowed by the Secretary of State for special reasons (reg. 11(1)). The matter is then referred to an insurance

---

90 *I.e.* stayed.

officer in the case of unemployment benefit, and to the Supplementary Benefits Commission in the case of supplementary benefit, with appropriate rights of appeal. If the amount recouped is found to be excessive, the excess is repayable to the employee (regs. 11(2) to (4) and 12).

In any proceedings by an employee under s. 103 of the 1975 Act for failure to pay remuneration under a protective award, and where an award is set aside or varied as the result of a review or appeal, account must be taken in the subsequent proceedings of the effect of what was done under the recoupment regulations in relation to the protective award or the original award, and any amount which proves to have been over-recouped is repayable to the employer or the employee by the Secretary of State, as may be appropriate (regs. 10(1) and 11(5)).

It is also important to note that the regulations apply only where an award is made by a tribunal, and not to payments made under a compromise settlement, whether the settlement is arrived at before the merits of a case have been decided, or is an agreement to settle the amount of compensation following a decision in favour of the applicant on the merits. Accordingly, the potential effect of the recoupment regulations should be taken into account by each side in assessing the monetary aspects of any settlement which may be under consideration.[91]

(3) **Protective awards**

The provisions of the regulations are in most respects identical to those relating to monetary awards. The main difference is that already noted, namely that there is no subdivision of the award between the prescribed element and the balance. Accordingly all payments are "sisted" under reg. 8(2) until the Department of Employment has either served a recoupment notice or notified the employer that it is not intended to serve one. But the employee's right to complain to an industrial tribunal of his employer's failure to pay money due under a protective award is not affected (reg. (3)). If he does so, however, reg. 3(2) comes into play, as already noted, to prevent any overlap.

On the decision of the tribunal being announced or, if reserved, when it is promulgated (in practice, usually the latter), it becomes the employer's duty to give the Department of Employment, in writing, the name, address and national insurance number of every employee to whom the award relates, and the date or proposed date of the termination of his employment. This must be done within ten days of the announcement or promulgation, as the case may be, or if not reasonably practicable to do so, within such period, as soon as reasonably

[91] As to settlement procedures, see Chap. 6, pp. 133 to 136.

practicable thereafter (reg. 7). On the decision being announced or promulgated, the Secretary of the Tribunals must notify particulars of the award to the Department of Employment, specifying the employer, the description of the employees to whom the award relates, and the dates of the protected periods (reg. 6(1)).

A recoupment notice must be served within 21 days from the date on which the Department receives the information which the employer has to supply under reg. 7, or as soon as practicable thereafter (reg. 9(5) and (7)). The recoupable amount is the amount of remuneration due to the employee under the award (less any tax or social security contributions which would fall to be deducted therefrom by the employer) up to the date on which the Secretary of State receives from the employer the information required under reg. 7, or the amount actually paid in respect of benefit in respect of the same period, whichever is the less (reg. 9(3)).

ALTERATION OF DECISIONS

(1) **Before promulgation**

Before a decision is drawn up and entered in the Register it is not complete, and until then a decision which has been announced verbally can be recalled or altered by the tribunal. This was decided in *Hanks* v. *Ace High Productions Ltd.* [1978] I.C.R. 1155. The Employment Appeal Tribunal said, however, that the power should only be used sparingly, in the type of case where there is an obvious error or omission which, if not corrected in this way, would lead to a review or appeal, but that it should not be used in effect to re-hear the case. Since, for the reasons explained above,[92] the "advance notice" letter cannot be regarded as a decision which can be entered in the Register, the principle in *Hanks* would also apply to the subsequent recall or variation of a decision intimated by such a notice, as well as to a decision announced verbally at the conclusion of the hearing.

In *Hanks,* after the industrial tribunal had announced the decision at the end of the hearing, the Chairman realised that a case which was in point had not been fully considered, and invited the parties to return and make further submissions. This procedure was approved by the Employment Appeal Tribunal, and should generally be adopted in any case where the proposed alteration to the decision previously announced is substantial or potentially controversial. Where it is not (*e.g.* where it consists of a recalculation of compensation) it may be sufficient merely to note in the written decision that there has been an alteration from what had previously been announced.

---

[92] See p. 194.

(2) After promulgation

After the decision has been entered in the Register, it can only be altered or set aside by an appellate court on an appeal,[93] or if varied or revoked as the result of an application for review,[94] or by a certificate of correction. The rules give the Chairman power by certificate under his hand to correct clerical mistakes or errors in a decision (which includes the reasons for it) arising from any accidental slip or omission. Where a decision is so altered (*i.e.* whether by appeal, review or certificate of correction), the Secretary is required to make the necessary correction in the Register (which in practice is done by the Chairman initialling the necessary correction in the original decision), and to send copies of the new or corrected entry to the parties entitled to receive the original decision.[95]

While clerical mistakes are usually self-evident, what constitutes an "accidental slip or omission" is a question of circumstances. Exercised with discretion, the power to correct mistakes is a useful one, which can save parties the necessity of appealing or applying for review. It is generally confined to cases where the mistake is obvious and relatively simple to rectify, and where correction is thus unlikely to give rise to controversy. It is particularly useful where the mistake relates to the remedy afforded, rather than to the merits of the case. But if the correction under consideration is relatively substantial, and particularly where there is any possibility that it might be controversial, parties should be asked to consent to the proposed correction: if consent is refused by either, the Chairman would probably refuse to issue a certificate, but allow the party in whose interest the correction would be to apply by way of review. Similarly, if a party were to object to a certificate of correction issued *ex parte* by the Chairman, an application for review or appeal would be competent.

There is no limit on the time when a decision may be corrected in this way. Where appropriate, a certificate of correction can be issued while a case is subject to an appeal, but in practice, this would only be done if the correction was straightforward and necessary for the purposes of the appeal.

ENFORCEMENT AND RECOVERY OF TRIBUNAL AWARDS AND OTHER DEBTS DUE BY EMPLOYERS

(1) General: preferential claims

Certain debts due by employers to employees under awards made by

93 See Chap. 12 below.

94 See Chap. 11 below.

95 The Industrial Tribunals (Rules of Procedure) (Scotland) 1980, r. 9(6) to (8); there are similar provisions in the other rules of procedure.

industrial tribunals, or by virtue of statutory provisions, are accorded special treatment under the Employment Protection (Consolidation) Act 1978.

(a) On application made by an employee under s. 106 or s. 122, certain debts may be paid by the Secretary of State, who then assumes the rights of the employee to claim payment from the employer, or out of his insolvent estate. These fall into three categories:

(i) Redundancy payments, and certain equivalent payments, as specified in s. 104(1) (called an employer's payment[96]). An employee who claims that his employer is liable to pay him an employer's payment may apply to the Secretary of State, either where he has failed to recover the amount due from the employer after taking all reasonable steps, short of legal proceedings, or if the employer is insolvent (s. 106(1)). "Legal proceedings" does not include proceedings before an industrial tribunal, but does include proceedings to enforce a decision or award of a tribunal (s. 106(7)): so an employee who has been found entitled to a redundancy payment by an industrial tribunal is not required to have resorted to enforcement procedure before applying. But although an employee may possess the statutory qualification for a redundancy payment, the Department of Employment may insist that he applies to an industrial tribunal for a declaration that he is entitled to one, before making a payment under s. 106. Refusal to make a payment would entitle the employee to refer the matter to an industrial tribunal under s. 108(1) and (2).

(ii) Maternity pay. Sections 40 and 43 contain similar provisions to those of ss. 106(1) and 108(2) in respect of maternity pay.

(iii) Various debts due by the employer to the employee, if the employer is insolvent. These are payable by the Secretary of State if he is satisfied that the employer is insolvent, and that on the date on which the employer became insolvent, or the date of the termination of the employee's employment, whichever is the later, the employee was entitled to the debt in question. They are listed in ss. 121(2) and 122(3). Those which may relate to industrial tribunal proceedings are a basic award of compensation for unfair dismissal and arrears of pay for a maximum period of eight weeks in aggregate. Arrears of pay for this purpose consist of the following (see s. 122(4)):—

> a guarantee payment;
> remuneration on suspension on medical grounds under s. 19 of the 1978 Act;
> any payment for time off under ss. 27(3), 31(3) or 31A(4); and
> remuneration under a protective award under s. 101 of the Employment Protection Act 1975.

---

[96] See s. 153(1) for definition.

Under s. 122(5) there is a variable limit on the weekly amount of any such debt, which with effect from February 1, 1981 was £130.[97] Refusal to make a payment would entitle the employee to complain to an industrial tribunal under s. 124(1).

For the purposes of ss. 40, 106 and 122, an employer is insolvent in Scotland if,—

(a) an award of sequestration is made on his estate, or he executes a trust deed for his creditors or enters into a composition contract;

(b) he has died and a judicial factor has been appointed on his insolvent estate under s. 163 of the Bankruptcy (Scotland) Act 1913; or

(c) where the employer is a company, a winding-up order is made or a resolution for voluntary winding-up is passed with respect to it, or a receiver of its undertaking is duly appointed (see ss. 40(1), 106(6) and 127(2)).[98]

(b) Any amount owed by an employer in respect of the items listed above as arrears of pay under s. 122(4), and which therefore qualifies for payment by the Secretary of State, also qualifies, by virtue of s. 121, for the preferences accorded to wages under s. 118 of the Bankruptcy (Scotland) Act 1913 (as also in England and Wales under s. 33 of the Bankruptcy Act 1914) and s. 319 of the Companies Act 1948. Other sums due under awards by industrial tribunals rank only as ordinary claims in the division of the assets of an insolvent employer.

It will be seen from the foregoing that, except in the particular situations mentioned above, statutory preferential treatment only applies where some formal act has occurred to render the employer insolvent in terms of the above definition. Unless and until this happens, a person in whose favour an industrial tribunal has awarded a payment of a sum of money, and who has difficulty in obtaining payment, can only enforce payment by legal enforcement processes (generally called diligence in Scotland) which, unfortunately but inevitably, are complicated and expensive, and may also be unproductive if the debtor is financially embarrassed.[99]

(2) **Enforcement of Scottish industrial tribunal awards**

(a) *In Scotland*

Paragraph 7(2) of Sched. 9 to the Employment Protection (Consolidation) Act 1978, as amended by the Employment Act 1980 (Sched. 1, para.

---

97 The Employment Protection (Variation of Limits) Order 1980 (S.I. 1980/2019).

98 For the procedural effect of an employer's insolvency in industrial tribunal proceedings, see Chap. 4, pp. 83, 84, 86.

99 At the time of writing, the whole law on the subject of diligence is under review by the Scottish Law Commission.

27), provides that any order for the payment of any sum made by an industrial tribunal in Scotland (or any copy of such an order certified by the Secretary of the Tribunals) may be enforced "in like manner as an extract registered decree-arbitral[1] bearing a warrant for execution issued by the sheriff court of any sheriffdom in Scotland". Para. 7(3) excludes any sum awarded under a decision or order which, on being reviewed, has been revoked, and provides that where a decision has been varied on being reviewed, para. 7(2) shall be construed as a reference to the decision or order as so varied. These provisions apply only to an order for payment: at common law a contract of service will not be enforced by a decree of specific implement and, on the same principle, while the unfair dismissal legislation makes provision for orders for continuation or restoration of employment, there are no provisions enabling physical compliance with such orders to be enforced. The sanctions for non-compliance are financial.

How may an extract registered decree-arbitral bearing such a warrant as is mentioned above be enforced in Scotland? This depends on the Writs Execution (Scotland) Act 1877, s. 2 of which provides that in all extracts of writs which contain a clause of registration for preservation and execution, and which are registered in the sheriff court books of any county in Scotland, the sheriff clerk shall insert a warrant of execution. There are similar provisions in s. 1 regarding writs which are registered for preservation and execution in the Books of Council and Session. Section 3 provides that it shall be lawful, by virtue of the warrant inserted in any extract under the two preceding sections, to arrest, to charge for payment, and to poind. The usual practice in drawing up a submission to arbitration is to include a clause by which the parties agree that the deed, and any decree-arbitral which may be pronounced thereunder, may be registered for preservation and execution. A clause in those terms will bring the decree-arbitral within the scope of the 1877 Act. Without such a clause, the holder of a decree-arbitral would have to raise an action in the court for "decree-conform", before he could enforce the decree. The amendment to Employment Protection (Consolidation) Act 1978, Sched. 9, para. 7(2) removes any doubt which may have existed under the previous wording of the paragraph as to whether an order by an industrial tribunal in Scotland is enforceable by summary diligence without prior recourse to a court action for decree-conform. It is to be noted, however, firstly, that there is nothing particular about a decree-arbitral in these respects. The obligation in any registered writ is enforceable under the 1877 Act, provided the deed contains a clause of consent to registration for preservation and execution. If it does not, a court decree must first be

---

[1] A decree-arbitral is an award made by an arbiter in a process of arbitration.

obtained. Secondly, the operation of diligence in relation to industrial tribunal proceedings must, by implication, be governed by the law of diligence as applying to writs registered for preservation and execution under the 1877 Act, and not the law applying to court decrees, if and so far as there is any difference between the two.

If difficulties are encountered in obtaining payment of an award, application should be made to the Secretary of the Tribunals. Normally he will first write to the party against whom the order was made. If this does not evoke a satisfactory response, he will issue a certificate of the decision of the tribunal to enable diligence to be operated.[2] Due to the absence of any express provision as to the effect of a review or appeal on the operation of an order of an industrial tribunal, as noted in Chapter 12 (at p. 252), and since wrongous use of diligence at any time may attract a claim for damages against the party using it, a certificate will not be issued, except on showing special cause, until the expiry of the period for appealing (42 days from the date of promulgation for an appeal to the Employment Appeal Tribunal, and for an appeal to the Court of Session[3]) or during the currency of an appeal or review application.

Most steps of diligence must be operated by a sheriff officer. When received, the certificate of the decision should be sent to an appropriate sheriff officer with instructions to take such steps as may be appropriate in the circumstances.

As indicated above, the forms of diligence available under s. 3 of the Writs Execution (Scotland) Act 1877 are arrestment and poinding, the latter of which must be preceded by the service of a charge for payment. Arrestment is a process whereby money or debts due to the debtor by a third party, or goods of the debtor in the hands of a third party, at the actual time of arrestment, are secured for the benefit of the creditor. The third party is called the arrestee. The arrestment does not transfer the arrested property to the arresting creditor to achieve this, and unless the debtor agrees to release it to him, the arresting creditor must go on to raise an action in court, called an action of furthcoming. Wages are probably the asset over which arrestment is most commonly used, but as an arrestment only attaches what is due at the date of the arrestment, the arrestment does not "lie on the table" to catch future wages as well, which must be the subject of further arrestments. This apart, the obvious asset for an employee to arrest would be the

---

[2] For detailed expositions of the law of diligence, see Gloag & Henderson *op. cit.*, Chap. XLVIII; Dobie, *op. cit.*, Chap. XII; Stewart, *Diligence*. Note that in the absence of a specific waiver and within various limits, foreign and Commonwealth states, diplomatic agents and consular officials enjoy substantial immunity from diligence (the State Immunity Act 1978, s. 13(2)(3) and (6); the Diplomatic Privileges Act 1964, Sched. 1, Art. 31; the Consular Relations Act 1968, Sched. 1, Arts. 43 and 45).

[3] See Chap. 12, p. 262 and p. 269.

employer's bank balance, but of course, if this is in overdraft at the time of the arrestment, nothing will be caught. Arrestments should therefore only be used where there is reason to believe that there are arrestable funds in the hands of the third party. Poinding secures goods in the hands of the debtor himself which are his own property (but not those of a third party, such as his spouse), and may be effected if the time specified in the charge for payment has expired without sufficient payment having been made. As with arrestment, poinding does not transfer the property to the creditor: it only stops the debtor from parting with the goods. If the debtor does not pay up, the eventual sanction is to apply to the sheriff for the poinded goods to be sold under warrant.

In addition, a creditor whose debt is liquid (which presumably would include the holder of an order for payment by an industrial tribunal[4]) may apply for letters of inhibition under the Signet against the debtor. Inhibition effectively prevents the debtor from parting with his heritable property (*i.e.* land and buildings), by making such a transaction voidable at the instance of the inhibiting creditor. The procedure is complicated, and would have to be initiated by a solicitor. The process by which heritable property is attached in payment of a liquid debt (subject to a right of redemption by the debtor) is called adjudication, and is initiated by a court action.

If all else fails, it is open to the creditor to apply to the court for the debtor to be sequestrated (judged bankrupt).

(b) *In England and Wales and elsewhere*

There are no provisions applying the Judgments Extension Acts (which make provision for the registration of decrees and judgments of the courts in the various countries of the United Kingdom in the courts of the other countries, to enable them to be enforced without the necessity of obtaining a decree-conform) to awards by industrial tribunals. A decree-arbitral registered in the Books of Council and Session for preservation and execution bearing a warrant for execution under s. 1 of the Writs Execution (Scotland) Act 1977 would be registrable in the High Court by virtue of s. 3 of the Judgments Extension Act 1868. But the amendment to para. 7(2) of Sched. 9 to the Employment Protection (Consolidation) Act 1978 precludes any possibility of the 1868 Act applying. Accordingly only the Inferior Courts Judgments Extension Act 1882 could apply. But ss. 3 and 4 of this Act extend the privilege of registration in the county court only to a certificate of judgment obtained in a sheriff court for any "debt, damages or costs"

4 Provided it is above the amount for which action by way of summary cause (as opposed to ordinary action) is appropriate (see Gloag and Henderson, *op. cit.*, p. 780).

and not (in contrast to the 1868 Act) to an extract of a writ registered for execution in the books of a sheriff court. Thus it seems that the 1882 Act cannot be said to apply by implication to an award by a Scottish industrial tribunal.

It would appear therefore that the only course open to the holder of such an award against a respondent who resides or has his place of business in England and Wales, and against whom diligence cannot be operated in Scotland, would be to raise proceedings in the appropriate court for judgment for the amount awarded, on which execution could then be levied. Para. 7(1) of Sched. 9 to the Employment Protection (Consolidation) Act 1978 provides for recovery by execution through the county court of *any* sum payable in pursuance of a decision of an industrial tribunal in England and Wales (*i.e.* irrespective of the financial limits on jurisdiction in the county court itself) but does not apply to any sum payable by order of a tribunal in Scotland. Thus the financial limits on jurisdiction in the county court would apply, and if the amount of the award exceeded those limits, it would seem that the proceedings would have to be taken in the High Court. So while it may be possible for an applicant resident in Scotland to initiate industrial tribunal proceedings there against a respondent who resides or carries on business in England and Wales[5], considerations of enforcement may indicate that the proceedings should be taken in the latter country.

Similarly, recourse could only be made to the appropriate national court where an award is made against a person resident or carrying on business elsewhere than in England and Wales (and who is not otherwise amenable to the jurisdiction of the English courts), if the award is not enforceable in Scotland. But (except in Northern Ireland[6] and the Isle of Man, and there only within the limits specified in ss. 157 and 158 of the Employment Protection (Consolidation) Act 1978 and s. 128 of the Employment Protection Act 1975 (*q.v.*)) it is improbable that an award by an industrial tribunal would be considered to afford a valid ground of action against a person within the jurisdiction of the court of the country concerned, at least in the absence of equivalent domestic legislation in that country. The expedient of first raising an action in the Court of Session for decree-conform, with a view to invoking the privileges conferred by the legislation giving reciprocal recognition to the judgments of the domestic courts of the United Kingdom and of other countries, would also be unlikely to be available, since *ex hypothesi* in most cases the respondent would not be amenable to the jurisdiction of the court.[7] In practice, therefore, an award would

[5] See Chap. 4, pp. 29 and 31.

[6] Where little of the employment legislation under which industrial tribunals in Scotland and England and Wales have jurisdiction applies directly.

[7] If jurisdiction in the Court of Session could be founded by arrestment, the fund which could be arrested for that purpose would also be arrestable in execution of the award.

probably be irrecoverable in such a situation. But it would appear that if the European Judgments Convention is ratified by Parliament, industrial tribunal awards would be enforceable in other contracting states.

(3) **Enforcement of English industrial tribunal awards in Scotland**

As already indicated, para. 7(1) of Sched. 9 to the Employment Protection (Consolidation) Act 1978 provides that "any sum payable in pursuance of a decision of an industrial tribunal in England and Wales which has been registered in accordance with the regulations shall, if a county court so orders, be recoverable by execution issued from the county court or otherwise as if it were payable under an order of that court."

It is understood that the way in which these provisions operate in practice is that an originating application is first taken out in the county court for an order equivalent to decree-conform. If the view were to be taken by the registrar of a county court that this order enabled him to grant a certificate under s. 3 of the Inferior Courts Judgments Extension Act 1882 (and no opinion is expressed on that matter), and such a certificate were produced to an appropriate sheriff clerk in Scotland, the certificate would be registrable under s. 4 of the Act, and under s. 5 process of execution would issue thereon against any goods or chattels of the defender (*i.e.* the defender's goods could be poinded, but arrestment would not be competent). But in most cases s. 10 of the 1882 Act would act as a stumbling-block. This provides in effect that where judgment is obtained in the county court against a person who, at the time when the proceedings are commenced, was domiciled in Scotland, the Act does not apply "unless the whole cause of action shall have arisen, or the obligation to which the judgment relates ought to have been fulfilled" within the jurisdiction of such county court *and*[8] the action was personally served on the defendant within that district. (But the section would not apply where the party in right of the award is the respondent in the industrial tribunal proceedings, *i.e.* where the award is one of costs against an applicant.[9])

Unless therefore the requirements of s. 10 could be satisfied, or do not apply, the holder of an English industrial tribunal award against a Scottish party who cannot enforce the award in England would appear to be in the same position as his Scottish counterpart. He could only raise an action in the sheriff court (where of course there is no overall upper financial limit on jurisdiction) for decree-conform, on which diligence would then be operable.

8 Author's italics.

9 See Dobie, *op. cit.*, p. 288.

(4) **On behalf of deceased employees**

The Industrial Tribunals Awards (Enforcement in case of death) Regulations 1976 (S.I. 1976/663) have been commented on in Chapter 4 above.[10] They provide that, in appropriate cases, the award of a tribunal shall be made in favour of the estate of the deceased employee. Where, however, a personal representative of the deceased employee has taken up the proceedings, the award should be made in favour of the personal representative in that capacity.

---

[10] See p. 85.

CHAPTER 10

EXPENSES

GENERAL

In each of the rules governing industrial tribunal procedure, the tribunal is given the power to award expenses (called "costs" in England), which in court proceedings consist of the cash outlays incurred by a party in the course of the proceedings, and (where legally represented) the fees incurred by him to his legal representatives, taxed on the appropriate scale (see below at pp. 240, 241 under "Taxation").[1]

CASES UNDER THE INDUSTRIAL TRIBUNALS RULES OF PROCEDURE (SCOTLAND) 1980

In civil courts, while expenses are always within the court's discretion, the normal rule is that a successful party will be awarded expenses against the unsuccessful party. This is not normal in proceedings under these rules, which govern the vast majority of cases before industrial tribunals. Rule 11(1) provides that, with the exceptions in paras. (2), (3) and (4) of the rule, which are referred to below, the tribunal shall not normally award expenses, but may do so where in its opinion a party *in bringing or conducting the proceedings*[2] has acted frivolously, vexatiously *or otherwise unreasonably*,[2] which in the case of a respondent may apply whether or not he has entered appearance. Where the tribunal is of that opinion it may:

(*a*) order that party to pay to another party (or to the Secretary of State if, not being a party, he has appeared under r. 7(5)) either a specified sum in respect of the expenses incurred by him or *the whole or part of those expenses*[2] as taxed (if not otherwise agreed);

(*b*) order that party to pay to the Secretary of State the whole or any part of any allowance paid by the Secretary of State to any person (other than to tribunal members or assessors) for the purposes of, or in connection with, his attendance at the tribunal.

---

[1] For the practice of the courts with regard to expenses reference should be made to McLaren, *Expenses* and Dobie, *Sheriff Court Practice*, Chap. XIV.

[2] The words emphasised did not occur in r. 10(1)(a) of the Industrial Tribunals (Labour Relations) (Scotland) Regulations 1974, which preceded the 1980 rules. Rule 10(1)(*b*) of those rules was also slightly differently worded.

The concepts underlying the above provisions are that a person who, in good faith, considers that he has a good cause of action or ground of defence, should not be inhibited from taking proceedings before an industrial tribunal by the fear of liability for expenses, which provides a formidable deterrent to civil litigation in the courts; and therefore that in proceedings under this rule each side should generally bear its own expenses.

It was held in *E. T. Marler Ltd.* v. *Robertson* [1974] I.C.R. 72 that a claim is frivolous if the applicant knows that it has no substance and is bound to fail, or is on the face of it so manifestly misconceived that it can have no prospect of success, and that it is vexatious if brought for some improper motive, *e.g.* out of spite to harass the employer. The same considerations apply to the conduct of a respondent. While a claim may be frivolous without being vexatious, and attract liability to expenses on that score only, it will generally be an ingredient in holding a claim to be vexatious that it is a hopeless one (See *Marler, supra* at p. 76E and *Prajapati* v. *Richard Thomas & Baldwins Ltd.* (1966) 1 I.T.R. 564. Compare the Vexatious Actions (Scotland) Act 1898, under which a person may be declared a vexatious litigant if he has "habitually and consistently instituted vexatious legal proceedings, without any reasonable ground for instituting such proceedings".) The introduction of the words "in bringing or conducting the proceedings" in the 1980 rules reflects the decision in *Cartiers Superfoods Ltd.* v. *Laws* [1978] I.R.L.R. 315 that vexatiousness and frivolity are not confined to the institution of proceedings. In that case it was also stated that it is not necessary that a party should know that the way in which a case is being conducted is frivolous. The correct test is to consider what he knew or ought to have known if he had gone about the matter sensibly.

The above definitions of a frivolous or vexatious claim fit the situation where an applicant insists on proceeding after it has been pointed out to him at a preliminary hearing that a tribunal does not appear to have any jurisdiction to entertain his complaint. As regards claims whose merits are hopeless, it has not in the past been the practice of tribunals to award expenses merely because they have decided that the application (or the defence) lacked merit. While it is inevitable that some applications are presented or defended more in hope than in expectation, the majority of parties have what is to them a genuine case, however misconceived the tribunal may eventually hold it to be. As was said in *Prajapati* v. *Richard Thomas & Baldwins, supra,* not every hopeless application is frivolous. And in *Bhardwaj* v. *Post Office* [1978] I.C.R. 144 it was stated (at p. 148) that many cases are only perceived to be groundless at the end of long proceedings; that the purpose of proceedings is to enable cases to be tested; and that (in an unfair dismissal case) the burden of proof is on the respondent and not on the applicant.[3] Statistics show that about 50% of the unfair dismissal complaints presented proceed to a hearing, the remainder being settled or withdrawn beforehand, and of that 50% about one-third succeed. The proportion of the unsuccessful claims in which the evidence discloses no possible point for consideration about the fairness of the dismissal is small: but such cases when they occur, are those which have been regarded by industrial tribunals as potentially appropriate for the exercise of their power to award expenses. This approach reflected the decision in *Marler, supra,* where it was held that while an employee is entitled to have the reasons advanced by his employer for his dismissal, and the reasonableness of his dismissal, adjudicated upon, it was nevertheless not the case that every dismissed employee could pursue such a claim without impunity. It remains to be seen, however, what effect tribunals and appellate courts will decide there should be on previous practice by the introduction of the pre-hearing assessment procedure, in cases where a warning is given about the risk of expenses being awarded, and by the introduction of the additional words "or otherwise unreasonably" in r. 11(1).[4] These words bring r. 11(1) closer to the equivalent rule in proceedings before the Employment Appeal Tribunal, and the practice of the Employment Appeal Tribunal may provide some guidance on the subject.[5]

The exceptions to the provisions of r. 11(1) are:

(1) The provisions in rr. 11(2) and 11(3) relating to expenses where a case is postponed or adjourned. These have been discussed in Chapter 7 at p. 166. (But the late withdrawal of an application, does not fall within these provisions, but falls within r. 11(1)).[6]

(2) In proceedings under the Docks and Harbours Act 1966, the tribunal's powers are expressed (in r. 11(4)) in similar terms to those in the other procedural rules referred to below.

Rule 11 applies to an order by a Chairman dismissing proceedings where an application is withdrawn (see r. 12(5)), so withdrawal of an application will not *necessarily* elide liability for expenses if they are sought by the respondent.

CASES UNDER OTHER REGULATIONS

In the other rules[7] the tribunal is given an unqualified discretion to

[3] Decided before the amendment of s. 57(3) of the Employment Protection (Consolidation) Act 1978 by the Employment Act 1980.

[4] See Chap. 6, p. 119.

[5] See Chap. 12, p. 272.

[6] See Chap. 6, p. 135.

[7] The Industrial Tribunals (Scotland) Regulations 1965 (as amended), Sched. 2, r. 13(1); the Industrial Tribunals (Improvement and Prohibition Notices Appeals) (Scotland) Regulations 1974, r. 13(1); and the Industrial Tribunals (Non-Discrimination Notices Appeals) (Scotland) Regulations 1977, r. 11(1).

order that a party shall pay to another party either a specified sum in respect of expenses or, in default of agreement, the taxed amount of the other party's expenses. In these cases the tribunal is therefore entitled to follow the general rule in litigation that expenses will normally follow success.

LIABILITY

It will be noted that in each of the various rules on the subject, the tribunal's powers in the matter of expenses are not limited to making an award in favour of a successful party, but are so framed that an award of expenses may be made to an unsuccessful party. This reflects the practice of the courts in Scotland, which is that if the court disapproves of the conduct of a successful party, either before or during the course of the litigation, it may refuse him expenses, or, exceptionally, find him liable in expenses to the unsuccessful party.[8] In Scotland unnecessarily lengthy hearings before industrial tribunals are unusual, and the occasion has seldom arisen, but if a party were to prolong a hearing unnecessarily, *e.g.* by insisting on leading a mass of evidence to prove a point on which the tribunal had indicated that they were already satisfied, or on matters which the tribunal had indicated that they regarded as irrelevant, an award of expenses might be made, and has been made in Scotland, on the ground that the conduct was vexatious.

Although r. 11(1) of the Industrial Tribunals Rules of Procedure (Scotland) 1980 (repeating the wording of its predecessor) applies expresssly to a respondent who has not entered appearance, the addition of the words "in bringing or conducting the proceedings", which did not occur in the preceding rule, seems to limit the application of the rule and exclude from the ambit of liability to expenses not only the conduct of either party prior to the initiation of proceedings (following the decision of the Employment Appeal Tribunal in *Orme* v. *West Midland (Insurance) Brokers* (EAT 27/2/1979), but also a respondent who has not entered appearance, and who thus has taken no part in the proceedings.

As to the question whether an award of expenses may be made against any person other than a party or a person entitled to be heard who has appeared, see below under "Solicitors and Other Representatives".

Under the predecessor to r. 11(1) of the Industrial Tribunals Rules of Procedure (Scotland) 1980[9] parties have been ordered to make a payment to the Secretary of State in respect of allowances paid for their

[8] See Dobie, *op. cit.*, p. 315 and cases there cited.

[9] *I.e.* r. 10 in the Industrial Tribunals (Labour Relations) (Scotland) Regulations 1974.

opponents' attendance at a hearing rendered abortive because of conduct held to be frivolous, such as where an application has been withdrawn at the eleventh hour before the hearing with no adequate excuse tendered. But in *Seel Garages Ltd.* v. *Byrne* (EAT 48/80) it was held by the Employment Appeal Tribunal in England that, on a proper construction of the English equivalent to r. 10 in the 1974 rules, it was not competent to make any order in favour of the Secretary of State in respect of the cost of convening a hearing which had to be adjourned as a result of conduct which was held to have been frivolous. That decision may be distinguishable on its facts, and technically it may no longer be authoritative, in view of differences in wording between the present r. 11(1) and its predecessor. That apart, it is difficult, with respect, to see why under the terms of r. 11(1)(*b*) a party who has acted frivolously or vexatiously should not be ordered at least to reimburse the Secretary of State for allowances paid to persons for attending an abortive hearing, and in practice such orders have been made in Scotland.

EXERCISE OF THE POWER

In each of the rules the tribunal's powers in the matter of expenses are discretionary. The discretion must be exercised in a judicial manner,[10] taking into account all relevant factors. In addition to the motives and conduct of the parties, already mentioned, these will include the practice of industrial tribunals in other cases under the same rules raising similar issues, the particular issues and evidence in the case under consideration, the means of the party against whom an award is being considered,[11] and the extent of the expense likely to have been incurred by the party in whose favour an award is being considered (see also below under "Amount of Award").

If an application is dismissed on a preliminary point and the respondent has been ordered not to attend, a tribunal may make an award of expenses if the circumstances appear to warrant it. In practice, it will rarely do so, as the respondent will not usually have incurred any substantial expense at that stage. But the applicant may be refused payment of allowances for attending a hearing (see below under "Payment of Allowances").

When an application is dismissed because an applicant has failed to appear at the hearing, a tribunal may also make an award of expenses in favour of the respondent, and in Scotland it is settled practice to do so: but the applicant's failure to appear may put the tribunal in difficulty

[10] See *Marler* v. *Robertson, supra.* For the principles applying in discretionary matters, see also Chap. 12, p. 257.

[11] See *Carr* v. *Allen-Bradley Electronics Ltd.* [1980] I.C.R. 603.

in deciding whether his conduct has been frivolous, vexatious, or otherwise unreasonable if there is no indication as to the reason for his absence. But the circumstances may be such as to justify an inference of frivolousness from the very fact of his failure to appear.[12] An award may also be made if an application is withdrawn at the eleventh hour.[13]

Similarly, failure to appear at a hearing does not elide liability for expenses on the part of the respondent, where the circumstances warrant an award being made. In *Rolfe* v. *Ray King Transport Ltd.* (1966) 1 I.T.R. 454 a respondent resisted an application for redundancy payment, entitlement to which had previously been conceded in correspondence, and then did not appear at the hearing, and an award of costs was made. But, as pointed out above, the position may be different under the 1980 rules where a respondent has not entered an appearance at all.

A tribunal will usually only consider awarding expenses if an application is made to that effect, although when announcing its decision it may indicate, where it is firmly of that opinion, that the conduct of a party appears to have been frivolous or vexatious. But situations may occur, however, in which the tribunal may raise the question of expenses on its own initiative, if it considers that the circumstances warrant it. Generally, expenses should not be awarded without affording the party against whom an award is under consideration the opportunity to oppose it. In *Bhardwaj* v. *Post Office, supra,* an appeal on the ground that this had not been done was not opposed. Conversely an attempt to move for expenses should not be stifled.[14] The exception is where expenses are awarded against a party who has failed to appear, but in such cases the tribunal will make it clear in its decision that the party against whom the award is made may apply for the decision to be reviewed.

A party who wishes to move for expenses should not delay doing so until the tribunal's decision is made known. The tribunal may reserve its decision, and the opportunity to apply for expenses and hear what the other party has to say in reply may not conveniently re-occur. Failure to do so, however, will not be fatal, as the tribunal is not entirely *functus officii* (*i.e.* its function is not completely discharged) at that stage.[15] In *Zakia* v. *Home Office* (EAT 28/79) the application for costs was not made until after the tribunal's decision had been promulgated. The Employment Appeal Tribunal rejected a submission that it was incompetent on that ground. All they said was that such an application should be made promptly, without stating any particular time limit. If, however, an

---

12 See *Prajapati* v. *Richard Thomas & Baldwins Ltd., supra.*

13 See Chap. 6, p. 135.

14 *Meagher* v. *Holland, Hannen & Cubitts (Southern) Ltd.* (1968) 3 I.T.R. 104.

15 *St. Mungo Community Trust* v. *Colleano* [1980] I.C.R. 254.

application for expenses is made after a tribunal has issued its decision on the merits, the reasons for the application would have to be submitted in writing, and the opposite party would also be given the opportunity of replying and submitting in writing why expenses should not be awarded. Thereafter the matter would be decided by the tribunal on the basis of the written submissions on either side, but it would appear that a further written decision would be necessary, and that it is not a matter which would fall within the Chairman's powers under r. 12(4), and would therefore have to be referred to the full tribunal. Moreover, where a question arises of awarding expenses in connection with some intermediate matter (*e.g.* an adjournment) the tribunal may reserve the decision until the merits of the case have been finally decided.

SOLICITORS AND OTHER REPRESENTATIVES

In sheriff court proceedings the rules provide that a decree for expenses may go out in the name of the solicitor who conducted the case. (Sheriff Courts (Scotland) Act 1907, Sched. 1, r. 99). A solicitor may on the other hand be found personally liable in expenses where he has conducted a litigation without authority from his client, or where expense has been occasioned by his own fault.[16] In industrial tribunal proceedings the rules of procedure dealing with expenses provide only for awards to be made to and against parties, or persons entitled to appear who do appear, or in favour of the Secretary of State if he is not a party. The definition of "party" in the procedural regulations is not capable of being construed as including a representative. In *Walsall Metropolitan Borough Council* v. *Sidhu* [1980] I.C.R. 519 the Employment Appeal Tribunal held that under the equivalent rule in the Employment Appeal Tribunal Rules (the wording of which is on similar lines) it was not competent to award costs to the Race Relations Commission, who had indemnified the party in whose favour an award might otherwise have been made, with the result that the party had not in fact incurred any costs. The situation is perhaps different where there is a question of awarding expenses *against* the party who has been financially supported by a body such as the Equal Opportunities Commission or the Race Relations Commission, or by a trade union or employers' association. *Carr* v. *Allen-Bradley Electronics Ltd., supra* showed that an award against such a party is competent, but that the amount of the award should be assessed by regard to the means and circumstances of the party concerned, and not on the assumption that it

---

[16] See Dobie, *op. cit.*, p. 330 and cases there cited.

will be met by the body supporting him. By the same token, where an award of expenses has been occasioned by the fault of a solicitor or other representative, there is no statutory warrant for finding the solicitor or representative personally liable for expenses,[17] nor, on the basis of the decision in *Carr* v. *Allen-Bradley Electronics Ltd., supra,* should the amount awarded be assessed on the assumption that the party against whom it is to be made will have a right of recourse against the solicitor or other representative.

FORM AND AMOUNT OF AWARD: TAXATION

As pointed out above, the rules provide that in making a finding for expenses a tribunal may either award a specified sum or may make a general award, to be taxed where not agreed. They go on to provide that any such expenses which require to be taxed may be taxed in the sheriff court "according to such of the scales prescribed by the sheriff court rules for civil proceedings . . . as shall be directed by the order".[18] As regards scales of taxation, there is a distinction in court proceedings between expenses taxed "as between party and party" and taxation "as between solicitor and client". The former is the scale on which the expenses of a successful litigant are taxed unless otherwise ordered. It extends only to those expenses which by established practice are regarded as necessary for the conduct of the case, commonly called "judicial expenses". The successful party is therefore almost invariably left to meet extra-judicial expenses incurred in excess of that scale, to a greater or a lesser degree according to the nature of the case and the way in which it has been conducted. Furthermore, expenses awarded by the court, on whatever scale of taxation, do not extend to expenses incurred prior to the commencement of the proceedings. Thus an award of expenses virtually never indemnifies the successful litigant. Expenses on the solicitor and client scale come nearer to doing so, however, since they extend to all expenses reasonably incurred by the party in whose favour an award is made from the time when proceedings commenced. They are only awarded in a limited number of types of case,[19] or, exceptionally, in the court's discretion for a particular reason arising out of the way in which a litigation has been conducted. It would only be in the most exceptional situation that an industrial tribunal would consider making an award of expenses on the solicitor and client scale: were it to do so, it would be appropriate to make the award on the restricted scale of "solicitor and client, third party paying".

---

[17] *Plant & Excavations (Salop) Ltd.* v. *Crocombe* (EAT 157/80).

[18] The Industrial Tribunals Rules of Procedure (Scotland) 1980, r. 11(5). There are similar provisions in the other rules.

[19] See Dobie, *op. cit.*, pp. 319 to 321.

In the sheriff court the scales of taxation differ also according to the nature of the case and the sum for which decree is granted, and any general order for expenses made by an industrial tribunal must therefore specify on which of these scales they are to be taxed. Taxation in the sheriff court of expenses awarded by a tribunal poses a number of practical problems, however. In court, expenses are taxed by the auditor on a remit by the court, which may issue specific directions on particular matters relating to the taxation, and remains the final arbiter in any objection which may be taken by either side to the way in which the auditor taxes specific items. When the expenses have been taxed (both sides having the opportunity to be present), and any objections have been disposed of, the court will grant decree for the taxed amount of the expenses if the party found liable does not make payment voluntarily. While orders in suitable terms to reflect this procedure can be made by a tribunal, the sheriff court auditor may have difficulty in applying to industrial tribunal proceedings the detailed items in the sheriff court scales of taxation, which are framed with specific reference to the minutiae of court proceedings. Where the party in whose favour the award is made is not represented by a solicitor, difficulties could also arise as to how far an award of expenses would extend, so that for instance a company represented by its personnel officer might only be entitled to recover cash outlays and expenses paid to witnesses, and not to any sum to cover the time spent by its representative in preparing the case and appearing at the tribunal.[20] Furthermore, where an order for taxed expenses is made, the case cannot be regarded as finally disposed of until taxation has taken place.

For all of these reasons, coupled with the desirability of keeping procedural formality to a minimum and (in cases under the Industrial Tribunals Rules of Procedure (Scotland) 1980) on the principle that awards of expenses are made primarily to reflect disapproval of the conduct of the party found liable, industrial tribunals usually award specified sums. This practice is more consistent with the concept that parties should normally bear their own expenses, and has the further advantages of flexibility and avoiding the further protraction of the proceedings which would be inevitable if expenses had to be taxed. In cases where r. 11(1) applies, therefore, the tribunal will take into account the factors mentioned above under "Exercise of the Power" which led to their decision to make an award, in order to arrive at a specified sum which they consider enough to inconvenience the party found liable, and deter him from frivolous or vexatious conduct in the future, while at the same time affording a reasonable measure of reimbursement to the party in whose favour the award is made, for the

---

[20] See *Forbes* v. *Whyte*, (1891) 18 R. 688.

expense to which he has been put by the conduct which has given rise to the award.

Cases under the other rules may be more appropriate for a general award if a finding for expenses is made, although here again convenience may indicate modification to a fixed sum. Where a general award is made, the relevant part of the tribunal's decision should be in the following form (or one approximating thereto):

> " . . . That the [applicant, appellant or respondent, as the case may be] be found liable to [the appropriate person] in the expenses of the application [or appeal, as the case may be] , to be taxed, failing agreement, by the auditor of the sheriff court at . . . as between party and party [or as between solicitor and client, third party paying, as the case may be] on the ordinary [or summary as may be appropriate] scale [here add any special directions which may be appropriate], and reserving the rights of either party to object to such taxation to the tribunal; and that the application [or appeal, as the case may be] be continued for such further orders as may be appropriate."

An order in the above form would provide the sheriff court auditor with a remit on which to act. It could include any special directions which the tribunal might consider appropriate to assist the auditor in relating the actual procedure which has taken place in the case to the detailed terms of the sheriff court scales of taxation, while preserving the tribunal's overall position as arbiters in the matter. The direction that the proceedings be continued would enable either party to object to the taxation of specific items, and would enable the party in whose favour the award is made to come back and apply for an order for payment of the taxed amount of the expenses, and generally would enable the tribunal to retain control of the case, in the event of undue delay in implementing the order. The primary initiative would rest, of course, with the party in whose favour the award was made to prepare an account, have it taxed (failing agreement), and seek payment from the party found liable.

PAYMENT OF ALLOWANCES

Paragraph 10 of Sched. 9 to the Employment Protection (Consolidation) Act 1978 makes provision for payment of allowances by the Secretary of State for the purposes of, or in connection with, attendance at industrial tribunals.

The sanctioning of the payment of such allowances to parties and witnesses is a matter within the discretion of the Chairman, and may be refused by him. They may be disallowed if a party's conduct is considered to be frivolous or vexatious (whether or not an award of expenses is also made), and in relation to persons brought as witnesses (whether actually called to give evidence or not) if the Chairman is of the opinion that there was no reasonable justification for so doing, *e.g.* where, having been told that a hearing is a preliminary one, and that it will not be necessary to bring witnesses concerning the merits of the case, a party nevertheless insists on doing so.

CHAPTER 11

REVIEW

GENERAL

Under each of the rules of procedure, except those in the Industrial Tribunals (Scotland) Regulations 1965 (as amended), Sched. 2 (for appeals against assessments to levy under the Industrial Training Act 1964), an industrial tribunal has power to review and to revoke or vary by certificate under the Chairman's hand any of its decisions, on the grounds that:

(*a*) the decision was wrongly made as a result of an error on the part of the tribunal staff; or

(*b*) a party did not receive notice of the proceedings leading to the decision; or

(*c*) the decision was made in the absence of a party or (in cases under the Industrial Tribunals Rules of Procedure (Scotland) 1980) a person entitled to be heard; or

(*d*) new evidence has become available since the making of the decision, provided that its existence could not have been reasonably known or foreseen; or

(*e*) the interests of justice require such a review.[1]

The word "decision" as defined in each of the procedural regulations expressly excludes an interlocutory order,[2] so that any order which falls into that category is reviewable only by way of appeal.

REVIEW PROCEDURE

An application for review may be made at the hearing, but if not, it must be made to the Secretary of the Tribunals at any time from the date of the hearing until 14 days after the date on which the decision is sent to the parties. The application must be in writing, stating the grounds in full.[3]

---

[1] The Industrial Tribunals Rules of Procedure (Scotland) 1980, r. 10(1); the Industrial Tribunals (Improvement and Prohibition Notices Appeals) (Scotland) Regulations 1974, r. 12(1); the Industrial Tribunals (Non-Discrimination Notices Appeals) (Scotland) Regulations 1977, r. 10(1).

[2] See Chap. 9, p. 192 as to the meaning of "interlocutory order".

[3] The Industrial Tribunals Rules of Procedure (Scotland) 1980, r. 10(2). The equivalent provisions in the other rules are in similar terms, except that in the Industrial Tribunals (Improvement and Prohibition Notices Appeals) (Scotland) Regulations 1974, r. 12(2), application for review must be made within 14 days from the date of the entry of the decision in the Register.

Under the Industrial Tribunals Rules of Procedure (Scotland) 1980, a tribunal may extend the time for applying for review, notwithstanding that it may have expired, under the general power to grant such extensions in r. 12(2)(*a*). In *St Mungo Community Trust* v. *Colleano* [1980] I.C.R. 254, the respondents failed to lodge a notice of appearance. They received notice of the proceedings but did not attend the hearing. After the industrial tribunal had decided the case in the applicant's favour and issued a decision to that effect the respondents applied for a review of the tribunal's decision, on the grounds that it had been made in their absence, and that the interests of justice required a review. Subsequently they lodged a notice of appearance setting out the grounds on which they sought to resist the case. The Chairman of the industrial tribunal refused a review on the ground that under r. 3(2) of the rules in force at the time (which did not differ in this respect from r. 3(2) of the 1980 rules) a respondent who had failed to lodge a notice of appearance could only apply for a review on the ground that he had not received notice of the proceedings, which was not so. The respondents then applied for leave to enter appearance out of time, relying on r. 3(3), which provides that a notice of appearance lodged late is deemed to include an application for extension of time. The Chairman refused to consider that application on the ground that, having reached a decision on the case, the industrial tribunal was *"functus officii"*. The Employment Appeal Tribunal held that there was no limit in time for lodging a notice of appearance and applying for it to be received late; that the industrial tribunal should decide whether adequate cause had been shown for allowing the notice of appearance to be received late; and that if it was to be allowed to be received late the tribunal should then go on to consider whether the application for review could also be entertained out of time. Needless to say, it was pointed out that a very heavy burden lay on respondents in such a position to justify such an application at such a late stage.

An application for review is first considered by the President, the Chairman of the tribunal which decided the case, or the Regional Chairman, any of whom may refuse it if in his opinion it has no reasonable prospect of success.[4] In *P. J. Drakard & Sons Ltd.* v. *Wilton* [1977] I.C.R. 642 it was stated that an application for review should set out not only the grounds on which the review is sought, but should also state in what respect the tribunal's decision was wrong. These, however, are matters which if not explicitly stated in the application can usually be inferred. *Drakard's* case turned to some extent on practice in the

---

[4] The Industrial Tribunals Rules of Procedure (Scotland) 1980, r. 10(3). The equivalent provisions in the other rules refer to a nominated Chairman and not to the Regional Chairman. They also specifically require the reasons for refusal to be stated, but in practice this is also done in cases under the 1980 rules.

English courts. In Scotland, the practice when considering whether an application for review discloses a reasonable prospect of success is to look at the apparent merits of the application in the light of the considerations discussed below (see under "Exercise of the Power"), and without any particular formality. If, however, the application is so inadequately framed that it is not possible to decide on what ground it is based, the party making the application would be given the chance to elaborate before a decision is taken as to whether it should be refused as having no reasonable prospect of success. Where the basis of the application is that new evidence should be allowed, the nature of the evidence should be specified. In all cases the reasons for making the application should be stated as fully and clearly as possible, and it should be stated upon which of the grounds specified in the rules the application is based.

If an application is not refused under the foregoing provisions, it is put out for hearing before a tribunal. This should normally be the tribunal which heard the case, but in the Industrial Tribunals Rules of Procedure (Scotland) 1980 provision is made (r. 10(4)) for the application to be heard by a different tribunal if it is not practicable for it to be heard by the tribunal which decided the case, or if the decision was made by a Chairman sitting alone under r. 12(4).[5] There is no requirement that an application for review must be intimated to the other parties to the case, but the Industrial Tribunals (Improvement and Prohibition Notices Appeals) (Scotland) Regulations 1974 (r. 14(2)(*b*)) and the Industrial Tribunals (Non-Discrimination Notices Appeals) (Scotland) Regulations 1977 (r. 12(2)(*b*)) provide that before granting such an application the tribunal may require the applicant for review to give notice to the other parties. In *Ali* v. *Nilgun Fashions* (1978) 13 I.T.R. 443 it was stated that as a matter of ordinary practice, when an application relates to a question of substance, it cannot be finally disposed of in the absence of a party who has not received notice of the proceedings. In Scotland, in all cases where the application is not refused as having no reasonable prospect of success, notice is invariably given to the other party so that he may be given the opportunity to oppose the application.

On hearing an application for review, the tribunal must first consider whether one or more of the statutory grounds for review have been shown, and if so whether the application should be granted. It may be necessary for factual matters to be investigated, and appropriate evidence to be led, before the tribunal can arrive at that decision, particularly where questions arise as to whether the application has been made in bona fide.[6] The rules provide that if the application is

[5] *N.B.* A Chairman may also sit alone to decide an application for interim relief under s. 77 of the Employment Protection (Consolidation) Act 1978 (see Chap. 3, p. 20).

[6] See *Morris* v. *Griffiths* [1977] I.C.R. 153.

granted, the tribunal shall either vary its decision or revoke the decision and order a rehearing.[7] What course the tribunal will follow will depend upon the nature of the point raised by the application, and the likely scope of a rehearing. In *Estorffe* v. *Smith* [1973] I.C.R. 542 it was held (at p. 545) that if an application for review is granted, the tribunal is free to review the whole of its decision. But the point raised by an application for review may relate only to a limited aspect of the tribunal's decision (*e.g.* compensation), and in such a situation it would be inappropriate, both on grounds of equity and expense, for the whole case to be reheard. In practice, therefore, regard will be had to the grounds stated in the application, and parties will be advised whether they should come to the hearing of the application for review prepared to deal only with the points raised in the application, or should also be prepared (on the assumption that the review is granted) to deal with the merits of the case again, whether in whole or in part. In effect, particularly where the point at issue does not involve any further factual investigation, the hearing of the application for review may also take in the question whether the tribunal's original decision should be varied, revoked or adhered to. Where, however, a successful application for review would involve substantial further investigation, it would be normal to order a rehearing at a later date if the tribunal decides to grant the application.

Having heard and decided the application, the tribunal issues a written decision in the usual way, as discussed in Chapter 9, recording its decision on the application for review: if the application is granted, the decision will record whether the original decision is varied or revoked, and will either record a substituted decision, or order that the case be continued for a rehearing, as may be appropriate. It is the duty of the Chairman to certify that a decision has been varied or revoked. In practice, this is accomplished by his signature of the tribunal's decision. The Secretary of the Tribunals then has to correct the original entry in the Register of Decisions and send a copy of the corrected entry to the parties and, in cases under the Industrial Tribunals Rules of Procedure (Scotland) 1980, to any person entitled to appear who did appear, and, where the case was originally referred by a sheriff, to that sheriff.[8] In practice this is done by issuing copies of the decision on the application for review and (if appropriate) any consequential decision after a re-hearing has taken place.

EXERCISE OF THE POWER

The wide variety of the grounds on which an application for review may

[7] The Industrial Tribunals Rules of Procedure (Scotland) 1980, r. 10(4). The equivalent provisions in the other rules are in similar terms.

[8] The Industrial Tribunals Rules of Procedure (Scotland) 1980, r. 10(5). The equivalent provisions in the other rules are in similar terms.

be made enables an injustice to be remedied without recourse to an appellate court if it has occurred from a cause for which the parties themselves cannot be reasonably held responsible. While decisions of industrial tribunals are appealable on points of law (as discussed in Chapter 12) it was stated in *British Midland Airways Ltd.* v. *Lewis* [1978] I.C.R. 782 that an obvious slip or error of law can be more conveniently corrected by review than by appeal, even if this involves overturning the original decision. As was pointed out in *Blackpole Furniture Ltd.* v. *Sullivan and Anr.* [1978] I.C.R. 558, if an appeal court overturns the decision of an industrial tribunal it often has to remit the case back to be reheard by the same or a differently constituted tribunal. If, therefore, the industrial tribunal has made an *obvious* error (such as a mistake in the calculation of compensation), the extra time and expense involved in an appeal can be eliminated by an application for review. Indeed, in the Scottish case of *William P. Harrower Ltd.* v. *Hogg* (EAT 215/78), the Employment Appeal Tribunal awarded expenses against successful appellants on the ground that they should first have sought a review of the industrial tribunal's decision before proceeding with an appeal. But if it is merely *arguable* that the tribunal has erred in law, it is more appropriate that the point should be taken before an appellate court rather than before the tribunal which decided the case. In *Dean* v. *Polytechnic of North London* [1973] I.C.R. 490, where an application for review was made after an appeal had been lodged, it was held that if the result of a review could be to remove or alter the grounds of appeal or alter the findings of fact, the application for review should be determined before the hearing of the appeal. *British Midland Airways* v. *Lewis, supra,* and *Blackpole Furniture Ltd.* v. *Sullivan and Anr., supra,* must be regarded as superseding the suggestion in *Simmons* v. *Medway Welding Ltd.* [1973] 8 I.T.R. 373 that it is inappropriate for an application for review to be considered if an appeal has been lodged.

Paragraph (*d*) of the rules, which provides that new evidence may afford ground for a review, is framed in terms which resemble the "*res noviter*" rule regarding the admission of evidence in civil litigation in the courts,[9] and is generally applied in the same way, with due allowance for the differences between tribunal and court procedures. Although the decisions referred to below were given on appeal, they also apply, where in point, to applications for review based on para. (*d*). New evidence will only be allowed in exceptional circumstances, and the review procedure is not intended to give a party the opportunity to have a "second bite of the cherry" in presenting his case.[10] It is the duty of parties to present all the evidence which they consider relevant to

---

[9] See Gloag & Henderson, *Introduction to the Law of Scotland,* 8th ed., p. 14.

[10] See *Sinclair* v. *S.C.W.S. Ltd.* (1972) 7 I.T.R. 185 at p. 187 and *Flint* v. *Eastern Electricity Board* [1975] I.C.R. 395 at p. 404.

the case which they have to make or refute, as the case may be, and even although a tribunal may indicate what evidence it considers appropriate, it has no duty, even where parties are not legally represented, to ensure that all relevant evidence has been placed before it. This was stated, and has since been reiterated, in *Craig* v. *British Railways* (1973) 8 I.T.R. 636. An application for review based on para. (*d*) will therefore only be granted if a reasonable explanation can be produced as to why the new evidence which is sought to be adduced was not placed before the tribunal at the previous hearing, and (assuming it to be credible) it can be said that it would or might have had a decisive effect on the tribunal's decision.[11]

In *Stevenson (Dyers) Ltd.* v. *Brennan* (1974) 9 I.T.R. 202 it was held that if an application for review based on one particular statutory ground has been refused, a further application is not afterwards competent based on the same ground. In *F. Raybright T.V. Service Ltd.* v. *Smith* (1974) 9 I.T.R. 28, however, a second application was allowed, but the circumstances were held to be exceptional. These cases left open the question whether (assuming no question of time bar arises) a subsequent application based on a *different* ground would be competent. But in *Flint* v. *Eastern Electricity Board, supra,* it was held that if an application for a review seeking the admission of new evidence is refused under para. (*d*) it cannot be granted on the alternative ground, under para. (*e*), namely that the interests of justice require a review. Absence of legal representation before the industrial tribunal is not sufficient ground for review or appeal except in very exceptional circumstances (see Chapter 12, p. 258).

In general, when considering an application for review, a tribunal has first to decide whether it comes within one or more of the grounds specified in the rules, which, as stated above, may involve a factual investigation. The onus of establishing this is of course on the party making the application. Thereafter, it will be within the discretion of the tribunal whether, and if so to what extent, its original decision should be varied, revoked, or affirmed. As in all discretionary matters, the tribunal's discretion must be exercised judicially.[12] All relevant circumstances should be taken into consideration in order to decide whether the balance of justice lies in granting or refusing the application. Regard must be had to the substance of the case which the party seeking review wishes to put forward, and whether, first, it could have had a decisive influence on the tribunal in arriving at its original decision,[13] and if so, secondly, whether in all the circumstances it is consistent with justice that the applicant for review should be allowed to put the case forward.

[11] See *Bagga* v. *Heavy Electricals (India)* [1972] I.C.R. 118 at p. 120.

[12] For the principles applying to discretionary matters, see Chap. 12, p. 257.

[13] See *Richter* v. *North Thames Gas Board* (1973) 8 I.T.R. 175.

Comment has already been made on absence of legal representation as a potential ground for review. An applicant for review who alleges that he has been misled as to his rights may be in a stronger position, however (see *Berkeley Garage (Southampton) Ltd.* v. *Edmunds* [1975] I.C.R. 228). The question of prejudice to the opposite party should be considered as well as that of prejudice to the party seeking review. And the conduct of the party seeking review, or his representative, may also have to be taken into account, so that a review may be refused if it is considered that he is to blame for the situation which has given rise to the application.

Where an application for review is based upon circumstances which have occurred since the tribunal reached its original decision, which is probably most likely to occur over decisions on awards of compensation, the test to be applied is whether the forecasts which the tribunal had made have been proved false to a sufficiently substantial extent, and whether this has occurred so soon after the decision that a review is necessary in the interests of justice. This was decided in *Yorkshire Engineering and Welding Company Ltd.* v. *Burnham* [1973] I.R.L.R. 316, and applied in *Studio Press (Birmingham) Ltd.* v. *Davies* (1977) 12 I.T.R. 93.

CHAPTER 12

APPEAL

GENERAL: AVENUES OF APPEAL

Appeal may be taken from an industrial tribunal in either of two ways, depending on the nature of the proceedings:

(1) Under s. 136(1) of the Employment Protection (Consolidation) Act 1978, an appeal lies to the Employment Appeal Tribunal on a question of law arising from any decision of, or arising in any proceedings before, an industrial tribunal under, or by virtue of:

(*a*) the Equal Pay Act 1970;
(*b*) the Sex Discrimination Act 1975;
(*c*) the Employment Protection Act 1975;
(*d*) the Race Relations Act 1976;
(*e*) the Employment Protection (Consolidation) Act 1978.

Appeal also lies to the Employment Appeal Tribunal on the grounds of jurisdiction introduced by the Employment Act 1980 (see ss. 2(7), 4(8) and 5(9)). As regards s. 4(8) (unreasonable exclusion or expulsion from trade union membership) the appeal may be on any question of law or fact. In the other two cases the appeal may only be on a question of law.

From the Employment Appeal Tribunal appeal lies in Scotland to the Court of Session, with leave of the appeal tribunal or of the Court of Session, and in England and Wales to the Court of Appeal with the equivalent leave.[1]

(2) In any other proceedings, by s. 13(1) of the Tribunals and Inquiries Act 1971, as applied to Scotland by s. 13(6), a party who is "dissatisfied in point of law" with a decision of an industrial tribunal may appeal to the Court of Session or may require the tribunal to state and sign a case for the opinion of the court. Section 13(2) makes provision for a case to be stated in the course of the proceedings before the industrial tribunal.

Decisions of the Court of Session in any of the foregoing proceedings are in turn appealable to the House of Lords, but in proceedings under the Tribunals and Inquiries Act 1971 only with leave either of the Court of Session or of the House of Lords.[2]

Nearly all appeals from industrial tribunals are now to the Employment Appeal Tribunal, as the proceedings for which the channel of appeal is s. 13(1) of the 1971 Act are not numerous and do not often occur in practice. Stated cases under s. 13 of the 1971 Act are virtually unknown.

---

[1] The Employment Protection (Consolidation) Act 1978, s. 136(4).

[2] See s. 13(6)(c).

Whereas enforcement of an order made by the Employment Appeal Tribunal is not suspended by an appeal to a higher court unless otherwise directed (see below, p. 269) there is no explicit provision in the legislation or the rules of procedure for industrial tribunals, or in the Employment Appeal Tribunal Rules, as to whether an appeal suspends the decision of the industrial tribunal, and there does not appear to be any judicial authority on the point. As explained in Chapter 9 (at p. 228), the Secretary of the Industrial Tribunals will not normally issue a certificate of the decision of an industrial tribunal, on which enforcement procedure depends, until the period for lodging an appeal has expired without an appeal having been taken, or during the dependence of an appeal. As to the effect of an appeal on reinstatement and compensation for unfair dismissal, see Chapter 9, p. 216 and *Qualcast (Wolverhampton) Ltd.* v. *Ross* [1979] I.C.R. 387.

THE EMPLOYMENT APPEAL TRIBUNAL

The Employment Appeal Tribunal was established by s. 87 of the Employment Protection Act 1975, now repealed. It continues in existence by virtue of s. 135(1) of the Employment Protection (Consolidation) Act 1978. In addition to its jurisdiction in appeals from industrial tribunals, the appeal tribunal has jurisdiction as a court of first instance under s. 5(2) of the Employment Act 1980 in claims for compensation by a person denied admission or re-admission to a trade union after a declaration by an industrial tribunal under s. 4 that he has been unreasonably excluded or expelled from the union in question, and has a further appellate jurisdiction in questions arising in any proceedings before, or arising from any decision of, the Certification Officer; some such appeals may be on questions of fact or law (Employment Protection (Consolidation) Act 1978, s. 136(3)), while others are on questions of law only (s. 136(2)). Strictly speaking, these proceedings are not within the scope of this chapter, but as applications under s. 5(2) of the 1980 Act follow industrial tribunal proceedings, reference is made below to the rules of procedure relating particularly to such proceedings.

The appeal tribunal is a superior court of record.[3] It has jurisdiction in Scotland and in England and Wales, and its members may (and do) sit in either country. Like industrial tribunals, appeal tribunals consist of a judicial member, who acts as Chairman, and "appointed members", who are persons with special knowledge or experience of industrial relations, as representatives either of employers or of workers. The

[3] The Employment Protection (Consolidation) Act 1978, Sched. 11, para. 12.

judicial members are judges of the High Court or the Court of Appeal in England, together with at least one judge of the Court of Session. The appointed members are appointed by the Queen on the joint recommendation of the Lord Chancellor and the Secretary of State for Employment. One of the judicial members is appointed President.[4] At the time of writing there is one Scottish judicial member.

The appeal tribunal has a Central Office in London, and a Scottish office at 249 West George Street, Glasgow G2 4QE, but it may sit anywhere in Great Britain. Proceedings must be before a judicial member and either two or four, but almost invariably two, appointed members (made up equally from employers' representatives and workers' representatives) unless parties consent to their being heard by a judicial member and one appointed member only.[5]

In relation to the attendance and examination of witnesses, production and inspection of documents, and all other matters incidental to its jurisdiction, the appeal tribunal has the like powers, privileges and authority as the High Court in England and Wales and the Court of Session in Scotland. But no person may be punished for contempt of the tribunal except by or with the consent of a judge.[6] Decisions or awards of the appeal tribunal have the same effect and may be enforced in the same manner as the decisions or awards of the body or officer from whom the appeal was brought.[7] (See Chapter 9, pp. 226 to 231, as to enforcement of industrial tribunal awards, and below at p. 260).

SCOPE OF APPEALS

(1) **General**

In order to succeed, an appellant must generally show that the decision of the industrial tribunal was wrong in law.[8] The onus in this respect is on him,[9] but there have been exceptional cases in which an appeal has been allowed where no error of law has been found on the part of the industrial tribunal.[10]

In *Melon and Ors.* v. *Hector Powe Ltd.* [1980] I.R.L.R. 80 the Lord President said:

---

4 The Employment Protection (Consolidation) Act 1978, s. 135(2) to (5).

5 The Employment Protection (Consolidation) Act 1978, Sched. 11, paras. 13-16.

6 The Employment Protection (Consolidation) Act 1978, Sched. 11, para. 22.

7 The Employment Protection (Consolidation) Act 1978, Sched. 11, paras. 21 and 21A (the latter paragraph having been added by para. 29 of Sched. 1 to the Employment Act 1980).

8 See *Central Scotland Water Development Board* v. *Johnston* (1971) 6 I.T.R. 86.

9 *Challinor* v. *Taylor* [1972] I.C.R. 129 (at p. 131).

10 See below under "New matter" at p. 259.

"The law is clear that where it cannot be shown that the tribunal of original jurisdiction has either misdirected itself in law, entertained the wrong issue, or proceeded upon a misapprehension or misconstruction of the evidence, or taken into account matters which were irrelevant to its decision, or has reached a decision so extravagant that no reasonable tribunal properly directing itself on the law could have arrived at, then its decision is not open to successful attack. It is of no consequence that the appellate tribunal or court would itself have reached a different conclusion on the evidence. If there is evidence to support the decision of the tribunal of first instance then in the absence of misdirection in law—which includes the tribunal's selection of the wrong question to answer—that is an end of the matter."

Appellate courts do not encourage appeals which, under the guise of raising a point of law, amount in effect to an attempt to obtain a reversal of the decision of an industrial tribunal on the facts of a case.[11] In *Palmer* v. *Vauxhall Motors Ltd.* [1977] I.C.R. 24 it was held that where the industrial tribunal has not overtly misunderstood the evidence or misapplied the law, the test is whether, on the facts found by the industrial tribunal, no person acting judicially and properly instructed as to the relevant law could have come to the decision reached by the tribunal. In *Retarded Children's Aid Society Ltd.* v. *Day* [1978] I.C.R. 437, Lord Russell of Killowen, agreeing with Lord Denning MR, warned at p. 444 against concluding that by not mentioning some point or breach an industrial tribunal had overlooked it, and against "searching around with a fine tooth-comb for a point of law in a situation where on the merits and the oral evidence the members of the Employment Appeal Tribunal would have taken a different view than that of the industrial tribunal."

Similarly, in *Jowett* v. *Earl of Bradford (No. 2)* [1978] I.C.R. 431 it was stated that where the language of a statute is unclear or ambiguous, the courts have to interpret it, and their interpretation becomes a binding precedent, but that tests, methods of approach or guidelines given by superior courts for the application of a given set of facts to a statutory provision which is plain in itself, are not intended to be rules of law or binding precedents; if inferior tribunals fail to adopt them they are likely to go wrong, but not to adopt them is not in itself an error of law which can be the subject of appeal. Similar observations were made in *Wells* v. *Derwent Plastics Ltd.* [1978] I.C.R. 424. In *Bailey* v. *BP Oil Kent Refinery Ltd.* [1980] I.R.L.R. 287 the Court of Appeal went further and said that it was unwise for appellate courts to set out guidelines and wrong to make rules and establish presumptions for industrial tribunals

---

11 See *Thomas Betts Manufacturing Co.* v. *Harding* [1980] I.R.L.R. 255 at p. 258.

to follow in considering whether an employer has acted reasonably in dismissing an employee, and emphasised that every such case must depend on its own facts.[12]

Unless an appeal lies on fact as well as law,[13] a finding-in-fact by an industrial tribunal is usually final and cannot be altered on appeal. The rule is not absolute, but in accordance with the general principles referred to above, an appellate court will only interfere if the industrial tribunal's conclusion on fact amounts to an error of law. In *Alexander Machinery* v. *Crabtree* [1974] I.C.R. 120 it was stated (at p. 122) that absence of evidence to support a particular finding is an error of law, and similarly that a finding of fact, or a refusal to find a fact, will involve an error of law if the finding or refusal is a conclusion which no tribunal, properly directing itself, could reach on the basis of the evidence which has been given and accepted by it. The word "accepted" was stressed because it is important that tribunals, in reaching findings of fact, should set out in substance what evidence they do or do not accept.[14] The test was stated to be: "Is the tribunal providing both parties with the materials which will enable them to know that the tribunal has made no error of law in reaching its findings of fact?". Failure to satisfy the test will in itself constitute an error of law, but an appellant will not ordinarily be allowed to contend that the decision was contrary to the evidence, or that there was no evidence to support the decision, unless full and sufficient particulars of the matters relied on are supplied to the appeal tribunal.[15] As to how the appeal tribunal will deal with appeals under s. 4(8) of the Employment Act 1980, where appeal is allowed on questions of fact, see below, pp. 259, 260).

Where a criticism by an appellant of a finding of fact, or a refusal to find a fact, by the industrial tribunal is based on an allegation that there was evidence before the tribunal which is not referred to in the tribunal's decision, or that evidence before the tribunal has not been accurately or fairly stated or summarised in the decision, recourse may have to be made to the Chairman's notes. But in a case where there was a conflict between certain findings-in-fact in the reasons in the decision and the Chairman's notes the NIRC held that they must be guided by the former, unless there were compelling circumstances which led to the conclusion that the reasons may inaccurately state the substance of the evidence.[16] In Scotland, contrary to the practice in England and Wales, the Chairman's notes are not transcribed in ordinary course, and

---

12 See also Chap. 9 at p. 204.

13 See above, p. 251.

14 See Chap. 9, p. 197.

15 Employment Appeal Tribunal Practice Direction, February 17, 1981, [1981] I.C.R. 287, para. 5(*b*).

16 *Ogidi-Olu* v. *Governors of Guy's Hospital* (1974) 9 I.T.R. 70.

are not supplied to the parties except on application to the appeal tribunal on cause shown.[17] The notes will not be supplied merely to enable a party's advisers to comb through them in the hope of finding a ground on which to appeal.[18]

The appeal tribunal's Practice Direction dated February 17, 1981, [1981] I.C.R. 287, reflecting the decisions in *Dexine Rubber Company Ltd.* v. *Alker* [1977] I.C.R. 434 and *Bhardwaj* v. *Post Office* [1978] I.C.R. 144, provides (para. 12(a)) that complaints of bias or of the conduct of an industrial tribunal will not normally be considered unless full and sufficient particulars are set out in the grounds of appeal. In any such case the Registrar of the appeal tribunal will give any appropriate directions for obtaining particulars of the complaint, which will be communicated to the Chairman of the industrial tribunal so that he may comment upon it; unless the appropriate procedure has been followed no such complaint will be permitted to be developed during the hearing of the appeal. In practice, however, intimation of all appeals is made by the Registrar of the appeal tribunal to the Secretary of the Industrial Tribunals in terms of the Employment Appeal Tribunal rules, whether allegations of bias or misconduct are made or not, and the Chairman is afforded at that stage the opportunity to make any comments which he may consider appropriate, whether by way of answers or of a less formal report on the proceedings before the industrial tribunal. The rules of the Court of Session also make provision for intimation of an appeal to be made to the Chairman in every case under s. 13(1) of the Tribunals and Inquiries Act 1971.

The courts will not decide points of law which do not arise in the context of a live issue. This principle was applied in *Secretary of State for Employment* v. *Nortons (Cardiff) Ltd.* (1972) 7 I.T.R. 136. Likewise, the Employment Appeal Tribunal held in *Harrod* v. *Ministry of Defence* [1981] I.C.R. 8 that s. 136(1) of the Employment Protection (Consolidation) Act 1978 did not entitle it to entertain an appeal concerned only with the reasoning of the industrial tribunal, but which did not seek to disturb its order.

On questions relating to compensation it was held in *Nohar* v. *Granitstone (Galloway) Ltd.* [1974] I.C.R. 273 that an appellate court can only interfere with an industrial tribunal's award if satisfied that the tribunal failed to take into account some element of compensation that they were legally bound to take into account, or assessed compensation at a figure manifestly unwarranted by the evidence led before them. While the industrial tribunal should show the reasons for their decision on such matters, the evidence on which the decision is based, and how

---

17 Employment Appeal Tribunal Practice Direction, February 17, 1981, para. 13(b).

18 *Hector Powe Ltd.* v. *Melon and Ors.* (EAT 5/12/77).

the award is made up, by reference to the various relevant categories of compensation,[19] the appeal tribunal will not interfere in respect of trifling amounts or unimportant errors.[20]

Interlocutory and other incidental procedural rulings by industrial tribunals, (whether fully constituted, or consisting only of a Chairman sitting alone), such as decisions on applications for postponement or adjournment, are appealable (as being a question arising in the proceedings), as are refusals of applications for review. Most matters of that kind are within the discretion of the industrial tribunal, which has to decide where the balance of justice lies between both parties.[21] In *Jacobs* v. *Norsalta Ltd.* [1977] I.C.R. 189 Phillips J said that provided a discretionary power is exercised judicially and not arbitrarily or capriciously, the industrial tribunal's discretion is complete. In *Ryan Plant* v. *Price* [1976] I.C.R. 424 he expressed the view that a decision in a discretionary matter is wrong, not if it is one of several decisions each of which is possible, but only if an appellate court can say that it is not really a possible view for the tribunal to have arrived at on the facts. In *Bastick* v. *James Lane (Turf Accountants) Ltd.* [1979] I.C.R. 778 Arnold J said that for the appeal tribunal to interfere with a Chairman's discretion it was necessary to show that he had taken into account some irrelevant matter or failed to take into account some relevant matter or that the decision was perverse. In *Carter* v. *Credit Change Ltd.* [1979] I.C.R. 908 the Court of Appeal approved the decisions in *Jacobs* v. *Norsalta* and *Bastick's* case, and declined to lay down any general principle, except that the industrial tribunal Chairman should attempt to do justice as best he can in each individual case.[22]

The Court of Session will not interfere with the decision of a judge of first instance in a discretionary matter unless it has been exercised in a way which is contrary to principle. This approach has been followed by the appeal tribunal in Scotland.[23]

Under r. 29 of the Employment Appeal Tribunal Rules the tribunal has the power to promote conciliation. For a case in which the power was exercised see *Pambakian* v. *Brentford Nylons Ltd.* [1978] I.C.R. 665.

(2) **New matter**

A party (whether appellant or respondent) will not normally be allowed to raise in an appeal an issue which was not canvassed before

---

19 *Fougère* v. *Phoenix Motor Co. Ltd.* [1976] I.C.R. 495; *Green* v. *J. Waterhouse and Sons Ltd.* [1977] I.C.R. 759.

20 *Fougère, supra* at p. 182.

21 See *Morris* v. *Griffiths* [1977] I.C.R. 153 and *Masters of Beckenham Ltd.* v. *Green* [1977] I.C.R. 535.

22 See also on this subject in Chap. 6 at p. 121.

23 *Bain* v. *George Lawson & Son* (1899) 1 F. 576; *D. C. Thomson & Co. Ltd.* v. *Alexander* (EAT 158/79).

the industrial tribunal, or to raise at the hearing of an appeal an issue not raised in the notice of appeal or the respondents' answer, as the case may be. But exceptions are admitted, as noted below.

As regards issues not raised before the industrial tribunal, in nearly all the reported cases the new matters have involved questions of fact which were not investigated by the industrial tribunal, and the refusal to allow the new question to be taken has turned particularly on that point.[24] In *Secretary of State for Employment* v. *Newcastle-upon-Tyne City Council* [1980] I.C.R. 407 the point was also taken that the new issue which the respondents were seeking to raise was contrary to their case as presented to the industrial tribunal. But it was held in *Kumchyk's* case, *supra* that there was nothing in the language of s. 88 of the Employment Protection Act 1975, now s. 136 of the Employment Protection (Consolidation) Act 1978 (and in contrast perhaps to appeals falling under the Tribunals and Inquiries Act 1971, as pointed out in *GKN (Cwmbran) Ltd.* v. *Lloyd, supra)*,[25] to exclude the consideration of a new point of law, but that in almost every conceivable case it would be unjust to do so. In *Land and Anr.* v. *West Yorkshire Metropolitan County Council* [1979] I.C.R. 452, however, where there was agreement on the further facts on which the new points depended, the appeal tribunal took the new points into consideration. And in *House* v. *Emerson Electric Industrial Controls* [1980] I.C.R. 795 it was held that where the new matter raised a question of the industrial tribunal's jurisdiction it would be contrary to the principles of justice not to allow it to be taken on appeal. An exception was made to the general rule in the Scottish case of *Sinclair* v. *SCWS Ltd.* (1972) 7 I.T.R. 185, where a case was remitted back to the industrial tribunal to hear evidence on a new matter, a major factor in the decision being that the applicant had not been professionally represented before the industrial tribunal. In *Dalton* v. *Burtons Gold Medal Biscuits Ltd.* [1974] I.R.L.R. 45, however, absence of legal representation before the industrial tribunal was held not to afford grounds for a rehearing, and a similar view was expressed in *Kumchyk, supra* (at p. 1123).

Similarly, although in *Leonard* v. *Fergus and Haynes Civil Engineering Ltd.,* 1979 S.L.T.(Notes) 38, the Court of Session did not rule out the possibility of entertaining a question arising out of a decision of an industrial tribunal which had not been taken before the Employment Appeal Tribunal, the court has subsequently ruled firmly that its sole concern is with questions of law arising from a decision of the appeal

---

[24] *Central Scotland Water Development Board* v. *Johnston* (1971) 6 I.T.R. 86; *GKN (Cwmbran) Ltd.* v. *Lloyd* [1972] I.C.R. 215; *Kumchyk* v. *Derby City Council* [1978] I.C.R. 1116; *Jones* v. *R. M. Douglas Construction Ltd.* [1979] I.C.R. 278.

[25] See also the Scottish case of *Stewart* v. *Alexander* (1969) 4 I.T.R. 234.

tribunal, and that it will not entertain a question which was not canvassed before that tribunal.[26]

As regards questions of law arising from a decision of an industrial tribunal which have not been canvassed in the notice of appeal or the respondents' answer, it was first decided that these could not be pursued in *Bagga* v. *Heavy Electricals (India) Ltd.* [1972] I.C.R. 118, and this remains the normal practice.

Where a question raised in a notice of appeal relating to a matter which was before the industrial tribunal would involve the admission of new evidence on the subject which was not before the industrial tribunal, the new evidence will only be allowed by an appellate court in exceptional circumstances because, as was stated in *Flint* v. *Eastern Electricity Board* [1975] I.C.R. 395 (at p. 404) it amounts to "a second bite at the cherry". The test for allowing such evidence to be led was formulated in *Bagga's* case as being that some reasonable explanation must be produced for not putting it before the tribunal of first instance; and that, if accepted as credible, it would or might have had a decisive effect on the decision. Moreover questions of this kind fall within the power of an industrial tribunal to review its own decision,[27] and, as pointed out in *British Midland Airways Ltd.* v. *Lewis* [1978] I.C.R. 782, should first be raised in that way. Where this was not done, the Employment Appeal Tribunal in Scotland awarded expenses against a successful appellant.[28]

Some cases where new evidence has been allowed because the circumstances are exceptional have not involved any error by the industrial tribunal on the material before it, whether the evidence has been allowed on a question already before the industrial tribunal (such as *William P. Harrower Ltd.* v. *Hogg, supra,* where it was alleged that perjury had been committed before the industrial tribunal, and *D. G. Moncrieff (Farmers)* v. *MacDonald* [1978] I.R.L.R. 112, involving new evidence relevant to compensation), or on a question not previously before the industrial tribunal (*Sinclair* v. *SCWS Ltd., supra*). These cases seem therefore to be exceptions to the normal rule that an appellant can only succeed if he establishes error of law on the part of the industrial tribunal.

It remains to be seen whether, in the one situation in which appeal lies to the Employment Appeal Tribunal on questions of fact (*i.e.* under s. 4(8) of the Employment Act 1980), the appeal tribunal will confine itself to considering whether, on the evidence which it had before it, the industrial tribunal was entitled to make the findings-in-fact which it did, as the Court of Session would normally do, based on the notes of evidence in the court below, or whether it will be prepared to rehear the

[26] *Tyrell* v. *Temple Farm Coal Co.* (First Division, July 1, 1980).

[27] See Chap. 11, p. 248.

[28] *William P. Harrower Ltd.* v. *Hogg* (EAT 215/78).

evidence which was led before the industrial tribunal, or hear other evidence which was not. The matter may depend upon whether the industrial tribunal has adequately set out in its decision the evidence which was before it, or whether the appellant can show good reason why evidence which was not before the industrial tribunal should be admitted at the appeal stage. In appeals from decisions of the Certification Officer, where there is appeal on fact as well as on law, the appeal tribunal hears evidence, but this is because the Certification Officer exercises a jurisdiction which is quasi-judicial and partly administrative, and does not hear evidence tested by cross-examination.[29] The decision in *International Air Services (UK)* v. *Jones* (see below) may be a pointer to what the appeal tribunal's approach will be.

DISPOSAL OF APPEALS: FURTHER PROCEDURE

(1) Under the Employment Protection (Consolidation) Act 1978, s. 136(1)

If an appeal is successful, the Employment Appeal Tribunal has wide powers to determine what further action to take. By para. 21(1) of Sched. 11 to the 1978 Act it may exercise any powers "of the body . . . from whom the appeal was brought" or may remit the case to "that body". Paragraph 21(2) provides that any decision or award of the appeal tribunal shall have the same effect and be enforced in the same manner as a decision or award of "a body . . . from whom the appeal was brought." By para. 21A(2)[30] an order for payment in Scotland, or a certified copy thereof, may be enforced in the same way as a decree-arbitral registered in a sheriff court with a warrant of execution. These provisions are in effect identical to those relating to industrial tribunals (see Chapter 9, pp. 226, 227).

In *International Aviation Services (UK)* v. *Jones* [1979] I.C.R. 371 the appeal tribunal rejected a contention that it could only hear new evidence if it related to what had happened before the industrial tribunal or to matters which had arisen since the industrial tribunal hearing, and held that since para. 19 of Sched. 6 to the Employment Protection Act 1975 conferred on the appeal tribunal all the powers of the industrial tribunal in connection with an appeal, it enabled it to exercise wider powers than that of the High Court, and that it had a discretion to admit fresh evidence within the principles stated in *Bagga* v. *Heavy Electricals (India) Ltd.* [1972] I.C.R. 118.[31] But in practice it is exceptional for the appeal tribunal to hear evidence,[32] and cases where

---

29 *Blue Circle Staff Association* v. *Certification Officer* [1977] I.C.R. 224 (at p. 226-7); *HSD (Hatfield) Association* v. *Certification Officer* [1978] I.C.R. 21.

30 Added by the Employment Act 1980, Sched. 1, para. 29.

31 See p. 259 above.

32 For a Scottish case in which the appeal tribunal did decide to hear further evidence itself, see *D. G. Moncrieff (Farmers)* v. *MacDonald*, *supra*.

any further enquiry is considered necessary are usually remitted. If the appeal tribunal considers it inappropriate to remit to the same industrial tribunal, the case is remitted to a differently constituted tribunal. In *Askew* v. *Victoria Sporting Club Ltd.* [1976] I.C.R. 302, it was held that the appeal tribunal had a wholly unrestricted power to remit a case for rehearing. The appeal tribunal has no power, however, to award interest on an award of compensation by an industrial tribunal.[33]

If an appeal from the Employment Appeal Tribunal to the Court of Session (or from the latter to the House of Lords) is successful, the case will come back to the appeal tribunal to make such further orders as may be appropriate in the light of the decision of the appellate court, accompanied, if need be, by directions on the subject.

(2) **Under the Tribunals and Inquiries Act 1971, s.13**

By R.C. 291 of the Rules of the Court of Session, R.C. 280 applies to stated cases under s. 13(2) of the Tribunals and Inquiries Act 1971 (but, not apparently, to appeals under s. 13(1)). Rule 280 provides that the court may at any time before the final disposal of the case, allow the case to be amended with consent of parties, and may remit the case for restatement or further statement in whole or in part; and that if for the disposal of the case any enquiry into matters of fact is competent and required, "the Division before which the case depends may remit to a reporter or to a Lord Ordinary or to one of their own number to take evidence". (The passage quoted has to be applied subject to the provisions in R.C. 291(3) (as amended) that such cases are disposed of by a single judge nominated by the Lord President).

There are no other provisions in the Rules of Court defining the powers of the court in disposing of appeals and stated cases under s. 13(1) of the 1971 Act. *Stewart* v. *Alexander* (1969) 4 I.T.R. 234 suggests that except within the ambit of R.C. 280 (which has very limited application) the court can only determine the points or questions of law in issue and, if the appeal is successful and any further matters require consideration in the light of the court's decision, remit the case back to the industrial tribunal which heard it, with any appropriate directions as to how to proceed.

EMPLOYMENT APPEAL TRIBUNAL PROCEDURE

(1) **General**

Proceedings before the Employment Appeal Tribunal are regulated by the Employment Appeal Tribunal Rules 1980 (S.I. 1980/2035), which came into operation on February 1, 1981, replacing the previous rules of

[33] *Nelson* v. *BBC (No. 2)* [1980] I.C.R. 110.

1976 (S.I. 1976/322). Subject thereto, the tribunal may regulate its own procedure.[34] There is also a Practice Direction by the President dated February 17, 1981, [1981] I.C.R. 287, replacing a previous Direction dated March 3, 1978 (as amended on February 22, 1979).

The rules are intended to operate in a flexible manner. The tribunal may alter the requirements for service,[35] and extend or abridge time limits.[36] Failure to comply with any requirement of the rules does not invalidate the proceedings unless the appeal tribunal otherwise directs, and the tribunal may dispense with or modify any steps specified in the rules if it considers that to do so would lead to the more expeditious or economical disposal of any proceedings or would otherwise be in the interests of justice.[37]

Preliminary and interlocutory procedure is dealt with by the Registrar, subject to a right of appeal from his decision to a judge or, if the judge so directs, to a fully constituted tribunal.[38]

(2) **Institution of appeal: time limits**

An appeal is instituted by serving on the appeal tribunal a notice of appeal in accordance with prescribed forms, together with a copy of the decision or order appealed from. This must be done within 42 days from the date on which the decision or order appealed from was sent to the appellant.[39] Institution of an appeal should not be deferred because the decision or order of the industrial tribunal is an interim one (*e.g.* where the industrial tribunal has dealt only with the merits and not with the remedy), or because an application has been made to the industrial tribunal for a review.[40] But an appeal will not be adjourned to let an application for a review be lodged out of time.[41] If an appeal is lodged out of time, the notice of appeal must be accompanied by an application for an extension of time setting out the reason for the delay. Conversely, applications for extension of time are not considered until a notice of appeal has been presented. As laid down in *Marshall* v. *Harland & Wolff Ltd.* [1972] I.C.R. 97, extensions will only be granted in rare and exceptional circumstances. In particular, it is not necessarily a good excuse that legal aid has been applied for or that support is being sought from an outside body (*e.g.* the Equal Opportunities Commission, or a

---

34 The Employment Protection (Consolidation) Act 1978, Sched. 11, para 17(2).

35 Rule 28(5).

36 Rule 30(1).

37 Rule 32.

38 Rules 3(2), 16 and 17; Practice Direction, para. 3, 6 and 7.

39 Rule 3(1).

40 Practice Direction, para. 4(g). See also *Firestone Tyre & Rubber Company Ltd.* v. *Challoner* [1978] I.C.R. 175.

41 *Rigby* v. *British Steel Corporation* [1973] I.C.R. 160.

trade union). In any case of doubt or difficulty the notice of appeal should be presented in time and an application should be made to the Registrar for directions.[42]

The notice of appeal should state all the questions which the appellant seeks to raise. As pointed out above,[43] an appellant will not normally be allowed to raise a point which has not been canvassed in the notice of appeal. But an appellant may apply afterwards for leave to add an additional ground of appeal, and provided that the application is made in sufficient time before the hearing to enable intimation to be made to the respondent, the application will normally be granted.

(3) **Doubtful applications**

Where it appears to the Registrar that the appeal tribunal may not have jurisdiction he must notify the appellant to that effect,[44] but may first seek clarification or amplification of the grounds of appeal from the appellant.[45] The appellant may then serve a fresh notice of appeal within the remainder of the 42 days' limit or 28 days from the date of notification, whichever is the longer period.[46] The fresh notice of appeal is considered with regard to jurisdiction as if it were an original notice of appeal.[47] Where the Registrar notifies an appellant under r. 3(2) that in his opinion the appeal tribunal does not have jurisdiction, no further action shall be taken on the appeal, but if the appellant expresses dissatisfaction with the Registrar's opinion the papers must be placed before a judge for his direction whether any further action be taken on the appeal.[48]

In addition, under the Practice Direction (para. 6), a case where the grounds of appeal do not appear to disclose an arguable point of law may be set down for a preliminary hearing, but in practice this is not done in Scotland, where doubtful points of law are either dealt with as a preliminary matter at the beginning of a hearing or during the hearing itself.

(4) **Service of notice of appeal: respondents' answer: cross-appeals**

It is the duty of the Registrar to serve a sealed copy of the notice of appeal on the appellant, on every person who is a respondent,[49] on the

---

42 Practice Direction, para. 4(*e*), (*f*) and (*h*).

43 See p. 259.

44 Rule 3(2).

45 Practice Direction, para. 5(*a*).

46 Rule 3(3).

47 Rule 3(4).

48 Rule 3(5).

49 *I.e.* the parties to the industrial tribunal proceedings (see r. 5(*a*)).

Secretary of the Industrial Tribunals, and on the Secretary of State in appropriate cases where he is not a party.[50]

The rules do not specify any period within which the respondent is to answer the notice of appeal. This is a matter for the Registrar to determine and notify to the respondent.[51] The normal practice is to allow 21 days from the date of service of the notice of appeal. Within the time appointed a respondent who is to resist must deliver an answer in writing in accordance with the form prescribed, setting out the grounds on which he relies (for which it is sufficient to state that he relies on the same grounds as those relied on by the industrial tribunal).[52] A respondent may cross-appeal in his answer to the appeal, in which case the appellant is given the opportunity to resist the cross-appeal and state the grounds upon which he does so.[53] As to where a respondent fails to deliver his answer in time, see below under "Default by parties". As with the notice of appeal, all points which the respondent intends to raise should be canvassed in his answer, otherwise he will not be allowed to raise them at the hearing.

(5) **Applications under section 5(2) of the Employment Act 1980**

These must be made in writing, following form 5 in the Schedule to the rules, and must be served on the tribunal along with a copy of the relative decision of the industrial tribunal (r. 8). For time limits, see Chapter 4, p. 52.

If it becomes clear that at the time the application was made the applicant had been admitted or re-admitted to the trade union concerned, the application should be made to an industrial tribunal, and the Registrar is directed to forward it to the Central Office of the Industrial Tribunals (r. 9). Otherwise he serves a sealed copy of the application on the applicant, and on the respondent trade union and the Secretary of the Industrial Tribunals (r. 10). If the trade union wishes to resist the application, it must enter appearance within 14 days of receipt of the application, by serving on the appeal tribunal a notice of appearance made out in accordance with form 6 in the Schedule to the rules, and setting out the grounds on which the union relies (r. 11). The Registrar then serves a copy of the notice of appearance on the applicant (r. 12).

(6) **Interlocutory applications**

These must be made in writing, specifying the direction or order

---

50 Rule 4.

51 Rule 6(1).

52 Rule 6(2).

53 Rule 6(3).

sought.[54] They are considered by the Registrar in the first place, who is to have regard to the just and economical disposal of the application and to the expense which may be incurred by the parties in attending an oral hearing.[55] The matter may be decided on the basis of written submissions.[56] Interlocutory applications are disposed of by the Registrar, but the Registrar may refer the matter to the President or a judge, who may dispose of it himself or give the Registrar directions on the matter.[57] Applications to strike out pleadings or debar a party from taking any further part in the proceedings are normally heard immediately before the hearing of the appeal itself.[58]

Interlocutory applications may be heard in public or in private.[59] Where both parties to an appeal were agreed that the decision of the industrial tribunal was wrong and as to the terms of the order which ought to be made by the appeal tribunal, it was held that the matter should be dealt with in open court, and not by the Registrar.[60]

A decision of the Registrar is appealable to a judge by notice given orally or in writing within three days of the decision.[61]

(7) **Directions**

The appeal tribunal may of its own motion or on application give directions regarding the future conduct of the proceedings for the purpose of securing their just, expeditious and economical disposal, and may appoint a date for doing so. The tribunal may also at any stage direct a party as to any steps to be taken by him in relation to the proceedings.[62]

Parties applying for directions must, if practicable, give particulars of any directions applied for, which are notified to the other parties by the Registrar, if practicable. Written representations may be submitted in relation to the application.[63] Application may also be made for further directions or for the variation of any directions already given.[64]

Although there is no restriction on the matters on which directions may be given, the following particular matters are specified:

(a) the amendment of any notice, answer or other document;

---

54 Rule 15(1).

55 Rule 16(1).

56 Practice Direction, para. 7(*a*).

57 Rule 16(2).

58 Practice Direction, para. 7(*b*).

59 Rule 18.

60 *Comet Radiovision Services Ltd.* v. *Delahunty* [1979] I.C.R. 182.

61 Rule 17.

62 Rules 19 and 20.

63 Rule 19(2) and (4).

64 Rule 19(6).

(b) the admission of any facts or documents;
(c) the admission in evidence of any documents;
(d) the mode in which evidence is to be given at the hearing;
(e) the consolidation of the proceedings with any other proceedings pending before the tribunal;
(f) the place and date of the hearing.[65]

Directions may also be made in pursuance of r. 29 (which makes provision for conciliation).[66] *Pambakian* v. *Brentford Nylons Ltd.* [1978] I.C.R. 665 was a case where this was done. (See also below under "Joinder of parties"). As to cases where complaints of bias of or the conduct of an industrial tribunal are made, see p. 256 above; para. 12 of the Practice Direction provides that if adequate particulars of the grounds of complaint have been given in the grounds of appeal, the Registrar will give appropriate directions for the hearing.

(8) Joinder of parties

Either of its own motion or on application by any person, the appeal tribunal may direct that parties may be added to or dropped from the proceedings, and give such consequential directions as may be necessary.[67] In *Pambakian* v. *Brentford Nylons Ltd., supra,* an order was made bringing in additional respondents under the equivalent rule to r. 29 (which provides that the tribunal may take steps to enable parties to avail themselves of opportunities for conciliation).

(9) Default by parties

If a respondent to any proceedings fails to deliver an answer or (in an application under s. 5(2) of the Employment Act 1980) a notice of appearance within the time appointed, or if any party fails to comply with an order or direction of the appeal tribunal, the tribunal may order that he be debarred from the proceedings, or make such other order as it thinks just.[68]

(10) Abandonment

With the consent of the respondent, an appeal may be abandoned at any stage before it is decided. If the respondent's consent is not obtained, the appeal will be heard in the usual way. No procedure is laid down in the Employment Appeal Tribunal Rules or the Practice Direction, but the Registrar and all other parties should be notified

65 Rule 19(5).
66 Rule 19(4) (where the reference is misprinted as being to r. 30).
67 Rule 14.
68 Rule 21.

immediately. A party who delays unreasonably in abandoning his appeal is liable to have an award of costs or expenses made against him.[69] It may be assumed that the same practice will be followed with regard to applications under s. 5(2) of the Employment Act 1980.

(11) **Service of documents**[70]

Notices or other documents which require to be served on any person may be served at his address for service or, where no such address has been given, to his registered office, principal place of business, head or main office, or last known address, as the case may be. Notices for an unincorporated body may be sent to its secretary, manager or other similar officers.

Notices and documents for the appeal tribunal may be sent by post or delivered to the Registrar: those instituting proceedings to or at the Central Office or any other office of the tribunal, and any others to or at the office where the proceedings in question are being dealt with.

Every document served by post is assumed in the absence of evidence to the contrary to have been delivered in the normal course of post.

The appeal tribunal may direct that service of any document may be dispensed with or effected otherwise than in the manner prescribed by the rules.

(12) **Hearings by the tribunal**

By r. 7, the arrangements for hearing an appeal (stating the date by which interlocutory applications must be made) are to be notified by the Registrar as soon as practicable to the parties, to the Secretary of the Industrial Tribunals and to the Secretary of State in appropriate cases where he is not a party. There are similar provisions in r. 13 in respect of the hearing of applications under s. 5(2) of the Employment Act 1980.

Paragraph 10 of the Practice Direction regulates the listing of cases, the arrangements for which differ between England and Wales and Scotland.[71] For Scotland the Direction provides that when the respondent's answer has been received and a copy has been served on the appellant both parties will be notified in writing that the appeal will be ready for hearing in approximately six weeks. The proposed date of hearing will be notified to the parties three or four weeks ahead. Any party who wishes to apply for a different date must do so within seven days of receipt of such notification. Thereafter a formal notice of the

---

69 See below under "Costs and Expenses", p. 272.

70 Rule 28.

71 See parts A and B of para. 10 respectively.

date fixed for the hearing will be issued not less that 14 days in advance, which will not be discharged except by the judge on cause shown.

The hearing is an oral one, in public unless for one of the reasons specified (which are in substance identical to those in the equivalent rule in industrial tribunal proceedings)[72] the tribunal decides to sit in private.[73]

In the case of appeals, the hearing normally takes the form of legal argument between the parties or their representatives, although as already pointed out[74], the appeal tribunal has the power to hear evidence, which may be given on oath.[75] The tribunal may order any person to attend as a witness or produce any document. But no person is to be treated as having failed to obey such an order unless at the time it is served he has been sent a sufficient sum to cover the cost of his attendance.[76] As to the matters which may be raised at an appeal hearing, see above under "Scope of Appeals", pp. 253 to 259. As regards applications under s. 5(2) of the Employment Act 1980, it is assumed that appropriate evidence will usually be heard.

Documents for the use of the appeal tribunal are prepared and indexed by the tribunal staff, a copy of the index being supplied to parties before the hearing, but it is the responsibility of parties or their advisers to see that all exhibits or documents which were before the industrial tribunal and which are considered relevant are sent to the appeal tribunal immediately on request, to enable this to be done.[77] In practice, such documents are usually retained at the industrial tribunal office, and are forwarded by the Secretary of the Industrial Tribunals to the Registrar. As to the Chairman's notes, see above at pp. 255, 256.

Special application must be made, as prescribed in para. 11 of the Practice Direction, for the admission of a document which was not before the industrial tribunal, including any note of evidence given before the industrial tribunal (other than Chairman's notes).

(13) **Drawing up and enforcement of orders**

The powers of the appeal tribunal in disposing of an appeal have been mentioned above (see p. 260). Compensation is the remedy in applications under s. 5(2) of the Employment Act 1980, the relative provisions being subss. (4)(*b*), (5), (6) and (8) of s. 5(*q.v.*). Sealed copies of every order of the appeal tribunal are served on every party to the proceed-

---

72 See Chap. 7, p. 139.

73 Rule 24.

74 See above, pp. 253 and 260.

75 Rule 23.

76 Rule 22. As to the tribunal's general powers in such matters, see p. 253 above.

77 Practice Direction, para. 13.

ings and on the Secretary of the Industrial Tribunals.[78] Rule 25(2) requires the appeal tribunal to give its reasons in writing for the order on application by any party within 14 days of an order finally disposing of the proceedings, unless it was made after the delivery of a reasoned judgment, but in practice reasons are invariably given in writing after a final order is made.

The statutory provisions regarding enforcement of orders by the appeal tribunal have been referred to above, at p. 260. Subject to any order made by the Court of Appeal or Court of Session, and to any directions given by the appeal tribunal, appeal from the appeal tribunal does not suspend the enforcement of any order made by it.[79]

(14) **Further appeal**

An appeal to the Court of Session from the appeal tribunal requires leave of the appeal tribunal or of the Court of Session.[80] The appeal must be made in writing to the Inner House and lodged in the General Department not later than 21 days after the decisions or order complained of was intimated to the appellant.[81]

Such appeals are regulated by R.C. 290 of the Rules of the Court of Session, as amended, and so far as applicable, by the Rules of Court generally,[82] to which reference should be made for the detailed requirements for the manner in which the appeal is to be set out and the further procedure involved.

For an appeal from the Court of Session to the House of Lords the petition of appeal must be lodged within three months from the date of the interlocutor appealed from, unless limited by order of the House or of the Court of Session. The procedure is regulated by the Directions as to Procedure and Standing Orders of the House of Lords,[83] to which reference should be made. Leave to appeal is not required.

PROCEDURE IN APPEALS UNDER S. 13(1) OF THE TRIBUNALS AND INQUIRIES ACT 1971

An appeal to the Court of Session must be presented within 42 days after the date on which the document recording the decision or order appealed from is sent to the appellant.[84] (*I.e.* the same time limit as for appeals to the Employment Appeal Tribunal).

---

78 Rule 25(1).

79 Rule 25(3).

80 The Employment Protection (Consolidation) Act 1978, s. 136(4).

81 Rules of the Court of Session, R.C. 290, as amended.

82 Printed in the *Parliament House Book*, Division C.

83 Printed in the *Parliament House Book*, Division B.

84 Rules of the Court of Session, R.C. 292(*b*).

The procedure is regulated by Rules of Court 290 (excluding para. (*h*)) and 292, and, so far as applicable, the other Rules of Court. Although the appeal is presented to the Inner House in terms of R.C. 290(*a*), by R.C. 291(3) (as amended) it is disposed of by a single judge nominated by the Lord President (in practice, usually the Scottish judicial member of the Employment Appeal Tribunal), before whom (or in vacation, the vacation judge) the appeal is placed for an order under R.C. 290(e) for intimation to the respondents and to such other person or persons as the court may think proper, and appointing answers to be lodged within such a period as the court may fix. The form of appeal and answers, and the manner of effecting service, are prescribed in R.C. 290. Any documents founded on by the appellant should also be lodged with the appeal, in so far as in his possession or under his control. Rule 292 provides for intimation also to be made to any other party to the proceedings before the industrial tribunal, and to the Chairman of the industrial tribunal.

After any answers have been lodged (with which should also be lodged any documents founded on therein) the case is enrolled for further procedure, and thereafter is put out for hearing in accordance with the usual practice, on a peremptory diet if arrangements are not made for a fixed diet.

In *Gordon District Council* v. *Hay* 1978 S.L.T. 2[85] the decision of the nominated judge was appealed to the Inner House. The appeal was taken in the usual way by which any decision of an Outer House judge is submitted to review, namely by reclaiming motion. No question was raised as to the competency of the reclaiming motion. Accordingly it may be taken that a decision of the nominated judge is reviewable by the Inner House as an Outer House decision. As it will normally dispose of the whole subject matter of the case, the period for enrolling a reclaiming motion would appear to be that provided by R.C. 264(*a*), namely not later than the 21st day from the date of the relative interlocutor, without leave, although cases of this type do not fall squarely within the rules, not having been "initiated in the Outer House either by summons or petition". No counter reclaiming motion is necessary on the part of the respondent to the reclaiming motion, and no grounds of appeal need be lodged, as the reclaiming motion submits all prior interlocutors of the Lord Ordinary to review at the instance of all parties (R.C. 262(*c*)).

For appeals from the Court of Session to the House of Lords under these provisions, leave is required, either from the Court of Session or the House of Lords.[86] A petition to the House of Lords for leave to

---

85 Outer House: the Inner House decision is not reported.

86 Tribunals and Inquiries Act 1971, s. 13(6).

appeal must be lodged within one month from the date on which the order appealed from was made. Otherwise there are no differences in procedure from appeals in proceedings under the Employment Protection (Consolidation) Act 1978.

PROCEDURE IN STATED CASES UNDER S. 13(2) OF THE TRIBUNALS AND INQUIRIES ACT 1971

This varies according to whether the case is stated by the industrial tribunal of its own motion, in which case the procedure is regulated by Rules of Court 279, 280 and 291(2), or whether it is stated on the application of a party to the proceedings. In the latter case, the procedure is regulated by R.C. 277 to 280. The application is made to the clerk of the industrial tribunal either before the issue of the tribunal's decision or within 14 days thereafter. It may be deferred if the industrial tribunal think that it is necessary or expedient that the facts should first be ascertained, and may be refused if the industrial tribunal are of the opinion that the proposed question does not arise, or that a decision on it is unnecessary for the purpose of the appeal or is frivolous.[87]

In such an event the party whose application has been refused may apply within 14 days from the date of such refusal to the Inner House of the Court of Session by written note for an order on the other party to show cause why a case should not be stated, and for an order requiring the tribunal to state a case.[88] Such applications are dealt with summarily, and if granted the case is stated and the further procedure in the Court of Session takes place in accordance with R.C. 277, 279 and 280. As already noted,[89] R.C. 280 makes provision for amendment or restatement of the case, and for the court to make any necessary inquiry into matters of fact.

As with appeals under s. 13(1), all stated cases and applications in respect of a refusal to state and sign a case are dealt with by a single judge nominated by the Lord President. Further appeal lies to the Inner House and thence to the House of Lords, as noted and discussed above with regard to appeals under s. 13(1).

COSTS AND EXPENSES

(1) **In the Employment Appeal Tribunal**

Rule 27(1) of the Employment Appeal Tribunal Rules provides as follows:

---

87 R.C. 277(c) and (*d*).

88 R.C. 278.

89 See p. 261 above.

> "Where it appears to the appeal tribunal that any proceedings were unnecessary, improper or vexatious or that there has been unreasonable delay or other unreasonable conduct in bringing or conducting the proceedings, the tribunal may order the party at fault to pay to any other party the whole or such part as it thinks fit of the costs or expenses incurred by that other party in connection with the proceedings."

The word "costs" has a technical meaning in English law equivalent to "expenses" in Scottish legal terminology, and means legal costs. The word "expenses" in r. 27(1) has thus been construed in England as meaning non-legal costs, resulting in an award to a party who was not legally represented towards the cost of opposing an appeal abandoned at an unreasonably late stage.[90] On the other hand in *Walsall Metropolitan Borough Council* v. *Sidhu* [1980] I.C.R. 519 it was held that where a party had not personally incurred costs, because the Commission for Racial Equality, who supported her case, had indemnified her, the appeal tribunal had no power to order a respondent to pay the costs incurred by the Commission on her behalf.

The rule is similar to that now applying to most industrial tribunal proceedings.[91] In *Coates & Sons Ltd.* v. *Kendrick* (EAT 178/79) it was held that "unnecessary" means something like that the outcome of the appeal can make no difference to the situation of the parties, and that "improper or vexatious" must mean something more than an error of judgment as to the prospects of success and probably must connote something to do with motive for bringing the appeal. Similarly in *Penrose* v. *Fairey Surveys Ltd.* [1973] I.C.R. 26 the opinion was expressed that it would require a very extreme case to justify the court making an order for costs on the basis that no part of the proceedings was necessary, and the NIRC declined to say what the words "unreasonable conduct" would cover. Most of the cases where costs or expenses have been awarded are fairly evenly divided between those where the reason has been unreasonable delay in prosecuting or abandoning an appeal and those where the reason has been that the appeal had no possible merit.[92] In *William P. Harrower Ltd.* v. *Hogg* (EAT 215/78), a Scottish case, an award of expenses was made against a successful appellant on the ground that he should have first applied to the industrial tribunal for a review of its decision, the appeal being concerned with the admission of further evidence.

Rule 27(2) provides that the appeal tribunal may assess the sum to be paid under an order for costs or expenses, or may direct that it be

---

90 *Rocha* v. *Commonwealth Holiday Inns of Canada Ltd.* (EAT 13/80).

91 The Industrial Tribunals Rules of Procedure (Scotland) 1980, r. 11(1). See Chap. 10, p. 234.

92 See *Wedge* v. *F. P. W. Finnigans Ltd.* (1973) 8 I.T.R. 476; *Maroof* v. *J. B. Battey & Co. Ltd.* (1973) 8 I.T.R. 489; *J. & H. Smith Ltd.* v. *Smith* [1974] I.C.R. 156; *Dacres* v. *Walls Meat Co. Ltd.* [1976] I.C.R. 44; and *Redland Roof Tiles Ltd.* v. *Eveleigh* [1979] I.R.L.R. 11.

assessed by the taxing officer (who in Scotland is the Auditor of the Court of Session) from whose decision an appeal shall lie to a judge, subject to the rules which apply to appeals from the Registrar.[93]

In appeals to higher courts, the ordinary rules of Scottish court practice as to expenses apply, namely that they normally follow success, subject to any directions made when leave to appeal was granted.

(2) **In appeals and stated cases under the Tribunals and Inquiries Act 1971**

There are no statutory rules regarding expenses, and the ordinary rules of court practice would apply.

REVIEW: CORRECTION OF CLERICAL MISTAKES

Rule 26(1) of the Employment Appeal Tribunal Rules provides that the tribunal may, either of its own motion or on application, review any order made by it and may revoke or vary such order on the grounds that:

(*a*) the order was wrongly made as the result of an error on the part of the tribunal or its staff;

(*b*) a party did not receive proper notice of the proceedings leading to the order; or

(*c*) the interests of justice require such a review.

The rule is similar in wording and concept to the equivalent rule in industrial tribunal proceedings, with the omission of the absence of a party and of new evidence as potential grounds for review.[94] Any application for review must be made within 14 days of the date of the order.

Rule 26(3) provides that a clerical mistake in any order arising from an accidental slip or omission may at any time be corrected by, or on the authority of, a judge or member. This rule is also similar to the equivalent rule in industrial tribunal proceedings.[95]

There are no equivalent provisions in the Rules of the Court of Session.

---

93 See above, p. 262.

94 See Chap. 11, p. 244.

95 See Chap. 9, p. 224.

APPENDICES

APPENDIX 1

THE INDUSTRIAL TRIBUNALS RULES OF PROCEDURE (SCOTLAND) 1980[1]

[June 26, 1980]

(S.I. 1980 No. 885)

Originating Application

1.—(1) Proceedings for the determination of any matter by a tribunal shall be instituted by the applicant (or, where applicable, by a sheriff) presenting to the Secretary of the Tribunals an application, to be known as an originating application, which shall be in writing and shall set out:

(*a*) the name and address of the applicant; and

(*b*) the names and addresses of the person or persons against whom relief is sought or (where applicable) of the parties to the proceedings before a sheriff; and

(*c*) the grounds, with particulars thereof, on which relief is sought; or in proceedings under section 51 of the 1966 Act[2] the question for determination and (except where the question is referred by a sheriff) the grounds on which relief is sought.

(2) Where the Secretary of the Tribunals is of the opinion that the originating application does not seek or on the facts stated therein cannot entitle the applicant to a relief which a tribunal has power to give, he may give notice to that effect to the applicant stating the reasons for his opinion and informing him that the application will not be registered unless he states in writing that he wishes to proceed it.

(3) An application as respects which a notice has been given in pursuance of the preceding paragraph shall not be treated as having been received for the purposes of Rule 2 unless the applicant intimates in writing to the Secretary of the Tribunals that he wishes to proceed with it; and upon receipt of such an intimation the Secretary of the Tribunals shall proceed in accordance with that Rule.

Action upon receipt of originating application

2. Upon receiving an originating application the Secretary of the Tribunals shall enter particulars of it in the Register and shall forthwith send a copy of it to the respondent and inform the parties in writing of the case number of the originating application entered in the Register

[1]Sched. 1 to the Industrial Tribunals (Rules of Procedure) (Scotland) Regulations 1980 (S.I. 1980/885).

[2]*I.e.* the Docks and Harbours Act 1966.

(which shall thereafter constitute the title of the proceedings) and of the address to which notices and other communications to the Secretary of the Tribunals shall be sent. Every copy of the originating application sent by the Secretary of the Tribunals under this paragraph shall be accompanied by a written notice which shall include information, as appropriate to the case, about the means and time for entering an appearance, the consequences of failure to do so, and the right to receive a copy of the decision. The Secretary of the Tribunals shall also notify the parties that in all cases under the provisions of any enactment providing for conciliation the services of a conciliation officer are available to them.

Appearance by respondent

3.—(1) A respondent shall within 14 days of receiving the copy originating application enter an appearance to the proceedings by presenting to the Secretary of the Tribunals a written notice of appearance setting out his full name and address and stating whether or not he intends to resist the application and, if so, setting out sufficient particulars to show on what grounds. Upon receipt of a notice of appearance the Secretary of the Tribunals shall forthwith send a copy of it to any other party.

(2) A respondent who has not entered an appearance shall not be entitled to take any part in the proceedings except—

(*i*) to apply under Rule 13(1) for an extension of the time appointed by this Rule for entering an appearance;

(*ii*) to make an application under Rule 4(1)(*i*);

(*iii*) to make an application under Rule 10(2) in respect of Rule 10(1)(*b*);

(*iv*) to be called as a witness by another person;

(*v*) to be sent a copy of a decision or specification of reasons or corrected decision or specification in pursuance of Rule 9(3), 9(7) or 10(5).

(3) A notice of appearance which is presented to the Secretary of the Tribunals after the time appointed by this Rule for entering appearances shall be deemed to include an application under Rule 13(1) (by the respondent who has presented the notice of appearance) for an extension of the time so appointed. Without prejudice to Rule 13(4), if the tribunal grants the application (which it may do notwithstanding that the grounds of the application are not stated) the Secretary of the Tribunals shall forthwith send a copy of the notice of appearance to any other party. The tribunal shall not refuse an extension of time under this Rule unless it has sent notice to the person wishing to enter an appearance giving him an opportunity to show cause why the extension should be granted.

Power to require further particulars and attendance of witnesses and to order recovery of documents

4.—(1) A tribunal may—

(*a*) subject to Rule 3(2), on the application of a party to the proceedings made either by notice to the Secretary of the Tribunals or at the hearing of the originating application, or

(*b*) in relation to sub-paragraph (i) of this paragraph, if it thinks fit, of its own motion—

(i) require a party to furnish in writing to the person specified by the tribunal further particulars of the grounds on which he or it relies and of any facts and contentions relevant thereto;

(ii) grant to the person making the application such a commission and diligence for the recovery or inspection (including the taking of copies) of documents as might be granted by a sheriff; and

(iii) require the attendance of any person (including a party to the proceedings) as a witness or require the production of any document relating to the matter to be determined, wherever such witness may be within Great Britain;

and may appoint the time at or within which or the place at which any act required in pursuance of this Rule is to be done.

(2) A party on whom a requirement has been made under paragraph (1)(*i*) or (1)(*ii*) of this Rule on an *ex parte* application, or (in relation to a requirement under paragraph 1(*i*)) on the tribunal's own motion, and a person on whom a requirement has been made under paragraph (1)(*iii*) may apply to the tribunal by notice to the Secretary of the Tribunals before the appointed time at or within which the requirement is to be complied with to vary or set aside the requirement. Notice of an application under this paragraph to vary or set aside a requirement shall be given to the parties (other than the party making the application) and, where appropriate, in proceedings which may involve payments out of the Redundancy Fund or Maternity Pay Fund, the Secretary of State if not a party.

(3) Every document containing a requirement under paragraph (1)(*ii*) or (1)(*iii*) of this Rule shall contain a reference to the fact that under paragraph 1(7) of Schedule 9 to the 1978 Act,[3] any person who without reasonable excuse fails to comply with any such requirement shall be liable on summary conviction to a fine not exceeding £100.

(4) If the requirement under paragraph (1)(*i*) or (1)(*ii*) of this Rule is not complied with, a tribunal, before or at the hearing, may dismiss the originating application, or, as the case may be, strike out the whole or

[3] *I.e.* the Employment Protection (Consolidation) Act 1978.

part of the notice of appearance, and, where appropriate, direct that a respondent shall be debarred from defending altogether: Provided that a tribunal shall not so dismiss or strike out or give such a direction unless it has sent notice to the party who has not complied with the requirement giving him an opportunity to show cause why such should not be done.

Time and place of hearing and appointment of assessor

5.—(1) The President or a Regional Chairman shall fix a date, time and place of the hearing of the originating application and the Secretary of the Tribunals shall (subject to Rule 3(2)) not less than 14 days (or such shorter time as may be agreed by him with the parties) before the date so fixed send to each party a notice of hearing which shall include information and guidance as to attendance at the hearing, witnesses and the bringing of documents (if any), representation by another person and written representations.

(2) In any proceedings under the 1966 Act in which the President or a Regional Chairman so directs, the Secretary of the Tribunals shall also take such of the following steps as may be so directed, namely—

(*a*) publish in one or more newspapers circulating in the locality in which the port in question is situated notice of the hearing;

(*b*) send notice of the hearing to such persons as may be directed;

(*c*) post notices of the hearing in a conspicuous place or conspicuous places in or near the port in question;

but the requirement as to the period of notice contained in paragraph (1) of this Rule shall not apply to any such notices.

(3) Where in the case of any proceedings it is provided for one or more assessors to be appointed, the President or the Regional Chairman may, if he thinks fit, appoint a person or persons having special knowledge or experience in relation to the subject matter of the originating application to sit with the tribunal as assessor or assessors.

Pre-hearing assessment

6.—(1) A tribunal may at any time before the hearing (either, subject to Rule 3(2), on the application of a party to the proceedings made by notice to the Secretary of the Tribunals or of its own motion) consider, by way of a pre-hearing assessment, the contents of the originating application and entry of appearance, any representations in writing which have been submitted and any oral argument advanced by or on behalf of a party.

(2) If, upon a pre-hearing assessment the tribunal considers that the originating application is unlikely to succeed or that the contentions or any particular contention of a party appear to have no reasonable

prospect of success, it may indicate that in its opinion, if the originating application shall not be withdrawn or the contentions or contention of the party shall be persisted in up to or at the hearing, the party in question may have an order for expenses made against him at the hearing under the provisions of Rule 11. A pre-hearing assessment shall not take place unless the tribunal has sent notice to the parties to the proceedings giving them (and, where appropriate in proceedings which may involve payments out of the Redundancy Fund or Maternity Pay Fund, the Secretary of State, if not a party) an opportunity to submit representations in writing and to advance oral argument at the pre-hearing assessment if they so wish.

(3) Any indication of opinion made in accordance with paragraph (2) of this Rule shall be recorded in a document signed by the chairman, a copy of which shall be sent to the parties to the proceedings and a copy of which shall be available to the tribunal at the hearing.

(4) Where a tribunal has indicated its opinion in accordance with paragraph (2) of this Rule no member thereof shall be a member of the tribunal at the hearing.

The hearing

7.—(1) Any hearing of or in connection with an originating application shall take place in public unless in the opinion of the tribunal a private hearing is appropriate for the purpose of hearing evidence which relates to matters of such a nature that it would be against the interests of national security to allow the evidence to be given in public or hearing evidence from any person which in the opinion of the tribunal is likely to consist of—

(*a*) information which he could not disclose without contravening a prohibition imposed by or under any enactment; or

(*b*) any information which has been communicated to him in confidence, or which he has otherwise obtained in consequence of the confidence reposed in him by another person; or

(*c*) information the disclosure of which would cause substantial injury to any undertaking in which he works for reasons other than its effect on negotiations with respect to any of the matters mentioned in section 29(1) of the Trade Union and Labour Relations Act 1974.

(2) A member of the Council on Tribunals or of its Scottish Committee shall be entitled to attend any hearing taking place in private in his capacity as such member.

(3) Subject to Rule 3(2), if a party shall desire to submit representations in writing for consideration by a tribunal at the hearing of the originating application that party shall present such representations to

the Secretary of the Tribunals not less than 7 days before the hearing and shall at the same time send a copy to the other party or parties.

(4) Where a party has failed to attend or be represented at the hearing (whether or not he has sent any representations in writing) the contents of his originating application or, as the case may be, of his entry of appearance may be treated by a tribunal as representations in writing.

(5) The Secretary of State if he so elects shall be entitled to apply under Rule 4(1), 13(1) and (2), 15 and 16(1) and to appear as if he were a party and be heard at any hearing of or in connection with an originating application in which he is not a party in proceedings which may involve payments out of the Redundancy Fund or Maternity Pay Fund.

(6) Subject to Rule 3(2), at any hearing of or in connection with an originating application a party and any person entitled to appear may appear before the tribunal and may be heard in person or be represented by counsel or by a solicitor or by a representative of a trade union or an employers' association or by any other person whom he desires to represent him.

Procedure at hearing

8.—(1) The tribunal shall conduct the hearing in such manner as it considers most suitable to the clarification of the issues before it and generally to the just handling of the proceedings; it shall so far as appears to it appropriate seek to avoid formality in its proceedings and it shall not be bound by any enactment or rule of law relating to the admissibility of evidence in proceedings before the courts of law.

(2) Subject to paragraph (1) of this Rule, at the hearing of the originating application a party (unless disentitled by virtue of Rule 3(2)), the Secretary of State (if, not being a party, he elects to appear as provided in Rule 7(5)) and any other person entitled to appear shall be entitled to give evidence, to call witnesses, to question any witnesses and to address the tribunal.

(3) If a party shall fail to appear or to be represented at the time and place fixed for the hearing, the tribunal may, if that party is an applicant, dismiss, or, in any case, dispose of the application in the absence of that party or may adjourn the hearing to a later date: Provided that before deciding to dismiss or disposing of an application in the absence of a party the tribunal shall consider any representations submitted by that party in pursuance of Rule 7(3).

(4) A tribunal may require any witness to give evidence on oath or affirmation and for that purpose there may be administered an oath or affirmation in due form.

Decision of tribunal

9.—(1) A decision of a tribunal may be taken by a majority thereof and, if the tribunal shall be constituted of two members only, the chairman shall have a second or casting vote.

(2) The decision of a tribunal shall be recorded in a document signed by the chairman which shall contain the reasons for the decision.

(3) The clerk to the tribunal shall transmit the document signed by the chairman to the Secretary of the Tribunals who shall as soon as may be enter it in the Register and shall send a copy of the entry to each of the parties and to the persons entitled to appear who did so appear and, where the originating application was sent to a tribunal by a sheriff, to that sheriff.

(4) The specification of the reasons for the decision shall be omitted from the Register in any case in which evidence has been heard in private and the tribunal so directs and in that event a specification of the reasons shall be sent to the parties and to any appellate court in any proceedings relating to such decision together with the copy of the entry.

(5) The Register shall be kept at the Office of the Tribunals and shall be open to the inspection of any person without charge at all reasonable hours.

(6) Clerical mistakes in documents recording the tribunal's decisions, or errors arising in them from an accidental slip or omission, may at any time be corrected by the chairman by certificate under his hand.

(7) The clerk to the tribunal shall send a copy of any document so corrected and the certificate of the chairman to the Secretary of the Tribunals who shall as soon as may be make such correction as may be necessary in the Register and shall send a copy of the corrected entry or of the corrected specification of the reasons, as the case may be, to each of the parties and to the persons entitled to appear who did so appear and where the originating application was sent to a tribunal by a sheriff, to that sheriff.

(8) If any decision is—

(*a*) corrected under paragraph (6) of this Rule,

(*b*) reviewed, revoked or varied under Rule 10, or

(*c*) altered in any way by order of an appellate court,

the Secretary of the Tribunals shall alter the entry in the Register to conform with any such certificate or order and shall send a copy of the new entry to each of the parties and to the persons entitled to appear who did so appear and where the originating application was sent to the tribunal by a sheriff, to that sheriff.

Review of tribunal's decisions

10.—(1) A tribunal shall have power to review and to revoke or vary by certificate under the chairman's hand any decision on the grounds that—

(*a*) the decision was wrongly made as a result of an error on the part of the tribunal staff; or

(*b*) a party did not receive notice of the proceedings leading to the decision; or

(*c*) the decision was made in the absence of a party or person entitled to be heard; or

(*d*) new evidence has become available since the making of the decision provided that its existence could not have been reasonably known of or foreseen; or

(*e*) the interests of justice require such a review.

(2) An application for the purposes of paragraph (1) of this Rule may be made at the hearing. If the application is not made at the hearing, such application shall be made to the Secretary of the Tribunals at any time from the date of the hearing until 14 days after the date on which the decision was sent to the parties and must be in writing stating the grounds in full.

(3) An application for the purposes of paragraph (1) of this Rule may be refused by the President or by the chairman of the tribunal which decided the case or by the Regional Chairman if in his opinion it has no reasonable prospect of success.

(4) If such an application is not refused under paragraph (3) of this Rule it shall be heard by the tribunal which decided the case, or

(*a*) where it is not practicable for it to be heard by that tribunal, or

(*b*) where the decision was made by a chairman acting alone under Rule 12(4),

by a tribunal appointed either by the President or the Regional Chairman, and if it is granted the tribunal shall either vary the decision or revoke the decision and order a re-hearing.

(5) The clerk to the tribunal shall send to the Secretary of the Tribunals the certificate of the chairman as to any revocation or variation of the tribunal's decision under this Rule. The Secretary of the Tribunals shall as soon as may be make such correction as may be necessary in the Register and shall send a copy of the entry to each of the parties and to the persons entitled to appear who did so appear and where the originating application was sent to a tribunal by a sheriff, to that sheriff.

Expenses

11.—(1) Subject to paragraphs (2), (3) and (4) of this Rule, a tribunal shall not normally make an award in respect of the expenses incurred by a party to the proceedings but where in its opinion a party (and if he is a respondent whether or not he has entered an appearance) has in bringing or conducting the proceedings acted frivolously, vexatiously or otherwise unreasonably the tribunal may make—

(*a*) an order that that party shall pay to another party (or to the Secretary of State if, not being a party, he has acted as provided in Rule 7(5)) a specified sum in respect of the expenses incurred by that other party (or, as the case may be, by the Secretary of State) or the whole or part of those expenses as taxed (if not otherwise agreed);

(*b*) an order that that party shall pay to the Secretary of State the whole, or any part, of any allowance (other than allowances paid to members of tribunals or assessors) paid by the Secretary of State under paragraph 10 of Schedule 9 to the 1978 Act to any person for the purposes of, or in connection with, his attendance at the tribunal.

(2) Where the tribunal has on the application of a party to the proceedings postponed the day or time fixed for or adjourned the hearing, the tribunal may make orders against or, as the case may require, in favour of that party as at paragraph (1)(*a*) and (*b*) of this Rule as respects any expenses incurred or any allowances paid by that party as a result of the postponement or adjournment.

(3) Where, on a complaint of unfair dismissal in respect of which—

(i) the applicant has expressed a wish to be reinstated or re-engaged which has been communicated to the respondent at least 7 days before the hearing of the complaint, or

(ii) the proceedings arise out of the respondent's failure to permit the applicant to return to work after an absence due to pregnancy or confinement,

any postponement or adjournment of the hearing has been caused by the respondent's failure, without a special reason, to adduce reasonable evidence as to the availability of the job from which the applicant was dismissed, or, as the case may be, which she held before her absence, or of comparable or suitable employment, the tribunal shall make orders against that respondent as at paragraph (1)(*a*) and (*b*) of this Rule as respects any expenses incurred or any allowances paid as a result of the postponement or adjournment.

(4) In any proceedings under the 1966 Act a tribunal may make—

(*a*) an order that a party, or any other person entitled to appear who did so appear, shall pay to another party or such person either a specified sum in respect of the expenses incurred by that other party or person or the whole or part of those expenses as taxed (if not otherwise agreed);

(*b*) an order that a party, or any other person entitled to appear who did so appear, shall pay to the Secretary of State a specified sum in respect of the whole, or any part, of any allowance (other than allowances paid to members of tribunals) paid by the Secretary of State under paragraph 10 of Schedule 9 to the 1978 Act to any person for the purposes of, or in connection with, his attendance at the tribunal.

(5) Any expenses required by an order under this Rule to be taxed may be taxed in the sheriff court according to such of the scales prescribed by the sheriff court rules for civil proceedings in the sheriff court as shall be directed by the order.

Miscellaneous powers of tribunal

12.—(1) Subject to the provisions of these Rules, a tribunal may regulate its own procedure.

(2) A tribunal may, if it thinks fit—

(*a*) extend the time appointed by or under these Rules for doing any act notwithstanding that the time appointed may have expired;

(*b*) postpone the day or time fixed for, or adjourn, any hearing (particularly as respects cases under the provisions of any enactment providing for conciliation for the purpose of giving an opportunity for the complaint to be settled by way of conciliation and withdrawn);

(*c*) if the applicant shall at any time give notice of the withdrawal of his originating application, dismiss the proceedings;

(*d*) except in proceedings under the 1966 Act, if both or all the parties (and the Secretary of State if, not being a party, he has acted as provided in Rule 7(5)) agree in writing upon the terms of a decision to be made by the tribunal, decide accordingly;

(*e*) at any stage of the proceedings order to be struck out or amended any originating application or notice of appearance or anything in such application or notice of appearance on the ground that it is vexatious;

(*f*) on the application of the respondent, or of its own motion, order to be struck out any application for excessive delay in proceeding with it:

Provided that before making an order under (*e*) or (*f*) above the tribunal shall send notice to the party against whom it is proposed that any such order should be made giving him an opportunity to show cause why such an order should not be made.

(3) Subject to Rule 4(2), a tribunal may, if it thinks fit, before granting an application under Rule 4 or Rule 13 require the party (or, as the case may be the Secretary of State) making the application to give notice of it to the other party or parties. The notice shall give particulars of the application and indicate the address to which and the time within which

any objection to the application shall be made being an address and time specified for the purposes of the application by the tribunal.

(4) Any act other than the holding of a pre-hearing assessment under Rule 6, the hearing of an originating application or the making of an order under Rule 10(1), required or authorised by these Rules to be done by a tribunal may be done by, or on the direction of, the President or the chairman of the tribunal or any chairman being a member of the panel of chairmen.

(5) Rule 11 shall apply to an order dismissing proceedings under paragraph (2)(*c*) of this Rule.

(6) Any functions of the Secretary of the Tribunals other than that mentioned in Rule 1(2) may be performed by an Assistant Secretary of the Tribunals.

Extension of time and directions

13.—(1) An application to a tribunal for an extension of the time appointed by these Rules for doing an act may be made by a party either before or after the expiration of any time so appointed.

(2) Subject to Rule 3(2), a party may at any time apply to a tribunal for directions on any matter arising in connection with the proceedings.

(3) An application under the foregoing provisions of this Rule shall be made by presenting to the Secretary of the Tribunals a notice of application, which shall state the title of the proceedings and shall set out the grounds of the application.

(4) The Secretary of the Tribunals shall give notice to both or all the parties (subject to Rule 3(2)) of any extension of time granted under Rule 12(2)(*a*) or any directions given in pursuance of this Rule.

Additional and representative respondents

14.—(1) A tribunal may at any time either upon the application of any person or, where appropriate, of its own motion, direct any person against whom any relief is sought to be joined as a party, and give such consequential directions as it considers necessary.

(2) A tribunal may likewise, either upon such application or of its own motion, order that any respondent named in the originating application or subsequently added, who shall appear to the tribunal not to have been, or to have ceased to be, directly interested in the subject of the originating application, be dismissed from the proceedings.

(3) Where there are numerous persons having the same interest in an originating application, one or more of them may be cited as the person or persons against whom relief is sought or may be authorised by the tribunal, before or at the hearing, to defend on behalf of all the persons so interested.

Consolidation of proceedings

15. Where there are pending before the industrial tribunals two or more originating applications, then, if at any time upon the application of a party or of its own motion it appears to a tribunal that—

(*a*) some common question of law or fact arises in both or all the originating applications, or

(*b*) the relief claimed therein is in respect of or arises out of the same set of facts, or

(*c*) for some other reason it is desirable to make an order under this Rule,

the tribunal may order that some (as specified in the order) or all the originating applications shall be considered together, and may give such consequential directions as may be necessary: Provided that the tribunal shall not make an order under this Rule without sending notice to all parties concerned giving them an opportunity to show cause why such an order should not be made.

Transfer of proceedings

16.—(1) Where there is pending before the industrial tribunals an originating application in respect of which it appears to the President or the Regional Chairman that the proceedings could be determined in an industrial tribunal (England and Wales) established in pursuance of the Industrial Tribunals (England and Wales) Regulations 1965 and that such application would more conveniently be determined by such a tribunal, the President or the Regional Chairman may, at any time upon the application of a party or of his own motion, with the consent of the President of the Industrial Tribunals (England and Wales) direct that the said proceedings be transferred to the Office of the Industrial Tribunals (England and Wales): Provided that no such directions shall be made unless notice has been sent to all parties concerned giving them an opportunity to show cause why such a direction should not be made.

(2) Where proceedings have been transferred to the Office of the Industrial Tribunals (Scotland) under Rule 16(1) of the Industrial Tribunals (Rules of Procedure) Regulations 1980 they shall be treated as if in all respects they had been commenced by an originating application.

Notices, etc.

17.—(1) Any notice given under these Rules shall be in writing.

(2) All notices and documents required by these Rules to be presented to the Secretary of the Tribunals may be presented at the Office of the Tribunals or such other office as may be notified by the Secretary of the Tribunals to the parties.

(3) All notices and documents required or authorised by these Rules to be sent or given to any person hereinafter mentioned may be sent by post (subject to paragraph (5) of this Rule) or delivered to or at—

- (*a*) in the case of a notice or document directed to the Secretary of State in proceedings to which he is not a party, the offices of the Department of Employment at Pentland House, 41 Robb's Loan, Edinburgh EH14 1TW, or such other office as may be notified by the Secretary of State;
- (*b*) in the case of a notice or document directed to the Board,[4] the principal office of the Board;
- (*c*) in the case of a notice or document directed to a sheriff, the office of the sheriff clerk;
- (*d*) in the case of a notice or document directed to a party:—
  - (i) his address for service specified in the originating application or in a notice of appearance or in a notice under paragraph (4) of this Rule; or
  - (ii) if no address for service has been so specified, his last known address or place of business in the United Kingdom or, if the party is a corporation, the corporation's registered or principal office in the United Kingdom or, in any case, at such address or place outside the United Kingdom as the President or the Regional Chairman may allow;
- (*e*) in the case of a notice or document directed to any person (other than a person specified in the foregoing provisions of this paragraph), his address or place of business in the United Kingdom, or if such a person is a corporation, the corporation's registered or principal office in the United Kingdom;

and if sent or given to the authorised representative of a party shall be deemed to have been sent or given to that party.

(4) A party may at any time by notice to the Secretary of the Tribunals and to the other party or parties (and, where appropriate, to the appropriate conciliation officer) change his address for service under these Rules.

(5) The recorded delivery service shall be used instead of the ordinary post:

- (*a*) when a second set of documents or notices is to be sent to a respondent who has not entered an appearance under Rule 3(1);
- (*b*) for service of an order made under Rule 4(1)(*iii*), requiring the attendance of a witness or the production of a document.

(6) Where for any sufficient reason service of any document or notice cannot be effected in the manner prescribed under this Rule, the

[4] *I.e.* the National Dock Labour Board, as reconstituted under the Dock Work Regulation Act 1976.

President or the Regional Chairman may make an order for service in such manner as he may deem fit and such service shall have the same effect as service in the manner prescribed under this Rule.

(7) In proceedings brought under the provisions of any enactment providing for conciliation the Secretary of the Tribunals shall send copies of all documents and notices to a conciliation officer who in the opinion of the Secretary is an appropriate officer to receive them.

(8) In proceedings which may involve payments out of the Redundancy Fund or Maternity Pay Fund, the Secretary of the Tribunals shall, where appropriate, send copies of all documents and notices to the Secretary of State notwithstanding the fact that he may not be a party to such proceedings.

(9) In proceedings under the Equal Pay Act 1970, the Sex Discrimination Act 1975 or the Race Relations Act 1976 the Secretary of the Tribunals shall send to the Equal Opportunities Commission or, as the case may be, the Commission for Racial Equality copies of all documents sent to the parties under Rule 9(3), (7) and (8) and Rule 10(5).

APPENDIX 2

ORIGINATING APPLICATION

Form IT I (Scot) as revised September 1980

Application to an Industrial Tribunal

NOTES FOR GUIDANCE

Before completing the application form please read—
THESE NOTES for guidance
LEAFLET ITL I which you were given along with this form

THE APPROPRIATE BOOKLET referred to under the relevant Act of Parliament—see paragraph 2 below.

1 **QUALIFYING PERIODS AND TIME LIMITS**

In order to make a valid application you must satisfy any appropriate qualifying period of continuous employment and your application must be received within the appropriate time limit. Information on both of these requirements is given in the booklets mentioned in paragraph 2 below. For example, if you wish to complain of unfair dismissal the time limit for the receipt of such an application is normally 3 months from and including the effective date of dismissal. There is no qualifying period of employment for certain jurisdictions eg Equal Pay, Sex Discrimination or Race Relations complaints or where dismissal is for trade union activities, but time limits for making an application apply.

2 **RELEVANT ACTS OF PARLIAMENT**

You can ask the Tribunal to decide various questions as provided for in relevant Acts of Parliament. Details of these questions, the relevant Acts of Parliament and the titles of booklets explaining in simple terms the provision of these Acts and what the Tribunal can decide are given in leaflet ITL I which should be issued to you with this form. These booklets are obtainable FREE from any employment office, jobcentre or unemployment benefit office. This form may be used for any of the matters referred to in leaflet ITL I.

3 **PREPARATION OF APPLICATION FORM**

When completing the application form you should fill in items 1, 2, 4 and 12 and any other items which are relevant to your case. If in doubt about the respondent to name in item 4 you may seek advice from any employment office, jobcentre or unemployment benefit office. A Citizens' Advice Bureau or Trade Union may be able to help you complete the form or advise you as to whether you have a complaint which an Industrial Tribunal could consider.

4 PREPARATION OF YOUR CASE AND REPRESENTATION AT THE HEARING

At the hearing you may state your own case or be represented by anyone who has agreed to act for you. If you intend to have a representative it is advisable that he or she should be consulted at the earliest possible stage—preferably before the application form is completed (but see note above regarding time limits). In cases under the Equal Pay and Sex Discrimination Acts the Equal Opportunities Commission, and in cases under the Race Relations Act the Commission for Racial Equality, may provide assistance or representation—see appropriate booklet. If you name a representative all further communications will be sent to him or her and not to you; you should arrange with your representative to be kept informed of the progress of your case of the hearing date.

Do not forget to sign the form.

PLEASE DETACH THESE NOTES before sending the application form to the Central Office of the Industrial Tribunals. **KEEP THE NOTES FOR FUTURE REFERENCE.**

APPLICATION TO AN INDUSTRIAL TRIBUNAL

UNDER ONE OR MORE OF THE FOLLOWING ACTS:—
EQUAL PAY ACT 1970
SEX DISCRIMINATION ACT 1975
EMPLOYMENT PROTECTION ACT 1975
RACE RELATIONS ACT 1976
EMPLOYMENT PROTECTION (CONSOLIDATION) ACT 1978 (as amended by the Employment Act 1980)
EMPLOYMENT ACT 1980

For Official Use	
Case Number	

THIS APPLICATION HAS BEEN REGISTERED AS A COMPLAINT UNDER THE FOLLOWING ACTS
EQUAL PAY ACT 1970
SEX DISCRIMINATION ACT 1975
RACE RELATIONS ACT 1976
EMPLOYMENT PROTECTION ACT 1975
EMPLOYMENT PROTECTION (CONSOLIDATION) ACT 1978 (as amended)
EMPLOYMENT ACT 1980

SECTION ....

IMPORTANT: DO NOT FILL IN THIS FORM UNTIL YOU HAVE READ THE NOTES FOR GUIDANCE. THEN COMPLETE ITEMS 1, 2, 4 AND 12 AND ALL OTHER ITEMS RELEVANT TO YOUR CASE.

TO:— THE SECRETARY OF THE TRIBUNALS
CENTRAL OFFICE OF THE INDUSTRIAL TRIBUNALS (SCOTLAND)
ST ANDREW HOUSE, 141 WEST NILE STREET, GLASGOW G1 2RU Tel.: 041-331 1601

1 I hereby apply for a decision of a Tribunal on the following question (State here question to be decided by the Tribunal and explain the grounds overleaf)

....

....

2 My name ....

Address ....

.... Telephone No................................

My date of birth is ....

3 If a representative has agreed to act for you in this case please give his or her name and address below and note that further communications will be sent to your representative and not to you (*See Note 4*)

Name of representative ....

Address ....

.... Telephone No................................

4 Name of respondent(s) (in block capitals) ie the employer, person or body against whom a decision is sought

(*See Note 3*) ....

Address(es) ....

.... Telephone No................................

(a) (Where the application relates to Maternity Rights)
When your absence began did your employers employ more than 5 persons?..........

(b) (In all other applications)
(i) When your employment ended did your employer employ more than 20 persons?

....

(ii) If not, had he during your employment ever employed more than 20?.................

5 Place of employment to which this application relates, or place where act complained about took place.

....

6 My occupation or position held/applied for, or other relationship to the respondent named above (eg user of a service supplied in relation to employment)

....

7 Employment began on..................and (if appropriate) ended on............................

8 **(a)** Basic wages/salary....................................

(b) Average take home pay..............................

9 Other remuneration or benefits.......................

10 Normal basic weekly hours of work..................

11 (In an application under the Sex Discrimination Act or the Race Relations Act) Date on which action complained of took place or first came to my knowledge.............

12 You are required to set out the grounds for your application below, giving full particulars of them.

13 If you wish to state what in your opinion was the reason for your dismissal, please do so here.

14 If the Tribunal decides that you were unfairly dismissed, what remedy would you prefer? (Before answering this question please consult the Notes for Guidance for the remedies available and then write one of the following in answer to this question: reinstatement, re-engagement or compensation)

....

Signature .... Date ....

APPENDIX 3

NOTICE OF APPEARANCE

Form IT 3 (Scot)

INDUSTRIAL TRIBUNALS (RULES OF PROCEDURE) (SCOTLAND) REGULATIONS 1980............

NOTICE OF APPEARANCE BY RESPONDENT

To the Secretary of the Tribunals
Central Office of the Industrial Tribunals
(Scotland)
Saint Andrew House
141 West Nile Street
GLASGOW G1 2RU
Telephone 041-331 1601

Case No. (S)/

For office use	
Date of Receipt	Initials

1 I *do / *do not intend to resist claim made by

2 My/Our name is Mr/Mrs/Miss/title* (if company or organisation)
address

telephone number

3 My representative/agent/solicitor † is
address

telephone number

4 (a) Was the applicant dismissed? YES/NO*
(b) If YES, what was the reason for the dismissal?

(c) Are the dates given by the applicant as to the period of employment correct? YES/NO*
(d) If NO, give dates of commencement
and termination
(e) (Where the application relates to Maternity Rights)
When the applicant left did you employ more than 5 persons?

(f) (In all other applications):—
(i) At the date of termination of employment did you employ more than 20 persons?
(ii) If not, have you ever employed more than 20 persons during the applicant's period of employment?

5 If claim is resisted, please state grounds on which you intend to resist.
You are required to give details of your reasons for resisting it.

*Delete as necessary
†Only to be completed where an agent etc. is used

Date .... Signature ....

APPENDIX 4

NOTICE OF HEARING

Form IT 4 (Scot)

THE INDUSTRIAL TRIBUNALS (RULES OF PROCEDURE) (SCOTLAND) REGULATIONS 1980

NOTICE OF HEARING

Office of the
Industrial Tribunals (Scotland)

CASE No. ....

NOTICE IS HEREBY GIVEN that the application of

dated will be heard by an Industrial Tribunal

at

on day of 19 at o'clock

in the noon or as soon thereafter as may be.

In his own interest each party should appear at the hearing with his witnesses (if any) at the above time and place and bring with him all documents on which he intends to rely eg a letter of appointment, contract of employment, working rule agreement, pay slips, income tax forms, evidence of unemployment and other social security benefits, wages book, details of benefits and contributions under any pension or superannuation scheme etc.

Each party (other than a respondent who has not entered an appearance) is entitled to be represented by anyone they choose.

If for any reason a party does not propose, or is unable to appear at the hearing either in person or by representative, that party should *immediately* inform me in writing at the address mentioned at the head of this notice, stating the case number of the proceedings and the reasons for the proposal not to, or the inability to, attend or to be represented. He should also state whether he wishes the hearing to proceed in his absence, relying on any written representations he may have made.

In cases where reinstatement, re-engagement or return to work is an issue, a respondent who without special reasons is unable at the hearing to provide the Tribunal with reasonable evidence as to the availability of comparable or suitable employment, may be liable for expenses incurred by a resultant postponement or adjournment.

If there are criminal proceedings pending or police enquiries which may lead to criminal proceedings then the above office should be advised immediately.

Dated .... Signed .... Secretary

To the Applicant(s) To the Respondent(s)

APPENDIX 5

SCHEDULE TO THE EMPLOYMENT PROTECTION (RECOUPMENT OF UNEMPLOYMENT BENEFIT AND SUPPLEMENTARY BENEFIT) REGULATIONS 1977 (S.I. 1977/677)*

TABLE RELATING TO MONETARY AWARDS

Column 1 PAYMENT	*Column* 2 PROCEEDINGS	*Column* 3 MATTER TO WHICH PRESCRIBED ELEMENT IS ATTRIBUTABLE
1. Guarantee payments under section [12 of the 1978 Act].	1. Complaint under section [17].	1. Any amount found to be due to the complainant and ordered to be paid under section [17(3)] for a period before the conclusion of the tribunal proceedings.
2. Payments under any collective agreement having regard to which the appropriate Minister has made an exemption order under section [18 of the 1978 Act].	2. Complaint under section [18(4)].	2. Any amount found to be due to the complainant and ordered to be paid under section [17(3)], as applied by section [18(4)], for a period before the conclusion of the tribunal proceedings.
3. Payments of remuneration in respect of a period of suspension on medical grounds under section [19 of the 1978 Act].	3. Complaint under section [22].	3. Any amount found to be due to the complainant and ordered to be paid under section [22(3)] for a period before the conclusion of the tribunal proceedings.
4. Payments under an order for reinstatement under section [69(2) of the 1978 Act].	4. Complaint of unfair dismissal under [section 67].	4. Any amount ordered to be paid under section [69(2)(*a*)] in respect of arrears of pay for a period before the conclusion of the tribunal proceedings.

*Adapted by subsituting references to the provisions of the Employment Protection (Consolidation) Act 1978 which re-enacted equivalent provisions in the Trade Union and Labour Relations Act 1974 and the Employment Protection Act 1975 which were in force and referred to in the regulations when they were made in 1977, and to indicate where reference is made to provisions of the 1975 Act which remain in force.

Column 1 PAYMENT	*Column* 2 PROCEEDINGS	*Column* 3 MATTER TO WHICH PRESCRIBED ELEMENT IS ATTRIBUTABLE
5. Payments under an order for re-engagement under section [69(4) of the 1978 Act].	5. Complaint of unfair dismissal under [section 67].	5. Any amount ordered to be paid under section [69(4)(*d*)] in respect of arrears of pay for a period before the conclusion of the tribunal proceedings.
6. Payments under an award of compensation for unfair dismissal in cases falling under section [68(2) of the 1978 Act] (cases where no order for re-instatement or re-engagement has been made).	6. Complaint of unfair dismissal under [section 67].	6. Any amount ordered to be paid and calculated under section [74(2)(*b*)] in respect of compensation for loss of wages for a period before the conclusion of the tribunal proceedings.
7. Payments under an award of compensation for unfair dismissal under section [71(2) of the 1978 Act] where reinstatement order order not complied with.	7. Proceedings in respect of non-compliance with order.	7. —ditto—
8. Payments under an award of compensation for unfair dismissal under section [71(2) of the 1978 Act] where re-engagement order not complied with.	8. —ditto—	8. —ditto—
9. Payments under an interim order for reinstatement under section [77(7) of the 1978 Act].	9. Proceedings on an application for an order for interim relief under section [77(1)].	9. Any amount found to be due to the complainant and ordered to be paid in respect of arrears of pay for the period between the date of termination of employment and the conclusion of the tribunal proceedings.
10. Payments under an interim order for re-engagement under section [77(8)(a) of the 1978 Act].	10. Proceedings on an application for an order for interim relief under section [77(1)].	10. —ditto—

Column 1 PAYMENT	*Column* 2 PROCEEDINGS	*Column* 3 MATTER TO WHICH PRESCRIBED ELEMENT IS ATTRIBUTABLE
11. Payments under an order for the continuation of a contract of employment under section [77(8)(b) of the 1978 Act] where employee reasonably refused re-engagement.	11. —ditto—	11. —ditto—
12. Payments under an order for the continuation of a contract of employment under section [77(9) of the 1978 Act] where employer fails to attend or is unwilling to reinstate or re-engage.	12. —ditto—	12. —ditto—
13. Payments under an order for the continuation of a contract of employment under section [79(2) of the 1978 Act] where reinstatement or re-engagement order not complied with.	13. Proceedings in respect of non-compliance with order.	13. Any amount ordered to be paid to the employee by way of compensation under section [79(2)(*b*)] for loss of wages for the period between the date of termination of employment and the conclusion of the tribunal proceedings.
14. Payments under an order for compensation under section [79(3)(*a*) of the 1978 Act] where order for the continuation of contract of employment not complied with.	14. Proceedings in respect of non-compliance with order.	14. Any amount ordered to be paid to the employee by way of compensation under section [79(3)(g)] for loss of wages for the period between the date of termination of employment and the conclusion of the tribunal proceedings.
15. Payments under an order under section 103(3) [of the 1975 Act] on employer's default in respect of remuneration due to employee under protective award.	15. Complaint under section 103(1).	15. Any amount ordered to be paid to the employee in respect of so much of the relevant protected period as falls before the date of the conclusion of the tribunal proceedings.

INDEX